The Womanly Art of Breastfeeding

The Womanly Art of Breastfeeding

La Leche League® International

Third Edition

A PLUME BOOK

NEW AMERICAN LIBRARY

TIMES MIRROR

NEW YORK AND SCARBOROUGH, ONTARIO

LA LECHE LEAGUE is a registered trademark of
La Leche League International, Inc.

This is an authorized reprint of a hardcover edition published by
La Leche League International. The hardcover edition was
published simultaneously in Canada by
La Leche League International.

Library of Congress Catalog Card Number: 83-61753

Cartoon illustrations by Joan McCartney

All Richard Ebbitt photographs are copyrighted by him.

First Plume Printing, September, 1983

1 2 3 4 5 6 7 8 9

We dedicate this book with much love to
the many caring parents who have helped make
La Leche League what it is today, to our patient,
loving husbands and children, and—in a very
special way—to Doctors Herbert Ratner and
Gregory White, all of whom helped the seven of
us to learn the womanly art of breastfeeding.

THE WOMANLY ART OF BREASTFEEDING
would not have been written and the basic
principles underlying the work of La Leche League
would not have withstood the test of time as
they have, had it not been for the unfailing counsel
of Doctors Herbert Ratner and Gregory White.
These two physicians have supported us from the
early days of the League when breastfeeding was
indeed an unpopular way to nurture a baby. For
this, we are most grateful.

Contents

PART TWO: NICE TO KNOW

CHAPTER

Foreword

Few pioneers are graced with seeing their efforts recognized by society at large. The founding mothers of La Leche League International, however, are such pioneers. They have seen their work flower and bear fruit. They have seen the impact of their work upon their culture.

From their own personal experiences, the founding mothers recognized the benefits of breastfeeding to both mother and child. They also recognized the widespread antipathy toward breastfeeding in the culture at large, and in the hospital environment in particular. They saw clearly the oppressive effect this antipathy had upon women who wanted to breastfeed their babies, and the deprivation it imposed upon mothers and their infants. To offset the detrimental effect of these negative attitudes, they banded together to share the joys of breastfeeding with other young mothers and, in 1956, organized La Leche League.

In La Leche League's early years, breastfeeding was a lost art, and bottle feeding was in its heyday. It was a time when doctors (but not infants) paid lip service to breastfeeding. "Breastfeeding is best," they proclaimed, "but bottle feeding is just as good." It was their success with artificial feeding of hospitalized sick infants, and other infants in unusual circumstances, that led doctors to this belief that bottle feeding was, in fact, just as good. Then, as indications for bottle feeding insidiously broadened, it was only a matter of time until the unusual—bottle feeding—became the usual, and the customary—breastfeeding—became the rarity. Such conversion is seen frequently in medical practice: in the shift of the place of birth from home to hospital; in the increase of circumcision, episiotomy, obstetrical analgesia and anesthesia; and the forceps and stirrup delivery. Unbelievably, the operative delivery—cesarean section—is, today, becoming the usual and the nonoperative delivery, the unusual.

Physicians, comfortable with modern science and technology, were, in the case of bottle feeding, misled by gross nutritional standards such as weight gain and apparent freedom from nutritional diseases. Unfortunately, they did not reflect on the boasting of the formula industry that each new discovery was **the** discovery that would make the artificial product equal to human milk. The very fact that there were "new discoveries" annually proved the futility of their claims. This should have suggested to physicians that the natural was a standard unattainable by the artificial; that the thousands of laboratories, the countless scientists, and the annual expenditure of millions and millions of dollars devoted to research were a measure of our extensive ignorance of the workings of nature. Although raised on the theory of evolution, which taught that survival meant fitness, the doctors of the day disregarded the tailor-made, eminent fitness of breast milk for the young of each species and ignored the fact that the species-specific breast milk had had the longest clinical trial of any food ever made for the young. Physicians were, in effect, pitting their knowledge and experience against nature's knowledge and experience. They were bound to lose.

The founding mothers and their legion of followers opted, not for science and technology, but for nature as the repository of wisdom. They did not entrust the development of the mother-infant relationship to the vagaries of scientific advance, but rather, they placed their faith in nature and the promptings of the heart, a mode by which nature communicates many teachings. It was in the seventeenth century that Blaise Pascal, in his famous *Pensées*, wrote. "The heart has its own reasons, which reason does not know." How wise LLL mothers were. Their faith, which led them to accept nature's obvious norms, kept them ahead of the scientists. As one LLL Leader wittily stated, "A fanatic is a breastfeeding mother who for twenty years and against great odds has been doing and believing what physicians have only now discovered is a scientific truth."

Twenty-five years ago, when THE WOMANLY ART OF BREAST-FEEDING first appeared, it was the only book on breastfeeding published in the United States which was written for breastfeeding mothers. In those days, in most parts of the country, the incidence of breastfeeding at the time of hospital discharge was less than ten percent, and the duration was short, a matter of weeks. Only a few hardy souls managed to nurse as long as nine months. The breastfeeding climate was oppressive. Mothers desiring to breastfeed were looked at askance by hospital personnel because of their refusal to enter the world of emancipated womanhood. Physicians, for the most part, were indifferent, unenthusiastic, and unhelpful. In the hospital and at home, when the slightest nursing problem arose, medical personnel, relatives, and friends were prompt to urge bottle feeding as the foolproof solution.

With the inception of LLL, a remarkable reversal occurred. The new mother, full of the maternal promptings of nature, was no longer alone, unassured, insecure in the newness of her relationship to her child, wanting success, but fearing failure. She now had someone to turn to for practical help, a woman who had been there, who could provide the encouragement and support she needed. The value of this woman-to-woman help is paramount, especially during the period of transition when the mother-infant relationship shifts from the invisible to the visible, from the bodily womb to the spiritual womb (the womb with a view), and from an involuntary, effortless, passive system of nourishment to a voluntary, dynamically active mode of nourishment. This transitional period, with the uncertainties that accompany it, is not unlike the honeymoon or any other period of interpersonal adjustment. In addition, LLL gave the new mother (as well as the old) a bible, THE WOMANLY ART, an invaluable resource for the breastfeeding woman.

Dramatic changes have resulted from twenty-five years of LLL activities. Today, instead of a small minority, the majority of women are opting for breastfeeding. Today, instead of one book on breastfeeding there are dozens, some better than others, but none matching THE WOMANLY ART—the distillation of the accumulated experiences of thousands of LLL Leaders and millions of mothers. Today, increasingly, hospital personnel, relatives, the mass media, and others are becoming friends of breastfeeding.

Finally, we must express our debt to medical scientists for their dramatic findings of the past decade and to the American Academy of Pediatrics and the Canadian Paediatric Society, which as a consequence of these findings, made an unreserved commitment to breastfeeding in a joint statement issued on the occasion of the International Year of the Child in 1979. The definitive establishment and acceptance of the unmatchable superiority of breastfeeding and breast milk were in a way, a coup de grâce to bottle feeding. Though the latter has its role, no longer can it be thought of as an equivalent substitute for the nurturing and nourishing qualities associated with nursing. The scientific findings were twofold.

One was the discovery and the recognition of the remarkable protective properties of breast milk against infectious diseases. This discovery will go down in the annals of medicine as one of the most striking examples of nature accomplishing multiple goals through a single means. It extends the healing power of nature *(vis medicatrix naturae)* to the preventive as well. What mothers knew all along—that breastfed babies are freer from illness than bottle-fed babies—scientists have not only affirmed for modern times, but have confirmed by discovering the mechanisms that bring it about. Nursing mothers knew the **fact**; medical scientists know the **reasoned fact**—the reasons why. Breast milk prevents a multiplicity of infections that modern medicine not only cannot prevent, but sometimes cannot even cure. Even when modern medicine can cure what it doesn't prevent, there are always the attendant problems: the sickness itself, the parental anxieties, the emotional trauma of hospitalization, and the expense and complications of treatment. Since a major part of the protective properties of milk center about the human immunoglobulins and countless numbers of live human cells, it is no longer possible for formula manufacturers to mimic breast milk. Unlike the apparent matching of the nutritive properties of breast milk, matching a living tissue such as breast milk with its living cellular capacity to manufacture its own antibodies is an entirely different order of probability.

The other striking advance was the uncovering and elucidation of the maternal attachment phenomenon. What nursing mothers did by natural inclination and intuition, and learned experientially, scientists corroborated experimentally. The mother knew the fact, the scientist, subsequently, the substantiated fact. It was not a case of science replacing art, but of science illuminating a natural, maternal act which is part of the art of motherhood. Researchers simply delivered the scientific backup for what nursing mothers were accomplishing all along. Of tremendous importance is that maternal attachment adds the affective to the cognitive; i.e., the emotional to the intellectual, the outreach of love to rational comprehension. Only now are we beginning to grasp the extent to which the undermining of the maternal attachment process with its reciprocal bonding of infant to mother has contributed to the maternal and adult delinquency of a sick society.

This brings me to the publication on LLL's twenty-fifth anniversary, of the new edition of THE WOMANLY ART OF BREASTFEEDING. It marks a milestone, namely a sign and a symbol of the universal acceptance of the unique benefits and superiority of breastfeeding. THE WOMANLY ART, with its womanly know-how, is bound to play a critical role (as in the past it has played a major role in the renascence of breastfeeding) in converting today's universal assent into actuality. The reward? Mothers and infants will become bosom friends, and society will reap the benefits. In the words of mid-eighteenth-century philosopher, Jean-Jacques Rousseau, "Would you restore all to their primal duties, begin with the mothers; the results will surprise you."

Herbert Ratner, MD
Editor, *Child & Family Quarterly*
Visiting Professor of Community and Preventive Medicine
New York Medical College

Foreword

When I first visited La Leche League in Franklin Park, Illinois, in 1960 with my own six-month-old breastfed baby, Warren, I heard Mary White, a founding mother, talking to a new mother on the telephone. What she said put the whole spirit of the League in a few short words and foretold the secret of its success. Her words were: "After all, people are more important than things."

It is women who believe "people are more important than things" who have worked untold hours expanding the mother-to-mother help of the League throughout the fifty states and in over forty countries. The outstanding quality of La Leche League Leaders is their willingness to give generously their time, effort, and loving concern to babies and their mothers.

The genuine call to help other human beings is a powerful message that attracts outstanding people. The League has been blessed by attracting to its ranks extremely able, ethically sensitive women who give their abilities and energy, first to their own families and then to helping other families through LLLI. They have had the courage to do this in a society that downgrades motherhood and in which most women are raised to ignore the importance of their biological heritage, making them feel they should act like men, even to muting their unique ability to totally nourish their infants themselves.

Example is the best teacher, and it is La Leche League mothers breastfeeding in their homes—and discreetly outside their homes—who have helped to awaken the industrial world to a value almost lost: the closeness of the breastfeeding mother-baby couple. Anyone attending a League meeting sees tangible evidence of the health and well-being of breastfed babies. How beautiful and alert and agreeable those babies usually are!

The work of the LLLI mothers is another example of the adage, "the hand that rocks the cradle is the hand that rules the world." Their intense interest has enrolled the support of those who love and admire them. Very often, physicians most helpful to breastfeeding mothers are those who have learned about La Leche League-style breastfeeding in their own homes. Researchers now documenting the many unique qualities of human milk are very often parents of breastfed babies. The League itself has shown how much ability women can manifest when organizing for the welfare of others. All the members of the Board of Directors since LLLI's inception have had personal experience with total breastfeeding. In addition, LLLI has been able to get and use the help of outstanding advisors from many fields.

Now that many self-help groups flourish, it is notable that LLLI started in 1956, long before it was widely recognized how much people with similar problems and loving hearts could help each other by organizing. Not only is LLLI now an outstanding model of a self-help organization, but surely it is notable that this organization of breastfeeding mothers now offers authoritative courses for physicians and other professionals which give them continuing-education credits.

Part of LLLI's secret of success is the mothers' willingness to serve as a team, carrying personal responsibility but muting personal glory. THE WOMANLY ART OF BREASTFEEDING typifies this tendency—many people contributed and worked hard on this book, but no individual authors are cited. It is "The League Manual."

As the League goes into its second quarter-century, no one knows its future. However, its base is strong because it flows from the deep concern for the well-being of people rather than material acquisitions. Miracles can be accomplished when the emphasis is in the right place. What could be more important than concern for the little people of this world and helping them to obtain their human birthright: mothering through breastfeeding?

This book can do much to help yet another generation of babies get a good start in life. The warmth and maturity of the authors shine out on every page—a remarkable document illustrating their philosophy in life and their broad and exceptional wisdom about babies and breastfeeding. This revised edition is probably the most authoritative text for mothers on breastfeeding that has ever been developed, since it is based not only on research, but on vast practical experience.

Niles Newton, PhD
Mother of four breastfed babies, and
Professor of Behavioral Sciences
(Department of Psychiatry and Behavioral Sciences)
Northwestern University Medical School

Introduction

Breastfeeding a baby—what could be more natural? Just cradle that precious newborn in your arms and offer him your breast. What could be simpler?

Breastfeeding a baby *is* simple and natural—*if* you know how to do it. But it takes information *and* encouragement and some motherly know-how to nurse a baby, as the seven of us who founded La Leche League quickly discovered with our first nursing attempts. How often should you nurse? How long on each side? How do you know if baby is getting enough to eat? What other foods does he need? And what if he seems hungry again only an hour after he has been nursed?

When the seven of us found each other in 1956 and formed La Leche League, answers to such questions were as scarce as mother's milk itself. But we had breastfed a combined total of twenty-four babies, and by then had a good idea of what did and didn't work, what was and wasn't helpful. The secret of success in nursing a baby, we had discovered, was having the right information and having another nursing mother to turn to for advice and reassurance.

In THE WOMANLY ART OF BREASTFEEDING we have attempted to put a philosophy about being a mother and nurturing an infant between covers. This book is our way of sharing the sense of satisfaction and fulfillment countless mothers have found through nursing their babies, and the special joys that are awaiting as you embark on the great adventure of motherhood.

Our first two editions, published in 1958 and 1963, were based largely on our own personal experiences. This third edition draws on the wisdom that has been accumulated through the many thousands of breastfeeding mothers who have so generously shared their experiences with us during the past twenty-five years. Our only regret is that we cannot include more of the many inspiring and informative stories that have come our way.

As you will notice, we write from the perspective of a household consisting of husband, wife, and child or children. Breastfeeding and good mothering, we are convinced, progress more easily in such an environment, and children naturally flourish under the loving care of both a mother and a father. But from personal experience, we also know that as right and natural as this picture is, it does not always hold true in real life. Sometimes the father is missing from the family, and mothering then becomes a solitary endeavor. It is not an easy situation for a woman to be in. But no matter what else happens in her life, a mother can take great satisfaction in nursing her baby and staying close to him. Her efforts in this regard comprise an accomplishment that will increase in value as time goes by.

Our wish is that every mother anywhere in the world who wants to breastfeed her baby will have the information and support she needs to do so. Yes, breastfeeding is simple and natural—and an exquisitely beautiful way to nourish and nurture a new life.

❖❖❖❖❖❖❖❖❖❖❖❖❖❖❖❖❖❖❖❖❖❖❖❖
We appreciate and applaud
the fact that babies
come in two genders,
male and female,
delightful he's and
charming she's.
In this book, we refer to baby
only as "he," not
with sexist intent,
but simply for clarity's sake.
Mother is unquestionably "she."
❖❖❖❖❖❖❖❖❖❖❖❖❖❖❖❖❖❖❖❖❖❖❖❖

PART ONE

BREASTFEEDING YOUR BABY

Photo by Harriette Hartigan

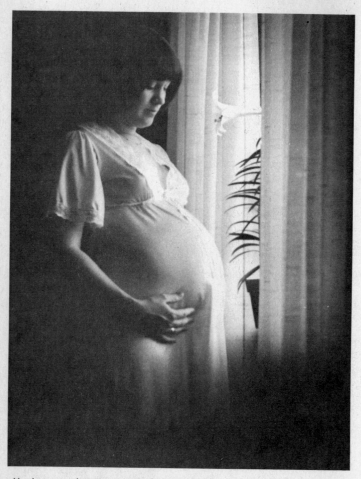

You have never been more aware of your womanliness than you are now as you nurture this new life within you. (Photo of Linda Heckman by Richard Ebbitt.)

Chapter I

You're Going to

Have a Baby

You are a woman who seeks a natural way of mothering and you want to learn as much as you can about breastfeeding, the most natural source of nourishment and security for your baby. For you, breastfeeding is an expression of what it means to be a woman. And you have never been more aware of your womanliness—you are going to have a baby. Pregnancy, childbirth, and breastfeeding comprise a special journey in the life of a woman. It is not the only one, certainly, but it is an important milestone, one bound up with extraordinary feelings.

Our heartfelt wish to you is for "A Happy Delivery and Plentiful Milk." This expression originated in centuries past and gave us the "La Leche" in our name. It undoubtedly sprang from the hopes and prayers of mothers themselves. As such, it is still meaningful to mothers today.

Having a baby is a wonderful, sweeping expression of trust and love, but the realization of the coming change in your life may take some getting used to. A father from Missouri, Tom Hanley, tells of some feelings that are probably common to many newly expecting parents.

> I think that the nine-month pregnancy is designed for more than the physical growth of the child; it is also a period of psychological preparation for the parents. Upon learning of this conception, we were not initially pleased, having made plans which would have to be altered. But as time went by, a mental metamorphosis took place in both of us, so that by the time our child arrived there was no question that what was happening was proper. As Elizabeth lay there with her arm encircling the baby, she was animated with a joy I had never seen before.

Your baby's stay in his first home, your womb, is comparatively short, but each new day adds tremendously to his growth and strength. Eighteen days after he is conceived, his heart is beating. About the fourth month or so of your pregnancy, you feel the flutter, the unmistakable stirring that is like no other. It's exciting and joyful—the revelation of a new life. Your body is superbly designed to meet his needs. There's the swelling readiness of your breasts, the expanding cradle of your womb. You are beautiful, as lovely as a tree that is heavy with fruit.

The last trimester—the seventh, eighth, and ninth months—are the "impatient months." You are eager to complete this stage and have the baby. You choose some things for the baby—diapers, of course, a baby carrier, baby clothes. How small they look! And you daydream—will it be a boy or girl?

Then, often when you least expect it, you feel a twinge. And another. The time is here. Mingled relief and anticipation can bring a catch in your throat. You might wonder at your own emotions, at the shadow of fearfulness you feel. Last minute preparations can be a blessing, for nature allows no turning back. Today, sometime soon, your baby will be born!

The doctor or midwife is contacted, and the preliminary details are taken care of. If your husband can be with you, you'll have the strength of two. You settle down to the work of giving birth, grateful for the pressure of his strong hand in yours. This day is like no other, and your mind, your whole body, centers on the process that is taking over inside of you.

The birth force rises, swells as a great wave, peaks, and recedes. Inexorably, rhythmically, it takes command. You try to concentrate on relaxing, on willing your muscles to cooperate. In the calm interim between contractions, there's rest.

The tempo quickens. Contractions are hard, come quickly. You've probably never worked harder in your life. Labor is a fitting term! Now is when you're most likely to feel exhausted and discouraged, and the reassurance of those with you is so important. "Don't give up!" you hear. "We'll soon have a baby!"

And, at last, there is the moment you've been waiting for all those months, the bursting forth, the moment of blessed birth! As you catch your breath, you hear his cry. Was a sound ever before so priceless? How vulnerable he looks, how indignant and wonderful!

The umbilical cord is cut, marking the first separation. Who is to bridge this change of worlds for your newborn, who will soothe him and let him know he is again secure? Who better than his mother?

Again your body cradles him. You touch him, kiss his cheek, stroke his damp little head. Will he nurse? Perhaps. At some time within the first hour or so he will take the breast. Gently you stroke his cheek with your nipple. He turns his head and nuzzles your breast. His tiny mouth grasps your nipple. Somehow, it seems no less than amazing! You and your baby can relax. Your tired body is not taxed by feeding your baby. After the enormous effort of giving birth, this is sweet reward.

In good time, without thought or conscious effort on your part, the milk will come. You can look beyond to the many days together as a nursing mother and baby. You'll begin to enjoy the "patient months." The security and warmth of your arms, the ready comfort of your milk, the familiar smell and pulse of your body are all precious food to fill out your baby's body and quicken his mind and spirit. Such accomplishments take time. But is there a more awe-inspiring task? This is the ageless beauty of mother and child—a time of grace and peace.

You'll hug him to you, intensely aware of his dependence upon you. Of course he will grow, will reach out, and eventually leave you. But not for a while. Give yourself time together; let there be no regrets. Together you'll begin to secure a new cord, one plaited simply and naturally of your

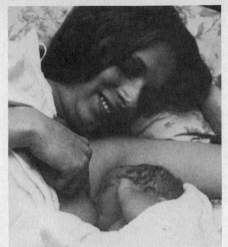

Breastfeeding immediately after birth is a wonderful way to welcome your baby into the world. Leigh Coryll and Teddy seem pleased with the idea. (Photo by Harriette Hartigan.)

continuing closeness through many unhurried days. Not to be cut, it will form the first link to all human love and understanding. And set firm and true, it will support and entwine new strands from father, brother, sister, family, all of society, through the years.

But perhaps, instead of the natural birth you prepared for, you have a cesarean delivery. Or the months of waiting are not long enough, and the baby arrives prematurely, to be whisked away for specialized care. It may be that your labor was long, and you are tired. For the moment there is little sense of rapport with the baby.

These things happen. They may slow down a mother's and baby's start as a nursing couple, but they need not end it. Given the right support, mothers and babies have untold levels of strength and adaptability. You can nurse your baby. Mothers through the ages have happily nursed their babies.

The groundwork is laid before your baby is born. Nothing is more important in your advance planning than your preparation for breastfeeding. There is no better time to start than now.

BEST FOR BABY—BEST FOR YOU

If you were to ask a group of nursing mothers to tell you what they consider the advantages of breastfeeding, they would most likely mention the points we bring up here. We will only touch briefly on the major benefits of breastfeeding in this section—we expand upon them later in Part Two of this book.

When you breastfeed your baby, you're providing him with the best possible infant food. No product has ever been as time-tested as mother's milk. Breast milk contains all the nutrients your newborn needs and is more easily digested and assimilated than any other infant food. Reassuring as this is, superior nutrition is only one of the many advantages you and your baby gain from breastfeeding.

There is no better safeguard for your baby against the onset of allergies than breastfeeding. A diet of your milk alone for about the first six months of his life readies his body for other foods. It protects him against infection as well as allergies. Living substances that are unique to your milk inhibit the growth of harmful bacteria and viruses in his still maturing system. With fewer problems, you can look forward to having a happier baby. And a happy baby is a smile on the entire household.

With his small head pillowed against your breast and your milk warming his insides, your baby knows a special closeness to you. He is gaining a firm foundation in an important area of life—he is learning to love.

As his tiny mouth eagerly milks your breast, your baby is performing an exercise that promotes the proper development of his jaw and facial structure. Breastfeeding also encourages a normal weight gain for your particular baby, which is good insurance against the millstone of modern life, obesity.

Putting your newborn to the breast within minutes after delivery helps prevent hemorrhage. Your infant's sucking causes the uterus to contract and reduces the flow of blood. It also results in the uterus getting back in shape more quickly than it would if you were not breastfeeding.

Since the beginning of time, mothers have instinctively cradled their newborn babies to their breast offering the warmth of their milk. Here Nash McLean Taylor, just minutes old, begins life nursing contentedly as he nestles against his mother's body.

The mother who is totally breastfeeding—not giving bottle supplements or solid foods—seldom becomes pregnant before her first menstrual period. This is usually six months or more following her baby's birth. It's a natural and safe form of birth control.

Breastfeeding—lactation—was meant to follow pregnancy and childbirth. The milk-producing breast represents a healthy progression in the natural sequence of pregnancy, birth, lactation. Many studies indicate that nursing your baby will improve your chances of avoiding breast cancer.

Breastfeeding results in an appreciable saving of time, effort, and cost when compared to formula feeding. Minutes and hours of a mother's time are not diverted to the preparation, sterilization, and cleanup of baby's milk. Feeding the baby is a time to relax. Day and night, automatically and accurately, milk is made and stored in the breasts. The temperature is always ideal; the supply is pure and practically unlimited. Nice, too, is the fact that this perfect food costs less than not-so-perfect substitutes. The good food you eat a little more of costs very little and nourishes both you and your baby.

Breastfeeding helps us, mothers and fathers, to recognize the different yet complementary ways in which we can relate to our new offspring. We mothers know that mothering through breastfeeding is the most natural and effective way of understanding and satisfying the needs of the baby. If you have older children, nursing the baby is an excellent form of sex education. For a parent, it is an educational process itself, of a rank and value equal to a course of study at any prestigious institution of learning.

Breastfeeding is the best start in life for a baby. Unlike so much that is considered "best" and is often beyond even one's wildest dreams, in this instance the best is yours to give.

YOU HAVE SOLID BACKING

If you had been a new mother living in Rome in the year 180 A.D., there is a good possibility that you would have heard the following advice from the physician Galen, who gave public lectures on anatomy and physiology. "For if one places the nipple in the mouth of the newborn, they suck the milk and swallow it eagerly. And if they chance to be distressed or to cry, the best appeasement of their unhappiness is the mother's nipple put in their mouth." Galen also advised mothers to rock and sing to their babies. "And whoever is able effectively to employ these arts," he observed, " will best develop both body and mind."

Closer to our own time, the man who is usually referred to as the father of the modern natural-birth movement, Dr. Grantly Dick-Read, said, "The newborn baby has only three demands. They are warmth in the arms of its mother, food from her breasts, and security in the knowledge of her presence. Breastfeeding satisfies all three."

Dr. Ashley Montagu, noted anthropologist and social biologist, wrote the following in 1971 in his book, *Touching:*

> Over the two or more million years of human evolution, and as a consequence of seventy-five million years of mammalian evolution, breastfeeding has constituted the most successful means of ministering to the needs of the dependent, precariously born human neonate . . . .
> For the newborn, what better reassurance can there be than the support of its mother and the satisfaction of suckling at her breast, what better promise of good things to come?

Still more recently, the American Academy of Pediatrics and the Canadian

Paediatric Society have stated that they "strongly recommend breastfeeding." Their joint statement, made in 1979, is widely recognized as a sweeping endorsement of breastfeeding.

The pediatricians stated, "We believe human milk is nutritionally superior to formula," and concluded that "the overall nutritional superiority of human milk remains unchallenged." As you might expect, the report stressed the importance of breastfeeding in those parts of the world where housing and sanitary conditions are inadequate. "For much of the population in developing countries," it reads, "both economic and health considerations speak conclusively for breastfeeding." A more surprising finding concerns areas that enjoy a high standard of living. Even in these areas less illness is reported among breastfed babies than among bottle-fed infants. The latest technological and medical advances notwithstanding, "new information suggests that significant advantages still exist for the breastfed infant." The report notes that breast milk is the only source of important elements that help to protect the newborn baby during the time his own immune system is maturing.

The pediatric groups also spoke of the emotional bond that develops between a breastfeeding mother and her baby. "Early and prolonged contact between a mother and her newborn infant can be an important factor in mother-infant bonding and in the development of a mother's subsequent behavior to her infant."

The Paediatric Society in New Zealand states, "Evidence continues to accumulate that an important contribution to child and possibly adult health can be made by an increased prevalence of breastfeeding."

The Kinderzentrum, the Institute for Social Pediatrics and Youth Medicine of the University of Munich, West Germany, considers breastfeeding "a primary measure in preventive pediatry."

A banner slogan at the World Health Organization reads, "Breastfeeding, a basic part of life." This multinational group issued a statement in Geneva in 1979: "Breastfeeding is an integral part of the reproductive process, the natural and ideal way of feeding the infant, and a unique biological and emotional basis for child development." The World Health Organization has also gone on record as urging, in strong terms, that steps be taken to counteract the spread of artificial infant feeding in high-risk populations.

Human milk has been in the limelight in recent years, as an information explosion has been removing some of the mystery surrounding its special properties. Scientists have long known that breastfeeding protects the infant, but now they are seeing how extensive this protection is and what makes it come about. Doctor T.E. Jarrett, Chairman of the Department of Pediatrics at the Chicago College of Osteopathic Medicine, points out that: "Recent research in the area of infant nutrition argues strongly for what we have known clinically for years. Breastfed infants have fewer serious or overwhelming infections, especially diarrhea and other gastrointestinal problems." These new discoveries are exciting, and additional details about them can be found in Part Two of this book.

Such background knowledge is valuable, for it can boost your confidence when your way of mothering is challenged. But knowing the special properties of breast milk is of little help in your first attempt to get your milk into your own very dear newborn. In the interest of keeping first things first, we have included in Part One of this manual the practical help you will need in order to nurse your baby. After all, mothers and babies were enjoying the benefits of breastfeeding long before proteins, immunities, or bonding were ever researched.

The mothers who sought out the physician Galen for advice were no better able to nurse their babies than you are. Your own determination is your most important asset. Look forward to being a breastfeeding mother.

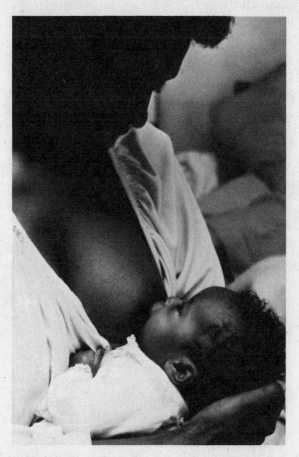

Michele McKinney and her daughter, Jorè, can attest to the special bond that exists between a mother and her breastfed baby (Photo by Harriette Hartigan.)

The months of pregnancy provide a special time for husband and wife to grow together into their new roles as parents. (Photo of Richard and Mary Wright by Richard Ebbitt.)

Chapter II

Planning for Your Baby

Planning for a new baby is one of the most exciting and forward-looking ventures in the life of a couple. You and your husband will dream the dreams that belong exclusively to parents, and your family's future is full of hope. But the status quo is up in the air. With the arrival of your newborn, your way of life will change as surely as the picture of your family that you so proudly display will change.

Planning usually begins with making practical arrangements. You'll select a doctor, look into childbirth education classes, locate breastfeeding help, and think about the things your baby will need. Then your attention will turn to the need for re-examining and rearranging the priorities in your life. Babies take time, and adjustments will have to be made. How can you change a routine here or eliminate an activity there in order to fit the new family member into your already busy life?

From long experience, we have learned that whenever a routine comes into conflict with the needs of one of the family members, it's the routine that has to give. Pursuits that had a prominent place in your life may be consigned to the background or even fade out of sight for the time being as you devote yourselves to your baby. "People before things" is a handy guide for picture taking and happy family making. Jim and Judy Good of Ohio, parents of eight and grandparents of eight, have led full, interesting lives, but they speak for many parents when they state with quiet conviction, "People are more important than things, especially when that person is a baby." More often than not, parents find that the old patterns and pleasures are not missed as much as anticipated. No doubt about it, the small new personality joining your family is guaranteed to add color, life, and sound to the setting!

It should be said, too, that this change of emphasis is not a temporary interlude, with life reverting to its former style once the baby is older. Having a baby, loving a child, is forever. You and your husband can no more return to the old ways than you can go back to life as it was before the two of you met and married. New experiences, endless opportunities, depths of feelings that you can know in no other way lie ahead of you.

True, the investment in a new baby is enormous. As you are probably well aware, the financial output is a definite concern for many young couples. But money is seldom the most critical or the rarest commodity that parents must provide. The coin that has greater value and is more difficult to part with is that which represents the continuous giving of one's self, emotionally and physically. Babies are unbelievably extravagant in this regard. They have no idea of how much it costs their parents to tend to them, worry about them, and love them day and night. They can't know, of course, until they themselves are one day parents. Then the gift is recognized and is passed on as lovingly as it was given.

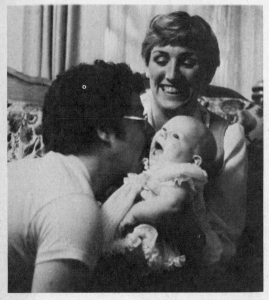

Life will never again be the same after your baby is born, but judging from the happiness Alicia Lindsay has brought into her parents' lives, who would want it to be any other way?

YOUR EXPECTATIONS

If you're like most first-time parents, you have some definite expectations of how a baby should behave. A favorite for many of us has to do with the "good baby," the baby who sleeps a great deal of the time and makes few demands. If his diaper is dry and his tummy full (the latter assured if he's been fed in the last hour), surely there should be no reason for crying. It's amazing that this image of a baby endures, considering that few, if any, adults would settle for such limited amenities in life. In answer to the inevitable question, "Is the baby good?" one La Leche League mother insists that all babies are good—some are just easier than others to live with at times. Aren't we all?

Another cherished idea in parenting is: "Don't let the baby rule your lives." The impression is that no thinking adult should allow a baby to "call the shots." It took some of us years of parenting to realize that this isn't a contest; it's a loving relationship. While babies cannot be outdone in loving, they need a little help with living. Your best guide is to listen to your own baby.

As mothers and fathers hope and struggle to be good parents, we must not be fooled into thinking that the "good baby" and the "parent in charge" offer proof of doing the job right. At times, it seems as if there is an inner pressure to be a perfect parent, although we'd all dismiss such an idea aloud as nonsense. It is nonsense, of course, and it takes away some of the fun of parenting. Be assured, the decision to just relax and enjoy your baby is much easier on both parents and babies.

Responding to your baby and enjoying him create the secure world that allows his body and soul to expand and thrive. Techniques in mothering are useful but secondary to your loving, unfailing concern. Have every confidence in your ability to care for your baby. A mother and father should realize that they are the most important people in their baby's life and the ones who will be best able to meet his needs.

FEELINGS—YOURS AND YOUR HUSBAND'S

Feelings—some positive, others negative—form a backdrop to the plans for your new baby. What are your husband's feelings about breastfeeding? What are your feelings about nursing the baby in front of others or when away from home? Questions and doubts are to be expected, and you and your husband should talk together about them and listen to each other.

When asked about breastfeeding, many men respond favorably or, at the least, are indifferent to the matter. Most recognize the natural way of feeding the baby as the best way.

A wife's enthusiasm for breastfeeding often sparks her husband's interest, so share your feelings with your husband. He can only begin to support your decision to nurse the baby if he understands what it means to you. Of course, not all husbands are pro-breastfeeding at first, and some, unfortunately, are downright unenthusiastic. Elton Kerness of New Jersey recalls his reaction to the prospect of his wife as a breastfeeding mother:

> When my wife, Bonnie, began to talk about nursing our expected child, I quickly realized that I had some fairly strong feelings on the subject, all of them negative.
> I knew nothing about breastfeeding. My feelings were mainly based on the fact that Bonnie had not nursed our other two children. Further, I had never known anyone who had nursed a child. I had some vague notions that this would disturb our man-woman relationship.
> I asked my wife why she was thinking of breastfeeding, who or what had influenced her decision. She said that one of her good friends was nursing her child and had talked to her about breastfeeding. This friend had also introduced her to an organization called La Leche League.
> I began to realize that most of my negative feelings were based on the plain and simple fact that I was ignorant of just what breastfeeding involved. Without real knowledge of the subject, I had fears of being tied down and not being able to go out with my wife, of being totally left out of her life because of the closeness of her relationship with the baby. And there was a natural anxiety about something new.
> "Just read the material," Bonnie said. "Don't have a closed mind. I believe if you read the book you will have a much better understanding of breastfeeding and then you will feel better about it."

So I promised her I would read the book, but that there were no guarantees.
Of course, I wanted to be able to help her as much as possible.
I read THE WOMANLY ART OF BREASTFEEDING rather surreptitiously,
for fear of being discovered by one of my male co-workers. It turned out
to be an enlightening experience.

Elton and Bonnie spoke with a knowledgeable pediatrician, one who "spent over an hour of his office time talking to us about the experience we were about to share." Elton was on his way to learning all he could about breastfeeding. "I was now a part of what was going on, and, like my wife, I spent time reading material and talking to others."

A little girl was born, and breastfeeding was off to a good start. The baby did "beautifully," and Elton concluded, "The peace and tranquility that a household experiences when a child is nursed is a wonder to behold. Everyone is less harried, and consequently everyone can enjoy the new addition as well as each other."

Of all the sources of encouragement a woman may receive in breast-feeding, her husband's support is the most meaningful to her. A woman looks for and appreciates her husband's interest, yet, for some, this kind of support is not easy to come by. Perhaps she is alone with her baby, or her husband is uncomfortable with the idea of his wife breastfeeding. The mother who has no such backing can still have a satisfying breastfeeding experience.

Sometimes the father who had misgivings before the baby was born grows to accept breastfeeding as the baby thrives on mother's milk. Renee Twombly of Illinois was expecting her third child when she made the decision to breastfeed. Her husband had some objections, but Renee decided to go ahead with her plans. "If God hadn't intended women to nurse their babies," Renee contended, "He would not have provided the equipment." Baby Aneta was a busy one-year-old, nursing only on occasion, when Renee felt her husband "had come around." She wrote, "It's the little things he says. Like the day when Aneta was nursing and suddenly said,

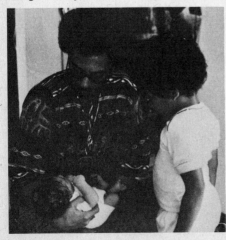

Al Colon introduces his newborn son, Jibari, to big brother, Adimu. (Photo by Donna Lyons.)

Fathers like Joe McGarry, with one-hour-old Kevin, know how easy it is for fathers to give their breastfed babies plenty of love.

'Mummmm.' Daddy looked over, laughed, and said,'The chocolate came in.' Or the genuine disappointment in his voice when he asked why she has virtually stopped nursing."

A discussion about breastfeeding, even when the husband has previously voiced strong reservations, can be a revelation. He may only want to spare his wife an undertaking that he believes will be too taxing for her. This was the case with the Metzes of Saskatchewan, Canada. Larry Metz was opposed to breastfeeding because a doctor had said his wife was high-strung and too nervous to nurse a baby. After a discussion with another doctor, one who had more experience with breastfeeding, Larry was reassured that women who may be labeled "nervous" or "high-strung" can nurse just as well as more relaxed women.

David Stewart, father of five from Missouri, offers this advice to other fathers in one of LLL's information sheets, *Father to Father:*

> Your support is so necessary. If forced to make a choice between her husband's wishes that she not breastfeed and her womanly desire to do so, she cannot feel happy with either decision. The outcome will be that either choice will adversely affect her relationship and attitude toward you. But if you are supportive, you will find that not only your wife, but you, too, will derive great satisfaction as she breastfeeds your baby.

Fathers Get Involved

One of the great things about today's fathers is that they really want to get involved with their babies. Some of them may think bottle feeding would have an advantage for them since they could help feed the baby. While we admit that an interested, involved father is a gem without price, we fail to see how dad is closer to his child just by giving a bottle. There are so many other things that dads and babies do so well together. A mother's contribution to her newborn is unique and the prototype of all other relationships throughout life. A father's gift is equally special, but different. Babies thrive on both. A story from Colorado by Mike Jackson is an example:

> It was hard to just stand by those first few months while the baby was almost totally wrapped up in mother and breastfeeding, but since she finally shed those wraps, we have been enjoying a relationship which is like no other I could imagine. Even though Kathy breastfed her until Jenny weaned herself at sixteen months, she has found herself almost having to fight for her share of the time with our baby. People gladly enlighten me as to her being a daddy's girl, and I love it. Whether we're playing on the swing set in the back yard, or she's helping me rearrange our rock garden, or we're raking leaves, we're always laughing and having a great time.
> Being a father is a thousand times more fun than I already knew it would be, because she is so secure in her early upbringing through breastfeeding. Daddy now gets his fifty percent of a loving child, Mommy gets her fifty percent, and baby gets one hundred percent of the love of both.

One mother, Pamela Benson of Washington, sums up her feelings simply: "There is no feeling like that in the middle of the night when I'm nursing the baby and my husband rolls over and puts his arms around us both. That is when I am happiest."

Discreet Nursing

Both you and your husband may have some uneasy feelings about what is still an uncommon sight in most parts of the western world—a mother nursing her child. You may worry about feeding the baby while you're away from home or when someone other than your husband is present. As the American Academy of Pediatrics noted, "It is a curious commentary on our society that we tolerate all degrees of explicitness in our literature and mass media as regards sex and violence, but the normal act of breastfeeding is taboo."

Embarrassment is one of the most common reasons mothers give for taking babies off the breast in a few weeks or months, even though the mothers enjoy breastfeeding. Interestingly, studies of breastfeeding mothers show that the mothers who stop early seldom know another nursing mother and have no one to confide in or help them in their new undertaking. Experienced breastfeeding mothers know how to nurse a baby so discreetly that only the mother and baby are the wiser. With such adeptness and the support of other level-headed parents, you'll find that your self-confidence soars. Breastfeeding can be as private as a mother wishes it to be, yet it need not unduly confine her and her baby.

There may be occasions when someone else in the room, a dear grandmother, perhaps, is extremely sensitive to the prospect of the baby being put to mother's breast when others are present. Breastfeeding mothers note that, at such times, discretion can be the better part of

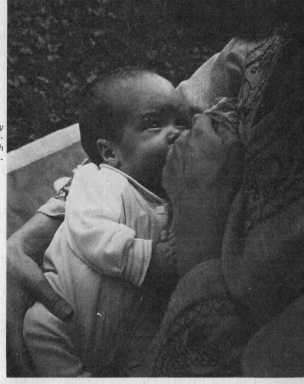

Only mother and baby are the wiser as twelve-week-old Elliot Smith nurses peacefully. (Photo by Martha Schulte.)

valor, and extra attention to modesty is a gesture of respect for others' feelings. Some mothers prefer to nurse the baby in another room, which is often less distracting for the baby, too. Dorothy Thorn of Alabama recalls breastfeeding her daughter:

Sometimes it's necessary, when visiting, to retreat to a friend's bedroom to nurse Summer, but this is a minor inconvenience when weighed with the many advantages of breastfeeding. I really believe a woman has to experience breastfeeding before she can truly realize the "hidden" advantages.

Although my husband was in favor of breastfeeding from the beginning, he has only recently been outspoken about it with friends. It's so easy to see why: all we have to do is look at our beautiful daughter!

On seeing the beauty of his wife breastfeeding their son for the first time, Tim Waltner of South Dakota was prompted to write:

It takes courage to nurse one's young. I suppose that we will not succeed for a long time in changing the distorted ideas of the breast. The most effective way to deal with the problem is to simply continue to encourage breastfeeding and not apologize for it. If there is a place for husbands and fathers in the breastfeeding relationship—and I am convinced there is—it is in being supportive of the mothers who do so.

A Pleasurable Experience

Women sometimes hesitate to breastfeed because, sadly, there are still a few mixed-up people in the world who will misinterpret the pleasure a mother experiences when nursing her baby. Nursing mothers tend to shrug a shoulder and dismiss innuendoes, since it's almost impossible to convey what they themselves know is normal and good to those who have no concept of this aspect of a woman's sexuality. A woman who breastfeeds with pride and satisfaction is aware that this is a sexual experience. She also knows that her feelings about it are on a totally different plane from the love she knows with her husband. Dorothy V. Whipple, MD, wrote in the *Journal of the American Medical Women's Association:*

> Suckling a baby, for the woman who accepts and enjoys her femininity, is a particularly moving experience. The physical sensation is pleasant, the guzzling eager mouth against the sensitive erectile tissue of the nipple is enjoyable in itself. It also brings peace, contentment, fulfillment to the whole body and personality. The sensation is not orgasmic; it is more like the peaceful afterglow of orgasm. It brings to the woman a deep and personal understanding of her role as a woman. It brings to her also a bond with women in distant times and cultures. The mature woman who carries out the totality of her feminine functions knows she has a niche in the ultimate scheme of things.

OTHERS IN THE FAMILY

The mother who is expecting her second child sometimes finds it hard to imagine that she will feel as close to the new baby as she does to the little one who is already here. Can there be the same strong love the second time around? The miracle of mother love is that it increases with each new birth. It is not diminished, not limited. It is not a pie that must be sliced into smaller pieces to accommodate extra plates at the table. With the new baby comes a resurgence of love for all of the family.

If you have older children, you're also probably wondering, "How can I possibly have enough time for them after the new baby arrives?" You ask if there won't be times when an older child will want your attention, and the baby will also need you. More than likely there will be, and this is when—and how—the mutual love and understanding that cement good human relationships are fostered. Learning to consider the needs of someone else who is helpless before one's own desires is an invaluable lesson in life for the older children. It is also one that you will want to help them with as much as you can.

In discussions about the arrival of the new member of the family, you and your husband can ask the other children to help you think of ways of managing and of helping each other. Encourage them to remember that the new baby will be the only member of the family who is completely dependent on you—just as they were at that age. When thought of in this way, it's easier for a young person to recognize (if not always accept) that the baby's needs must certainly come first.

Children usually understand the helplessness of a young one and accept it more readily than you might think. It has been revealing and gratifying to many of us to find that a crying baby is almost always disturbing to older children. They sense that something is not right, and they are happy again only when baby is happy. Looking ahead, you'll find that cheerfully putting the needs of the baby first, as a matter of course, is really an example of caring for others that benefits everyone concerned. It's truly a good way to educate your children for their future roles as loving parents.

At the same time, it's important for older children to know how precious they are to you and how much you love them. Telling your preschoolers the story of how you prepared for their coming and how important it was to you and their dad to give them the best care you could when they were babies is delightful reminiscing. It is also a positive way to help them understand that they were, and are, very special to you.

School-age youngsters in the family are generally very accepting of a new baby. They enjoy babies, and vice versa. Potential problems usually come from the variety of outside activities in which this age group is often involved and which demand a parent's participation. There's driving to and from games or lessons, attending programs, or working together on special projects. It can be a hectic pace for a mother who also has a new baby.

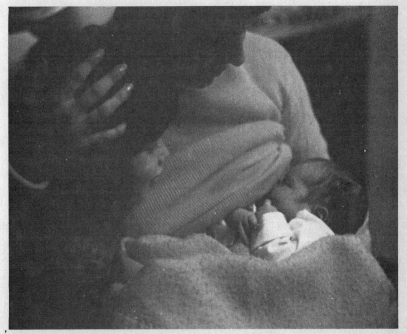

Parents are often amazed—and always delighted!—to see the special rapport that exists between an older sibling and a tiny baby. (Linda Schultz with her children.)

Many of these activities are attractive and worthwhile for your child, but here, too, you will have to be realistic and firm in setting limits for the time being. Do only those extras that you and the baby can honestly manage. Your husband can be a big help here, spending extra time with the older ones' activities whenever possible. But when both of you are too busy, your older children will still not be cheated; they're benefiting every day from the experience of having a younger brother or sister. If a particular program is very special to an older child, and neither you nor your husband can participate, be assertive in asking another parent to help you. For instance, a friend or neighbor could drive to and from functions; you can reciprocate later.

Babies are small for such a short time.

CHILDBIRTH

We learned early in the League's existence that a discussion about breastfeeding makes sense only if childbirth is also included. A woman's experience in giving birth affects the beginning of breastfeeding and mothering.

Childbirth can be a rich, joyful, and maturing experience. Those of us who have given birth without drugs and the medical instruments which so often follow their use know that helping her baby to be born and hearing his first cry can be a crowning moment of achievement in the life of a woman. It is not the only way for a baby to be born nor for a woman to feel this particularly strong sense of motherliness, but it is the most natural, and the easiest, for most of us. Doctor William Hazlett expressed the thought well when he wrote, "The more a woman accomplishes in her feminine, natural functions knowingly and willfully, particularly in labor, in the birth of her infant, and in its nourishment, the more she learns, both intuitively and consciously. The more she appreciates herself in so doing, the more her self-appreciation radiates toward her infant and others—her husband, her other children, and society."

For a new, expecting mother, it's reassuring to know that having a baby is a natural, normal function for which a woman's body is superbly designed. Almost all mothers are physically able to deliver their babies without medical assistance most of the time. A cardinal rule is to always have a doctor or trained midwife at the birth of your baby, as a lifeguard in the event of complications. But in the natural, normal birth, it is not the doctor who delivers the baby; it is the mother.

When you work with the birth forces within you during childbirth, your labor is shorter and more effective, and there's less need for the drugs that are often given when a mother is frightened and tense. The analgesics may seem inviting at the time, but keep remembering: *The healthiest birth situation for both mother and baby is one that is completely drug-free.* Advance preparation can pay off for you, your husband, and your baby by resulting in a shorter, safer, happier birth experience.

Your husband's presence and support can be a source of great comfort and strength to you in childbirth, and, we're happy to report, this is possible more and more often today. Your satisfaction in the labor of bringing your child into the world is more meaningful when reflected in your husband's eyes. Women need their husbands with them when their children are being born, and husbands take a giant step in feeling like fathers by being there.

You and your husband can begin to prepare for this truly momentous event in your lives by learning as much as you can beforehand. Read up on childbirth, and if at all possible, attend childbirth education classes. (Childbirth education associations are listed in the appendix, and books about childbirth are listed in the book list at the end of this book.)

Many of the fears, doubts, and misconceptions you may have about childbirth will disappear as you become better informed and more confident. In a childbirth class you can learn some simple exercises and helpful tips for staying on top of your contractions when the big day arrives and you know, "This is it!"

With concentration and practice, you can learn to make yourself relax, a technique that is invaluable in the first stage of labor. Your husband is a source of support that may be particularly welcome at the transition, the end of the first stage of labor. Then in the second stage of labor, by pushing with contractions, you move your baby out of the womb and into the world, perhaps even into his father's hands. The experience of seeing and holding his newborn bonds a father to his child and to the mother of his child in a special way. When you are all together—mother, father, and baby—you "claim" each other for your own.

You'll be able to hold your baby immediately after birth and put him to your breast. This step in mothering your newborn comes as naturally as day follows night. The outflow of love and warmth to your child at this time is an orderly continuation of the comfort, security, and warmth he has known for so long before his birth. This early contact between your baby and you can be very soothing and satisfying for both of you. Nursing the baby immediately after birth also encourages your milk to come in and starts you on your way as a breastfeeding mother.

Childbirth can and should be a family experience, shared by a husband and wife as they join together to greet their baby. As such, it is a wonderful beginning for a new family. The next step in your planning is finding the health professionals—doctors or midwives—who understand your hopes and can help you achieve your goals.

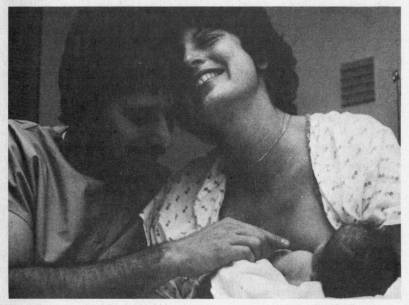

The moment of joy that John and Jan McIntosh experience following the birth of their daughter, Jenna, is the reason more and more couples are seeking hospitals that will allow them to share the entire birth experience. (Photo by Harriette Hartigan.)

YOU AND THE MEDICAL COMMUNITY

There's no doubt about it—your choice of doctors makes a difference. The doctor or trained midwife who attends you in childbirth will greatly influence how your infant is delivered, and the physician caring for your baby afterward can affect the course of breastfeeding. Even the doctor who prescribes for you should you become ill must take both you and your nursing baby into account. A doctor who has had little opportunity to learn about breastfeeding may be readily inclined to take the baby off the breast when treating either you or your baby. Such a move is bad for both of you and rarely necessary.

Many young couples are devoting a considerable amount of time and care to finding health-care professionals whose priorities in childbirth and baby care are similar to their own. For the parents who are eager to learn how to get what they want, there are numerous books written from a lay person's point of view on choosing health-care professionals, different methods of childbirth, and ways to communicate with doctors and hospital personnel. (See the book list at the end of this book.)

Attendance at La Leche League and childbirth education meetings is a good way to learn of other parents' experiences. As you become better informed, through reading and talking to others, you'll know the questions to ask in order to learn more about a doctor's or a hospital's practices.

Your first step will probably be to select the doctor or trained midwife who will attend the birth of your baby. Ask questions. Does the doctor encourage husbands to be with their wives for the birth? Seek out a doctor who does *not* routinely use medications or IVs during labor, who does not routinely induce labor or use fetal monitors, who does *not* routinely give anesthesia or do episiotomies.

Talking to Your Doctor

You and your husband may want to meet and talk to one or more doctors before selecting one. Before the interview, you can pave the way by sending a letter to the doctor stating two or three of your main concerns. For example:

> *Doctor, my husband and I feel strongly about being together when our baby is born. We prefer that as few drugs as possible be used during my labor.... It is very important to us that I have time with the baby right after birth.... Can arrangement be made so that our baby is not given supplements?... Being able to room-in with my baby is important to me.*

Even if unmedicated childbirth and breastfeeding are rarely seen in your community, think and act positively. Doctors can only assume that the standard routines they follow are acceptable to mothers and fathers unless informed otherwise. Jacqueline Palmenberg of Oklahoma had heard that the doctors she was considering would respond with "Not here" to her requests for different procedures. She decided to find out for herself and now strongly advocates asking for alternatives. "I communicated my desires, and the reasons for them, to the obstetrician and pediatrician. Permission was granted on all sides in advance," she reported. "What others assumed were 'rules' were only 'preferences.' There is an element of flexibility in preferences."

Your doctor, of course, is associated with a hospital and may also be in a group practice with other doctors. You'll be interested in knowing if an associate physician, rather than your doctor, may attend the delivery of your baby. Be sure to find out if the associates are also willing to respect your wishes.

You'll want to find out if the hospital takes kindly to husbands being in the delivery room and inquire about hospital arrangements for baby. Can babies room-in with their mothers?

The Baileys from Alabama were living in a new community for only a

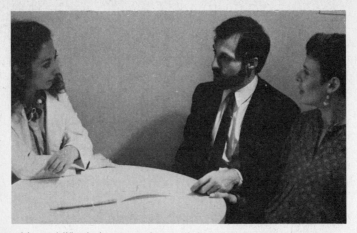

A happy, fulfilling birth experience begins with discussing your expectations with your doctor. Here Marc and Margie Davis talk over their desire for a shared, unmedicated birth, breastfeeding in the delivery room, and rooming-in with Dr. Cecelia Musso. (Photo by Pat Crosby.)

short time when they discovered they were expecting their second baby. Fran learned from a La Leche League Leader that the local hospital allowed fathers in the labor room but not in delivery. "Since Tony was present for Jessica's birth, I wanted the same experience with this baby," Fran told us. "We discussed ways of changing this policy for the better. I typed several petitions, which were then circulated in the local area. In just three days we had nearly two hundred signatures, and we presented them at the hospital's monthly staff meeting. The next day, I was notified that the petition was accepted and the hospital would admit fathers into delivery. I was ecstatic. Melissa was born a few months later with her proud father in attendance."

After discussing your concerns with your doctor, it's a good idea to put in writing what is acceptable to all of you and ask the doctor to indicate his or her agreement by signing your list. Such a simple memorandum could be the most important item you take with you to the hospital. Mothers say that producing their signed list was often all the authority needed to stay the hand that was ready to administer a routine procedure or medication in childbirth or give the baby the usual supplemental bottle in the nursery. If bottles are standing orders for the babies in your hospital, ask that an exception be made. Exceptions to hospital regulations are constantly being made, and you have nothing to lose by asking.

Birth Centers

A number of hospitals are responding to what George J. Annas, MD, MPH, writing in the *Medicolegal News,* calls "the patient influence on the way childbirth services are delivered." In an innovation called the "birth center," a husband and wife can be together, and labor and delivery can take place in one room that compares favorably to a bedroom in a home. Yet in an emergency, the full backup of the hospital system is just down the hall. Many of the usual "prep" routines, such as shaving and draping, have been eliminated. The mother stays in the same bed during labor and birth. Gone, and happily forgotten, is the delivery table with its cold, restrictive engineering and uncomfortable stirrups.

When there are no complications, mothers and babies often leave the birth center within twenty-four hours or less. Jerry and Elizabeth Rickert of Illinois drove seventy miles home the day following birth, with baby Charles in the infant safety seat in the back, his two-year-old sister, Julia, in her car seat, and mother between them.

Early and frequent nursings, unhampered by traditional hospital routines, are among the reasons that more and more mothers are choosing to have their babies in birth centers. Susan Jaffer nurses her newborn daughter, Gillian.

The Stephens of Kentucky were looking for a new doctor when their third baby was on the way. Ellen wrote of her efforts:

I didn't know a pro-natural childbirth physician, and our hospital doesn't allow fathers in the delivery room. Spinals, medications, and mother-infant separation are routine. After much searching, I found an obstetrician and pediatrician in a city twenty miles away who agreed to let me "do it my way."

Sarah was born fifteen minutes after we arrived at the hospital, at nine P.M. My husband hurried into the delivery room seconds after her birth and just in time to support me while I held her for the first time. Sarah came to the recovery room with me, thanks to a note from the pediatrician allowing this. There were a few raised eyebrows, but the nurses were very helpful. The doctor checked the baby and we were home by midnight, greeted by my parents and our very excited four-year-old Amy. Andrew, two years old, slept through the homecoming.

The moments we shared with him the next morning when he awoke to the squeaks of his new sister were most precious. I believe the bonding of mother and infant, and family and infant, are very important, and I wouldn't trade those first few hours with my newborn for anything!

My advice to anyone wanting a different experience than what is routine for their area is, be persistent.

Home Birth

One alternative to a hospital delivery is a "new" old approach, a home birth, with the mother staying in her home and the doctor coming to her. A cooperative doctor or midwife and a pregnancy that is serenely free of complications are prerequisites for a home birth. Those of us who have had our babies at home remember it as a simple, joyful experience that disrupted the flow of family life very little. When dear ones are nearby, a sense of closeness and solidarity is generated all around. Sisters, sisters-in-law, or her own mother often attend the new mother. Granddad and uncles can help with the young children, run errands, support, encourage, and sometimes pray. The whole family celebrates with the parents when the newest family member arrives in their midst.

A pioneer in delivering babies at home in an urban area is Dr. Gregory White, president of the American College of Home Obstetrics. Eight of the Whites' eleven children were born at home, either in Franklin Park or in the big white house with the red door in River Forest, Illinois where the Whites now live. The first patient of Dr. White's to have a home birth was Edwina Froehlich, one of the founders of La Leche League, when she and her husband, John, welcomed their firstborn, Paul, into the world in 1950. Since that time, both the number of doctors doing home births and the mothers enjoying them have increased greatly. Cindy Blease from

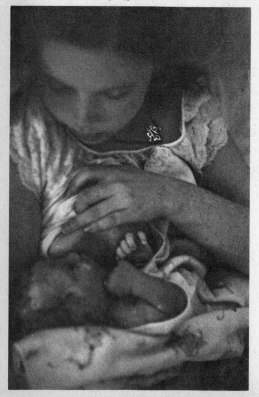

Home birth can be an enriching experience for the entire family. Here, Marie Hawbecker nurses Paul just minutes after he was born at home.

Maine writes about her home birth:

> After considerable debate and seeking of opinions from knowledgeable people, Jack and I decided to have our sixth child at home. Our doctor, Dr. Eva Reich, was happy to cooperate, so we went ahead with our plans. Darryl's birth was simple and beautiful. I never felt the need for any medication—I felt really "with it" and in tune with nature.
>
> Darryl started nursing after the first ten minutes. It took him a little while to get used to his new surroundings, then he nursed for forty minutes, and again for forty minutes before we finally settled down for the night—something that would never have happened in a hospital. He was as warm and snug as could be. For the first week or so he nursed every two hours pretty much around the clock.
>
> I wouldn't recommend home birth to everyone, but it gave me no problems. When I think of Darryl's birth it is with a warmth and closeness I never really felt when our first five children were born in the hospital.

If you would like to learn more about the choices parents have in regard to childbirth options, such as home birth, you might want to contact an organization called NAPSAC (National Association of Parents and Professionals for Safe Alternatives in Childbirth). See Appendix.

The Cesarean Question

According to a report by the National Center for Health Statistics, the number of cesarean deliveries performed in the United States in the years from 1973 to 1976 moved this operation onto the list of the ten most commonly performed surgical procedures, an increase that is viewed with alarm by many doctors and parents.

The decision to perform a cesarean is a serious one, often made at a critical point in labor when parents are not likely to question their doctor's decision. Parents will want to thoroughly discuss their doctor's views on cesarean deliveries early in pregnancy. A few doctors have come to feel that cesarean deliveries are always necessary for twins, babies who are breech, and so-called "prolonged" labor. Other doctors view cesarean deliveries as only a last resort and find that in many such cases all that is needed is a little more time and patience. With proper medical support and care, most babies, even the big ones, can be successfully delivered vaginally with greater safety for both mother and baby.

The incidence of prematurity, respiratory distress syndrome, and other complications is far higher with cesarean deliveries, and the likelihood that the baby and mother will be separated from each other, often for some time, is much greater. The mother is more likely to experience infection, pain, and discomfort, as well as psychological effects such as depression after a cesarean delivery.

If your doctor feels a cesarean delivery may be necessary for your baby, don't hesitate to consult another doctor before making such a major decision.

If you have already had a previous cesarean delivery you should know, too, that many such mothers have had subsequent vaginal deliveries with a much happier outcome than they could have enjoyed with another cesarean. Frequently the reason for the first cesarean delivery does not apply to subsequent births. Organizations such as C-SEC or VBAC can offer further information about this. (See Appendix.)

When a cesarean delivery must be performed, general anesthesia is usually not necessary. One of the regional anesthetics (spinal, epidural, or local) will allow you to be awake during the operation and involves fewer risks. A growing number of doctors and hospitals permit husbands to stay with their conscious wives during the cesarean birth. Mothers appreciate their husbands' comfort and support, and the fathers are glad to be able to participate in the birth of their babies. Discuss these things with your doctor.

The Baby's Doctor

When you are choosing the doctor who will care for your baby, you'll want to comb the area for someone who is knowledgeable about breastfeeding or at least has a positive attitude toward it. For many of you, a family doctor will be caring for both you and your baby and you can discuss breastfeeding at your prenatal visits. But many others will be selecting a pediatrician to care for the baby after birth. Make an appointment to talk to the doctor before the baby is born and let him or her know that you plan to breastfeed your baby. Ask questions. Are most of the doctor's patients breastfed? How does he or she deal with situations such as slow weight gain? A doctor who has not dealt with many breastfed babies may want you to give supplementary bottles or recommend that you start solid foods too early. If you are not satisfied with the answers you receive, shop around for another doctor. If this is not possible, discuss your concerns openly with the doctor and explain why nursing is so important to you.

You may want to ask La Leche League Leaders in your area about doctors who are helpful to breastfeeding mothers. Your choice of a doctor does make a difference.

Speak Up

When dealing with the health professionals in your area, you may have to take the initiative in letting them know what you want. A doctor who sees mostly bottle-fed babies may think that a mother would only want to nurse for a few months. This doctor may not realize how upsetting the offhand directive. "Wean the baby" is to a breastfeeding mother—and her baby! The doctor won't know that you prefer to continue to breastfeed unless you speak up. A simple, direct statement can begin a dialogue between the two of you. "Doctor, I need to discuss this with you. It's important to me." When there's a need for medication or hospitalization for the baby, you need a doctor who will treat him yet not interrupt breastfeeding—or do so as little as possible. Staying close to your baby at a time of illness, nursing him when possible, is always best.

Occasionally parents and the doctor find themselves at cross-purposes, perhaps over the treatment of a sick child, and the situation is enough to make the doctor throw up his hands and a mother dissolve in tears. Some emotion can be good, really—it relieves the tension and expresses more forcefully than words (which can be hard to find at such a time), how strongly a mother feels her baby's need for her.

If the doctor you are consulting is not able to understand your position, you are always free to consult another and, if necessary, change doctors. The American Medical Association calls this right of the patient the Fifth Freedom. Such instances are rare; we have many glowing accounts of parents and doctors learning from each other. Many doctors frankly admit that their views on breastfeeding have changed completely since getting to know happy nursing mothers and their healthy babies.

Most questions about problems of the breastfeeding mother are not medical, and even if your doctor is not knowledgeable about breastfeeding, you can count on having all the information you'll need to nurse your baby from a source such as La Leche League.

PREPARING YOUR NIPPLES AND BREASTS

Many women do nothing out of the ordinary to prepare their nipples and have no problems when they begin nursing their babies. Other women, usually those with fair skin and often blonde or redheaded, seem to have difficulty with nipple tenderness or soreness when they begin nursing. (Unfortunately, being a brunette with a dark complexion doesn't guarantee there won't be problems.) Most women reading this book have probably worn a bra since the first signs of womanhood, and their nipples have received little exposure to the naturally toughening effects of air, sun, and friction. The nipple soreness that sometimes develops in the early days of nursing will go away in time, but why not avoid or minimize the problem with some advance preparation?

A Daily Routine

A few precautions and some simple routines in the last three months of pregnancy serve as good conditioners for your nipples. First, it is important to avoid anything that is drying to the skin, because dryness encourages cracked nipples. Your normal routine for keeping the breasts clean is all the washing needed, both before the baby is born and afterward. Soap is drying, so use it sparingly, if at all, and rinse well. Many mothers avoid soaping the area around the nipple.

When you were newly pregnant, your breasts may have been tender and even sore to the touch, but that feeling will go away, and you can then begin the preparations that will help bring your nipples out. This will make them easier for your baby to grasp. Nipple preparation also helps you to feel comfortable handling your breasts and expressing your milk, a technique that may be helpful to you later on.

After bathing, rub each nipple with a terry cloth towel briskly, but gently. To bring the nipple out, place a thumb and forefinger near the base of the nipple and gently press together. You'll be able to feel where the larger mass of the breast tissue ends and the nipple begins. Then, holding the nipple, slowly pull it out, and gently, turn it up and then down. Do this exercise several times with each nipple, but only until it feels slightly uncomfortable, never painful. Gradually increase the number of nipple pulls, or rolls.

Gentle breast massage can also be helpful. Cup the breast with your hand and, pressing your fingers and thumb together slightly toward the chest wall, circle the breast with this gentle massaging motion.

Some mothers also apply a lubricant to their nipples. Any skin cream you already have should work well. Safflower oil (without preservatives), the oil used for salads and cooking, is another inexpensive choice you may want to try. It doesn't contain perfumes and is excellent for the skin all over your body. Pour a small amount in a couple of clean containers to keep in your bedroom and bathroom, and store the large bottle in the refrigerator.

This routine will take you only a few minutes each day. The important thing is to do it regularly. If you can go without a bra for part of each day, your nipples will benefit from the air and the light friction of your outer clothing. Some women are uncomfortable going braless and wear an old bra with the front cut out or use a nursing bra with the flaps down. Direct sunlight on the breasts, in very carefully-timed amounts to prevent burning, is also excellent to toughen the nipples.

For some couples, a normal part of their love-making, caressing the breasts and sucking the nipples, also serves as a form of nipple preparation. They see it as a natural help in preparing the wife's breasts for the coming work of nourishing their child.

Flat And Inverted Nipples

If you try the above nipple pulls and find that your nipples do not come out far enough for you to grasp them easily, you may have flat or inverted nipples. Squeezing or pinching gently at the base of the nipple should cause the nipple to project away from the breast. Flat nipples react by being shy. They just barely come out, a not uncommon situation among mothers who have never nursed before.

A highly recommended method for encouraging the flat nipple to be more outgoing was developed by Dr. J. Brooks Hoffman of Connecticut and was passed on to us by Dr. Richard Applebaum of Texas. With the "Hoffman technique," draw an imaginary cross on the nipple. Place a thumb on each side of the nipple along one line of the cross. Your thumbs should be directly at the base of the nipple, not the edge of the areola, the larger dark skin area surrounding the nipple. Press in firmly against the breast tissue and at the same time pull the thumbs *away* from each other. You'll be stretching out the nipple and loosening the tightness at the base, which will make the nipple move up and outward. Dr. Hoffman

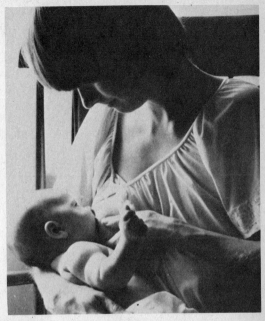

Preparing your nipples and breasts during pregnancy will help you to enjoy special moments such as those shared by Charlotte McPherson and six-week-old Amy Joy.

recommends that you repeat this stretch five times first thing in the morning, first along one of the imaginary lines of your cross, and then along the other. This preliminary step makes it easier for you to then grasp the nipple at the base and proceed with the pulling action described above.

Completely inverted nipples can be a problem, but they are rare. An inverted nipple shrinks back into the breast when the areola is depressed. Some inverted nipples appear as though they're pushed in all the time. One mother who had this type called it "the folding model of the nipple world." A full-size nipple is there, ready and able to do the job for which it was intended, but left on its own, it folds back into the breast instead of coming out when the baby tries to nurse.

Inverted nipples do respond to care, with the best treatment for the truly inverted nipple being the use of breast shields. Breast shields can also be used to correct flat nipples, since they're designed specifically to draw the nipple out. (They are worn for several months during pregnancy and should not be confused with the nipple shields sometimes used when feeding a baby and which, incidentally, almost always create more problems than they solve for the breastfeeding mother.) Breast shields are comfortable to wear, lightweight, and inconspicuous under your bra. You can begin wearing them as early as the third month of your pregnancy for a few hours a day and gradually increase the time to eight hours a day. There are two sections to each shield, the bottom part, which has an opening for the nipple and fits directly over the breast, and the top part, which holds the bra away from the emerging nipple.

The shields are available from La Leche League, and complete instructions come with them. They do perform well, so don't worry if you have flat or inverted nipples; you can breastfeed your baby. If you have this condition, you'll have to make the effort to bring them out so that your baby is able to begin nursing. Once he gets started, he'll soon draw the nipple out further, and, as only baby can, make it into a fine working model.

Occasionally, when flat or inverted nipples are discovered after the baby is born and there's a problem getting started, these shields can be worn between feedings to correct the condition. We tell about this in the section "Breastfeeding Gadgets."

Hand, or manual, expression is one way of milking the breast. Some authorities recommend that a little hand-expression be used during the last six weeks of pregnancy to squeeze out a few drops of colostrum, the first milk, which looks thick and creamy at this time. They believe this practice will keep the ducts open and prevent swelling, engorgement, and sore nipples. Opinion is divided on the matter, so ask your doctor if he or she wants you to hand-express colostrum. The procedure is the same as when expressing a quantity of milk, and we explain this in detail in "How to Express and Store Breast Milk." You will only express a few drops of the colostrum, and you may not get any—some mothers don't. But there's no reason to worry; the colostrum is there, and even if you can't express any, your baby will know just how to get it out.

SPECIAL PRECAUTIONS

Diet

If you already have good eating habits, there is no reason for you to make any major changes now. On the other hand, if you know that your eating habits could stand improvement, the period while you are pregnant and then nursing your baby is a good time to do this. Your baby's well-being during pregnancy depends to a great extent on good nutrition; your own health and well-being are also at stake. You now have a real investment in your baby's welfare as well as your own—and changes made because of strong motivation are easier to make and more likely to stick.

If you upgrade your diet while you're pregnant and then continue to prepare the same good foods when you're breastfeeding, they will soon be standard fare for the family, to the benefit of all. For a summary of the basics of good nutrition see "Nutritional Know-How."

Smoking

There's a cloud on the horizon for the baby whose mother smokes during pregnancy and afterward. You probably already know some of the disturbing statistics on smoking. Heavy smoking is a known cause of miscarriage, prematurity, and low birth weight. If you do smoke you are probably seriously thinking of quitting. Take heart—many women find that pregnancy is all the additional motivation they need to stop smoking. Do your best to quit. If you can't stop altogether, at least cut down. We heartily support your good resolutions and suggest that you encourage all other smokers in the house to put away the cigarettes along with you. Breathing secondhand smoke can affect a baby's health. If you can clear the air, your baby is less likely to develop respiratory problems.

As for marijuana, using it during pregnancy and when breastfeeding is courting trouble. New evidence on this drug clearly indicates that its effects on both mother and baby are far more serious than was previously thought to be the case. For one thing, the use of marijuana has been found to cause significantly lower levels of prolactin, the "mothering" hormone that is important not only to an adequate milk supply but to the whole mother-baby relationship. Again, be aware of the possible dangers of passive (secondhand) smoke.

Drugs

You should make it a practice not to take any medication whatsoever unless it is definitely necessary and has been prescribed or approved by a physician. Our medical advisors stress that this rule applies throughout life, but that the consequences of ignoring it can be particularly devastating during pregnancy. We live in an age of overmedication with an increasingly high incidence of serious drug allergies and other sometimes tragic reactions. This fact was sharply underscored some years ago by the thalidomide tragedies.

During the last six weeks of your pregnancy, you'll also want to guard against the use of aspirin (salicylate). A publication of the U.S. Department of Health, Education, and Welfare stated in 1978:

> Aspirin and other drugs containing salicylate should not be taken during the last three months of pregnancy except under a doctor's supervision. Salicylate, a common ingredient in many over-the-counter painkillers, may prolong pregnancy and labor and may cause excessive bleeding before and after delivery.

Cleaning out the medicine cabinet can be a part of your before-baby-arrives preparations. Being very cautious about taking any medication—aspirin, antihistamines, diet pills, and any other over-the-counter medications—unless prescribed or approved by a physician is a good health practice for all members of the family. Following this simple rule will help protect your family's health and, in addition, will have a noticeably beneficial effect on the family budget.

In recent years, a great deal has been learned about drugs in human milk and the effect, if any, that this may have on the nursing mother's baby. In the few cases where drugs are medically indicated, each situation must be considered individually. In general, there are only a relatively few medications that must be totally avoided by a nursing mother. For more information, see "When Mother Is Ill."

Alcohol

Alcohol, when used to excess, must also be included on the list of drugs that may harm your baby before he is born. Moderation at all times is extremely important; binges and babies don't mix.

While breastfeeding, an anxious, overtired mother may find that an occasional glass of wine, beer, or other alcoholic drink helps her to relax. Of course, as mother becomes less tense, so does her baby. Nursing itself is an excellent tranquilizer, and relaxing is the key. Many mothers who choose not to drink alcohol find that tension drains away with a cup of hot or iced tea, or another favorite beverage. Lying down can do wonders, and listening to music is soothing. Especially nice is having your husband's reassuring arms around you when you're nervous about your new responsibilities.

WHAT YOUR BABY NEEDS

Of course you'll be getting things for the new baby. There are so many different kinds of furniture, clothing, and other articles for a baby, you can indulge your inclinations to the limits of your own pocketbook and the generosity of friends and relatives. Very little specialized baby equipment is really necessary; more important to the baby are mother's sweet milk and loving arms. The items we mention here have been consistent favorites with parents for years. Many of them may be found at resale shops or rummage sales, or you may be able to obtain some on loan from friends.

Heading our list is the baby carrier, a simple device popular in all parts of the world. The carrier is a snug holder that suspends from mother's shoulders. Rediscovered in the past twenty-five years in the western world by nursing mothers in particular, the baby carrier was reported as "the one item mentioned most often by all mothers" in an informal survey conducted by *Potomac Potpourri,* a local insert to LLL NEWS, La Leche League's bimonthly publication. Editor Mary Redenius of Virginia had invited readers in the four-state area surrounding Washington, D.C. to give their views on baby equipment. The favorite style of carrier among the Potomac mothers was the soft, fabric, knapsack type, preferably the kind that can be worn either on the back or front.

Another popular choice is the large, sturdy, pouch-like carrier with openings for the baby's legs and perhaps a lightweight metal frame for extra support. There is also a simple sling variety that goes over one shoulder and holds the baby against the opposite hip. It folds into a small packet that can be tucked into a bag for ready use at any time. The young baby lies in it, hammock-style, his head supported against your arm or hand. Once he sits up well, the carrier is a sling seat from which he can survey the world.

Helen Nichols of Massachusetts described life with a little passenger aboard in a letter to the League "in praise of the baby carrier." Helen wrote, "As with breastfeeding itself, the benefits of the baby carrier are not entirely for the baby. In fact, as I discovered, mother receives a

Baby carriers and slings, from simple to sophisticated, all serve to keep baby snug and contented in the place he most loves to be—right next to his mother.

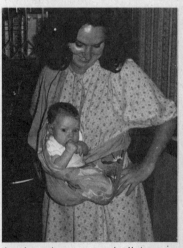

generous portion of them. I could cook, clean house, wash dishes, care for the older children, even sew while Benjamin slept blissfully in his cozy nest. It was, purely and simply, the very easiest thing to do."

As may be expected, Helen's use of the carrier elicited some dire warnings that the baby would surely be "spoiled." She writes, "Now that I can look back from my present position as mother of a happy, independent, cooperative fourteen-month-old, I realize that subconsciously I was running an experiment to see if constantly holding a newborn really would 'spoil' him, or would create problems when he became too big to carry around all the time. I discovered that as his body size grew, so did his ability to be on the floor trying to crawl or learning to walk. The less I was able to carry him around, the less he needed to be carried around."

A suggestion for taking the weight off the shoulders when carrying a child in a carrier on an extended trip comes from Nancy Shefelbine of New Mexico. Nancy's husband, Hank, an outdoorsman, suggested adopting the backpacker's technique of using a hip belt with the carrier. A couple of holes were drilled into the metal frame of their carrier in order to attach the hip belt.

With all carriers, it's a good practice to periodically check the straps, rings, and other parts for signs of wear. A break could result in a nasty fall for baby.

For the family with a car, an infant auto safety seat is a must. If you use it faithfully, beginning with baby's first ride (possibly the trip home from the hospital), you and your baby will soon accept the procedure as a matter of course. Whenever possible, plan to nurse the baby before starting out in the car, so you and baby will be more relaxed.

A member of the League, Jean Jewett, prepared the information on auto safety for children for the Michigan Office of Highway Safety Planning and recommends an impact-tested infant safety seat that faces toward the back for the young baby who is not yet old enough to sit up. Check with the Highway Safety Division in your area or *Consumer Reports* for information on the crash-resistant ratings for safety seats and devices. You cannot know if a safety seat is satisfactory by looking at it or feeling the padding.

Before selecting a seat, make certain that it will fit in your car and that the car seat belts are long enough to hold it in place. Jean cautions, "Be sure to fasten the harness around the baby and the safety belt around the

It's important to use an auto safety seat routinely every time you take your little one in the car. Here, Julia and Chuck Rickert are securely fastened into their auto safety seats and ready to go!

seat." When the weather is cold, dress the baby in a warm garment with sleeves rather than bundling him in blankets so you can bring the harness around him. Tuck any extra blankets on top. She also suggests that a rolled-up blanket or towel be placed on each side of the newborn to keep him from "slouching down into a little ball."

The auto safety seat, Jean points out, "costs less than an office visit to the doctor and a prescription for a minor problem, and auto safety is *not* a minor health problem. The automobile accident is the number one killer and crippler of children today."

A comfortable rocking chair is another popular item, and we'd go so far as to say that a rocker is every mother's and baby's due. Be sure to try out your selection for size and "feel" before purchasing it for the nursing corner. Judy Kahrl of Ohio suggests that you test the height of the armrest by placing your arm as you would while nursing the baby. "The one I had was too low, and I needed to have a pillow under my elbow," Judy discovered. And Mary White suggests that your rocker be "a nice wide one with room enough to tuck a toddler in beside you." Mothers also find the rocker is worth its weight in gold during the last months of pregnancy, and it can be a most comfortable spot in the early stages of labor, too.

A stroller or carriage also makes our list of things for the baby. The lightweight, collapsible strollers are popular, and some of these can hold both the baby and a toddler. Bear in mind, though, that convenient as these strollers are, they tip over rather easily and must be used with care. Many mothers like the versatility of a carriage-bed that accommodates a small baby and can be used to rock him gently to sleep.

The mothers in the Potomac survey expressed a number of other preferences. Changing tables were "loved or hated." Sue Arnold of Virginia used an unfinished kitchen cabinet for a changing table, finding it the right height, sturdy, and useful later for toys. The Redeniuses placed an old pillow on top of the baby's changing surface. Their newborn was more secure and did not startle as easily. A word of caution is in order when placing the baby on a table, counter, or any high surface. Fasten your young baby securely or take him with you if you go for a forgotten item or to answer the phone or door. In just a few seconds, the baby who supposedly does not roll over can fall and be seriously injured. The safest changing surface of all is the floor.

A word of warning is in order, too, regarding infant seats and walkers. Never leave your baby unattended in an infant seat on a table or counter. An active baby can easily scoot the seat across the smooth surface until, crash!, baby and seat are on the floor. A walker, a seat on wheels, also poses a danger. Too many babies have fallen down the stairs in them. A walker also restricts the baby and denies him the opportunity to naturally develop his coordination of arms, legs, and eyes that comes with crawling. Safer and more comfortable for the baby is a type of infant seat that rests on the floor and has a cloth back and seat on a slightly springy, metal-tubing frame.

In many homes, the full-size, expensive baby crib is losing ground to a mattress on the floor or space in mom and dad's supersize bed. In her excellent book, *Good Things For Babies,* Sandy Jones writes:

> The crib as we know it is a new and novel device. Historically, members of the human race gathered warmly together to sleep. Baby and mother slept together, with the baby nursing whenever she wanted to throughout the night. It is only in very recent history—the past hundred years, perhaps—that it has become the mode to put baby in a room to herself, in a wooden cage (the crib) and to give her a bottle rather than her mother's warmth.

If you do decide you want a crib for your little one, be sure to check into current safety standards for them. Older cribs may not meet these.

Playpens did not get a good press in the Potomac survey, and few of these mothers would put out the money for one. A mother who was given a used playpen set it up in the basement and found it useful to keep the baby off the damp floor while she did laundry. Another mother said her playpen was "a must" in her basement—to store the winter supply of squash.

A highchair can be a convenience for parents when the baby is older and ready to be eating solid foods, but a highchair can also be dangerous. Be sure the one you select has a wide base to prevent tipping over as well as a safety strap to insure that baby can't climb or fall out. Fasten the safety strap faithfully—it takes only a few seconds.

Baby clothes, too, come in for their share of attention from League mothers. In her LLL NEWS column, "Notes from Grandma," Betty Wagner suggests that you purchase as few baby outfits of one size as is practical, since your baby will outgrow them before you know it. Betty also questions the use day and night of one-piece suits which leave only the baby's head and hands uncovered. What a wasted opportunity for skin-to-skin contact! If you do use the one-piece suits with feet, Betty advises that you make sure the baby's toes have ample room to wiggle. And turn the outfits inside out when washing or check the foot portion to remove all threads or strands of hair before putting them on your baby. A length of hair wrapped around a small toe has been known to cut off circulation. Also snip the thin elastic bands on the wrists and ankles, since these too can bind.

Baby clothes made of natural fabrics such as white cotton cause fewer skin reactions and are preferred over synthetics. Be cautious when using fabric softeners for baby articles; they're a common cause of skin rashes.

A report on things for the baby would not be complete without some mention of diapers. The nursing baby needs a diaper that keeps the soft breast-milk stool from escaping out the sides—a particularly troublesome occurrence when visiting. An extra pin on each side of a cloth diaper will hold it close around the baby's legs. Some disposable diapers have a snug fit, but the special inner liner may prevent the necessary absorption.

There is something about settling into a comfortable rocking chair that seems to invite a relaxed, intimate dialogue between mother and baby. Linda White is shown here, enjoying such a dialogue with her daughter, Lindsay.

Removing the liner may help. A sensitive baby could also have a problem with the materials or fragrances used in certain disposables, as well as the plastic, outer covering that prevents air circulation.

If your baby develops a diaper rash, try using a vinegar rinse when washing the diapers. Just add a cup of vinegar to the final rinse. Ammonia and fungus-like organisms will not build up.

Speaking of diapers—a handy tote bag is invaluable. Mothers fill these bags with diapers, a change of baby clothes, an extra sweater, mom's purse, small toys, and snacks and books for a toddler. On the way home such treasures as shells from the beach or pinecones from the forest are added to the general inventory. The bag is an indispensable addition to your wardrobe, so keep it filled and ready to go.

All in all, babies need very few material things, and life is simpler for everyone involved without the extra furniture, fancy clothes, and complicated feeding equipment. Of course you won't need bottles or a sterilizer.

When considering things and babies, Lee Stewart of Missouri sums up the subject well: "Children's natural values are very human and simple. They want to be held and loved. They want to be with those who care for them. They want to be comfortable. Given a choice between the warmth of human values and material values, babies will almost always choose the human."

HOUSEWORK AND THE NEW BABY

The Best-Laid Plans

Top household efficiency and a new baby mix about as well as oil and water. Meeting baby's unscheduled needs makes a strict household schedule pretty much a thing of the past. This is not to say that a well-ordered life automatically becomes chaos at the moment of birth, but it is fair warning that you will want to reorder your thinking and reorganize your approach to household chores before your due date arrives.

The key to survival is to simplify. Pick an afternoon now to take a walking tour of your house, critically examining each room for items that should be removed, rearranged, or discarded. Do you hate to see the knickknacks on the bookshelf covered with dust? Then put them away and replace them with a fresh new plant that will brighten both the room and your spirits. Will you feel pangs of guilt if you see your silver trays or tea service covered with tarnish after baby arrives? Then secure them tightly in plastic bags and pack them away for a while. How about that overstuffed closet where everything from ski gear to broken lampshades seems to end up? You and your husband can work together now to clean it out, so that it won't get on your nerves later. Discard the things that are beyond repair or that you no longer need—don't just move them somewhere else where they will soon be in your way again. Box up as much of the rest as you can and store it in the attic or basement. You'll feel good about having such a big chore out of the way, and you'll be ever so grateful for that extra space to keep the baby items you'll soon be acquiring.

Whatever the season, do as much "spring cleaning" now as you can, so that you can let things slide for a while after baby is born. Light household chores are good exercise for you now, and having them done will be a godsend later when you'll want to devote your time and energy to the baby. This sudden zeal for cleaning and readying the house so often felt by mothers during the last months of pregnancy is referred to familiarly as the "nesting instinct."

Give some thought to rearranging your cleaning supplies so that they are readily accessible (but stored in a high, child-proof cupboard). You'll want your supplies to be handy so you can quickly clean a bathroom mirror or scour a sink if you have a moment before stepping into the shower or while keeping an eye on a three-year-old in the tub. Your bathroom will be company-presentable in minutes following bath time if you quickly wipe the mirror (already fogged), take a swipe over the sink and counter, and wipe up the water on the floor with a large towel, one that was already consigned to the laundry hamper.

Go Oft Astray

In households where there is a baby, housework is nearly always done in quick snatches—a series of mini-cleaning sprints. Five to ten minutes at full speed in the kitchen, devoted to whatever is most bothersome to you—perhaps the breakfast dishes on the table or the grubby floor in

How long does this "nesting instinct" last?

front of the sink or refrigerator—will improve the looks of the house and give you a sense of accomplishment. Throughout the day, center your attention on what you have accomplished, beginning with the all-important work of nurturing your baby, rather than dwelling on the tasks that still need doing.

Make your bed or not, as it pleases you. Plumping up the pillows and tossing the covers back to air is a time-honored custom. Without a spread in place, you'll probably lie down to nurse the baby more often during the day. Keeping up with the dishes is about as easy as keeping up with the Joneses, but we have some time-tested hints to at least give you a fighting chance. If baby is not agreeable to having you do the whole job when the meal is over, fill the sink with hot soapy water and let everything soak until you can get back to it later on or the next morning. If you have a dishwasher, reload it during those times when baby is wakeful and wants to be held in your arms or snuggled into his baby carrier. Babies usually love the constant up-and-down and back-and-forth motions that accompany the loading and unloading process. Don't rush it. And many a fussy baby has fallen asleep in a baby carrier while mom vacuums.

Bless This Mess

Little people and clutter seem to be inseparable. But clutter can be picked up and put out of sight amazingly quickly if you are equipped with a clutter-catcher—a cardboard box or other suitable container to carry with you as you whiz through each room depositing all the odds and ends that have been scattered about. This system enables you to de-clutter an entire house in fifteen minutes or so. The contents of the box can be sorted later when you have more time, but for now the house looks fairly straightened, and a visitor will be able to walk in the door without fear of skidding on a stray truck. Concentrate on immediately putting away the especially important items such as the car keys, which will drive you frantic when misplaced. A handy hook for keys just inside the door could be one of the best investments you make. For safeguarding other small, valuable items picked up during the day, the pockets in your jeans or an apron are indispensable.

Early in the morning, perhaps while you're relaxing with baby for an after-breakfast nursing, make a list of the "must do" chores for that day. Further refine your choices by selecting one, or possibly two, of the most important, (perhaps making an appointment with the eye doctor or replacing the broken zipper on your husband's favorite jacket.) Box off these top-priority items and plan on getting to them at the first opportunity, before you are caught up in the morass of everyday chores. If it's something you can't do until later in the day, set your alarm clock or oven timer to ring at the appropriate time. Beware of making a practice of going all out for cleaning, cooking, and scrubbing whenever the baby is taking a nap. Give some of that time to the other children, take a nap yourself, or relax with a project you enjoy.

Little Helpers

Toddlers love to help, and clever mothers find lots of things for little ones to help with. If you use nonbreakable dishes, your little one may enjoy setting the table, carrying one item at a time from the stack of dishes set out. Young ones never tire of the repetition of walking back and forth, especially when a smile and "thank you" accompany each dish that is delivered to the table. Shining the glass in a low window that has been sprayed with cleaner (or plain water) is another enjoyable pastime for budding artisans, (a task that is often signed by the young polisher pressing a small nose against the pane!).

Many toddlers seem to be fascinated with a hand brush or whisk broom and dust pan, so put yours to work under the kitchen table or some other open area. Old mittens and socks make great dusting mitts for little hands. If mother helps, too, even children who are barely walking will learn to put toys back in the toy box when it's time to clean up.

If you have children who are a bit older, the period before the new baby arrives is an excellent time to teach each one a new household skill. Select chores that match each one's ability and continue to work along with the child whenever possible. The children will learn from you, and humdrum chores, such as doing the dishes, can be transformed into special moments for sharing youthful hopes and problems. Children do not make appointments with their parents to talk over their deeply felt concerns. Such sharing takes place in the context of normal activities, during a time when parent's and child's hands are busy, but their minds and hearts are in touch with each other.

But don't be surprised if your young helpers are less than enthusiastic at times. That's normal for kids. Pour on the praise and be patient with

I started the Laundry for you!
Is 3 cups of detergent enough?

your apprentice. We all need to feel needed, and children benefit from knowing that the family is depending on them to carry out their assigned jobs. We parents overlook a golden opportunity if we don't help our children learn to accept responsibility and to enjoy the self-esteem that comes with being expected to do a job and doing it well.

Meals

When there is a new baby in your life, mastering the art of advance meal preparation is as vital as knowing how to relax in a rocking chair. Many women prepare double recipes of stews, casseroles, spaghetti sauce, chili, and the like during the last weeks of pregnancy and put the extra portions in the freezer. We've heard of thoughtful friends giving the mother-to-be a "casserole shower," presenting her with meals which they have prepared and frozen in disposable pans, complete with instructions for cooking or reheating. And the lovely practice of bringing a meal to the new baby's family has certainly not died out.

After the baby arrives, let simplicity in menu-planning be your watchword. Make a list of your favorite one-step, no-fuss meals and keep as many of the necessary ingredients on hand as possible. A dessert or snack of fresh fruit is always quick and nutritious.

If you don't already have a slow cooker, put it at the top of your list for the next gift-giving occasion. These marvelous cookers allow you to prepare your meat, potatoes, and vegetables at any convenient time during the day, and there's no frantic last-minute rush at suppertime when you're tired and the baby is most likely to need your undivided attention. Another helpful, inexpensive item for the mother whose attention is often distracted from her cooking is the metal plate that fits between a cooking pot and the stove burner and keeps the food from cooking too rapidly and burning.

For help in meal planning, you might want to read the League's cookbooks, MOTHER'S IN THE KITCHEN, and WHOLE FOODS FOR THE WHOLE FAMILY. Both are collections of mother-tested recipes which may give you some new ideas.

It pays to remember that nursing mothers should eat at regular intervals, and active children need to eat twice as often. To keep young temperaments soothed and tummies satisfied until mealtime, consider instituting salad snacks. Simply assemble an assortment of fresh, raw vegetables and fruits (excluding raw carrots and nuts if there is a toddler in the house). Preschoolers can be happily occupied in the preparations by washing and tearing greens, pulling the strings from celery stalks, breaking the cauliflower or broccoli florets, shining the apples, and arranging them all on a platter. Prepare these early in the day and keep in the refrigerator for quick munching later on. The addition of cheese, slices of hard-cooked eggs, or strips of cooked meat will add protein and staying power.

Sitting down for a few minutes for a snack is a positive measure to divert youngsters when they're tired and hungry and perhaps irritable. You can create a happy atmosphere with music—a favorite recording or, better yet, a sing-along with mom. The songs from your childhood are fresh and dear to your children and can become a part of their heritage.

When it comes to getting your husband and older children off to work or school on time, some judicious timing and advance planning can save the day. Betty Wagner, one of the LLL founders, managed by setting her alarm for about twenty minutes earlier than usual. Still resting in bed, she'd reset the clock for the regular time and nurse the baby. When she had to get breakfast and help the older children, she at least knew the baby would not be hungry in the midst of the morning rush.

One last thought on meal preparation: Now is the time to reinforce safety rules! When using the stove, turn in the handles of all pans so that children cannot grab them. Even babies still in their mothers' arms can reach surprisingly far. Store knives and other sharp utensils where children cannot reach them.

Laundry

We are all amazed at how much laundry a new baby makes and at how quickly adult laundry stacks up once a baby joins the family. Before the baby arrives, try to be sure that all of you have the most ample supply of clothing that your budget will permit, particularly underwear and socks, so that you won't have to do laundry every day or two.

Eventually the laundry has to be done, of course, and your own approach undoubtedly will depend on the kind of facilities available to you. Whether you depend on the neighborhood laundromat or have your own equipment, enlist your husband's help whenever practical. If your husband isn't

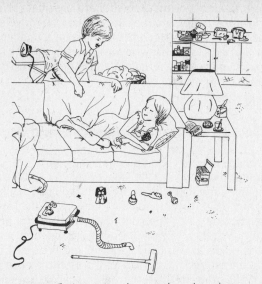

You know, I think I liked the nesting stage better.

already familiar with the intricacies of a washer and dryer, the hour is at hand for him to learn! When you are doing the laundry, you can use a baby carrier to good advantage. When it comes to trips to the laundromat or doing the laundry right at home, baby will be held and comforted, and you'll get clean clothing!

Consider investing in two or three inexpensive plastic buckets. You can use them to soak clothing that might stain and run it through the washer at a time that is convenient. Some system of pre-sorting laundry is a great help, too. As a container fills, you can quickly assess when you have a load of white or colored items, and you can drop them into the washer as you are passing by. Your toddler will love to be in on the action of transferring laundry from the dryer to the basket and then helping to fold the clothes. Long ago, many of us decided that a considerable amount of the laundry is just as serviceable when left unfolded. Undergarments, in particular, can be sorted—tops and bottoms—and quickly put away in an individual container such as a box, in a drawer, or on a shelf. Clean socks can be sorted into two baskets—one for white and the other for colors—and the older members of the family can each match their own pairs.

If you're in the habit of ironing some things, now would be the time to give it a second thought. Try the ten-minute test. Wear an ironed piece of clothing for ten minutes and notice how it takes on a more lived-in, rumpled look. The same item, left as is straight from the dryer or line, often "shakes out" or folds smooth, and looks just as good after a ten-minute wearing. You'll wonder if it's worth the time and energy (your own and the electrical power) to take to the ironing board.

As you make plans for keeping up with the laundry, concentrate on ways to lessen it. To start, you may find that the large bath towels that are used for drying when jumping out of the tub can be recycled if they're spread out and hung to dry instead of bunched on a small towel rack. A towel fastened around a towel bar with a large safety pin or grip snaps, for children to use when drying their hands, will not end up on the floor and then inevitably in the hamper.

WHAT TO WEAR—NURSING FASHIONS

You'll probably be glad to shed your maternity garb after your baby is born and your figure changes to the smaller tummy and the temporarily fuller bust of a breastfeeding mother. Actually, you can make almost any clothes do for nursing, but a few special items make life easier.

With pregnancy, and when the milk first comes in, the breasts often enlarge, and the support of a well-fitted bra can be most welcome. Let comfort be your guide. If you usually go braless, you may not need to wear one while breastfeeding. Or you may prefer to wear a regular bra, one with cups made of stretch material that you can lift up or pull down for nursing. Be sure that it does not press or bind. An inexpensive elastic extender, inserted in the back closure of a bra that otherwise fits well, could provide all the extra room you need.

You may find that you are more comfortable with a bra designed for nursing mothers. The traditional nursing bra has a flap on the cup that is opened for feedings and also has tucks in the back that can be let out if you need the extra room. We suggest that you start with two or three bras and try them for fit and ease of use before purchasing more. An LLL Leader, Kaye Lowman, made the following recommendations in an article that appeared in *Maternity Matters:* "Bras purchased during the last weeks of pregnancy should have extra room both in the cup and around the rib cage. The breasts will enlarge noticeably after the baby is born and the milk comes in, and nursing bras must be fitted with this in mind." Kaye noted that many mothers need "at least a cup size larger during lactation than they wore before or during pregnancy." A bra that is too tight, either around the ribs or in the cup, can cause a plugged milk duct or even a breast infection, and you don't want that to happen!

When trying on nursing bras in the store, be sure to note how the flap is attached in front. You'll want a fastener that you can manage with one hand so that you don't have to put the baby down every time you open or close the cup. If the bra you choose has a plastic liner in the cup, we recommend that you remove it, since plastic stops air circulation and seals in moisture, a combination that can lead to sore nipples. You can purchase nursing pads which fit inside your bra and absorb the milk that may leak from the nipples between feedings. A folded cotton or linen handkerchief works well, too, but avoid using the no-iron variety—the finish often retards absorbency.

Half-slips are probably the handiest while nursing, but you can adapt full slips to your needs by replacing the adjustment clip with a small piece of a Velcro-type fastener. For outer apparel, two-piece outfits—skirts, slacks, or shorts plus a top—are the nursing mother's all-time favorites. Choosing print or patterned tops provides camouflage against milk leakage. (And babies love the designs, especially those with bright colors!) With your knit top, blouse, or sweater lifted from the waist for nursing, all is in place on top, and the baby covers any bare midriff. When wearing a blouse that buttons down the front, you can unbutton from the bottom up. If you wear a three-piece outfit, with a jacket or shawl, you will be able to nurse so unobtrusively that the person sitting next to you won't know that the dear baby in your arms is having lunch.

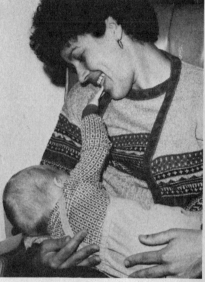

A three-piece outfit enables Heidi Plett to nurse Lennie comfortably and discreetly.

Your one-piece dresses with back openings don't have to gather dust in your closet if you—or a friend—are handy with a needle and thread. Look for a detail on the bodice that could conceal the addition of a small zipper, snaps, or dots of Velcro. Tucks on either side of the front, a dart, or a seam running from the side seam to the bust lend themselves to your alterations. Make an opening about six to eight inches long and face each side with seam binding of the same material, if you can find some somewhere (in a pocket or hem for instance). Carefully sew in the fasteners. If you choose the Velcro, which is handiest in many ways, remember to keep it to a minimum. It makes a ripping noise when pulled apart, which seems even louder if everything is quiet and you're trying to start nursing with no one taking notice of the fact. Just a dot of Velcro on one side, with a somewhat larger circle on the other side, can be managed easily with one hand. You and your baby can then be off and running.

When looking over your wardrobe, don't forget sleep wear. Long or short pajamas are easy and comfortable. The pretty nighties you already have may also be adapted for nursing the baby.

If you're looking for something new in either daytime or night wear—to celebrate the arrival of the baby—you may find just what you want in La Leche League's *Nursing Fashions Packet*. The packet includes sewing hints, as well as flyers describing commercially available nursing bras, nightgowns, dresses, and other apparel. And some lingerie manufacturers and maternity houses carry a line of nursing fashions that make feeding the baby a breeze. The breastfeeding mother has her choice of comfortable lounge wear, robes, blouses, nighties, and dresses, including styles for special occasions. All have concealed openings for discreet nursing.

BREASTFEEDING—THE KEY TO GOOD MOTHERING

Breastfeeding is more than a method of feeding your baby, even though your milk is important to your baby as a food and a source of elements that protect him against infection. Breastfeeding can be a springboard to good mothering. It is the most natural and effective way of understanding and satisfying the needs of the baby. An experienced mother made the observation, "Nursing the baby is the do-it-yourself kit for learning good mothering."

One explanation of breastfeeding's effectiveness lies in the fact that a nursing mother is physically different than a non-nursing mother. She is in a different hormonal state. Because she is breastfeeding, she has a high level of prolactin—the "mothering" hormone.

We all know that motherhood can be very demanding, and breastfeeding helps balance the give-and-take of caring for a young child. It serves as a bridge from mother to child, child to mother. Lucy Waletzky, MD, a psychiatrist who breastfed her children, explains: "The more intimate bodily communication inherent in the breastfeeding situation leads to a feeling of psychological 'oneness' with the child, which allows the mother to satisfy her own dependency needs (needs to be cared for and loved) at the same time she meets the baby's dependency needs. A mother's dependency needs may be accentuated postpartum by pain, fatigue, and the psychological stress of adjusting to new motherhood. When her dependency needs are thus met, her resentment of the child's dependency (often a very difficult problem) is alleviated, and the positive maternal feelings can flourish unencumbered."

What is "Mothering"?

"Mothering" is mother in action, caring for her baby, communicating with him and encouraging him to communicate back. It encompasses all of the many things that you will do to keep your baby healthy and comfortable, to help him grow in body and spirit. Breastfeeding is an unequaled form of communication between mother and baby. All of the senses can be brought into play. Your baby tastes your milk. He knows you through the smell of your skin and your milk. He experiences a sense of closeness to you by feeling your skin next to his. In the nursing position, he can easily look into your eyes. He hears your voice. What mother does not talk to her baby while he is nursing! As it is, the many

A nursing mother is physically different from a non-nursing mother because of the "mothering" hormone, prolactin. Linda Plummer enjoys comforting her baby at her breast. (Photo by Richard Ebbitt.)

times that you nurse your baby tell him in a way that words cannot, "Yes, you are safe. You are doing all right!" And he, of course, communicates back to you that he feels loved and is reassured. It is a learning and comforting experience for both of you.

From time immemorial, mothers have comforted their babies at the breast. They know that a few minutes of nursing often soothe an upset child's feelings of fear or anger, and that following the hurts that are an unescapable part of life, nothing is more reassuring to a small one than being close to mother and tasting her warm milk.

Good mothering means babying the baby, accepting that his wants and his needs are the same. It includes holding him when he is too full to nurse, but he is not yet ready to sleep. Mothering is changing a diaper or playing peek-a-boo. It means recognizing that each child has an inexhaustible need to be loved for what he is—a person with his own individuality. As he grows, his needs will change. A toddler needs freedom and guidance, gentle but with an ever-watchful eye. The manner in which these early needs are met, or not met, often has a great deal to do with a child's good or bad response to people and situations in later life. The way the child is mothered is important not only to mother and child, but to society as well. Marian Tompson, one of La Leche League's founders, observed, "No matter how far our world advances technologically, the decisions of how to use that technology still have to be made by people. And so the kind of people we produce is crucial to the direction our world takes. You know that raising a loving, caring child is probably the most important contribution any of us can make to the progress of the world."

Getting To Know You

Mothering is not something you can learn from a book. We can tell you, for instance, that most young babies like the secure feeling of being snugly wrapped up and cuddled. We can tell you that at about three months, another need begins to emerge—most babies like company. They like to be propped up in the midst of the family. Instead of wanting to be fed or cuddled, what they often want is just to be sociable. These may be perfectly true observations for many babies—but *your* newborn may prefer to have his arms and legs free, or *your* three-month-old may be over-stimulated by the busyness of a large family gathering and end up feeling miserable. You have to be sensitive to the individual needs of your own baby.

This sensitivity that helps you do the right thing at the right time comes from knowing your baby. It develops as you spend time with him, but it develops more quickly, and to a greater degree, if you are nursing your baby. The very closeness and intimacy of breastfeeding give you a quicker and surer perception of the feelings and needs of this tiny person, and how to meet them.

Your joy in mothering grows as you experience the quick, strong feeling of affection so natural between a nursing mother and her baby; as you develop an understanding of your baby's needs and gain confidence in your own ability to satisfy them; and as you see the happy dividends

The joy she has found in mothering is readily apparent in Shanda Bertelli's eyes, and in baby Mara's glowing smile.

from this good relationship as the baby grows. As one nursing mother expressed her feelings:

> After three bottle-fed babies I am finally able to nurse. The striking difference is the tremendous feeling of satisfaction that this baby has given *me*. Up till now I have been always completely baffled by the phrase "enjoy your baby." Not so with my breastfed baby. In three short months, she and I are already great friends. I feel as though I have finally arrived at motherhood. It's such a lovely warm glow that nursing imparts. And the nicest part of all is that this warm glow seems to be endless. It spills over into my relationships with all the rest of my family; there's always some to spare.

Breastfeeding is not a *guarantee* of good mothering, and bottle feeding by no means necessarily rules it out. The most important thing is the love you give your baby and the fact that you are doing your best to be a good mother. This does not mean that you must be a "super mom." As Mary White, another of LLL's founders, philosophizes:

> We're all learning, all the time. We're all still reaching up to the top of the ladder, and we've all got a long way to go. But for each and every one of us, the person from whom we can learn the most is our own baby; listen to him. Give to him; in the giving we are growing, as mothers and as women. As we watch him grow and bloom, we are watching an achievement to be really proud of.

The dividends will come. The effort you give to good mothering is never wasted.

MOTHER-TO-MOTHER

How can we adequately convey to you the tremendous value of being in touch with other nursing mothers? No book about breastfeeding can equal talking to an experienced nursing mother and seeing her happy baby. When you know a woman who enjoys being a mother, you have access to a continuing source of information and inspiration. It is our hope that you can join with other mothers and together find the same reinforcement and satisfaction that we have known. Mother-to-mother, you will create your own supportive environment for good mothering.

A supportive environment is so important to you as a new mother. In your first attempts to nurse your baby, you may feel like the new student in school, unsure of yourself and aching to have someone to talk to, someone to "show you around." Almost everything in those early weeks is a concern to you and, of course, you worry. As surely as a baby cries, a new mother worries. Talking to and meeting with other mothers can be a tremendous lift.

We share with you a few of the comments from mothers who have found such support from a La Leche League group. For more information see "About La Leche League" at the back of this book.

Mothers find companionship, information, and mother-to-mother help at a La Leche League group meeting in Birmingham, Michigan. (Photo by Dave Draxler.)

It was like a door opening welcoming me in. And in I rushed. I remember not so much of what was said; more I was caught up in the sight of gentle mothers in love with their babies; in the sounds of contented children; in the smells of coffee brewing and home-baked things.

Again and again, I am amazed to see from a few boxes and bags, a member's home be transformed into La Leche League. The League transcends. It is confined neither by time nor by space. La Leche League is portable and yet constant. Moving from month to month and series to series, it inhabits humble surroundings and elegant ones. But it is mainly because of the people involved in La Leche League that it will continue to grow and prosper.

—Mary Quinn, Quebec

The warm atmosphere of a room full of mothers, babies, and mothers-to-be sharing thoughts of nurturing and nourishing the newborn in a most natural way, through breastfeeding, left a wonderful impression. We saw mothers nursing their babies in a relaxed and comfortable way and picked up a variety of hints on establishing a satisfying breastfeeding relationship with our baby.

—Maryann Malecki, Florida

You come to LLL to find out about breastfeeding as such and you end up getting involved in the whole philosophy of child rearing in general. I know that I feel more of a sense of fulfillment as a wife and a mother because of my contact with LLL and the reading I have done.

—An LLL member

My deepest feelings of gratitude for this sensation of mothering success go to La Leche League which has in philosophy and example supported my natural mothering instincts.

I do not measure up to those ideals of mothering that I held in the early days of being a mother for they were quite unrealistic. I am not supermom material. I have my bad days when my temper tyrannizes the house, but they are fewer than they might have been. LLL has provided me with a healthy, sane, and practical mode of mothering that has helped me attain a sense of confidence and pride in my mothering ability.

—Sylvia Laale, Ontario

La Leche, what would I have done without you! I thank you and my husband thanks you, but the ones who benefited the most are still too young to even know how important you are.

I'd like to think that eventually I would have gotten this "good mothering" feeling through experience and time but doubt that I would have. When I first attended League meetings and expected to receive breastfeeding information, I never dreamed that I would somehow be gently helped to find this relaxed child-rearing attitude.

—Judy Moore, Georgia

I received a delightful call this morning from our family doctor which made me feel that my LLL work was especially appreciated and worthwhile. Dr. Jan Oosterhuis expressed his thanks to LLL Leaders who have done so much to help mothers happily breastfeed their babies. Dr. Oosterhuis fully supports LLL, he is an LLL Medical Associate, and in his practice encourages all mothers-to-be to breastfeed. He is especially supportive of LLL because he feels that we reach mothers in ways which are closed to him as a physician.

—Linda Lawrence, Ontario

The opportunity to share the concerns as well as the joys of motherhood is reason enough to attend LLL group meetings. Betsy Broesamle talks things over with Linda McCarthy. (Photo by Dave Draxler.)

I have a background in psychology, but it was attendance at LLL meetings and the example of a wonderful Leader, Norma Beazley, that showed me alternatives to many of the typical ways of handling children in our culture. The "psychology of mothering" is learned best from other mothers and comes through loud and clear at La Leche League meetings.

—Betty McLellan, Ontario

Sixteen-month-old Laila Shamszad "never misses an issue" of LLL NEWS, according to her mother, Meredith.

La Leche League News

Many mothers find a great deal of mother-to-mother help in the pages of LLL NEWS. This bimonthly publication features articles, poems, and stories written by mothers themselves about their own experiences. Many of the personal stories in this book first appeared in the pages of LLL NEWS. Elena Hannah, from Newfoundland, Canada, tells how it helped her:

When I was almost overwhelmed with problems I was having with my first baby, a friend sent me her two-year collection of LLL NEWS. As soon as I started reading them I felt I had found what I needed. Reading others' stories, many of them with problems more serious than mine, put everything back in perspective for me, and the main message seemed to be: *You can do it! You can overcome the difficulties!* By the time I finished devouring the collection I felt calmer and more confident.

The NEWS made me feel part of a large family who were one hundred percent behind me, who really cared. I subscribed immediately and eagerly waited for my very own first issue. Five years and two more children later, I still await eagerly my bimonthly "shot in the arm."

Gradually, I shifted from needing the basic how-to advice to needing the support for my way of mothering. As I grow in motherhood, I know the NEWS is there to help me out. So today I say: Thank you to all the moms that shared their stories with me, and thank you LLL for having such a wonderful publication.

For further information about LLL NEWS, see the Appendix.

Chapter III

Are You Thinking of Going Back to Work?

Deciding whether or not to work outside your home after your baby is born is a far more complex step than is usually portrayed in popular accounts of working mothers. You'll want to take your time making such an important decision. The familiar sign at a road crossing will serve you well in this situation—"Look Both Ways—Proceed with Caution."

The question of working (or going back to school) has been the subject of numerous sessions at La Leche League Conferences in recent years. Typically, a group of about thirty mothers fills the room, many of them with babies in their arms or toddlers playing nearby. As different women speak, it is obvious that they represent a wide range of experiences. Some currently have jobs and leave their children with sitters. Others take their babies with them on the job, and others have put their careers on hold until their young children are older. There are mothers who have done both—worked when one child was a baby, stayed at home with another.

As diverse as their situations may be, they share a common bond, their interest in breastfeeding and good mothering. The mothers are eager to make the most of the options available to them to give their babies the best possible start in life. The exchange of ideas is lively, and the mothers are not hesitant about examining some of the commonly held ideas on working and mothering. The following subjects come up time and again. How valid are these often heard comments?

—With a little adroit management, a mother can successfully combine motherhood and a career.
—For her own sense of well-being, a woman has to get out of the house.
—In today's economy, it takes two salaries to stay above the poverty level.
—If you don't leave your baby, he'll never learn to get along without you.
—Breastfeeding is nice, but it really isn't practical if you cannot be at home with your baby.

Let's begin with this last statement. Since you may have to return to work after your baby is born, you naturally want to know if you can breastfeed.

YOU CAN BREASTFEED

By all means, look forward to being a nursing mother. Not only is breastfeeding possible, many working mothers consider it easier than bottle feeding. Nursing is a joy for both mother and baby. For many, a quiet time with baby at the breast is the last thing on the agenda before mother goes off to work and the first upon her return home. While providing the baby with breast milk is always worthwhile, it is not the only matter of importance. If it were, we could give you a list of suggestions for keeping up your milk supply and wave you off to your job with a light heart. There are other concerns. The most persistent have to do with the separation from the baby that often goes with having an outside job or going to school. What does it mean to the baby when mother leaves him, even when it is in the care of another loving person? And how much does a mother miss by not having a continuous role in her baby's life? The mothers at the League sessions asked these questions and took a hard look at the saying, "It is not the *quantity* of time a mother spends with her child, but the *quality* that counts."

Quality vs. Quantity

In the practical context of mothering a young child day after day, of changing and feeding him, returning his smiles, applauding his efforts to reach a toy, distracting him at times, or consoling him when tears appear, the mothers we have talked to make no distinction between the quantity and quality of time they spend with their babies. Mary Ann Kerwin, a founder of La Leche League, has observed, "Babies need quantities of quality time."

The mothers agreed with pediatrician and mother Sally Shaywitz, MD, who recounted her own experience of returning to work in an article in the *New York Times Magazine:* "I learned that while it is true that the quality rather than the quantity of mothering is of paramount importance, nevertheless, a mother must be there all of the time in order to be there at those unpredictable times when it really matters."

A husband, Clint Brown of Maryland, expresses his views on the question of how much of a mother's time is enough for her baby.

> I am beginning to feel more and more unusual in today's society. The reason is that I would rather see my wife raise our children full-time than see her work outside the home.
>
> Before Christy's birth, we discussed priorities. Which was more important—extra income or constant, reliable care of our child; investment in a professional career or investment in the mental and physical growth of our child; budgeted quality time or abundant quality time with our child?
>
> I feel fortunate and very thankful that my wife is in control of our child's development. We can determine and implement character qualities. We can stimulate and reinforce behavioral aspects of her personality. We can answer questions and share spontaneous experiences.

Clint's wife, Linda, tells of her reaction to the prospect of quitting her job to be an at-home mother.

> Even before Christy was born, my husband and I decided that I would quit my job and stay at home with the baby. We knew it would mean a financial setback and a real tightening of our budget, but my husband's enthusiasm for an at-home wife and mother made me eager to try. However, I wasn't really as confident about it as he seemed to be. I had been in the teaching profession for six years and thoroughly enjoyed my job; it had given me a great deal of personal satisfaction. And now the thought of staying at home—with no adult conversation and no one to tell me what a fantastic job I was doing—didn't excite me. But I was in for a surprise. After just a few weeks, I became aware of a new freedom and many new opportunities for self-fulfillment.

WHY WOMEN WORK

"I work because we need the money" is the most common response from the mother who is going back to work after her baby is born. Sometimes, it's a case of either working or not eating. Then again, for many women, there is more to working than money. As was true for Linda Brown, emotional and intellectual satisfaction are good reasons for working. Women find that a job brings them not only money, but also a sense of accomplishment, even status. Some feel that they have a greater degree of control over their lives because they are wage earners. And many women have special skills that they have spent years acquiring. They know that they can make a valuable contribution in the work world.

How does a mother reconcile her own need for a healthy sense of self-esteem, achievement, and self-confidence with the needs of her baby? Determined mothers are finding that the two sets of needs are surprisingly compatible. Home offers countless possibilities. Contrary to what many had heard, the grass is not always greener in the marketplace than it is in the plot around the homestead.

Betty Trent Freeman of Washington worked when her first child was a baby, then switched to being an at-home mother with her second baby. Betty tells her story:

> When our first child was born, I was immersed in my job as a counselor for delinquent boys. I was so involved that I insisted on working until just a few hours before our daughter was born. I had two months at home with Jessica before I returned to work. At the time, I told myself that we needed the money, but the "liberated woman" in me also felt that I had to have the challenge and stimulation of an outside career. And I felt so needed at work, helping those troubled kids to find themselves.
>
> At the same time, I wanted to be a good mother. In spite of the long hours and odd shifts required by my job, I continued to nurse Jessica. I wanted her to have breast milk. So on the days that I worked, I expressed my milk into bottles for her. She got the nutritive benefits of mother's milk, but

we both missed out on the emotional benefits of full-time nursing. In trying to be "all things to all people," I often came up short on emotional energy.

Now, with our second baby seven months old, I realize how much I missed as a working mother. So many moments of Jessica's babyhood are forever lost to me. Most of all, I missed the closeness that full-time mothering and nursing affords. With our son, Jude, I'm finally able to see what an exciting time infancy is, and I'm reveling in the unique relationship we have. I know how special and fleeting those moments are, and, having missed many of them with Jessica, I'm treasuring them now.

For Betty, there came a new-found sense of personal well-being in having made the decision to spend her emotional and physical energy on her family. Her delight in her son's infancy was an added bonus.

Jobs in the marketplace have a highly visible rating system: usually, the higher the pay, the greater the prestige. The at-home mother has only one title, and there are no periodic raises telling her that she is doing a good job. But the rewards are there, right in the family, though they are much more subtle. A California mother, Emily Holt, discovered unexpected enjoyment in mothering and in the sense of personal growth she experienced in nurturing her baby. She had worked as an officer of a large bank before she had her baby, and she recalled her position as, "a wonderful job—interesting, exciting, a true career." She said, "I thought I had everything I'd always wanted." But when she reflects on the changes in her life that came with the birth of her baby, Emily writes, "Now I sit holding our five-month-old daughter, who is nursing so sweetly at my breast. I watch my husband's face light up with joy as she grabs his beard, laughing aloud. Oh yes, my job was wonderful as jobs go, but in these five short months, I have seen myself grow in a hundred ways, reaching for what is best in me to greet this beautiful new life. Sharing every delightful moment of our Sarah's discovery of our world, I realize how blessed I am to be a mother."

Like many mothers-to-be, Jean Smith of New York says that she could see no reason why she would not want to work after her first child was born. She describes how her attitude changed:

To work or not to work? For me, that had never been a debate. After our baby was born, and I had rested sufficiently, of course I would return to work. I had taught for thirteen years and was employed during the pregnancy. No baby was going to change my lifestyle. He would just have to fit in. I had planned to nurse—my mother had. I would quit at six months—my mother had. Besides, that was long enough to be tied down.

So I told myself, my husband, and my colleagues. Surprisingly, no one argued with me or tried to change my mind. (Later, my husband told me that his heart had stopped when I told him my plans. He had not been pleased, but didn't want to argue with a pregnant and determined wife!)

The baby has an intense need to be with his mother which is as basic as his need for food. Two-month-old John White finds comfort in the warmth and closeness of his mother, Shay. (Photo by Richard Ebbitt.)

I quit teaching in December; baby was due in February. I had two months to sit around, growing bigger and clumsier, justifying to myself the need to return to work so that my brain wouldn't die after being dormant. After all, how could diapers, spit-ups, and screeches be a challenge? Challenges were found in the hallowed halls of higher education.

Then, on February 19, at 12:07 A.M., after a twenty-hour labor, my husband and I delivered Jason Gerard. At midnight, in the back of my mind swirled those ideas of getting this birthing over with and taking up my old routine. At 12:10 A.M., as I was holding Jason in my arms, John and I crying and blubbering about the incredible miracle of creation, I knew, at that very moment, that my destiny had changed paths. Although it took me until April to say it out loud, truly I knew then that I would be a full-time mother.

Instead of that being the end of my story, it was really the beginning, because, since I had been a career woman for so many years, my new lifestyle, philosophy, and attitudes confused my friends who were full-time career women with children. So I became devoted to LLL meetings. I loved them! So did Jason! There I found other mothers who had chosen to stay at home—gladly, not begrudgingly. There I found other mothers who, at various times in their lives, came to know that an infant, a toddler, and "even" a newborn, are fascinating and very social creatures, who will respond from day one if someone (hopefully mother) is there to initiate the relationship.

THE MOTHER-CHILD RELATIONSHIP

The mother-baby relationship has fascinated the scientific community for a long time, since a child's early years hold the clues to his future behavior as an adult. Society stands to gain or lose, depending on the soundness of the mother-baby attachment. As more mothers asked questions regarding mother-baby separation, we searched out studies on child development.

Scientists hold that the child's initial one-to-one relationship with his mother is the foundation for emotional growth. From the security of the baby's ties to his mother he learns to relate to others. "The only true basis for the relationship of a child to mother and father, to other children, and eventually to society," Dr. W. Winnicott, a pediatrician from Great Britain, says, "is the first successful relationship between mother and baby."

Can a baby be "trained" to accept others and not always expect mother to care for him? Won't this make him more "independent"? No, say the experts. A baby's need for mother is not a habit; it's biology.

In her book *Oneness and Separateness,* Dr. Louise Kaplan, psychologist and Director of the Mother-Infant Research Nursery of New York University, explains that an infant does not have an identity of his own at birth. Baby is in a state of oneness with his mother. Based on her work in mother-infant research, Dr. Kaplan states, "From the infant's point of view, there are no boundaries between himself and mother. They are one." The child must negotiate the move from oneness with his mother into separateness and a sense of individuality. It is a second birth that unfolds gradually in the first three years of life. Maintaining the early mother-baby relationship is extremely important to the successful completion of this journey.

The young child who is separated from his mother exhibits all of the classic symptoms of grief. He may cry unconsolably or withdraw into unnatural quietness. Regarding this separation anxiety, Humberto Nagera, Professor of Psychiatry at the University of Montana, points out "When the child is confronted with the mother's absence his *automatic response is an anxiety state* that on many occasions reaches overwhelming proportions. Repeated traumas of this type in especially susceptible children will not fail to have serious consequences for their later development." Dr. Nagera goes on to say, "No other animal species will subject their infants to experiences that they are not endowed to cope with, except the human animal."

When women who plan to work ask Dr. Jack Raskin, a University of Washington child psychiatrist, how they can be sure that their children's needs are also met, his answer is:

> Only with difficulty. Even when parents have a great deal of time and energy to devote to caring for a young child, it's a hard job. When both parents work, the limited time available to the child and the other pressures on the parents can make it very hard to meet the child's needs.

The child's one-to-one relationship with his mother is the foundation for all future relationships. Eighteen-month-old Malcolm Speller is happy and secure when he is close to his mother, Ernestine. (Photo by Emil Warncke.)

The stakes are high, and ultimately the happiness of the child and of the parents will hinge on the quality of love and care the parents provide the child.

Dr. Raskin speaks of the ways in which a child acquires the skills and strengths needed to handle the stress that occurs in everyone's life. "The key," he emphasizes, "is the child's close, unbroken attachment in the early months to the people who care for him. Too much disruption of this," Raskin says, "embeds in the personality traits that can be destructive for a lifetime."

Cornell University's Uri Bronfenbrenner, an authority on child development, has said, "Children need enduring emotional involvement from people who are irrationally attached to them. In plain language, someone has to be crazy about kids, and it's best if it is the same someone. When this need is met, a child has the equipment to live up to his potential."

Says Dr. Raskin, "All the strengths in the growing child that allow him to cope with hard times and frustration, that allow him to play, go to school, and work, come from his involvement with people."

A Canadian, Donna K. Kontos, PhD, consultant psychologist, comments, "There is at present no known substitute for a family environment for child rearing....Prolonged maternal separations cause distress to the child. All the research and all of the literature tell us that the best thing for an infant is to have a consistent good mother around most of the time."

Another psychologist, Dr. Joyce Brothers, recognizes the pressures on young mothers to work, yet notes, "I realize that the economic necessities of life often force us to do things differently than we would like. But when it comes to child raising, I am convinced that a woman should make every possible effort to spend the first three years with her child. It *does* make a tremendous difference."

To describe the concept of a child's dependence on the mother, La Leche League says, "In the early years, the baby has an intense need to be with his mother, which is as basic as his need for food." Philosophizes Dr. Herbert Ratner, "It is **love** that holds together the delicate membranes of human society...and **love** is taught essentially through a one-to-one relationship."

A growing child is full of surprises. The moments of new achievement cannot be prearranged, and there are no replays. A baby's first steps can never be as meaningful to a sitter as they are to mother. Sharing the excitement and wonder of such everyday triumphs is payday for a mother with a little one, and there is a sense of sadness when it's missed.

Priceless moments like this one are part of the reward of full-time mothering. (Photo of Caitlin Reynolds by Richard Ebbitt.)

Deborah Fallows wrote in the *Washington Monthly* of her son's accomplishments the summer when he had turned two, and she had returned to work full-time:

> I convinced myself for quite a while that we still had many hours in the day together, enough that I wouldn't miss any important steps in his development. But late one afternoon, we went to play at a neighbor's house. My son hopped on his playmate's tricycle, and I expected to see him scoot off in his normal manner—two feet at a time, feet on the ground rather than on the pedals, moving in fits and starts. But he set his feet on the pedals—clearly a practiced and mastered skill—and zoomed off. I knew that somehow I'd missed all the trial and error, the skips and skids, along the way to becoming an expert pedaler.

Perhaps you would like to stay home with your baby, but you can't see how you can manage without your paycheck. Home is where your heart is, but a job is where the money is—or is it?

Does It Pay to Work?

Many of the women who are in touch with the League note that it is easy to think of one's take-home pay as "pure profit." Often the costs involved in working are overlooked, and some quick calculations of expenses versus income yield surprising results. There is the cost of a working wardrobe and transportation expenses getting to and from work each day. When you spend the day on the job, you probably prepare more expensive convenience foods or eat out more often. Figure out what child care for an infant would cost you. Then sit down and approximate how much money these things add up to and subtract this amount from your income. You may very well find that there would be little net gain if you continued to work after the baby arrived.

When tallying up the funds that will be available to you if you stay home, consider the likelihood that you will drop into a lower tax bracket after you stop working. The tax savings alone may be substantial. Many mothers find that it doesn't "pay" for them to work outside the home.

SOLVING FINANCIAL PROBLEMS

Even though a mother may be convinced of the importance of staying home, she and her husband may face the problem of finding a way to keep mother at home mothering the baby, while keeping the wolf from the door.

Occasionally, when finances are tight, the husband will consider taking on an additional part-time job. This solution needs much thought, though, since families need and want the father home, too, as much of the time as possible. As one husband put it, "It would have to be a case of not having bread to put on the table, and not having the table either." A better solution to financial strain is for mother to help make ends meet by the time-honored practice of being an astute household manager. Together, husband and wife pool their resources of time, energy, and skill in order to support the family. The mother's efforts can be a very real financial contribution to the family.

The Soderbergs of Missouri found the old proverb, "A penny saved is a penny earned," makes a lot of sense. Susan Soderberg writes:

> When Bill and I decided to buy a house and have a family, there was no question of my going back to work, for we have always believed that babies and small children have a constant need for their mother. We decided my job would be to earn money by saving money. We now have three children, and I have found that this job has become more challenging, and also more fun, as our family has grown. Not only have I learned to make a lot of things that I never knew I could make or do, but I have also found out much about myself and my capabilities and gained a lot of self-respect in the process. I have found that one can achieve a great feeling of pride and freedom by becoming even a little self-sufficient.

There is a major fact about saving money I have learned in my "business," which is helpful to keep in mind when laying out the budget. Just turning off the lights and hanging out the wash won't save you a whole lot of money, although every little bit helps. What one needs to do most is to economize on nonbasic needs—in other words, to stop buying so many non-essential things. We have developed a method to help cut down on these big expenses and I would like to share this method with you. Before we buy something we first ask ourselves these four simple questions: 1. Do we really need it? 2. Can we make it? Do it ourselves? Grow it? 3. Can we find it? 4. Can we borrow it?

Betti Jo Wilson of North Carolina, worked when her oldest child, Tracy, was a baby. The experience set her thinking:

I vowed that I would *never* leave another baby. When our second child Matthew, was born, I resigned from my job. These are some of the things I did in order to achieve my goal of staying home with my children.

Step One: Plan Ahead.
By saving every extra cent, my husband and I were able to put aside a small emergency fund before Matthew was born. This is quite helpful, but if your baby is already here and you weren't able to plan this far ahead, don't give up. Go on to step two.

Step Two: Make Money at Home.
By doing a few calculations I realized that after deductions, child care, and work expenses I would only bring home about a quarter of my salary. I then began to explore ways to make this smaller amount at home.
a) I became coordinator of a weekly Mother's Morning Out program at my church. (My children go along.)
b) I have made plans to baby-sit for another child in my home beginning when Matthew is six months old.
c) Also, my local LLL group sells baby carriers, which I have begun to make on consignment.
My husband helps out by doing occasional night and weekend work. One word of caution—don't try to take on too much, too fast, or you will become exhausted.

Step Three: Economize.
My husband is an avid gardener, so I freeze all our vegetables as an economy move. We buy our staple foods through a food co-op. We have turned down the heat, cut off excess lights, and when possible we dry our clothes outdoors. I pack my husband's lunch and drive a lot less. The children have fewer clothes and toys, but nobody seems to mind. (I might add that one of my friends sold her silver and another sold the second car in order to remain at home.) The possibilities are endless.
If all this sounds drastic, think of the benefits. I am more relaxed and much happier. Consequently, my husband and children are also happier. It is well worth the effort.

Earning Extra Money

What if your financial situation is such that you feel you absolutely have to bring in some extra income? Happily more and more mothers have been able to combine working and keeping their babies with them, given compatible conditions on the job, much determination, and help from their husbands and families. Many school buses make their runs with mothers behind the wheels and their babies securely in car seats behind them. Taking care of other mothers' children is a time-honored way to bring in extra income, although such women are pitifully underpaid, we feel, when other workers earn several times more than a "sitter" overseeing a young life. In a society where women regularly work outside the home, Pia Olsen of Denmark manages to be with her young son by being a day-care mother in her home. Pia is one of many mothers who are determined to be with their young children.

Many kinds of office work can be done just as well at home, so you might be able to interest your employer in having you do part-time work at home, coming into the office just long enough to pick up and deliver your work. It's this kind of flexibility in the working world that could be of great help to more families if it were more readily available to the trained woman who is also a mother.

If you are a good typist, get in touch with several different companies or secretarial services about free-lance typing at home, or run an ad in the newspaper. If you have a specialty like art, writing, photography, or public relations, you can develop a free-lance clientele and work out of

Kaye Lowman returned to her part-time community relations job after the birth of her baby and found that baby Carrie was easily accepted as "part of the decor." Kaye's work continued as usual without any need for mother and baby to be separated. (Photo by Paddock Publications.)

your home. Giving music lessons is another good option. Or, if you are a teacher, contact local schools about tutoring in your home. Another possibility, take baby along with you to your job. Given the right circumstances, an increasing number of women are finding that mothering the baby is compatible with their jobs.

Barbara Sullivan of Washington taught for a year at The Little School with baby Rachel as part of the classroom scene, much to the delight of the four-year-old pupils. A mother whose children attended the independent elementary school, Linda Steveley, tells of a conversation she had with Barbara before her baby was born. "She and I spent some happy times talking about birth and mothering and, of course, breastfeeding," Linda recalls. "At the time, her plans were indefinite; she knew she would not want to leave the baby every day when she went to work, but she was reluctant to give up teaching altogether."

Linda relates that the next time she saw Barbara, it was autumn, "and there she was at school, tiny Rachel snuggled close in her carrier! I saw that Barbara's room now had a rocking chair and a few baby things. Rather than detracting from the normal classroom routine, as some feared, having the baby at school has added a new and valuable dimension to the children's experience."

As her baby's first birthday drew near, Barbara confided to Linda that she would not want to be at school unless she could have Rachel near, but she also realized that a toddler in the classroom would require a tremendous amount of energy. Barbara's final decision was to take a leave of absence for the coming school year and continue to enjoy being with her baby.

From Oklahoma, Jackie Settlemyre tells of her experience in going back to work after her baby was born:

Being a working mother before Jamie Jo's birth, I knew that there was a strong possibility that I would have to return to work again. But I had already made up my mind that she would be breastfed. I had faith that when it was time to return to work all things would work out. I had very strong feelings about leaving her to work, and mixed emotions about whether it was worth it.

As J.J. approached five months of age, the opportunity to work was available. As I began to discuss the job with my prospective employer, I felt I should express my natural and most important reasons why I felt breastfeeding came first. By being honest with him and talking freely about how much I wanted to continue to breastfeed, I found a very receptive man. He was interested in my feelings and admired my convictions about the needs of my baby.

After I explained that immediate withdrawal from a breastfed baby is neither recommended nor healthy for mother or child, my employer suggested working only part-time and *bringing baby* with me for those few hours. I was thrilled! Not only would I be providing those necessary extra dollars, but I wouldn't be separated from my daughter.

Barbara Sullivan found that baby Rachel was a welcome addition to her preschool class.

SOME PRACTICAL PROBLEMS

Women who have had firsthand experience juggling husband, children, and career quickly learn how to read between the lines in the glamorous stories of working mothers. It's pretty rough trying to greet the business world at 9:00 A.M. when you were up most of the night with a teething baby. What do you do when the babysitter calls at 7:00 A.M. and says she cannot come, or calls at noon and says the baby is running a fever, and you are expected to stay on the job until 5:00 P.M.? Another problem, a red flag of worry for parents, is finding and keeping a suitable caretaker.

When mother has an outside job, housework may be postponed or eliminated altogether with no one suffering unduly, but baby care cannot be overlooked. A reliable sitter is needed every working day. A baby needs a loving, nurturing person, and this person should be the same someone, not an often changing parade of new faces and personalities.

Constancy in nurturing is the means by which the child learns to trust others. While a working mother naturally hopes to find such a reliable, loving sitter, she should also be aware that over a period of time, her baby will inevitably grow to love this "other mother." Some little ones cry for the sitter on weekends. In regard to the possibility of such a transfer of affection from the parent to the sitter, Dr. T. Berry Brazelton of Harvard Medical School comments, "Parents do grieve. They're no longer important to that child. Jealousy of the caretaker is inevitable, and they act it out in various ways."

On the other hand, the patient, caring sitter you have this morning may announce at nightfall that she is moving away or taking another job. Such a disruption can be difficult for an adult to cope with. It can be a serious loss of a loved one for a young child.

Because of the unpredictability of finding and keeping a private sitter, working mothers often turn to the day-care center as a solution to the sitter problem. While there is a degree of permanence in a day-care center, here, too, workers come and go. And while the decorations may be charming, children under the age of three are too young for group living. A young child was not meant to compete for attention with a large number of children of much the same age. Often a child will enjoy short play sessions in a nursery school, but all-day day care is a threatening situation. Group care in a day-care center falls far short of meeting a baby's or toddler's need to relate to one person, to count on one person for loving attention all of the time, at any time.

Basically, little ones are homebodies. They revel in a regular routine and familiar surroundings. During the summer that she worked and left her two-year-old, Deborah Fallows noted:

> Signs of strain surface in various ways—our son's whining insistence that *no,* he doesn't want to go to the babysitter's; asking hopefully whether it's Saturday today; his determination to slow down the whole hurried morning process; screaming when I try to change his soggy pajamas and put on clean street clothes; pulling his shoes and socks off as soon as I put them on; and doing everything possible to postpone our departure through the front door.

> I would love to humor him at these moments, to let him sleep late on overcast mornings, to let him play with his trucks and dawdle over his breakfast; but there is no time. I must be at my job before 9:00, which means we must leave the house before 8:30, which means we must start moving before 7:30 without fail. Certainly some of his balkiness is part of being two years old, and certainly he would do many of these things whether or not I worked. But I can't help feeling that my decision to work full-time this year had something to do with it. A child seems to sense unerringly when he is being rushed, when there is something on mommy's mind other than reading him a book or helping him assemble his train. Sometimes a child must be rushed, but I hate the thought of rush becoming the norm, replacing the sense that the child's parents have all the time and love in the world to give. . . .

An Illinois mother, Cynthia Cuevas, tells how she gradually came to understand the importance—and magnitude—of her at-home job with her baby.

> When our son, Phillip IV, was born, I joined a La Leche League group and decided to breastfeed for six months. I asked my doctor to prescribe breast milk as best for my baby. My company accepted this as a valid reason for a six-month compensated leave of absence.

> At League meetings, I saw the effects of full-time mothering and love. The seed was planted, but, in my case, took lots of time to grow. Despite all of the good advice, I was determined to return to my former job. Still, I decided to keep nursing my baby.

My company was moving to another state. I was promised flexible hours and substantial severance pay to return to help with the move. Money was an important factor in my decision. My husband was still an apprentice, and it was difficult to make our mortgage payments and to try to furnish our new home.

My husband was very mature and loving, and he felt that our baby needed me then. There would be lots of time to do the things we wanted later. However, I convinced him that I needed to do this. After all, I had worked full-time, attended college at night, and tutored in my spare time before my pregnancy. After that, an outside job and a baby seemed very easy to manage.

My mother offered to take care of little Phil. She was very experienced and loving, but I found our ideas were not the same. She insisted on giving him bottles. Even though he refused most of them, he cut down on his nursing. When I left for work, I would feel hurt to see him pacing in his playpen. I knew, instead, he could be crawling and exploring around our child-proofed home. My interesting and demanding job wasn't as exciting as Phil's first tooth, and my mother saw his first steps. My co-workers grew bored with my proud chatter about my baby. I became unhappy and whenever I thought about my baby I would have a let-down.

It became harder for me to cook or to shop. My husband wisely kept quiet and did more than his share of everything. I realized what was happening to our lives when I began to get angry about having to get up at night to soothe my teething baby. I decided to resign from my outside job. I did not want anyone else to raise my child, and I realized that I was sacrificing a good marriage and good mothering for money.

I wish I could say my decision to resign came about when I saw that the emotional and physical needs of my child should come first. Actually I only realize this now after having been a full-time "twenty-four-hours-a-day" mother for many years. It's the old myth of "quality time versus quantity time." Quality doesn't count if you're not there when they need you.

WILL YOU GO "STALE"?

If you enjoy your job, and the stimulation that comes with working, you may wonder how much of a challenge you'll find at home with just you, baby, and the four walls. Look for some unexpected and delightful surprises. "I was certain that I'd be bored to tears," was Shirley Callanan's first reaction to the prospect of staying at home. This Utah mother said she was "anxious to work on some kind of a part-time basis." But after her baby was born, she wrote, "I really didn't know what to expect of motherhood or how I would feel, and it's hard to describe the feelings that flowed through me those first few days, weeks, and months of my daughter's life. I was needed by this tiny person; I knew I could not leave her with someone else, no matter how loving."

Mothers find that they need not "go stale." The years at home with preschool children are a unique time in their lives for exploring new avenues of interest. If you keep your eyes open, you'll soon find activities that are right for you and are totally compatible with your first concern, mothering your baby.

This may be the time to use your education and become a self-directed learner, moving farther in an earlier interest or discovering a new one. How about gardening, sewing, and do-it-yourself projects that don't fit into a job schedule? Arlene Rossen Cardozo's book, *Woman at Home,* provides many insights into the challenges of staying at home. It may take creative thinking on the part of you and your husband to find ways to satisfy your own emotional and intellectual needs while caring for a young family, but the challenge, when met, is an exciting and stimulating one. Often the whole family benefits from mother's newest project.

GOLD IN THE BANK

The value of good parenting is never denied, but all too often it is unsung. What parents are learning to do for themselves (and in so doing, to help their children) is to become their own cheering section.

Mary White, a La Leche League founder, emphasizes, "Our society prizes people who achieve. We prize those who produce. All of us—mothers especially—ought to recognize very clearly: Nurturing a baby *is* producing. Mothering is the way of producing a healthy, strong personality in a child."

Carolyn Keiler Paul of New York says, "I think it's time we stop apologizing for being 'just a mother.' Child rearing is *not* a menial job. It calls for all of our talents and resources. My college education isn't going to waste, because it has enriched me so that I may in turn enrich the lives of my children."

True as that is, there are many pressures on mothers to seek a place in the public world of the marketplace. Judy Kahrl of Ohio appreciates the fact that it takes courage for a woman to stand in the face of such pressure and say, "At this time in my life, and with this new person as my responsibility, I am going to use my resources of time and physical and emotional energy in the most effective way possible for the nurturing of that new life." Judy adds, "Yet, the self-esteem which results from doing the job well is immeasurable."

As the 1980's emerge, many young women are opting to put their careers "on hold" when the baby arrives. They see motherhood as a special season in their lives, one that they do not want to miss. The working world will still be there two or three, five or ten years from now. Stay-at-home mothers of young children often see themselves resuming their working careers once their children are older. They view the time at home as a short period, "a sliver of time" when gauged against the many years that they can, and probably will, work outside the home.

As you await the arrival of your baby, you are probably thinking about what you should tell your employer regarding your future plans. From

Babies need continuing, ongoing care and affection from one person in order to thrive. Providing a reassuring hug or a soothing touch when baby is feeling bewildered or unhappy is what mothering is all about. (Photo of Veronica Castillo and Sebastian by Richard Ebbitt.)

experience, many mothers insist: "Do not make any commitments before your baby is born. Be very firm on this."

You do not want the specter hanging over your head of having to return to a job by a certain date because of an agreement you made while still pregnant. Most businesses give a maternity leave, and will hold your job for you for a specified period of time after the baby is born. By all means take advantage of it, and give yourself that time to assess how much you and your baby need each other. For someone to expect you to promise away your future and that of your baby before you even have a chance to meet is tantamount to signing a blank check—no, it is worse.

Be as cautious in your decision-making as you would be with a major investment—the investment here is this critical period in your life and that of your baby. The early months and years set the course for the rest of your child's life, and they can never be recaptured. And as Dr. Marilyn Bonham, the psychiatrist who wrote *Laughter and Tears of Children,* reminds us, "The outflow of (a mother's) love and affection for the very young child is pure gold in the bank."

We hope that these suggestions are helpful to you and that you will be able to stay home with your baby. But if you can't be an at-home nursing mother, we hope we can help you to breastfeed your baby as a working mother. For more information see, "Breastfeeding and Working."

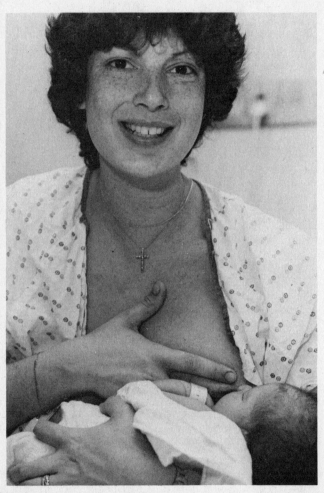

For Jan McIntosh, a happy birth experience helps get breastfeeding and mothering off to a good start. (Photo by Harriette Hartigan.)

Chapter IV

Your Baby Arrives

When your baby is born, his features may seem somewhat compressed, giving him the expression of a wise little old man. Traces of vernix, the creamy coating that protected him in the watery atmosphere of the womb, may still be in evidence. His appearance is days and weeks away from that of the usual baby pictures one sees—but no picture ever captured the wonder of a newly born baby.

To his parents, the newborn child is a rare and incredible sight. He seems so tiny and helpless, yet he is also more fully developed and has greater survival skills than had been generally recognized before the research of the last decade. Held up close, a baby who is not sleepy from drugs can see his mother's face clearly, and in fact has a preference for the human face. He can also hear quite well. For a period during the first hour of life, most newborns are quietly alert and receptive. A lively and intricate exchange of messages passes between the mother and baby who are together at this time.

When doctors from a number of European countries and the United States met to compare findings in their research, "The most surprising thing to emerge," said Dr. Myron Hofer, professor of psychiatry at the Albert Einstein School of Medicine in New York, "was the tremendous role the baby plays in the mother-infant relationship."

Films of a mother face-to-face with her newborn reveal the baby intently watching his mother and repeating her actions. She extends her tongue—the baby does likewise. He moves in rhythm to the tone of her voice. The recurring, back-and-forth responses between the mother and her baby have been described as a ballet. It is apparent that a delicate courtship is taking place. Mother and baby are "falling in love."

The hours and days immediately after the birth seem to be an especially sensitive period for a mother to form an attachment to her newly arrived baby. This bond may be made quickly in a flash of emotion, as a Washington mother, Carol Vines, describes:

> How does one explain that exhilarating feeling that follows a completely natural birth? You want to tell the world how great it is to have pushed that baby out. Who can explain that enormous, powerful surge of love that one feels upon first sight of that pink little life, when she is just two

seconds out of her warm hiding place? How can her bottom be so round and tiny? I wonder so much about her. Does she want to nurse? "Oh, please, can I hold her?"

But others of us find that our initial feelings for the baby immediately after delivery are at a low ebb. The small newcomer seems a stranger and may be howling lustily. Nonetheless, he is a needy little stranger, to be taken gently into a mother's arms and soothed. Gradually in these quiet times together, the magical wand of mother love imperceptibly brushes over, and strong bonds are formed between mother and child.

Says Dr. Hugh Jolly of London, "A normal baby should be delivered straight to his mother's arms where he can be caressed at the breast."

The important consideration is not whether it is love at first sight or a slower unfolding of loving emotion for your infant, but that being with your baby enables this natural bonding to begin to take place.

BREASTFEEDING — HOW SOON?

The sooner you put your baby to the breast, the better. Most babies are ready and even eager to nurse at some time within the first hour after birth. The sucking reflex of a full-term healthy newborn is usually at a peak about twenty to thirty minutes after he is born, provided he is not drowsy from drugs or anesthesia used during labor and delivery. If this prime time to begin nursing is missed, the baby's sucking reflex may be less acute for about a day and a half.

Early nursing is mutually beneficial to mother and baby. Aside from getting breastfeeding off to a good start, your newborn's immediate nursing hastens the delivery of the placenta. You will have less blood loss than you would have without this help from your little friend. For the baby, being so close to his mother is comforting, and the first milk, the colostrum, is priceless as a source of protective immunities against disease.

If your baby is born at home or in a birth center, he can usually be put to the breast without delay. Since you remain together in these circumstances, you and baby have all the time in the world to get off to a good start. In cultures where mothers regularly greet their newborns by cuddling and nursing, and infants remain with their mothers to nurse at will, breastfeeding progresses with few problems.

A hospital delivery may be a different story, of course. A delivery table is not the roomiest or most comfortable location for your baby's first nursing session, but nursing while still on the delivery table is preferable to waiting for this special event. A South Dakota mother, Cathie Walker, describes her experience:

What if the baby is uninterested? Will it be awkward on a narrow delivery-room table? The many questions I'd wondered about vanished from my mind as I held my newborn baby to my breast. Immediately, and so very naturally, little Alison latched on. Her big, dark blue eyes gazed into my

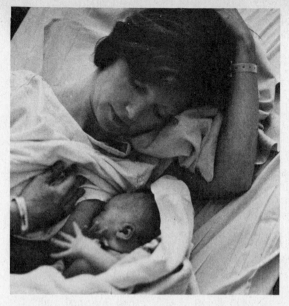

For healthy, full-term babies like Nash Taylor, mother's body heat and a lightweight receiving blanket, are all the warmth needed to maintain the baby's body temperature.

face as I stroked her beautifully round, wet head.

After about ten minutes the nurse carried Alison around the table to nurse on the other side. There was nothing awkward about it. I just leaned slightly to the side and cradled Alison in my arm.

Your first attempt at feeding the baby may proceed as smoothly and simply as Cathie described, but there are many variations of first-time nursings. Some babies only lick the nipple—a gentle way to practice for the nursings ahead. Others look, but don't try. Your baby may prefer to sleep. You may feel awkward or tense. Mary Ann Kerwin, one of La Leche League's founders, explains that the first time she tried to nurse her baby, "I was too insecure to relax."

If your first nursing session does not go as smoothly as you would like, don't worry—just look forward to the next feeding. Hopefully your newborn will be with you most of the time, if not all of the time, and the two of you will have ample opportunity to get used to being a nursing couple.

Need for Extra Warmth

If early breastfeeding is not a common practice in the hospital where you give birth, the staff may be hesitant about encouraging you. Mothers are sometimes told that their babies need to be in a heated bassinet or under an overhead heat lamp, a procedure that is rarely necessary. The premature infant under three pounds can well benefit from the heated bassinet and, in any case, will probably not have the strength to nurse. But, a study of 115 babies in the United States showed that a healthy, full-term baby, dried and swaddled following birth and then placed in his mother's arms, maintains his body temperature as well as a baby in a heated bed. Kathy and Dennis Hanley tell us of a hospital in Wisconsin where both the mother and father are encouraged to hold their newborn skin-to-skin soon after birth. The parents' body heat stabilizes their infant's temperature just as quickly as a warmer.

If your baby is healthy and full-term, and your doctor still orders special warming procedures, request that a heat lamp be placed over both you and your baby. You can then proceed to cuddle and nurse him.

Fear of Choking

Fear that the baby may choke while nursing is another reason often given for waiting six, twelve, or even twenty-four hours before starting breastfeeding. While choking can be a problem with babies who are experiencing the depressant effect of drugs, the same is not true for babies whose mothers have not been medicated. Dr. Gregory White of the LLLI Professional Advisory Board, who has delivered thousands of babies in his thirty-four years of practice, comments:

> The problem of choking on mucus present at birth is one I've never seen in a healthy, full-term baby. If the baby is born naturally, his throat reflexes are as good as yours are. If he has a little extra mucus, he will sneeze or cough or swallow to get rid of it. I think probably a little colostrum is pretty good stuff to wash it down with.... I've never seen a child have a problem with mucus from early nursing.

Another objection to early nursing is based on the possibility (one in four thousand births) of the baby being born with what is commonly called T-E (tracheoesophageal) fistula, an abnormal opening between the windpipe and the esophagus that allows something taken by mouth to enter the lungs. Water, or water and glucose, is often the first fluid given to babies, since water is preferable to cow's milk or a formula in the event that there is a T-E fistula. But, again, practices that may be advisable for bottle-fed babies do not necessarily apply to the breastfed baby. Colostrum is a natural bodily substance, like tears, and does not produce the irritating effects of a foreign substance such as glucose and water. At the first nursing, the baby gets only a very small amount of colostrum, approximately two tablespoons. According to Dr. James Good, another physician of long experience with breastfeeding mothers and a member of the LLLI Professional Advisory Board:

> There is a very simple test the doctor can do in the delivery room which takes maybe thirty seconds if he fumbles and even less if he's pretty adept. He can do this easily *if* a cardinal symptom makes him suspect T-E fistula. There is no need to do this on all babies. If the baby were to drink water, and get it into his lungs, this could be more damaging than colostrum.

Times Are Changing

Possibly the biggest hurdle you'll have to overcome in the hospital is established custom. The practice of keeping the newly born baby in the nursery originated at a time when mothers were heavily sedated and could not be expected to hold or nurse their babies for some time after the birth. In this regard, too, change is coming, and progress has been made in bringing mothers and babies together immediately after birth. One mother, Debi Sparks of Kentucky, recounted her experience in a hospital with "a long-standing policy of no nursing until twelve hours after delivery." During a prenatal visit, she spoke to her doctor of her desire to nurse right after delivery. Even though he had never heard of its being done, and no one had ever asked before, Debi said that he agreed. She describes her hospital experience:

> One of the first things I did after we arrived at the hospital was to mention to the nurses that I wanted to nurse my baby soon after delivery. No one had seen it done, but they were very curious. Labor was hard and fast and before I knew it we were in the delivery room. It felt great to push. Then it happened, the head, the shoulders, the whole body and there was my precious baby boy, weighing in at eight pounds and seven ounces and beautiful!
>
> I reminded the nurse about bringing the baby to me and was told that they wanted to do the blood tests and clean him up and they would bring him to me in the recovery room.
>
> The moment arrived, there was my sweet baby. I held him close and offered him my breast while lying down. He latched on like a pro! The nurses and aides were amazed. Since I felt so good, I then sat up and offered the other breast and all went beautifully. In fact, he didn't want to let go. I requested that no formula or sugar water be given in the nursery, and they brought him on demand, even if they had just brought him twenty minutes before.
>
> My milk came in about thirty-two hours after I started nursing my son, and he gained one-half ounce before leaving the hospital. My pediatrician was delighted, and so was I, since many babies lose weight at first.

Advance planning, whenever possible, will give you and your baby a head start in breastfeeding, but exceptional conditions can and do occasionally come up that may make it impossible for you to nurse as soon as you would like to. If this happens, modify your course of action and do the best you can at the moment; at least you'll know how breastfeeding normally proceeds. With such knowledge, you can quickly make up for lost time when you and your baby can be together and breastfeeding begins.

A NURSING SESSION IN SLOW MOTION

Getting your baby started at the breast smoothly and easily will soon be second nature to you. Nursing a baby, once you get the hang of it, is simplicity itself—much less involved than any description of the process. In addition to reading the basic information here, it will be helpful if you are in contact with an experienced breastfeeding mother and can see how she eases her baby through a feeding or two. Of course, no two mothers or babies are alike, so from the start look to your baby and do not be afraid to follow his preferences and your own motherly instincts.

In the hospital (and at home, too), take advantage of the fact that you can nurse your baby lying down. You will probably have to experiment a few times to find the most comfortable position for you and baby. It helps to have a couple of extra pillows at hand to tuck under a shoulder or behind your back. If this is your first baby, you may be a little scared and nervous. Take a few deep breaths and relax. Remember that other new mothers have felt the same way and have done just fine!

Lie on your side, slightly curved so your baby fits next to you comfortably. Have the baby on his side, his blankets loosened, his mouth in line with your nipple. Place your arm on the bed, above his head. Or try putting your arm under him, with his head in the crook of your elbow; this position brings the baby's head up closer to the breast.

Now, with your other hand, pull your baby's feet in close to you, lining his body up at a slight angle to you, his chin closer to your breast than his nose. His head will be tilted back a little, putting him in a good position to take the nipple well and, at the same time, to breathe freely. As you and baby get settled, talk to him or just make those little cooing noises that mothers and babies understand so well.

To make it easy for baby to grasp your nipple, form a V with two fingers, placing one above and the other below the areola, the dark area surrounding the nipple. Press down gently with the top finger and you'll make the nipple turn slightly upward. It will then be aimed toward the roof of baby's mouth and will be at a good angle for him to suck effectively.

Next, lean toward baby enough to be able to stroke his cheek (on the side nearest to you) with your nipple. The baby will turn toward any pressure on his face, a reflex that you want working with you. Trying to direct his head toward the breast by pressing against his face on the opposite side will cause him to turn away from you. So relax, and do nothing more than touch his cheek with your nipple, assuring him all the while that he will do very well at nursing, as he most certainly will. He'll soon turn toward the nipple, perhaps taking it and letting go a few times; then he'll take it into his mouth. Pull him in close enough to you so he is not straining to hold onto the nipple. It is important for a baby to take some of the areola along with the end of the nipple. If he is having difficulty getting hold of the areola, it may be because your breasts are quite full, and you will have to express some milk first, then offer the breast. (See "How to Express and Store Breast Milk.") If your nipple seems flat, you can draw it out by holding a cold washcloth or some ice against it for a few moments. Once baby is nursing, make sure your breast is not pressing against his nose, which will interfere with his breathing. You may have to hold the breast back slightly with your finger.

Breastfeeding while sitting up is basically the same as when lying down. Baby should be held facing your breast with head up close, yet tilted back slightly. Baby should be looking up at you. Cup your breast in your hand and press down on the areola with your thumb. This should point your nipple out and upward. Again, baby should get your nipple and part of the areola well into his mouth. He will be able to grasp the nipple well if you hold him close to you. If baby chews only on the end of the nipple, he may develop a style of nursing described by one mother as the "cliff-hanger." Baby won't get as much milk, and mother is likely to get sore nipples. As your baby grows older and holds his head well, you won't have to take such careful notice of angle and position; he'll get where he wants to go, all on his own.

When choosing your spot for nursing, pass up the straight-back, armless chair and settle into a comfortable armchair or rocker. You'll be in this position for some time, so arrange things for your comfort. Have a pillow handy to support your arm or cushion your back, if needed. You should be relaxed, with none of your muscles straining to hold yourself or baby. Many mothers become thirsty while nursing, so it's nice to have something to drink close at hand.

Some newborns nurse steadily without stopping until full, but many others seem rather lackadaisical, sucking for a minute or two and then resting with the nipple still in their mouth. Mother's milk lets down in spurts in response to baby's vigorous sucking, which explains the on-again, off-again manner of feeding. It often takes a newborn a few days to learn how to activate the flow of milk. You can encourage your "rester" to stay on the job by rubbing his back or feet, stroking him under the chin, or, of course, by talking to him. A never-fail starting technique is to gently tug at your nipple, alerting baby to the fact that it is there for a purpose, and he has work to do. Switching him to the other breast may spur him on.

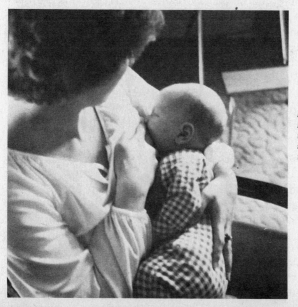

Becky Herbin holds her son Michael close with his body facing her, and uses her fingers to shape her nipple so he can grasp it properly.

The Let-Down

After the baby has been nursing well for several minutes, many mothers will feel a slight tingling sensation and notice a strong surge of milk. This is known as the let-down reflex, and may occur several times in one feeding. Some mothers do not notice this at all, but it is still occurring if their babies are nursing well. Other mothers feel the tingling sensation very strongly in the early weeks. For more information about the let-down reflex see "How the Breasts Make Milk."

If you must end a nursing session while baby still has a firm grip on your nipple, you can comfortably remove your baby either by gently pressing the breast away from the corner of his mouth or by pulling back on his cheek near the corner of his mouth, thereby breaking the suction that firmly holds the nipple. Merely pulling your baby off the breast may be painful, and it can also be damaging to your nipples.

Burping The Baby

During a feeding a baby sometimes swallows air that needs to be expelled or burped if the little one is to be comfortable. A bottle-fed baby usually takes in quantities of air, often because of the way in which milk flows from an artificial nipple. As a consequence, burping the baby is often thought of an an almost indispensable part of infant-feeding routines.

Swallowing air is not common among breastfed infants, so you may not have to worry about burping your baby after every nursing. Your experience with your own baby will be your best guide as to when and if he needs burping. Some breastfed babies never seem to need burping, while others will swallow air on occasion, often when mother's breast is very full and the milk comes quickly. The baby who by nature is a "gulper" is always a likely candidate for burping.

One of the reasons many babies spit up is simply that there is some air trapped inside with milk on top of it. In order for the air to get out, as it wants to do, the milk must come out first. In the interim, the baby may be quite uncomfortable and complain loudly. Anytime a baby has been crying long and hard—a situation you will certainly try to avoid—he will not nurse as calmly as he would normally and will probably swallow air. Burping is one of the things to try whenever the baby is fussy.

There are any number of ways to burp a baby. You can try placing your baby on your shoulder and gently patting his back. A clean diaper or receiving blanket tossed over the shoulder will absorb any milk that comes up. Just holding your baby in a more or less upright position will bring up most air bubbles in an easy and relaxed way. Another tried and true method is to raise baby, slowly, to a sitting position. When he is very small, take care to support his head and back, and hold him in this position for only a few moments. Some mothers rest the baby, tummy down, across their knees and rub or pat his back.

In the early weeks, try burping the baby when you switch from one breast to the other during a feeding and again when your baby is through nursing. If there is no burp after a few moments, you can forget the idea—unless, of course, he is fussy. You never really need an excuse for holding your baby, but the possibility that an air bubble is bothering him is as good a reason as any for extra comforting. Dads, too, are excellent baby soothers and burpers, especially as the baby gets bigger and can relax against those wonderful wide shoulders.

Anytime your baby burps especially loud and heartily, see if he wants a little more milk. The big bubble may have made him feel full when he really wasn't. But if baby falls asleep at the breast while nursing, it's usually best not to disturb him with the burping routine. Lay him down carefully, either on his side or stomach, not on his back. Often the right side is better than the left, since in this position the air will probably come up spontaneously. When he is lying on his side, the milk he might spit up will run out of his mouth and not upset him.

We'd also like to mention hiccups here. Little babies seem to be prone to them, often hiccupping after every feeding. Don't worry about them; they're perfectly normal and more upsetting to the parents than the baby.

IN THE BEGINNING

How Long to Nurse?

A common precaution given to new mothers is to limit nursings in the first few days to three or five minutes on each side at each feeding, and to work up to about ten minutes on the third or fourth day. More than one person may tell you not to let the baby nurse too long or too often for fear of getting sore nipples. Such advice does not take into account the fact that it may take two or three minutes for the milk to let down in any quantity, especially in the early days. Nursing for less than five minutes could mean that the feeding would end almost before it started. And once the milk is flowing, the slight soreness that may be felt when the baby starts to nurse subsides. Keep in mind that, in the beginning, nursing frequently—every two hours or so—is easier on the nipples and at the same time stimulates the production of milk, a primary concern.

Such advice about drastic limiting of nursing times should be put into perspective. Many women are never bothered with sore nipples at all, no matter how long or how often their babies nurse. Soreness may never be a problem for you, particularly if you have followed the suggestions for nipple care during pregnancy. (See "Preparing Your Nipples and Breasts.")

If you do develop tender nipples, there are a number of tried and true remedies to prevent them from becoming worse and to ease the discomfort. (See "If Your Nipples Get Sore.") Nipple soreness, like muscle soreness after a workout, is temporary. With continued exercise (or continued breastfeeding) it goes away. Limiting nursing may only prolong the conditioning period and the length of time that the nipples remain sore. It also depresses the milk supply. What an empty accomplishment it would be if a program of restricted nursing kept a mother's nipples from getting sore, but she was then left with insufficient milk for her baby.

One Side or Both?

While breastfeeding is being established, we recommend that you offer both breasts to the baby at each feeding. Nursing on one breast only could mean a four- to six-hour lapse before a breast is again nursed—too long a period in the beginning. The added stimulation of suckling baby on both breasts is a way of keeping pace with his increasing interest in nursing and his need for more milk. In addition, the breasts will not become painfully overfull, a condition that can develop quickly in the early days.

At each feeding, alternate starting sides. For instance, if at one feeding you start nursing on the right and then switch to the left, reverse the order for the next feeding. You'll be using the last used side first and the first, last. To help remember the starting order, mothers have come up with all kinds of ideas from fastening a small safety pin on the bra on the side used last to transferring a small ring from hand to hand. You'll soon figure out your own method. If you do forget, your baby and your own full breast will probably soon let you know—oops!—you've offered the "wrong" side. No harm is done if this happens from time to time; there's no need for you to worry about it.

"Emptying the Breast"

Sometimes mothers are told to empty their breasts completely after each feeding by pumping out whatever milk the baby may leave. This is not really practical because, first of all, the lactating breast is never empty; there will always be another drop of milk, and yet another. Secondly, we have yet to find a mother of a normal, healthy baby who found such emptying to be necessary in order to build up a good milk supply. Most women who start this sort of pumping soon give it up because it is a great bother and quite time-consuming.

If you should have a baby who does not at first suck well, as might be the case with some premies or an occasional full-term baby, you might have to pump after each feeding in order to provide sufficient stimulation to keep up your supply. Normally, though, the most urgent reason we know of for pumping is to provide breast milk for your own baby when he has to be separated from you for some reason. For further information, see "Special Circumstances." Often, too, the breastfeeding mother who is able to (and whose own baby will not lack for mother's milk or attention) will pump in order to help an ill baby who needs breast milk. Other than for one of these good reasons, you should not have to be concerned about pumping and emptying your breasts.

Keeping the Nipples Clean

Ordinary washing with plain water is all that is necessary for your breasts and nipples. There is no need for special cleansing techniques, either before or after nursing. When you do bathe, we recommend avoiding the use of soap on the nipples; it isn't necessary. Soap is drying

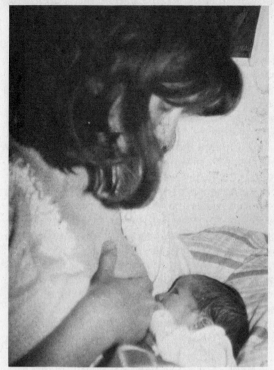

Newborn Tuga Maria Müller gazes lovingly at her mother, Christiane.

to the skin, as are alcohol and tincture of benzoin, and dryness encourages cracked nipples.

Since most of the germs your baby is exposed to both in the hospital and at home are airborne (from person to person), washing the nipple area won't help to protect the baby against them. Your milk acts as an antiseptic agent on the skin of your nipples. And, for your baby, breast milk is an excellent source of valuable antibodies against those germs.

WHEN THE MILK COMES IN—THAT FULL FEELING

Your milk will "come in" at some time between the second to the sixth day after delivery. Before that time, your baby will get colostrum, which will provide him with all of the nourishment he needs, plus elements to protect him against disease. (See Part Two.)

A combination of factors influences when a mother's milk comes in. Nursing the baby soon and often after birth encourages early and good milk production. An unmedicated delivery and having your baby with you (either rooming-in at the hospital or at home from the beginning) make an important difference. It also helps if you are reasonably at ease. For most mothers, being in the familiar surroundings of home, with the freedom this gives you to cuddle and nurse your baby frequently, is all that is needed to bring in the milk.

When the milk comes in, your breasts may seem fairly bursting. You feel as though you could satisfy twins—or triplets! The fullness is often due to a condition called engorgement. It comes about because additional blood has rushed to the breasts in order to assure that there will be adequate nourishment for the new baby. It is like the marshaling of the grand army—all the forces come to the fore to get things in good working order. The extra blood, along with some swelling of tissues, produces the engorgement. It occurs most often in first-time mothers, although this also varies among individuals. Some mothers notice only moderate or little fullness with their first babies, while other mothers who have nursed previously become engorged the next time around.

In the usual course of events, engorgement subsides in a matter of days. But while the breasts are engorged, it is especially important to continue to nurse the baby frequently, since emptying the breasts relieves the congestion. A comfortably warm shower, followed by a nursing, often reduces engorgement quickly. Sometimes the engorged area is mainly in one part of the breast, perhaps high up toward the arm. With the palm of your hand, gently stroke the breast downward toward the nipple. This is most effective when done under the shower or while leaning over a bowl of warm water and sloshing the water over the breasts. Hand-expressing some milk can also help to ease engorgement. (See "How to Express and Store Breast Milk.")

HOSPITAL ROUTINES

When you arrive at the hospital, be sure to tell the hospital staff that you plan to breastfeed your baby and you do not want what may be considered a routine shot or pill to dry up your milk. Your doctor and the baby's doctor may need to be reminded to leave word with the nursery that, right from the start, bottles and supplements of all kinds are off limits for your baby. A ban on bottles will make it much easier for you and baby to get off to a good start breastfeeding.

We hope you have the good fortune to be helped with breastfeeding by some of the many knowledgeable and enthusiastic nurses who care so much about helping mothers with those first nursing sessions. Of course, you can contact La Leche League with any questions you may have. A local Leader can give you the most direct help, but you're always welcome to call the International Office. Take telephone numbers with you to the hospital for reference if needed.

Hospitals want what is best for the patients, but often their size and bureaucracy come between their good intentions and the kind of care you need. Be prepared to speak up for what you want. Often, getting what you want is simply a matter of dogged persistence. One mother said that whenever she was told "I'm sorry, we can't do that" in answer to a request, she would say that she did not want anyone to go against hospital policy, but that she would like to talk to someone who had the authority to alter the policy. Carrying her appeal up the line did at times result in a happy resolution of the problem.

You May Need Help

Assertiveness takes energy, of course, and may be an effort that you aren't up to at the time. The other member of the parental team, your husband, remains your partner in helping to bend or bypass routines that hamper your breastfeeding efforts. You concentrate on caring for the baby, and he can take the position of running interference against red tape and regulations that get in your way. After all, this is *your* baby, yours and your husband's, a fact that is sometimes obscured in the delicate balance between institutional and parental authority.

Susan and Larry Kaseman of Virginia were looking forward to a home birth with their second child, but instead, baby Peter was born by cesarean in the hospital. Susan writes:

> As my husband, Larry, and I planned for the birth of our second child, our major concern was that our family be together as much as possible. We felt strongly about this for several reasons: we could support each other and strengthen family bonds; the baby would need the reassurance and stimulation of my touch, heartbeat, voice, the solace of nursing, and the physiological benefits of colostrum and milk; and the sooner Larry and our three-year-old Diede could touch the baby, the sooner (and perhaps more easily) these relationships could begin. For these and other reasons, we planned a home birth.

> When a cesarean became necessary, we quickly changed plans, but not priorities. In the hospital, with a combination of diplomacy and determination, Larry communicated our wishes to the pediatrician and the head nurse, and began a dialogue with the hospital staff. They would state hospital policy, we would offer an alternative, and they would consider and sometimes cooperate. Having an obstetrician who understood our requests was an invaluable aid.

> "May I please have my baby?" became my theme throughout my hospital stay. I had been reluctant to refer to our first child as "my baby" for fear of being thought an over-possessive mother. I have since decided it is an effective way of emphasizing to myself and the staff exactly who has the primary responsibility.

> Again and again I found that exceptions could be made to many of the rules. Peter was brought to us in the recovery room, two hours old and sleepy, but eager and able to nurse. What a tremendous help that contact was! When a nurse said an injection of painkiller would make me too woozy to be trusted with Peter, I declined the injection and she found a milder, oral drug that worked well enough. Declining a professional photograph because it would have meant another trip to the nursery for Peter, seemed to convince the staff that I was very serious about keeping him with me.

> Throughout our hospital stay, I had to keep asking for Peter. If one

person refused to bring him, I'd ask someone else. Staff members were generally cooperative in responding, but seldom offered to bring him. I felt like a minority of one because of my "unusual" ideas, and was grateful for the reassurance of those who agreed with me.

My initial concern had been that Peter be with me so I could meet his needs, but I was continually amazed at the strength of my need for him—how much better I felt, physically and emotionally, when he was in my arms, and how difficult it was when he was in the nursery.

No Supplements—Frequent Nursings

In the hospital your constant refrain should be that you *do not* want your baby to be given bottles of water or formula in the nursery, and you *do* want to be able to nurse him often. This is very important, because supplementary formula is one of the greatest deterrents to establishing a good milk supply, and frequent nursing is one of the greatest helps. **Your milk is regulated by what your baby takes, and the more he nurses, the more milk your breasts produce.** If your baby is given a bottle, he will take less from the breast, and your supply will diminish or will never be well-started. Also, your baby will be confused by the change from mother's soft nipple to the harder rubber nipple.

Tell everyone who will listen that you want to nurse your baby as often as he wants to be fed. He will not need formula, tea, sugar water, or plain water if he has you. Even one bottle of formula could lead to the development of an allergy when cow's milk is reintroduced into his diet months later. The nurses will want to avoid whatever could cause a problem for your little one, so explaining as often as necessary to the nurses on each shift that you are concerned about allergies will help them to remember that yours is the baby who does not get formula.

Rooming-in, which allows you to have your baby in your room for all or most of the time, is the ideal arrangement in the hospital. You care for the baby, and others care for you. Next best is having the baby brought to you at least every two or three hours during the day. As LLLI Professional Advisor, Dr. R. M. Applebaum, wrote in *Pediatric Clinics of North America:* "Hospitals geared strictly to the bottle routine of 'every four hours' should make the exception for the breastfed infant, who may be far too hungry to wait and soon exhausts himself from crying."

Babies also need nourishment during the night, and you will want your newborn brought to you for at least one night feeding. Some nurseries are not geared to bringing babies out for night feedings, so you may have to make an extra effort to let the night nurses know that you want your baby at night, too. Margaret Peyton from Ontario, Canada, was disappointed, but not daunted, when the nursing staff forgot to bring baby Kevin to her the first night in the hospital. Her solution:

The next night and every night until our release I pinned a note to Kevin's nightgown before they took him to the nursery at 10 P.M. I wrote a different note each night and kept them humorous.

Dear Night Nurse,
Please wake my mommy to feed me tonight.
She gets lonely. Besides, she has to learn
who's boss.   *Thank you,*   *Kevin*

The nurses taped the note each night to Kevin's bassinet, and I got to feed him every night thereafter.

Sleeping or Screaming?

If you are able to nurse your baby on demand, you won't be bothered with problems that can be caused by hospital feeding schedules. Such schedules, especially those with four-hour intervals between feedings, seldom coincide with a baby's appetite. Your newborn may often be either sound asleep or screaming his head off when brought to you. We don't know which is more disconcerting!

If your baby is sleeping when brought to you, try gently to awaken him; rough handling is very disturbing to the newborn. Joggle him a bit, rub his head, talk to him, stroke his cheek with your nipple. (Please don't let anyone snap at the soles of baby's feet sharply with their fingernails! Try rubbing his feet — or blowing on them!)

The late Ellen Hubbard, RN, an experienced obstetric nurse, passed on some tips for working with little sleepyheads in *RN Magazine:*

> To awaken the babe, I sit him on the bed, his chin in one of my hands, his back supported by the other (classic burping position), then bend him forward at the waist. Within a few seconds — usually by the count of seven — he stretches, opens his eyes, and raises his chin. I then quickly pop him into position for nursing by placing him on his side with the blankets loosened, feet close to mother's body, and head slightly away in an oblique line.

In reference to giving the baby a supplement when he wakes before the appointed time to be brought to his mother, Ellen commented:

> It is important not to give any bottles to the sluggish breastfeeding baby. The act of drawing the nipple in by making a trough with the tongue is bypassed with a bottle nipple. The baby who bottle-sucks develops a measurably weaker sucking reflex by four days of age, and gives less vigorous sucking to the breast when he is applied. If the baby can be taught to grasp the breast correctly, and obtain nourishment just one time, the rest is relatively easy.

If your baby doesn't wake up for a feeding, it is not the end of the world or of your chances to breastfeed. Cuddle baby, rock him, sing to him. Handling him in this way is a form of stimulation and is an important contribution to getting him moving and active. You might try undressing him or changing his diaper. With all this stimulation, he'll soon be awake and hungry. In the meantime, enjoy him. Newborns can make some outlandish faces in their sleep, and you may be laughing at your little clown. When the nurse comes in to take him back to the nursery, ask that he be brought to you as soon as he is awake, so he and you can start to "catch up."

If your baby is crying very hard, a little patience will be needed to first quiet him before putting him to the breast. Hold him in the nursing position against your breast. This may be all that's needed to quiet him. Rock him—with your body if there is no rocking chair in your hospital room—and sing a soothing melody. Try putting him on your shoulder and patting his back. After a little calming mothering, offer him your breast again, but don't push. Easy does it. He'll soon stop scolding the world and find that there are better things to do.

With either the sleeping or screaming baby, squeeze a few drops of your milk into his mouth to give him a taste of what he's missing. We do not advise putting anything, such as honey, on the nipple to entice the baby to take it. Anything other than your milk can cause a reaction in a sensitive baby. Also, these products may have impurities in them which would not faze an adult, but could cause problems for baby—a certain type of botulism spores, for example, can be found in honey. To quote from Father Fox's *Pennyrhymes,* "Honey is sweet, but love is sweeter."

Rooming-in

Problems caused by hospital routines can often be avoided if it is possible for you to room-in with your baby. Connie Horenkamp of Illinois tells of her experience:

My first two children were totally nursed, but forced to live those first precious days behind the glass wall of the hospital nursery. I spent many hours standing at the window making sure everything was all right. Then Marissa was born. Hospital policy was more relaxed, and I was more determined; we roomed-in together. We nursed frequently, napped together, and just cuddled. The first day she slept very little as she adjusted to her new life, but I was able to phone a Leader for the reassurance I needed. Now I keep remembering (three months later) how Marissa slept in my arms and in the arms of my husband. Those first days were ours in which to grow together. I went home confidently knowing my baby.

My husband and I were relaxed and better able to introduce her to the other children. The two times before, we had been clumsy and nervous over the baby even though I am a registered nurse. This time I came home rested since there weren't two days of worrying over who was crying down the hall behind the glass wall.

People are still commenting—"But didn't you need your rest?" My answer is that I was able to rest, knowing that my baby had the most concerned and observant caretaker in the world. No one wants to look at a baby as much as his own mother. I hope that someday the wall will be removed

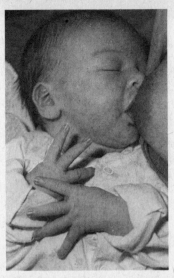

The tiny mouth, the graceful fingers, the obvious contentment of a breastfed baby are clearly displayed by Lineé Henning. (Photo by Harriette Hartigan.)

and rooming-in will be truly the accepted way of doing things. Our babies would certainly be much happier and mothers more confident. Rooming-in is a giant step in the right direction for good mothering.

Laurel Cohen of New Jersey planned on having rooming-in when her daughter, Debbie Sue, was born, but she was informed that the required private room was not available. The baby would have to be in the nursery, and feedings could be only every four hours. Laurel was in a double room with another patient, but when the woman left soon afterward, Laurel went immediately to the supervisor's desk. Could she pay the private room charge and have her baby with her? A call to the business office procured the needed permission, and a delighted Laurel reported, "I had my dear little baby with me all day." While the hospital did insist that Debbie Sue had to be in the nursery at night, at Laurel's request the nurses agreed to bring her to her mother for feedings on demand throughout the night.

Weight Loss And Jaundice

There are two common concerns for mothers while they're in the hospital that, fortunately, are seldom major problems—the baby may be losing weight or perhaps he is jaundiced. At times, these two conditions go together. In the vast majority of cases, when the baby is healthy and full-term, there is no better way of turning the tide in either condition than by uninterrupted, frequent nursing. Anything that interferes with breast-feeding every two or three hours in the first week should be avoided. Giving bottles of water or formula instead of nursing the baby frequently only complicates and worsens either situation.

Weight Loss. Some weight loss, up to a pound in a large baby, is not unusual especially if mother and baby are separated and baby is not nursing often. Babies are meant to gain, though, and a continuing loss of weight should not be ignored. (See "Slow Weight Gain.")

The fact is, a mother can supply ample milk for her baby. Dr. Richard Applebaum, a member of LLLI's Professional Advisory Board, wrote in *Pediatric Clinics of North America,* "A healthy (normal) mother can produce far more milk than the infant needs." And as mothers, we can tell you that the output of breast milk can be increased quickly and surely. The only effort it takes is nursing your baby leisurely and often. **The more you nurse, the more milk you will have.**

Weighing a baby before and after feedings is a common practice in some hospitals. Such weighings have many drawbacks, since baby's intake from the breast varies considerably from feeding to feeding, especially if he's "sleeping or screaming" when brought to his mother. In the very touchy first few days after delivery, it only takes one or two low readings on the scale to undermine a mother's confidence in herself. Actually, your baby does not need as great an amount of breast milk as he would of formula, since mother's milk is so well assimilated by the baby.

Jaundice. Many healthy, full-term babies have normal (or physiologic) jaundice, a yellowing of the skin and eyeballs, which appears when the baby is two or three days old. This jaundice is *not* a sickness. An excellent way to help your baby is to make *very sure* that he is getting what all newborns need—frequent nursings of their mother's colostrum and breast milk. Colostrum especially helps get rid of the jaundice. For more detailed information, see "Jaundice."

Early Discharge

Consider, too, an early discharge from the hospital. Even the most progressive hospital cannot duplicate the relaxed atmosphere and the freedom you have at home to mother your baby as you choose.

Karen and Larry Stange of Nebraska had wanted a home birth, but their doctor did not agree, so Karen next asked if she could go home from the hospital soon after birth if there were no problems. "To my surprise," she related, "he replied, 'I don't see why not.' Each visit after that, I reminded him of our plans." All went well for Karen and baby, and they were home again the same day the baby was born. Karen explains:

> The doctor said the baby should be observed for twelve hours, so after that we were allowed to go home. Thus began three of the best days in eleven years of marriage. The evening of Clay's true birthday all five of us sat in our home and, I'm sure, glowed with the love we all felt.
>
> Larry took three days off and we did nothing but be a family. We had few visitors as no one realized we were home. I was free to rest as I chose, and needless to add, breastfeeding went very well. All of us got to know each other better than ever, and Clay seemed to thrive on the added love of five-year-old Sean and three-year-old Eric. For us it was a great time that will be remembered fondly all our lives. Incidentally, this was the earliest our doctor had released a mother and infant in seventeen years of practice.

BREASTFEEDING GADGETS

Experience has taught us that breastfeeding proceeds most smoothly when kept as simple and natural as possible. Except for unusual circumstances, gadgets and gimmicks should be avoided, as they can interfere with the natural interaction between mother and baby.

Nasal Spray

You may have heard of a nasal spray that is supposed to bring on the let-down. Such artificial intervention is rarely necessary though sometimes suggested for a tense and nervous mother or one who is very doubtful of her ability to breastfeed. A seriously delayed let-down in the first weeks of breastfeeding is almost always the result of too long a wait before the baby is put to the breast or feedings that are too few and too short, and the resultant anxious mother. If you do find yourself in this situation, you would do as well to trust your womanly makeup and your own natural hormones as to turn to artificial methods. Head for home with its more relaxed atmosphere and nurse to your heart's content. The situation will be overcome as soon as baby continues to suck long enough to naturally bring on the let-down. Many of the suggestions in the section "Losing Your Milk?" can be used to build up your milk supply.

Nipple Shields

You should also be cautioned against using nipple shields. A nipple shield looks like a regular rubber nipple with a flange and is worn over the mother's own nipple during a feeding. A well-meaning but misinformed nurse sometimes suggests a nipple shield as a way to promote healing when a mother's nipples are sore. Occasionally, one may be offered at the first feeding, supposedly to prevent sore nipples, or because someone has decided that the baby isn't nursing "correctly." Some hospitals even go so far as to routinely hand out nipple shields to every nursing mother.

From our years of experience, we know without a doubt that nipple shields are an invitation to trouble. Their use is almost never justified, and they create many more problems than they supposedly solve. We cannot tell you how many mothers have called, upset and worried after a few days or weeks home with the baby and the nipple shield. The baby gets hooked on it, and breastfeeding is never fully satisfying. The impulses to the brain that normally come from a baby sucking directly on his mother's nipple are fewer, and the secretion and let-down of the milk is slowed. Baby may not gain as well as he should, and the doctor starts talking about a formula supplement.

Besides coming between a mother and her baby and interfering with the establishment of breastfeeding, nipple shields can also harbor germs. Cleaning them thoroughly is a time-consuming chore. They rarely help sore nipples anyway, and sometimes make them worse. In short, a nipple shield is an extra bother that continues long after the mother's nipples would have healed with the more natural measures for clearing up sore nipples. (See "If Your Nipples Get Sore.")

Occasionally a baby who has started on a shield is upset when his mother tries to take it away. With patience and understanding, a baby can be weaned from the rubber nipple and be none the worse for it. One successful method is to cut a small portion off the top of the nipple shield, then after a day or two, snip off another piece, and each day a little more. Another method is to start a nursing on the shield, and after one or two minutes when the milk is flowing well, whisk it away and quickly put baby directly on mother's nipple. Soon the baby is accustomed to the real thing, mother's nipple, and the shield can be thrown away.

Breast Shields

Nipple shields should not be confused with breast shields, which are recommended for mothers with flat or inverted nipples. These are normally used during pregnancy to gradually draw out the mother's nipples. (See "Preparing Your Nipples and Breasts.")

Breast shields can also be used after the baby is born to help draw out flat or inverted nipples that were not discovered or treated during pregnancy. The breast shields are worn between feedings. It may only be necessary to wear them for a day or two, but in more severe cases, the mother may have to wear them for two or three weeks. They should not be worn continually; the nipples should be exposed to air for fifteen minutes or so several times a day.

The breast shields should be washed frequently in hot soapy water and rinsed thoroughly. The mother should not save the milk that leaks into the breast shields. It should not be given to the baby as it is quickly susceptible to bacteria growth.

ELECTIVE SURGERY FOR YOU OR BABY

If you are going to be in the hospital anyway for the birth of your baby, you or your doctor may suggest that you have some other medical matter attended to. Examples of elective surgery for the mother include stripping the legs of varicose veins or tying the fallopian tubes (tubal ligation). As for the baby, it may be considered almost routine to circumcise boy babies when they are only a few hours or days old. But circumcision is elective surgery and you have a choice of whether or not to have your baby circumcised. You can also choose to wait a while before having this done. We bring these subjects up because, physically and emotionally, these procedures all take their toll on mother and child. Since they represent elective surgery, their appropriateness at this critical time must be questioned.

Circumcision is as painful a procedure to a newborn as it is to an adult. As a religious rite, circumcision is not performed until the baby is eight days old, when he is less apt to hemorrhage. The reasons given in the past for the non-religious, almost routine circumcision of the newborn were generally hygienic and are no longer accepted by many physicians and parents. If you're interested in learning more about this subject, see the Book List at the end of this book.

The most important reason for deciding against elective surgery following childbirth is that it interferes with a mother and her new baby being together and getting to know each other. While a mother may feel very good following the birth of her baby, her body nevertheless has some recovering to do. Adding the strain of recovering from a surgical procedure might lessen her enjoyment of these early days with her baby.

In regard to tubal ligation, there can often be an unexpected emotional reaction in the mother. When it dawns on her that the baby in her arms is her last, there may be feelings of deep sadness. It might become difficult for her to keep a normal perspective on her mothering of this baby. She may become exceedingly anxious about doing everything just right.

Whatever the inconvenience you may experience by postponing such operations for you or your baby, it is slight compared to the upheaval such surgery can cause in your life at this time.

LEAVING THE HOSPITAL

You can do yourself and your baby a favor by not taking any formula home from the hospital. You won't need it, and if it isn't in the house, you won't be tempted to use it at one of those moments of doubt that most mothers have. The take-home packs of formula are simply advertising, a promotion for artificial infant feeding. Some hospitals, recognizing this fact, are no longer routinely offering the formula to breastfeeding mothers.

Hospitals have become much more consumer-conscious in recent years and want to know what patients like or dislike about their hospital stay. By taking a few minutes to write a personal letter or fill out a patient questionnaire stating your preferences, you can support the practices you found helpful and point out the ones you'd like to see changed. Your suggestions could make it easier for the next breastfeeding mother giving birth in that hospital and, who knows?—you may find a delightfully improved atmosphere during *your* next visit.

By the time you leave the hospital, the nurses know of your interest in breastfeeding, so it would be most appropriate for you to leave them a copy of this book or the LLLI booklet for nurses, *How the Maternity Nurse Can Help the Breastfeeding Mother.* (See the Book List at the end of this book.) It's a nice way to say "thank you" by itself or with another gift, if such is customary. Nurses are not always aware that this kind of information is available and are happy to receive it.

If for some reason your breastfeeding experience in the hospital has not been the best or if you could not relax, don't fret. The hospital stay is now in the past. When you are at home with your baby, you will be able to nurse him. Thousands and thousands of mothers have done so in similar circumstances. The drive home, with baby secure in his safety seat, will be an especially exciting trip for you and your husband!

The early weeks are a period of adjustment, a time for you and your baby to settle into your new relationship as a nursing couple. Shown here are Martha Regan and six-week-old Jennifer. (Photo by Richard Ebbitt.)

Chapter V

At Home with

Your Baby

There is a sense of joy and satisfaction on everyone's part when your newborn is settled at home, in the heart of the family. Things are as they should be—you are all together. For you and your husband, a new phase of parenting begins. You'll find your mothering skills improving every day. But don't be surprised if you feel unsure of yourself and even a bit panicky at times. Once home, the care of this tiny baby is yours day and night, and the realization can seem overwhelming at times.

Most of us can say that we've been there; we know the feeling. One of La Leche League's founders thinks back with amazement at her own ineptness when she and her husband brought their firstborn home:

> The picture is vivid in my mind. Baby was lying in her basket, which was beautifully done up with a frilly, ruffled liner that I had made before she was born. She was crying her heart out, oblivious to this finery, and I, her mother, was sitting beside her, at a loss to know what to do. She had been fed and changed and was supposed to sleep. I remember thinking, "If only she were old enough to talk. She could *tell* me what is bothering her." Unfortunately, I was not yet aware of a far more basic form of communication with a little baby—a caring touch. How much more effective than speech! How simple if only I had picked her up! Instead, as a new mother, I was feeling somewhat put out at the turn of events, at myself, and my baby.

Think of the baby's first four to six weeks as an adjustment period for both of you, a time of getting to know each other. Your baby is mastering the skill of nursing to bring in milk, and your body is fine-tuning the system for producing it. It's not unusual for a new mother to feel as though her breasts are "bursting" with milk one day, and then be frantic a few days later because "there's nothing there."

Is the baby getting enough? Why is he crying? Haven't we all asked ourselves these questions and more? A good many of us announced firmly at some point in those early weeks that breastfeeding was "impossible." But at the urging of a supportive husband or with the help of another nursing mother, we decided to keep going for just a few days more. It's amazing how these early difficulties straighten out with a little time and patience.

BABIES ARE TO LOVE

Through doubts and anxious moments, remember—babies are to love. The task of caring for your new baby will not seem nearly so awesome if you keep this thought in mind. "Tender loving care" is what the very best authorities recognize as the prime need of babies. Look to your own baby. Is he happiest when snuggled close to you, nursing very often, perhaps even every hour? Or does he respond best when laid down after a nursing and patted to sleep? Your baby's well-being, comfort, and security are your guides.

In his helpful book for parents, *The Child Under Six,* James Hymes capsulizes the world of a baby: "He needs mothering. He needs nurturing. He needs someone who will care for him—someone big and strong, able and willing and ready. He needs—the old term is probably best—tender loving care."

Two well-known authorities on infant care, C. A. and Mary Aldrich, speak out for the little ones in *Babies Are Human Beings:* "Loving care and consistent, prompt response to their needs is tremendously important to their successful progress." The Aldriches explain that a baby's physical, mental, and emotional growth are interdependent. Emotional growth, they point out, profoundly influences the other two.

There is a beautiful simplicity about the care of the young baby that does not apply at any other stage of child rearing. With sureness we can say that **a baby's wants are a baby's needs**. The wants of a two- or three-year-old, however, may not always be what he needs. Parents will not respond any less lovingly then, but their approach will adjust to the changing world of the mobile child. (But we're getting ahead of ourselves. See "Gradually, With Love" for more on mothering the older child.)

With your newborn, "giving in" to him is good parenting. Feed him according to his own time schedule. Comfort him when he is upset. But, you may ask, won't such permissiveness spoil the baby and lay the foundation for problems later in life? This question is asked by many parents who are sincerely concerned about their children and want to do what is best. "Most spoiled children," say the Aldriches, "are those who, as babies, have been denied essential gratification in a mistaken attempt to fit them into a rigid regime."

A mother, grandmother, and League Leader, Marion Blackshear, thoughtfully considered the matter of spoiling and babies. From the experience she and her husband, David, a minister, have gained in rearing their own children, and from their contacts with many other young people, Marion writes: "When you think of a piece of fruit as spoiled, you think of it as bruised, left on the shelf to rot, handled roughly, neglected. But meeting needs, giving lots of loving care, handling gently, is not spoiling. I could carry this a step further and say that a piece of fruit is at its best when left to ripen on the tree, its source of nourishment—and a baby is at his best when held close to his source of physical and emotional nourishment—his mother."

Go right ahead and nurse your baby any time he seems to need it. Pictured here are Janet Repucci and her two-month-old son, Michael.

HOW MANY TIMES DO I FEED THIS BABY?

Throughout this book, we refer repeatedly to feedings "every two or three hours" since it is a common time span for babies' appetites. And it is a fact that when baby's tummy is filled often enough, and mother's breasts are emptied regularly enough, most breastfeeding problems are avoided. But no timetable can tell you how often you should nurse your baby. Some babies, some of the time, will nurse more often than every two or three hours. Such an increased need is an indication that the baby is lively and growing and is not a cause for worry. "Ad-lib nursing" can be very relaxing. You should not worry about putting baby to the breast "too often."

Mothers who live in a world that is not as mechanized and scheduled as ours would be aghast at the thought of regulating the comfort their babies receive at their breasts. A scientist, D.S. Matthews, described breastfeeding practices among mothers of Nigeria in the late 1940's:

A strict breastfeeding routine would be difficult to attain because the mothers, determined and obstinate, are not easily separated from their babies for long. Cots or cradles are not welcomed. The baby will remain from birth until about the second year of life almost constantly in close physical contact with the mother, who will feed it at irregular intervals, usually determined by the onset of crying.

A modern-day mother, Beth Leanza of New York, reflected on her own attitudes about mothering and the fact that her third daughter is "no trouble":

Rachel Marie is an easy-going baby—she is no trouble—and part of the reason, I've been thinking, is my changed attitude. It is quite different from what it was six years ago when our first daughter was born.

I had always felt that something must be wrong if she had to be held all of the time. After all, I thought, a baby should sleep in her crib. Nowadays, if Rachel can't get to sleep immediately after she nurses, I put her in a baby sling and hold her. Sometimes a bubble comes up, but most of the time she falls asleep on my shoulder. I no longer have a hang-up about where a baby should be.

When my second baby fell asleep nursing, I remember taking great pains to keep her awake so she would nurse longer. After all, I thought, a baby should get a bigger feeding and not have to be fed too often. Now, with Rachel, I no longer have a predetermined idea about the length of a baby's nursing. I find life much less frustrating with this attitude. If Rachel falls asleep nursing, even after a short nursing, I might put her down in her cradle. If she awakens shortly after, that's okay, too—I just nurse her again. Also, it helps not to think of nursings as "feedings." Nursing is caring for and comforting. The milk? That's the extra bonus that we mothers have for our babies.

With Rachel I am finding it a lot easier to accept help from others when they offer to cook, wash dishes, and do laundry, while I enjoy being available for Rachel and my older ones, too.

In the *Journal of Tropical Pediatrics and Environmental Child Health,* a guest editor, Babette Francis, wrote:

Successful lactation is an expression of a woman's femininity and she doesn't need to count how often she feeds the baby any more than she counts how often she kisses the baby.

About The Pacifier

Be forewarned that the pacifier can create more problems than it solves, often because it works too well. Pop it into a crying baby's mouth, and the room is suddenly blanketed with silence. What could be handier? But therein lies trouble. The use of a pacifier has a way of sneaking up on you by making it so simple to take the easy way out. While a pacifier can sometimes substitute for mother's breast, it is never a substitute for mother. A League Leader from Great Britain, Christine Blissett, explains that the English term for a pacifier is "dummy." "This is exactly what it is!" she adds.

If your baby has to settle for a "dummy" instead of nursing at your breast, stay with him. He still needs to be close to you, to be with a familiar voice and face. You don't want "it" taking over for you.

Used judiciously, however, for a short period of time and in a limited number of circumstances, a pacifier can be a help to the breastfeeding mother. In the early weeks of breastfeeding, a pacifier can be helpful if you have sore nipples and temporarily have to limit how long your baby sucks at the breast. As soon as the soreness begins to fade, increase the nursing time and throw out the pacifier. If your baby is sucking on a pacifier daily, your milk supply could be adversely affected and, as a result, the baby will not gain well.

Sucking can be very soothing to a newborn, and a pacifier may be convenient when you find yourself in a formal situation such as a religious service or wedding. If the baby starts to cry in the middle of the ceremony and you can't nurse him, a pacifier may satisfy him briefly until you can. It can also sometimes ease a tense situation when your infant starts to fuss on a crowded bus, in the checkout line at the store, or during the last ten minutes of driving home in the car.

The "pacifier habit" develops when it's used routinely, for instance, as a way to put the baby back to sleep. Ordinarily, if your baby likes to fall asleep sucking, let it be at the breast. You have the best pacifier in the world from baby's point of view. And more nursing at the breast means more milk for the baby. Among other drawbacks, routine sucking on a pacifier may lead to orthodontic problems in your child later in life.

If you use a pacifier for short periods and only in situations where it is impossible to nurse, your baby will not need it after the first two or three months. By that age, a baby can often be distracted and soothed in other ways than just by sucking. Also, you'll be a more experienced mother by then, so neither of you will miss it. And if you happen to have one of those babies who refuses that plug of rubber from the start, be thankful. You'll manage fine without it.

IS BABY GETTING ENOUGH?

Some babies never lose an ounce from the day they're born, and put on weight with the greatest of ease. Most babies lose some weight during the first week but get back to birth weight by about three weeks of age. In rare instances, perfectly healthy babies take as long as six weeks to recoup their birth weight. Dr. E. Robbins Kimball, one of LLLI's Professional Advisors, tells of a family with six children. All were breastfed, all required a full six weeks to regain their weight loss after birth, and all grew up to be fine and healthy.

How will you know if your baby is getting enough milk? He is probably getting enough to eat if he nurses every two or three hours. Is he "filling out" and putting on weight? Growing in length? Active and alert? A "yes" to these questions is an indication that your baby is thriving.

A quick, easy way to reassure yourself that your infant is getting enough milk is to check the number of wet diapers. If he has six to eight really wet diapers a day, he is doing fine. (For this purpose, keep the baby in cloth diapers. It's easier to judge wetness with cloth, rather than disposable, diapers.)

From time to time, you and your doctor will weigh the baby as a way of measuring his physical progress. A pound (453 grams) a month, or four to seven ounces a week is an acceptable gain, although some babies add a pound or more a week. Family characteristics and the baby's individual makeup need to be considered. Remember—healthy, happy babies come in all shapes and sizes. Both the quite fat and the very slim baby can be normal and healthy. Neither bigness nor smallness is a reason for concern as long as the baby's food is breast milk and nursings are according to his needs. If you feed your baby in the way that is naturally intended for the human infant, his weight gain will be what is natural for your particular child.

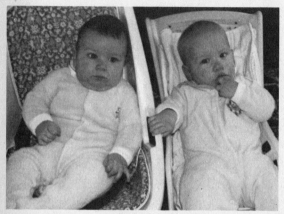

Babies come in all sizes! On the left is three-month-old Stephen Oliver and on the right is his cousin, five-month-old Erik Franke. Both are happy, healthy, and completely breastfed!

With regard to baby's size and appetite, Malinda Sawyer of Missouri noted, "Mothers who give birth to large babies and mothers who give birth to small babies have at least one thing in common: they can expect to have their ability to totally breastfeed the baby questioned." Two other Missouri mothers echo Malinda's thought. Mary Burdick's baby was a "lightweight" and her first to be breastfed. Her story begins with her pregnancy:

> How I wished I could breastfeed this third child! I had tried with my first child but it didn't work out, and I never even tried with our second child. An LLL Leader, Lois Hunziker, told me, "Mary, you can—almost any woman can. I've nursed all three of my children." With that, a whole new world opened up for our family.
>
> I gave birth to a tiny six pound, one-half ounce red-haired baby boy, Samuel David. Our first boy had weighed over seven and a half pounds, and our second boy had been a pound more than that, so this "little" baby was a surprise to us!
>
> On his second day he was down to five pounds, nine ounces, but my milk came in on the fourth day, and he gained an ounce a day. When Sammy was two weeks old, he weighed six pounds and six ounces. My mother was concerned that he wasn't gaining fast enough and urged me to give him a bottle, some juice, or cereal. Although I believed my baby was fine, I agreed to ask the doctor what he thought. He examined Sammy and

told me, "Your baby is doing fine; he's a very healthy baby. He is small, but every baby is a different person."

At his six-week checkup, he weighed seven pounds, one-half ounce, a weight gain of one pound over his birth weight. Sammy was a small baby and a very slow gainer, but fully breastfed. My doctor didn't believe that he even needed vitamins. I did receive some advice from concerned family members who believed that I should start early solids—one aunt was convinced that I was stunting his growth and he would be a midget!

My mother was worried for the first few weeks about Sammy but eventually became a strong supporter of my breastfeeding him. She realized when Sammy began to eat solids (after seven months), how much better he could use his tongue to swallow than our first two boys had.

For Kathy Whitney, the fact that she has large, rather than small, babies was the reason others were concerned. She writes:

Nora Tiffany was born weighing ten pounds, eight ounces. I always had plenty of milk, despite those who said I would need to give her supplemental feedings. None at all were needed, and she was always a healthy, happy baby. We offered her solid foods from the time she was five months old, but she refused them until she was nine and one-half months old. By this time, Nora had ten teeth and was able to eat finger foods.

Eighteen months after Nora's birth, I had ten pound, two ounce Eli Jeffrey. We brought him home when he was four days old, topping the scales at ten pounds, eleven ounces. At three months he weighed seventeen and one-half pounds. I offered solids to him at four months, but he refused them. He is now seven months old, weighs twenty-three pounds, all on breast milk.

When Alice Wohler of Illinois decided to breastfeed her third baby after bottle feeding the first two, she was unprepared for her doctor's alarm at the baby's slow weight gain. So she had him look at the files for her two bottle-fed babies, and sure enough, they had had the same slow pattern.

Marian Tompson, one of La Leche League's founders, remembers when two of her nieces had identical weights of seventeen pounds—but one baby was six months old and the other was one and one-half years old. Yet the doctor for each was satisfied that the baby was healthy.

CARING FOR YOUR BABY

As a very new little person, your baby continues to need many of the same conditions that helped him to grow in the womb. He needs to be close to you most of the time, whether awake or sleeping. Being close to you is very reassuring to your newborn. The rhythms of your breathing and heartbeat are familiar to him. In addition, he has been hearing your voice since about six months before he was born, so talking to him in soft, loving tones is especially soothing. For the time being, you are his world.

In her thought-provoking book, *The Rights of Infants,* Margaret Ribble defends the infant's right to good mothering. She stresses the importance of bodily contact between mother and baby. With a wonderfully practical touch, she states, "In addition, mothering includes the whole gamut of small acts by which an emotionally healthy mother may consistently show love for her child."

From time immemorial, mothers have expressed their love for their babies in many mundane tasks that are repeated countless times a day—bathing, changing, dressing. With all of these routines, simplicity is best. Let's look now at a few of them.

Bathing the Baby

A complicated bathing ritual may focus more attention on the apparatus and procedure than on the baby. Of course, babies must be kept clean, but this can often be taken care of with a minimum of fuss, sometimes just a quick dunking from the waist down in a washbowl filled with warm water. Sometimes mothers tend to overdo bathing and consequently wash away much of the natural oil on the baby's skin. A number of mothers have noticed that when less time was devoted to scrubbing, their young children's skin was in better condition.

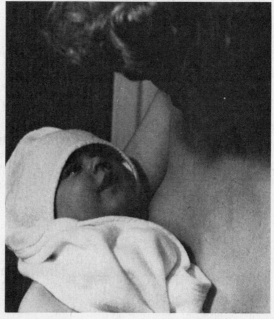

A relaxed and uncomplicated bath-time often provides some special moments between mother and baby. Six-week-old Adam Nelson is warm and cozy as his mother Sharon wraps him in a soft towel.

In some households, the baby is bathed by the father. Not all fathers feel at ease in handling a small baby, and we know of many fathers who prefer to wait and learn about baby care "gradually and with love." But if your husband is interested, try to arrange some of baby's routines to suit his schedule.

Wrap Him Up

A young baby sometimes startles himself when awake with a sudden movement of his arms or legs, and being securely wrapped is calming to him. Wrapping him snugly is often a good way of keeping your tiny baby happy. Think about how he was living before he was born. You can see how imitating that warm snugness may help him feel more secure in the big, impersonal world in which he is separated from you part of the time. The "swaddle wrap" has been used by mothers in all parts of the world.

You may find that after you have held your baby, wrapped snugly, in an unhurried way for a while, he will quietly drift off to sleep. Lay him down, blanket and all, with the blanket up behind his head. Otherwise the shock of a cold sheet against his head may be enough to wake him.

Adapted from Niles Newton's The Family Book of Child Care.

Diapers and Other Clothes

Another aspect of "tender loving care" is keeping your baby reasonably dry and comfortable. Fairly frequent changes of wet diapers during the day, with limited use of plastic protectors, should prevent diaper rash. Many mothers use double diapers at night. They find that the extra padding means fewer middle-of-the-night changing sessions. And if night feedings are low-key and quiet, baby will begin to associate nighttime with sleep—eventually.

When dressing your young baby, choose items that are loose and can be put on and taken off easily. We all love to see babies dressed up, but displaying a fancy bonnet or jacket is less important than keeping the baby comfortable. As for frilly, ruffled basket liners and such, while they are lovely to look at, none has ever been known to quiet a fussy baby, and all make extra laundry.

Bowel Movements

For the first few days after birth, baby's stool will be very dark—greenish-black—and sticky. It may be a nuisance to wipe off his little bottom, but it's a reassuring sign that all is well with baby's digestive system. This first stool is called meconium. Nursing the baby soon after birth assures that

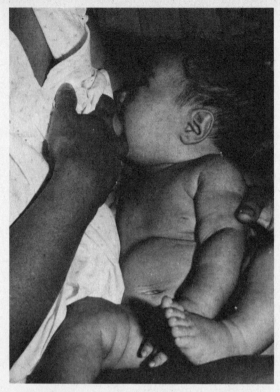

Two-month-old Andrea Cohen doesn't care a bit about impressing people with her baby finery. She is securely wrapped in what she likes best of all—her mother's loving arms!

baby will be getting your colostrum. Colostrum's cathartic properties help get rid of the meconium and thereby reduce his chances of becoming too jaundiced.

Once the meconium is cleared out, the stool of the baby who is receiving only mother's milk differs a good deal from that of the formula-fed infant. The stool of the breastfed baby is usually quite loose and unformed, often of a pea-soup consistency, and may be yellow to yellow-green to brownish in color. The odor, unlike that of the bottle-fed baby's stool, is mild and not unpleasant.

Frequency of bowel movements varies from baby to baby and even from week to week with the same baby. Sometimes there are frequent movements, each one just a stain on the diaper. At first, your baby may have a bowel movement with every nursing. This is definitely not diarrhea in the breastfed baby. Or, perhaps, he may have only two or three large movements a week, or sometimes only one a week. There is room for considerable variation among perfectly normal breastfed babies. Even an occasional green, watery stool is not a cause for worry in the otherwise healthy baby. Bowel movements can also change in color after exposure to the air.

Happily enough, because breast milk contains enough water for his needs, your breastfed baby does not get constipated. Constipation (hard, dry stools) has nothing to do with the time interval between bowel movements. Some breastfed babies go five to seven or more days between bowel movements and have perfectly normal, though naturally profuse, stools.

Babies sometimes fuss just before or at the time they have a bowel movement, and a change of position may help them. Some can get down to business more easily when in a semi-reclining position, either in your lap or in an infant seat. Others want to brace their feet against something. If you hold the baby against your shoulder, hold one hand under his feet. If your baby is one who seems to have a difficult time with this, you might try helping him by sponging the rectal area gently with warm water. If that doesn't help, some doctors suggest inserting just the tip of a rectal thermometer. This is seldom necessary, and there's no need to bother unless your baby has a real struggle and seems very uncomfortable.

Keep Your Baby Close

Just a reminder here about a few things we mentioned earlier that make it easier for you to have baby near you. The baby carrier is one example. Says Rose Sax of Tennessee: "For those of you who find that you can't do much those first weeks—you're right—you should take it easy. But after a while, I found that the carrier did give me two free hands for meal preparation and doing things with my daughter, Christy, while at the same time keeping the baby very happy and satisfying his need for me. When we went outdoors in the cold weather, I would tuck Joe into his carrier and pop my poncho over both of us, keeping us warm and cozy."

Also helpful is a portable crib, cradle, or basket, making it possible for baby to sleep near you, wherever you might be in the house. Some of the baskets come with wheels and can be moved easily from room to room. Keep baby's cradle close to you so you can reach over and rock or pat or jiggle him gently every now and then.

Along with whatever else you are doing during the day, you will want to have your baby close to you as a matter of course. You don't have to have him in your arms every minute, although you will be holding him often, both when you are nursing and between times (as he needs this contact). But you will just want to be there because what your baby needs most of all is you. No one else can take your place. To him, there is nobody quite like his mother.

Viola Lennon, one of La Leche League's founders, tells a story of a young mother who had what seemed to her a hundred and one problems. Vi recalls: "I invited her over for a visit. As she sat down in the living room with me, she immediately began asking questions. Soon I noticed she was not listening to my answers but was watching me handle my baby, Marty, who was rather fussy that day. I nursed him, walked him, bounced him, rocked him, and carried him with me to the kitchen while I made a pot of tea. Finally, she blurted out, 'Does he often act this way?' When I said yes, she smiled and said, 'I don't think I have any real problems. I just didn't know that babies needed all that attention.'"

NURSING MANNERS

As parents soon learn, babies have distinct personalities, and nowhere is this more apparent than in the way each little person approaches the important matter of eating. With our first babies some of us had preconceived ideas of how babies should nurse—beautifully-mannered, of course, with no starts and stops or spitting up. With later babies, we found it much more revealing and entertaining to relax and observe each new stylist. Your may find that your baby will fit one of the following descriptions. On the other hand, he may create a style that is strictly his own.

The Leisurely Diner

This young miss or mister thoroughly enjoys mealtime, which may be just about all of the time, especially in the early weeks. Intervals between nursings will lengthen as he grows older, and while he will probably always enjoy unhurried dining, he'll become much more efficient about drinking his fill. Once you are sure that he is gaining well, you can on occasion end a nursing after twenty minutes or so, feeling confident that he will not go hungry. A bonus with this type of baby is the opportunity to take it easy and cuddle lots with your leisurely nurser.

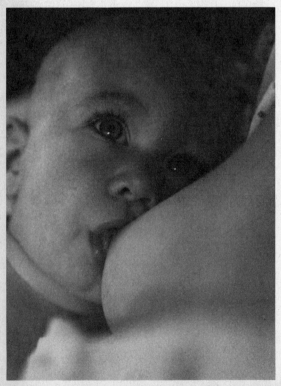

Leisurely diner, Mara Bertelli, tells her mother just how special these early days are.

The Nip and Napper

The nip and napper has much in common with the leisurely diner, although he tends to drop off to sleep (nap) after a few minutes of nursing (nip) and repeats this sequence rather often.

The No-Nonsense Nurser

Feedings are a down-to-business operation with this youngster. Once beyond the early stages of learning about breastfeeding, nursing time may be over in ten or fifteen minutes or less. There is little opportunity for a dinner time tête-à-tête with the no-nonsense nurser. But look for a big smile, sometimes with milk trickling from the side of his mouth, at the end of a nursing and before he moves on to the next challenge.

The What-Goes-Down-Tends-To-Come-Up Tyke

Is this a personality or a physical trait? No matter, it is unmistakable. While almost all babies bring up a little milk occasionally after a feeding, this little one spits up regularly after feedings and in-between time. He is happy enough and gains well. As long as he has six to eight wet diapers a day you can be sure he is getting enough milk.

He may or may not speed through nursings. If he does, try to slow him down. Some babies spit up because they're getting too much milk too quickly. If your baby gulps and gasps just after you have a let-down, try taking him off the breast for a moment or two as the milk rushes down. Have a diaper handy to catch the overflow. Let baby start nursing again as the milk flow slows to a rate he can handle. Some babies may even let the overflow trickle out of their mouths, which is a nice way of alleviating the problem. Your main response to this characteristic should be very gentle handling, with no sudden movements. Too vigorous burping can bring up milk that would otherwise stay in the baby's stomach. Gentle handling after a feeding will help your baby keep down his lunch. It may help to raise the pad or mattress in baby's bed or basket by an inch or two at the head end.

Occasionally a baby will finish nursing as usual and promptly bring up what seems to be the entire feeding, perhaps even with jet-like force. If the baby does not show any signs of illness—no fever or unusual crying—it is probably just one of those things. Of course, you'd want to check with your doctor if this happens often.

A handy supply of diapers or small towels is a help in protecting your clothing with a spitter in the family. And along with diapers, take extra changes of clothing for baby when going out. As Dr. Gregory White has observed, "in a healthy baby, spitting up is a laundry problem, not a medical problem."

Getting bigger is a sure cure for this tendency in a baby. While spitting up is a nuisance at the time, there is less odor and staining with breast milk than there would be if baby were formula-fed. And really, what's a little milk between a mother and her bosom buddy?

As the months go by, any early breastfeeding problems fall by the wayside. Nursing times are punctuated by beaming smiles from your precious baby. Four-month-old Jonathan Parker's dancing eyes tell his mother Barbara more clearly than any words ever could how much he enjoys their special breastfeeding relationship.

And So It Goes

Breastfeeding becomes easier as it continues. As your baby's personality emerges, the fun increases. There are shy smiles and love pats. At eight months or even sooner, your little nurser may be so reluctant to miss any goings-on that he relinquishes the breast to watch the cat stroll by. Don't misread this as a sign of readiness for weaning. Just choose a more secluded spot for some nursings, and he'll soon settle down. The nine-month-old allows for no such nonsense, but he may surprise you by losing his outgoing ways and clinging to you even when dear grandparents stop by. Breastfeeding is not the reason; being nine or ten months old is. He is not overly dependent on you. The nursing relationship is a safe harbor from which he can explore the world in his own good time.

TAKING CARE OF MOTHER

As a brand-new mother, you may find yourself concentrating so completely on your baby that you forget about taking care of yourself, so a quick review of the basics of "mother care" is worthwhile here. Mother care isn't elaborate or demanding: it involves mostly common-sense things that are important to any new mother, breastfeeding or not.

Good food, plenty of fluids, and adequate rest come quickly to mind. We also include in our list the need for plenty of loving exchanges—if only a hug or a quick squeeze of a hand—between the new baby's parents. Such shared moments will keep you and your husband going during this demanding time in your lives.

New nursing mothers usually try to eat well, and the nutritious dishes that generous friends or your gourmet husband prepare are consumed with relish. Choose between-meal snacks carefully. A nursing mother gets hungry almost as often as her baby, and there's the temptation to nibble on sweets. Choose instead nutritious snacks such as fresh fruit, raw vegetables, or cheese. Getting enough to drink can be taken care of by keeping unsweetened juice or water handy at all times. For more information, see "Nutritional Know-How."

Sufficient rest is right up there with the most important recommendations for a new mother. In the days immediately following your baby's birth (and when you first come home from the hospital), you will want to spend a good part of your day relaxing. A certain amount of being up and about provides needed exercise, but forgo long periods of bustling around. This is the time to enjoy being pampered, like the queen bee you are. "Mothering the mother" is an integral part of the care of a new mother and baby in many cultures.

Take Ten

A handy rule of thumb for a new mother is to sleep, or at least rest, whenever baby dozes. Even the baby who "never sleeps" catnaps more often than parents may realize. True, the times when the baby sleeps are probably not when you are accustomed to sleeping, and it will take some discipline on your part to set aside what interests you at the moment, close your eyes, and think "sleep." When baby's eyes close at the breast, settle back in your chair with your feet up, your little bundle still in your arms, and try to drop off to sleep. Even a few minutes of sleep can make you feel like a new person. And even if you can't sleep, just closing your eyes, forgetting work that needs to be done, and relaxing can be refreshing.

You might want to keep a stack of diapers, a diaper container, and a few other baby items (wipes, changes of undershirts and gowns, and a couple of small blankets) close at hand. With these essential supplies always nearby, you can feed and change baby with a minimum of effort.

If friends or relatives offer to help, explain that you can manage the baby's care, but an extra pair of hands is always welcome with the older children or the ever-present dishes in the sink and laundry in the hamper. Be appreciative of your husband's efforts to take up the slack in running the household. As for those things that don't get done—ignore them.

Visitors

When company comes, it's a good idea to keep an eye on the clock as well as on the baby. Having well-wishers stop over to see the new family member is a delight, of course, and the conversation may be stimulating, but keep the visits short and sweet. Hours may fly by before you realize it. Invariably, when the visitors leave and you long to crawl into bed and sleep, the baby is awake and needs your attention.

There is no end to the strategies couples have devised to avoid overextending the new mother. One very effective technique is for you to announce at the beginning of a visit how long you will be up. When guests arrive, and after you first tell them how pleased you are to see them, say something to this effect: "if only for a half hour," or however long seems wise. The length of the visit is your decision, but it never hurts to emphasize "doctor's orders." Any doctor would agree that the woman who is holding down a daytime and nighttime job, as you are with your new baby, must guard her rest. Enlist your husband in your plan, if he is at home, to remind you that, for a new mother, "rest is best."

Oblivious to the cares of the world, Rebecca Howard and twelve-day-old Elizabeth enjoy that special blissful sleep that comes when you are snuggled close to someone you love.

Another easy and self-preserving measure is what one mother calls "robe play." Slip into your robe when the company knocks on the door, even if you have been wearing daytime clothes. Without saying a word, the message is conveyed that you are not yet up to entertaining as usual.

In general, a new mother can be as active as she wants to be, provided that she stops whatever she is doing the instant she begins to feel tired. You will find that this little reminder covers a multitude of new-mother indiscretions. By taking care of yourself in the early weeks, you will feel better in the months ahead.

New Baby Blues

Occasionally, a woman feels down or depressed for no particular reason following the birth of her baby. "There I was, holding my beautiful new daughter in my arms, knowing that I had everything to be thankful for, yet I was dissolved in tears," one mother remembers. Another mother described the feeling as "combat fatigue following delivery." Dr. James

Good points out the similarities between the depression a mother may feel following the delivery of her baby and that which often sets in the day after a special occasion. The anticipation and planning that filled the months before have come to an end. A high point of participation is over, and a period of adjustment follows. This emotional seesaw may also arise as a result of the change of hormones in your body from a pregnant to a nonpregnant state. It is usually short-lived, but if the feeling persists, you may want to check with your doctor. Breastfeeding and having your baby close to you will help you to deal with this transition. The old standbys, eating well and getting enough rest, are important in making you feel well, both physiologically and emotionally.

Leaking

One thing that can be a nuisance for the nursing mother is milk leaking at inopportune moments. This is most likely to occur during the first weeks of nursing. Suddenly, to your dismay, you realize that milk is leaking from your breasts. Often, it is nearly time for a feeding and the sight, sound, or even the *thought* of your baby triggers the let-down reflex.

If you have some leakage, you can work out ways to take care of it. What milk does seep out won't be a problem if you wear nursing pads in your bra. Nursing pads, which are usually made of a gauze-like material and often are disposable, can be purchased wherever nursing bras are sold. (Avoid the kind with plastic liners, since air can't get to the nipples.) Some mothers make their own pads by stitching together circular pieces cut from old diapers or other absorbent material. The pads can be washed along with baby's other things and reused. A folded cotton or linen handkerchief works well, too.

When leaking begins, pressure applied against the breasts will keep the milk from dripping out. If you notice the tingly, stinging sensation of the let-down—or if you feel milk starting to leak—fold your arms across your chest and apply pressure with the heels of your hands against the breasts. Another unobtrusive way to stop leaking is to rest your chin on your hands and press against your breasts with your forearms.

At times, milk may drip from one breast when baby starts to nurse on the other. If your breasts are very full or engorged, there is good reason to let the milk come out rather than hold it back. It's a great way to relieve that full feeling and perhaps prevent a plugged milk duct. To catch the overflow and keep yourself dry, hold a diaper or something equally absorbent under your breast. A fresh washcloth will do nicely. Some mothers stock up before the baby is born with a dozen or more lightweight, inexpensive washcloths ("seconds") that often come packaged in bundles. They're handy for all kinds of mop-ups, and since they are thinner than regular washcloths, they are easy to use when washing behind delicate, small ears and in the creases of chunky arms and legs.

But Where Has All The Milk Gone?

When the milk comes in and your breasts feel quite full, you are of course overjoyed and supremely confident that you will have plenty of milk for your baby. Then the engorgement goes away, and you may find yourself thinking that the milk must be gone, too. At this point you may feel discouraged. You begin to wonder, "Have I lost my milk?"

You haven't, we can assure you. The absence of that full feeling and dripping is no indication that the amount of milk you have for your baby has diminished. The making of milk is an almost continuous process. As the baby takes some out, more comes in. Just keep nursing, and your eager eater will be rewarded with milk, even though you do not feel "full."

The more often your baby takes milk, the more milk you will have. When a mother has twins, there is twice the stimulation to the breasts to produce milk, and so she has enough for two babies. When your baby nurses less often or with less vigor, the amount of milk you produce decreases accordingly. If it drops too low to suit his needs, he will want to nurse more often. With added nursings, your breasts will respond by making more milk.

As you will see, breastfeeding is an excellent example of the law of supply and demand in operation. *Problems arise when rigid feeding schedules, bottles of water, or supplementary feedings hamper the natural balance.* It takes a little while to establish a good balance between baby's appetite and your milk supply, so be patient. The first six weeks are sometimes the most challenging; just take it easy, let nature take its course, and soon you and your baby will be feeling like "old pros."

TIME FOR THE OTHER LITTLE ONES

If this is not your first baby, you will have other little ones at home to consider as you respond to your new baby's needs. You will find that generous portions of love and reassurance will go a long way toward helping your older child, the ex-baby, accept the demands that the new baby is making on your time. When the baby is fussy you can remind an older child, "Mary, when you were little and hungry, I'd ask Timmy and Elizabeth to be patient and wait because you needed to be fed (or rocked, or held, or whatever)." The child loves the idea of once having been the "star," and it's a happy thought that can always be reinforced with a hug. When feeding the baby, a nursing mother usually has an arm free for quick hugs or other important tasks.

There's a peace of mind in keeping the "old-young" child near you when you're nursing the baby, rather than risk having him off somewhere on his own. A popular suggestion is to arrange a nursing corner that accommodates at least three—mother, baby, and an older brother or sister. Have an extra chair or stool next to your rocker, with some interesting play items nearby. Change the assortment regularly; surprises

Your older child, the ex-baby, needs to know he still has a special place in your heart. Encourage him to get acquainted with the baby. Two-year-old Aaron Cryan "helps" baby sister Holly nurse.

are always fun. One creative mom, Marge Bazemore of Georgia, added a small table for a work surface, and she and son Russ enjoy a variety of activities while the baby nurses. Marge describes their favorite choices:

- A cassette tape recorder. It's easy to operate and Russ enjoys hearing his voice as well as Phil's cooing.

- Simple puzzles.

- Play dough. I also keep a cookie cutter handy.

- Finger puppets.

- Crayons, paper, pencil, and coloring book.

- Pegboard. I made one out of a piece of ceiling board and used golf tees for the pegs.

- Viewmaster and slides.

- Books and family photo albums.

- Spools and a cord for stringing.

From time to time, sit on the floor while nursing. You'll be at eye level with your toddler, and the whole floor is the play area. It's great for building with blocks or rolling a soft ball. This is especially helpful when the ex-baby is looking for extra attention. Jealousy toward the new baby often shows up when the baby is three or six months old, if it hasn't happened sooner.

An understanding husband is one of a nursing mother's most treasured assets. He can step in to provide you with a welcome respite when he is home, and your older one will thrive on the extra attention from daddy.

Dads are often masters at keeping toddler minds and hands busy when mother needs some time alone with the baby, or when she decides to take advantage of baby's nap time for a relaxing bath or a much needed rest. Daddy and the toddler will both enjoy some toddler-size roughhousing, and who but daddy can add such excitement to stories by putting in all of those low, rumbling noises?

Jerry Sparks helps three-year-old Stuart run off some toddler energy—and thoroughly enjoys himself in the process!

Daddies and older children often develop a new and very special relationship when a new baby joins the family. Let your husband know how much he is needed and appreciated, encourage him to spend some extra time with your toddler or preschooler, and be prepared to watch the two of them become the best of friends.

GOING OUT? TAKE BABY ALONG

You don't have to be a stay-at-home with a breastfed baby. Baby can go right along with you almost everywhere you want to go. In the early weeks, it's a good idea to pace yourself—take things easy—for your own sake. A brief shopping trip or a visit to see the proud grandparents are good starters and can be a refreshing break in the everyday routine. When you're ready to go, baby and a diaper bag are easy bundles to take along.

Feeding your baby or comforting him at the breast is no problem, since it is possible to nurse inconspicuously almost anywhere. In most parts of the world no one gives a second thought to the sight of a nursing mother. But of course you are living in *your* part of the world, and if you feel more comfortable nursing your baby without drawing attention to the fact, you have a lot of company in other mothers who feel this way.

It's a simple matter to conceal the whole operation. You will need only a minute or so of privacy to get baby started at the breast. Once he's nursing, your baby could be sleeping in your arms for all anyone knows. When visiting in another home or when guests come to your home, you may want to find a quiet spot where baby can get started. You can then arrange a lightweight blanket around both of you before rejoining the group. In a public place, you can always turn your back to the mainstream of traffic and screen yourself and baby for a moment, behind a large potted plant for instance. In seconds you can settle baby at the breast.

Many large stores, airports, and train stations have rooms set aside for mothers and small babies. Another possibility when shopping in a large store or shopping center is a visit to the women's clothing department. If it isn't too crowded, you can relax in a fitting room while you nurse the baby. If you sew or just enjoy looking at fashions, take a nursing break in the pattern department—one with comfortable stools at the pattern-book counter.

Two-piece outfits are probably the most convenient for nursing away from home. (See "What To Wear—Nursing Fashions.") A loose-fitting, bulky sweater or overblouse can be quickly lifted from the waist for easy nursing. You remain covered on top, and a diaper or small blanket can be a casual cover-up. The never-out-of-fashion shawl also lends itself to discreet nursing. Many maternity shops now feature special tops for nursing mothers with concealed openings for nursing.

You will soon be able to devise a way to nurse inconspicuously to suit any occasion. At the beach, a large beach towel thrown casually over your shoulders and arms can serve as a kind of private tent for your nursing baby. Relax. You'll look no more unusual than the woman who is covered by a towel to protect herself from the sun or wind.

As a new breastfeeding mother, you may feel more at ease about nursing in different situations if you practice inconspicuous nursing at home first, with your husband or a good friend as critic. Mothers find that it doesn't take long to smooth out their performance. A Nevada mother, Charlene Brown, wrote:

> After the birth of our daughter, Dawn Michelle, Fred and I were invited to speak about our experience at a Lamaze class. Toward the end of the meeting, Dawn decided that she wanted to nurse. I continued answering questions as I put her blanket over her head and my shoulder, and she took the breast. One of the expectant mothers commented that I certainly had a unique way of quieting her—throwing a blanket over the baby's head! I explained that it wasn't so much unique as natural—the baby was nursing. Fred later said that I was getting to be such a pro, I didn't even pause in mid-sentence.

Marian Tompson, one of LLL's founders, tells the story of a picture-taking session for a feature story about breastfeeding. The photographer asked Marian to pose holding her baby "just as if you were nursing him." When she held the baby in the familiar position, he started nuzzling at her blouse in a frustrated sort of way. She excused herself for a minute, went into the next room to start the baby nursing, then returned and posed obligingly for the pictures. The photographer was completely amazed to learn later that he had gotten some real "action" pictures.

Alone Is Lonely

Try not to leave your baby any more than you have to. Babies need their mothers. It's a need that is as basic and intense as the need for food. "That's all well and good," you may be thinking, "but what about mother? What mother hasn't wanted to get away from her baby at times?" We'd readily agree that probably all mothers have had the feeling at some point that they'd love to walk away from the day-in, day-out demands of child care. In fact, on a particularly trying day, you may find yourself mentally packing your bags for a one-way trip to a tropical island!

When you find yourself in such a frame of mind, recognize it for what it is, a feeling that besets all parents at times. And then go on from there. Little children challenge their parents ever so relentlessly to be more giving. The process is not always an easy one, even for the most loving mother. But you have tremendous resources to call on, not the least of which is your closeness to your baby. We mothers grow along with our children. From Ohio, Judy Kahrl tells of her own experience in gaining an understanding of her baby's need for her:

> One thing that helped me when I wanted to leave the baby was to remember that a baby has no sense of time. When he is left, he thinks it is *forever*. He can't understand that his mother will be back later tonight or whenever. Also, what seems like a short time to parents, for instance a weekend, is proportionately speaking, a long time in the baby's life. It has helped me to try to look at this from the baby's perspective, his sense of time, his understanding of the world. Of course, we mothers have needs, too, but because of our maturity, we are better equipped to cope with ours, to postpone them for a bit. A baby's needs are immediate.

Three-month-old Melanie Webster enjoys her lunch as much as her mother enjoys sailing.

Georgine Christensen pauses to nurse seven-month-old Jessica high up in the Cascade mountains.

Breastfed Babies Go Everywhere

Those of us who bottle fed at one time and then breastfed our babies found that we were, in fact, much freer with a nursing baby. We could join in all kinds of doings, yet have the satisfaction of meeting our babies' needs. You'll probably find that home is still best, for both you and baby, since you are usually better able to relax in your comfortable rocking chair in familiar surroundings than anywhere else. Sometimes the very young baby seems happier amid the sights and sounds of home. But when you want to venture forth, the possibilities are endless.

Your babe in arms is a great moviegoer. He'll snuggle down and nurse or sleep through a full-length feature. In the darkness, no one but you, your husband, and the baby knows what's going on (other than that the baby is "being so good"). Jody Nathanson and her husband, Sherman, completed the opera season with their new baby. Jody wore a long cape, which covered her and the baby. "Ushers thought I was still pregnant," she says.

The women in the League group of Hull, England, recently drew up a list of the places they had gone with their nursing babies. In many of the situations, they felt it would be difficult to feed or comfort a bottle-fed baby. Lynne Emerson wrote the following account:

> Bridget said that she'd nursed (in common with many of us) in restaurants, doctors' and dentists' surgeries, and in church. Christina took the minimum of equipment on a canalling holiday compared with another bottle-feeding mum on another boat. She has also nursed baby Sarah in the changing rooms at the local sports centre. Lynne, one of our keener

League mums (she regularly travels sixty miles there and back to meetings), said she has nursed at a wedding reception, in a snow blizzard, while stuck in her car when her ten-minute car trip turned to all day after the car broke down, whilst football spectating, and on the beach.

Another brave mum nursed her baby while on supply teaching, while others have nursed in trains, at parties, at clinics, on mountain tops, and even in the bank.

I have nursed Lucy, when only three months old, at a one-day yoga seminar. The yoga teacher was skeptical at first, but I assured her Lucy wouldn't distract the class. The last excursion (to see the local pantomime) was really exciting. The whole family went, and there were a few raised eyebrows when we walked in, but afterward people remarked how good she had been. We hope this will help dispel the myth that breastfeeding is confining.

How is a baby apt to be received at adult gatherings? For the most part, very well. Most people love to see babies, and there isn't a better conversation starter. Occasionally there may be surprise or a question. Terry Liebowitz of California relates two experiences at restaurants with baby Sarah:

Upon arriving at a very well-known San Francisco spot, the doorman greeted us with a very worried, "Have you spoken to the management about your baby, Madame?" My husband unabashedly replied, "We're attending his private party." This statement silenced the doorman, the hat checker, and the maître d'. Sarah was her most charming self and giggled from her baby carrier while we walked determinedly through the restaurant.

A few weeks later, we were eating at a much friendlier establishment. Sarah began to object to our "quiet little dinner away." We were obviously struggling to make her happy when the maître d' came over. He assured us, "We have thrown out some rowdy folks, but never any babies. Just let me know if anyone is bothering this beautiful baby."

Advance Planning

A little advance planning or innovative thinking will often save the day and keep a young one and his mother together and happy. When Mary White was the matron of honor at a wedding, she brought a baby-sitter along for the specific purpose of holding her three-month-old baby during the ceremony. Between church and the reception, Mary slipped off, nursed the baby, and was back in the receiving line in time to shake a few hundred hands.

Attendance at religious services can put a mother in a bit of a quandary, particularly if it is customary to leave babies in the nursery, usually in the care of strangers—kindly people, but strangers nonetheless. Brenda Toomey of Alabama was determined to continue attending church, but did not want it to be an upsetting occasion for her young son. She kept him with her when he was small, which she says was easier for her

Breastfed babies do go everywhere!

Kathi Runkle, baby Kyla, and three-year old Susan enjoy the beach.

Monica Treder snuggles close to her mom while Doug, Greg, and Sara enjoy a trip to the playground.

Beth Skala finds nursing ten-month-old Amity convenient anywhere.

because another La Leche League Leader (also a member of her church) had "laid the groundwork." Brenda describes the Toomey's plan:

> As a tiny baby, Jamie either slept or nursed. As he grew older, church time coincided with nap time. This worked out well also, since he slept in the nursery and I left word that I wanted to be signaled when he woke up. It was strange the first time I had to get up and leave during church—but my strong feelings and my pastor's understanding helped make it a workable solution for me. Jamie is now three, and my husband is able to stay with him at church, too. When Jamie is in the nursery, I still have the same signal schedule worked out. Even at three, he still needs me in many ways. My being with him during this time at church becomes more important when I witness one of his little friends crying for his mother. Then I know that what I'm doing is best for me and my family. It's also helpful to have an older child (Leslie is six) who turned out "normal" even though she went through the same dependency, and we met her very important needs in the same way we now take care of Jamie's.

Another mother, Barbara Rozek of Texas, solved the problem in an ingenious way. She brought the Bible Class to the nursery:

> As a mother of a toddler who needs me on Sunday mornings as well as during the rest of the week, I have run into difficulties with church attendance. Our family of five has always attended worship services and Bible school on Sundays. But I found there is no place for the mother who must take care of the needs of her child during the Sunday-school hour. A toddler's noise is not appreciated in the Adult Bible Class, and the alternative of staying home during that time does not help to set a good example for the older children in the family. After speaking to our Board of Elders and the Superintendent of the Sunday School, we have set up a class for mothers and babies together in a room in the church. The room contains a couple of rocking chairs, a crib, and toys. Each mother is encouraged to attend with her child and to tend to the needs of her child as the hour of class progresses. You will find mothers changing diapers as needed, nursing or bottle feeding as is normal routine for that mother and child, providing finger foods for the more active toddlers. The class is slow-paced with the idea that we can learn together in Christian fellowship while also fulfilling our God-given roles as mothers.

Travel Plans

On longer excursions, babies make good travelers if some thought is given ahead of time to their special needs. Breastfed babies have logged a phenomenal number of hours in the air. Judy Sanders of Washington flew halfway around the world to New Zealand with her thirteen-month-old daughter, Maria. Judy reports that it was easy to travel with Maria because she was breastfed. Wearing a caftan-type long dress with hidden zippers was comfortable and convenient for discreet nursing.

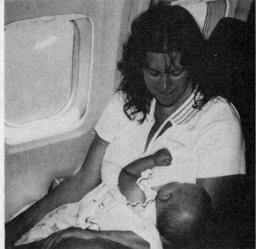

When traveling by plane, Kay McFerrin suggests nursing your baby at take-off and landing as she does here with six-month-old Monica.

Kay McFerrin of Texas tells of her family's vacation:

> Last summer we traveled to Acapulco, Mexico, with our infant daughter, Monica. Thanks to breastfeeding our little girl was a delightful travel companion.
>
> Monica was six months old then, and still on just mother's milk. All she needed for the trip was her mother, some diapers, and a bathing suit. We all had such a marvelous time. I had no worries such as what if the room doesn't have a refrigerator, or what if I don't take enough formula, or how to warm formula, or how to take formula and feed baby away from the hotel, or any other problems a bottle-fed baby and mother might face. No matter where we were—beach, sight-seeing, poolside, or plane, wherever Monica got hungry, she just did what came naturally.
>
> At night we never had to bother with baby beds, we just tucked our baby in with us as we do at home. She didn't care where she was—no insecurity for her! She was happy just being with her mother and daddy. It never even occurred to us to leave her out of this adventure.

You'll want to check with your specific air carrier for the regulations before planning a trip by plane. Generally speaking, children under the age of two fly free if they do not occupy a separate seat. Reserving a bulkhead seat will give you some extra room for an infant seat or baby carrier. Pack your tote bag with baby's diapers, soft toys, and a change of outfits—just in case your luggage does not land at the same time or place that you do. Nursing your baby at takeoff and landing will lessen the pressure on his ears.

If You Must Leave

If you must leave your tiny baby for a short time—and the shorter the time the better—leave him with someone he is happy with when you are around. Be sure to leave baby well fed and contented. Don't rush—babies can sense when mother is in a hurry to get away. When he is happy and settled, then go off. For some time you won't leave him for longer than an hour or two, and then only occasionally. Since you don't want your little one to miss you or go hungry, you'll want to be back soon.

Mothers often ask about leaving a bottle of formula when they're gone, "just in case." Does one bottle make that much difference? We wish we could say that it doesn't, but we can't. Even one bottle can be a problem for some babies. Pam von Gohren recalls her first evening out: "One never expects to have problems. When I read in the La Leche League manual about hand-expressing for the baby if you left him, my reaction was, 'Oh, bother.' After six weeks of 'mother only' for my daughter, my husband and I left Gretchen Estelle with grandma for an evening, along with a hospital-provided bottle of formula. The previous evening, instead of nursing her completely, I began the feeding with a bottle so she would not protest the following night." Pam relates that Gretchen became very ill from the formula and had to be hospitalized. Her story has a happy ending, with a healthy little girl who was, however, found to have an intolerance to cow's milk, as well as soy and eggs. The doctor requested that she be breastfed "at least eighteen months." Pam tells all new mothers, "Granted, our little one was an exceptional case, but if you're tempted, don't slip—mother's milk only those first six months." The von Gohrens have become very adept at keeping up an active social life while taking the baby along.

With all of their babies over many years, the Whites have never found it necessary to leave a nursing baby long enough to require a bottle. Tied down? An Indiana mother, Mary Long, offered the following thought on the matter. "Everyone is 'tied down' in some way; to a mate, a job, a pet, houseplants, housework. For me, one of the best ways in the world to be 'tied down' is with a nursing baby."

In regard to hand-expressing, storing, and preparing breast milk to be given in a bottle, see "How to Express and Store Breast Milk." It is invaluable for those very rare situations in which you have no choice but to be away from your tiny baby. Some mothers like to keep an "emergency bottle" of breast milk stored in the freezer. Hopefully, it will never be needed, and baby will always have mother.

NERVOUS, PLAIN TIRED, OR TOO BUSY?

If your baby happens to be one of those fussy, active babies who are always looking for mother's attention and who thrive on change, you may find it hard to follow our advice to relax and take it easy. If this is the case, you have our sympathy, because we've had this kind of baby too, and we know how trying it can be. The very busy, alert baby is almost always more content as he gets older and can do more for himself. He can't wait to conquer the world on his own! In the meantime, a few suggestions may help you relax if you and baby are giving each other the jitters.

First of all, ask yourself if you are trying to pack too much into your day. We hope you have taken to heart our remarks about the baby being more important than the house or other commitments. But if you do find yourself tense and jittery and you know the baby will want to nurse again soon, take a breather for a minute or two to help you relax. An exercise break can do wonders. It doesn't have to be a strenuous workout—more the bend-and-stretch variety or a lively dance routine. The activity will loosen tight muscles and perk up the blood circulation.

Other times, mothers find that lying down, closing their eyes, and listening to soft music for ten minutes or so is refreshing. Try it! Think of tension draining away as water drains from a basin. Or snuggle with baby and a book. Or nurse and watch a television program. The important part is to forget about those things which "must be done." Remember, "people before things," and that includes you! (See the section on "Housework and the New Baby.")

Weather permitting, look forward to a walk outdoors each day. Take baby with you, of course, in his carriage or in the always convenient baby carrier. The fresh air, sunshine, and change of scenery will do both of you a world of good.

It may be that, when you begin to feel on edge, you could be hungry. How long has it been since your last meal? Why not eat a piece of fresh fruit or nibble on a tasty piece of cheese? A hard-cooked egg, ready in the refrigerator, will furnish you with the staying power of protein. A slice of whole-grain bread with peanut butter is also quick and good. Or brew a fragrant cup of hot tea to drink as baby nurses.

Don't forget the old standby, which was so helpful during the early weeks before you were completely back to par, lying down with baby for nursing. If you want to keep one eye on the other children, stretch out on the couch with the children and toys nearby. This last suggestion is especially recommended for the late afternoon when life is apt to crowd in on both you and the baby.

The end of the day is often a troublesome time for mothers and babies. Clare Vetter of Kentucky tells of one particularly trying time at her home:

> After a very big day, my eighteen-month-old nursling, Isaac, was too exhausted, too "wired-up," that is, to nurse. Of course, I was worn out also and perhaps a bit low on milk supply. I dropped on the couch and Isaac would start to nurse, then he would sit up and fuss loudly.
>
> My husband Tom came in and put on his new record, a lovely relaxed piece, Pachelbel's Kanon. The music seemed to be just what our family needed. I stood up, and with Isaac in one arm and supported by Tom, the three of us began a lively yet soothing waltz. Our dance was spontaneous and improvised, and our aching muscles seemed to work out their pains. Gazing into Tom's eyes I remembered our first dance at a college waltz party ten years ago. There is so much more to our lives now than then!
>
> The canon ended too soon. Bath time, story time, then bed and lights out. Isaac and I lay nursing and the melody played itself again inside me; and there was milk. Sometimes a little romance helps.

Anytime you begin to wonder if things are going as they should, nothing is more reassuring than talking to another experienced nursing mother. If there is no League Leader in your area, you are always welcome to call the La Leche League office in Franklin Park, Illinois. (See "About La Leche League.") Every so often, take a moment to think through the ways to make the most of this time in your life. Use your own good judgment as to what is or is not important. Your baby and the rest of the family, too, need and appreciate a mother who is relaxed and feels good about herself.

"FREQUENCY DAYS" — GROWTH SPURTS

During the first week or two (often when you have just come home from the hospital), the baby who has been nursing every three hours may suddenly want to dramatically increase the number of feedings. No sooner does he drift off to sleep than he is up again, nuzzling the bedding or his fist, looking for something to eat. You may hear comments to the effect that it was a nice try, but breastfeeding just isn't working. Tune out such remarks. There is no need to reach for the baby bottle.

This increase in the number of nursings is normal. Medical writers in old textbooks referred to it as "frequency days." They recognized that such spurts in nursing build up the milk supply to meet the growing baby's increasing need. So settle in with baby for a few "frequency days" of nursing. Even the skeptics would be hard-pressed to think of anything else you could be doing at this time that is more important than giving your baby the best possible nourishment.

Twenty minutes of fairly vigorous nursing every hour or so is more effective than less frequent, longer sessions at the breast with baby sleepily holding the nipple in his mouth. Most babies eventually settle into a fairly consistent pattern of nursing, one that is right for each particular child. An increase in frequency will show up every so often, usually in relation to growth spurts. Like the rest of us, babies are hungrier at some times than others. Rather than check out the refrigerator, baby looks to mom. A growth spurt may mean that a baby's appetite temporarily gets ahead of his mother's milk supply.

Mothers commonly report such a fussy period coinciding with a growth spurt between the third and sixth weeks. If this happens, put baby to the breast as often as he will take it. With extra nursings, it isn't long before your milk production steps up to meet his increased need. The interval between nursings will soon lengthen, and baby will be his old self again. The extra rest that comes to you with more frequent nursing may be exactly what the doctor would order. It may be that the tempo of all you are doing has picked up a little faster than is good for a new mother. Nature and your baby combine forces to help you get much needed rest.

When your baby is three months old, more or less, there is often another fussy period. It is probably due (at least in part) to a jump in appetite, and again, increased nursing will generally take care of this part of the difficulty. It is still too early for solids for most healthy babies, so don't risk an allergy to new foods by introducing solids too early.

Another factor in the three-month fussy period, which you may or may not experience with your baby, is that he stays awake longer and is taking a greater interest in the world around him. Fussing may then indicate a need for company and action, rather than hunger. Keep him in the center of activity. Settle him near you in a safe spot on a blanket on the floor where he can really stretch out. He will enjoy music, movement, and people going by. As he gets older, he thrives on change and variety. As he becomes more aware of the world around him, the sights and sounds of the family group are wonderful stimulation for his senses. People often notice and comment on the early alertness and responsiveness of the baby who is part of the family group, who is talked to and sung to and smiled at often.

THE BABY WHO IS PLEASINGLY PLUMP

If your breastfed baby is a round little fatty, some may say he's gaining too much. While he may weigh more than the average shown on the doctor's charts, the baby on breast milk alone will not be overweight. According to Dr. Derrick Jelliffe, a totally breastfed baby who is "overweight" is not necessarily overfat (obese). Still, in a weight-conscious world, even baby fat is suspect, and the mother of a plump, fully breastfed baby may be told that her child should be put on a diet.

Heredity plays a definite role in determining a child's growth pattern, as became obvious in the Nixon family in Florida. Baby Alena weighed almost eighteen pounds at three and a half months, and her mother, Janice, was told that the development of a large number of fat cells in infancy would cause Alena problems later in life. This was Janice's first child and first breastfeeding experience, and she was understandably upset. "But I thought back over all I had read or heard at the LLL meetings I had been going to since my eighth month of pregnancy," Janice recounted. "Was Alena happy and alert most of the time? Yes. Was she developing well in all other aspects? Yes."

Janice also remembered her mother telling her that she herself had been a very large baby, and she and her mother searched the family album for baby pictures. "A picture of my mother when she was a baby also showed her to be extremely chubby, and she was completely breastfed." Their findings were meaningful because, as Janice points out, "Neither of us has had a weight problem as an adult."

At the four-month checkup, Alena weighed in at almost nineteen pounds and was twenty-five inches long—way above the norms. Janice showed the doctor the family pictures:

When the doctor saw the pictures, he was so impressed that he called in another doctor to look at them. They talked about the loopholes in the "fat cell" theory, and the obvious fact that fat babies do not always become fat adults. It had been their observation that breastfed fat was indeed different from formula-fed fat, and the difference could even be felt in the silky smooth skin of the breastfed infant. They both agreed that there was no reason for me to alter Alena's present care in any way. Absolutely no diet!

Janice concludes, "Thank you, LLL, for giving me confidence in my ability to nurse my baby and to believe that nature's way is still the best."

There are hazards in limiting growth by putting a baby on a diet. The young child is a dynamic body builder, producing cells of all kinds, brain and nerve cells as well as fat cells. Researchers have observed that the flesh of the breastfed baby is firmer than that of a bottle-fed infant. There are no "empty" calories in breast milk, as there are in highly processed foods.

It must be remembered here that fat accumulated in the relatively inactive pre-toddler stage is preparatory for the highly active time when the busy toddler hardly has time to eat. It is not unlike the extra weight that a woman puts on during pregnancy in preparation for the extra demands of motherhood.

As a breastfeeding mother, you are not going to fall into the anxiety trap of monitoring how many ounces of milk your baby takes. You will not get into the habit, as can happen with bottle feeding, of coaxing him to finish the last few ounces in a bottle. When you start solids, your child will probably be a grown-up six months old. You will have bypassed the unnatural situation that comes when solids are given to the younger child, who automatically pushes out whatever is spooned into his mouth, making it difficult for a mother to know if her baby is hungry or not.

Breastfeeding is the first preventive measure against obesity in adult life. When your baby is ready for solids, follow nursing with wholesome foods. Avoid sweets, white bread, and most dry cereals. (See "Nutritional Know-How" and "Introducing Other Foods.") Offer good foods freely and casually, but don't push and prod the baby to eat. We have found that by age two or three, the heavyweights among the tiny tots usually slim down beautifully.

WHY IS HE CRYING?

The sound of a baby crying is not easy to ignore. It is not intended to be. Your baby's cry is *meant* to be disturbing, for it is his most important means of communication. Only by crying can he let you know that he needs you to help him—to come to his rescue. Something is bothering him or frightening him. It may be that he is hungry, or he may be lonesome for you. He only knows the security of your presence when his body is next to yours; as far as your baby is concerned, you might as well be on Mars as on the other side of the house. Holding him may be all that is needed to set his world aright. Vi Lennon, one of LLL's founders, recalls that she once asked an older child to pick up the baby, who was crying, while she finished frying chicken. Her helper responded, "I already tried that, but it's no use. He's having an attack of loneliness for you."

If your baby is fussy, don't hesitate to put him to the breast again, even if his last nursing may have been only minutes ago. In her book, *Nursing Your Baby*, Karen Pryor tells a new mother to think of the breast as a way to comfort her child as well as feed him. Remember that your baby derives a great deal of comfort from sucking and being held close to you.

A rocking chair can be soothing for both mother and baby. Behavioral scientist and mother of four children, Dr. Niles Newton, notes, "The time-honored tradition of rocking the baby to sleep is very effective." Smooth

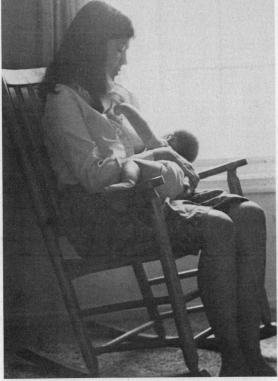

Susan Clarke and her six-month-old son John prove that a rocking chair can be soothing to both mother and baby. (Photo by Anne Nenninger.)

out the blankets around him, and settle in your rocker. One mother, Becky Conley from Illinois, calls hers a "magic rocker":

> No matter how hectic the day or how frantic the world may seem, we can retreat to the arms of our rocker, assume blast-off position with nipple and mouth engaged, and be suddenly inviolable to it all. Peace descends on us; tensions float away; and love surrounds us like a cloud.

> We can go anywhere we please in our rocker. Over the year since Eli was born, we've been to desert islands, a number of mountain ranges, endless beaches and on a few, very special occasions, to what surely must have been heaven.

Is He Uncomfortable?

But what if mother's warm breast and trusty rocker are not the answer? Could he be crying because he's too warm? Babies perspire quickly when crying hard. Leave him in just a shirt and diaper and see if this helps. On the other hand, very young babies in particular often feel snug and safe when wrapped in a soft blanket. An air bubble could be what is bothering him. See if any of the burping positions helps him to get it up. It may be that he will soon have a bowel movement, and he is fussing because he is still getting used to this bodily function.

Perhaps something he is wearing is causing the problem. Try removing all of his clothes—you'll probably change his diaper at least once anyway if he's fussy. Look for a pin or rough label, or something binding around his leg or arm—sometimes a hair from mother's head can wrap tightly around baby's toe. Look him over carefully from top to bottom, just to be sure that nothing is hurting him or irritating his tender skin.

Once he is snug and dry, offer him the breast again. This time, he just may drift off to sleep. But sometimes the baby doesn't want to nurse, or has downed so much milk he repeatedly spits it up, and still he cries. What then? Try holding him against your shoulder (not in the nursing position if he is already full of milk), and with a background of soft music or your own lullaby, glide through the house doing the "baby waltz." Some mothers put the baby in a baby carrier and vacuum the rugs. The droning noise of the vacuum cleaner and the accompanying body movements often lull the baby to sleep. How about a drive in the car? Or a stroll outdoors? A warm bath may soothe and relax both of you—try taking baby into the tub with you.

Babies are sometimes fretful for reasons that no one, not even the mother, can understand. Even if you can't calm your baby right away, try not to let it upset you. "Don't take it as a personal rejection of you," a mother who has gone through the experience advises. Your baby will always benefit from a calm, loving mother. In handling any tiny baby, you have to move slowly and gently and quietly. Fast, jerky motions and loud noises may startle him. If he is already upset for some reason, accept the fact and work from there—slow and easy.

Overtired?

Some babies cry because they are overtired, but aren't happy being held as they fall asleep. Try laying your baby in his cradle or on a blanket on the floor and talk or sing to him softly as you pat him gently. He may continue to fuss for a few minutes, then close his eyes, and to ever less urgent cries, drift off to sleep. You'll soon know if he is truly tired and ready to sleep or not. If he becomes increasingly more anxious (even five minutes is a long time for a baby to cry), pick him up again.

By carefully noting when her usually content baby became tense and was not easily comforted, one mother realized that the fussy period started about an hour after the older children returned home from school. "The baby was delighted to see them, and they were eager to play with her, but the hubbub sometimes overstimulated Mary. She ended up being what her grandmother called 'overtired.' If I intervened a little earlier, and Mary and I settled in the rocker in the corner of the kitchen for a nursing, she relaxed. After a little nap, she was her old happy self again."

Fussy Spells

It is quite common for a baby to have a regular fussy period, often late in the afternoon or during the evening, that occurs predictably day after day at just about the same hour. At other times, the baby is good-natured, and there doesn't seem to be any particular cause (and no cure, other than time) for these fussy spells. The baby is not unduly uncomfortable, as with colic, but is not content, either. Folklore refers to this time as the "Granny Hour,"—meaning that a loving grandmother is needed who has nothing more urgent to do than rock and cuddle the baby till the fussiness is over.

While husbands may not always be home at baby's fussy time, it can be a great comfort to a mother and a fussy baby if father can take over for a spell. The change of loving arms and voice often relaxes an upset child. While your husband and baby watch the fish swimming in the fish tank or the cars passing by, you may want to take a refreshing shower—it can really help wash the tension away.

After you have changed him, fed him, and done all the usual things to soothe your fussy baby, ask yourself these questions: "Have I had a big day? Done something extra tiring? Left the baby with someone else? Had any upsetting incidents?" The answers to these questions might give you a clue to his behavior.

Crying It Out

While holding and carrying the baby may comfort him, it may also elicit some stern advice from concerned friends and relatives. The notion still persists that the baby who cries when put down, but is soothed when held, should be laid down gently but firmly to "cry it out."

Sometimes a mother wonders if it really makes a difference if the baby cries in her arms or in a crib. It makes a considerable difference. Jan Wojcik of Florida puts the matter in a different light by asking how any of us would feel if we were the ones who were upset. "If we were crying, wouldn't we feel better if someone were around to reassure us? To care that we were upset? Wouldn't we wives feel rejected if our husbands were to say, 'Go into the bedroom. I don't want to be around you until you regain control of yourself.' Don't we want to be loved in times of stress as well as in times of happiness?"

Our suggestion to the mother of a fussy baby is: Don't let your baby cry alone. The comfort and security extended by your loving arms is never wasted. Love begets love. Then, too, the next thing you try may be just the right thing to ease baby's discomfort and restore peace and serenity to the house.

Baby The Baby

As we mentioned earlier, you cannot spoil a baby; his wants are his needs. **His need to be lovingly held when he is upset is as strong and important as his need to be fed and kept warm and dry.** So, if your infant stops his crying when you pick him up and hold him, just keep on holding him and be happy that you are there to satisfy this important emotional need. By all means, "baby" the baby.

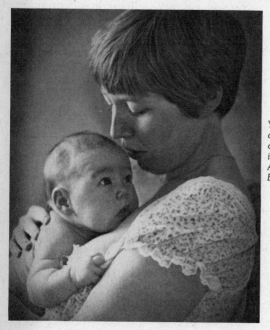

Your gentle touch and soothing voice are important reassurances to your little one that you are nearby, ready to lovingly tend to his needs. (Photo of Mary Ann Sember and Erin by Richard Ebbitt.)

Dr. Lee Salk, Pediatric Psychology Director of New York Hospital-Cornell Medical Center, has written, "The baby whose cries are answered now will later be the child confident enough to show his independence and curiosity. But the baby who is left to cry it out may develop a sense of isolation and distrust, and may turn inward by tuning out the world that will not answer its cry. And later on in life, this child may continue to cope with stress by trying to shut out reality." As for crying being good exercise for a baby's lungs, Dr. Salk says, "If crying is good for the lungs, then bleeding is good for the veins!"

The Crying Will End

By observing and responding in different ways to your baby, you will learn the varied language of his cry. You will be able to differentiate—most of the time—the cries of hunger, of fatigue, of frustration, of pain, or of discomfort, just as you have learned to understand the unspoken needs of your husband and friends.

When the baby is crying it may seem as though it will last forever, but this fussy period *will* pass. And baby will sleep.

THE "COLICKY" BABY

When a tiny baby has long periods of hard crying, and seems to be in some sort of physical discomfort for which there is no apparent reason that you or your doctor can discover, he is often said to be colicky.

"Colic" is a catchall word meaning essentially "loud, persistent screaming for undetermined reasons." As many causes of colic are put forth as there are doctors who have studied it. As far back as the turn of the century, colic was referred to in one widely used pediatric text as "a scientifically inaccurate and unsatisfactory term which serves such a useful purpose in practice and covers so well a multitude of abdominal pains that it maintains its place in our medical books." The same loose definition could apply today; doctors still seem to know little or nothing about the true cause of this kind of crying.

Perhaps the best guess is that some babies have more delicate digestive systems than others, and this factor, combined with tensions and stress introduced from the outside, is the likeliest cause of colic.

What can you do about colic? We'll repeat what you already know to be fundamental—calm, gentle handling is essential. Your colicky baby may also have an almost constant need to suck, and many doctors believe that frequent, small feedings geared to the baby's small intestinal tract are easier for him to handle than fewer, larger feedings. Dr. Gregory White makes this observation:

> The sucking needs of some babies may lead them to take in more milk than they can comfortably handle at one time. Offering the breast more often, with shorter feedings, may help in this case. Since colicky babies are often tense and anxious, frequent feedings may help in this way, too, as they give baby more contact with mother and more cuddling.

Try feeding your colicky, but thriving baby from one breast only during a two- to three-hour period. He may want to nurse a number of times during that time span; just keep to the "empty" breast. After two to three hours, switch to the other breast and again limit nursings to one side.

Occasionally, something taken by the mother might be considered as a possible cause of colicky restlessness in her baby. Some possibilities include certain vitamins, food supplements such as brewer's yeast, large amounts of caffeine or foods or drinks with artificial sweeteners. In rare instances, a food such as milk (or foods containing milk), or eggs in the mother's diet can make her baby uncomfortable. (See "Allergies.")

When the baby is so obviously in distress, you will no doubt be holding him a great deal. The following account from Sue Nobriga Buckley of California tells of a "colic hold" that helped her baby feel better:

> Although Lara gained weight quickly and proved to be alert and healthy, every evening found us rocking or walking her back and forth for hours before her crying and wailing gave way to sleep. After five weeks of

steady evening and occasional daytime crying sessions, we were hesitant to visit her grandparents. When we did visit, Lara typically acted pleasant during most of the day, only to start in loud and long in the early evening. As usual no one could comfort her until her grandfather picked her up, laid her astraddle his arm with her head slightly higher than her feet, and proceeded to immediately rock her to sleep. Amazed, we imitated his way of holding her whenever Lara began to act colicky, and almost every time the new way of holding her quieted and comforted her.

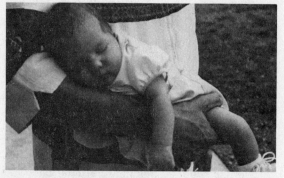

Lara Buckley is held by her grandfather in the "colic hold" position.

A soothing, pleasant bath proved to be a refuge for Judy Wesockes and her baby daughter. Judy, who lives in Florida, writes:

When Amy has an attack of colic, usually between eight and ten in the evening, we go into a warm, deep tub and stay there for the duration of her attack. The moist heat, holding her, and relaxing all help. She gets almost immediate relief, but if we get out of the tub, the symptoms return. So we stay in, and I add more hot water as needed.

Dr. James Good strongly recommends skin-to-skin contact, "for instance, baby against mother's abdomen," for the warmth and closeness a colicky baby often needs for relief.

Colic usually subsides after the baby reaches three months. It is thought that by this time he has matured enough to be able to cope somewhat better with whatever is bothering him. The colicky period can be a very trying time for a mother, but the stress is halved when there is someone close at hand to reassure her, or, at times, to hold and comfort the baby.

When the baby is colicky, a father can feel very needed. The fresh touch a father brings to the situation when he takes the baby for a spell may calm baby and will surely help mother feel more relaxed. An Ohio mother, Nancy Law, speaks from experience when she says, "If anyone needs the father's involvement, it is the mother of a colicky baby. She needs a 'dragon,' in the person of her husband, to freely spew fire at critical relatives and support her. He should feel free to ask visitors to leave so mom and babe can rest. And since colicky babies have not mastered the art of peaceful sleep, father can have unlimited contact with his young child."

Knowing that your breast milk is the best possible diet for your baby will help you to be relaxed and calm. It's one less thing to worry about, and baby will be spared the trauma that comes with changing formulas. Also, the warm closeness of the nursing relationship is the best possible situation for easing stress and tension. Your gentle, loving ministrations will help ease your baby through this period.

NIGHT FEEDINGS

When your baby wakes at night, just tuck him into bed with you, start nursing him, and the two of you can drop off to sleep again together. It is quite safe—we have all done it, and so have mothers all over the world for centuries. The babies love the warm closeness, which usually helps them drop off to sleep sooner than they might otherwise.

During the first two months, it is especially desirable for the baby to nurse at least once during the night. Your young baby is growing at a phenomenal rate and has a physical need to be fed during the night. Also, your breasts can become engorged and uncomfortable if you go for five, six, or more hours without a feeding, and in the morning baby might have trouble getting started at the breast because of the fullness.

A study of nursing mothers in West Nigeria by Jelliffe and Jelliffe revealed that babies as old as ten months received not less than twenty-five percent of their breast milk at night. So if your baby wakes up for night feedings, figure that he needs them, either because of an empty spot in his stomach or one in his heart. He may need the reassurance of your closeness, which comes with a middle-of-the-night snack.

Nighttime nursings in bed allow for greater skin contact and touching. Mother and baby are not encumbered by layers of clothing. In his book on the importance of touching to the development of the person, anthropologist Ashley Montagu states, "The infant's need for body contact is compelling." Montagu further quotes J. Lionel Taylor, "The greatest sense in our body is our touch sense. It is probably the chief sense in the processes of sleeping and waking."

Following the tips for nursing while lying down is your passport to restful night nursings. (See "A Nursing Session in Slow Motion.") If you feel awkward when you first try to nurse in bed, continue to experiment with different positions. Once you can feed the baby while comfortably stretched out, you've eliminated much of the work of mothering for about eight of the twenty-four hours in a day. In order to see what you are doing in the early weeks without turning on a bright light, consider keeping a small flashlight on the nightstand or under your pillow. To change sides with a minimum of strain when nursing while lying down, simply hold baby close to you with both arms and roll over.

You've probably heard stories of a parent rolling over on the baby in bed. Don't worry; your baby is safe. Your healthy, normal baby, even when very small, can move his head and in some way let you know if a

Christopher, Alita, and Liana Shipley enjoy waking up in their family bed. (Photo by Pat Crosby.)

blanket is over his face or if he is feeling closed in. Fathers and mothers say that they quickly develop a sixth sense for allowing room for the baby, in much the same way as one knows not to roll off the bed when asleep.

If you're worried that the baby may fall off the bed there are a number of ways to protect your precious bundle. Pull his cradle or bassinet next to your bed. When close by, it's convenient to scoop him into your bed when he cries. If it is high enough it serves as a guardrail to keep baby from falling when he's in your bed. A resourceful mother in Pennsylvania, Pat Muschamp, uses a blanket to keep her little baby from moving away from her after she has drifted back to sleep. Place baby's blanket diagonally on the bed, like a kite. You lie down with the inner corner under you and baby next to you on the blanket. Pull the outer corner of the blanket across baby's body and tuck it under your body. Your baby is wrapped snugly against you, and there is no worry about falling. You'll find this helpful in the daytime, too, when your husband isn't sleeping on the other side of the baby.

Some mothers wear a bra to bed at night. This is not necessary, but if you find you're more comfortable with some kind of support, choose a bra that is big enough or stretchy enough to allow for expansion when your breasts fill during the night hours.

When Will He Sleep Through The Night?

Probably the reason this question ever assumed the proportions it has is because of the inconvenience of nighttime bottle feeding—getting up with the baby into what may be a chilly house in winter, waiting while the bottle warms, fighting sleep, and being fearful that baby or bottle may be dropped. As a nursing mother, you are spared such inconvenience, so when you hear that a neighbor's baby sleeps through the night and yours doesn't, ask yourself, "Is it really that important?" Isn't the important thing that your baby is content and happy and you can satisfy his needs at night as well as during the day? To a baby, it makes no difference whether the sun is up or the world is hushed in darkness. His need for mothering remains. It is never less important at one time than another.

As to when he will sleep through the night, it's impossible to say. Babies are human beings, and each and every human being in the world is different from every other. Some babies will sleep through the night at an early age, and some will not. This is as true of bottle-fed babies, by the way, as it is of breastfed babies. And not infrequently, the little one who sleeps through the night one week is waking the next. This wakefulness is not a sign of problem behavior. If there is anything that can be learned by studying the sleep patterns of large numbers of children, it is that many more wake at night than don't. Over the years mothers have also found that giving solid foods early is no cure-all for wakefulness. (Babies are usually ready for solids at about six months.)

We mothers often ask when our babies will sleep through the night because we are frantically wondering when we can sleep without interruptions. Getting up in the night is never a favorite part of parenting. But there are ways to cope, to come to terms with the situation. How you think about night waking can make a considerable difference in how it affects you. We know the truth of this because many of us learned it the hard way. Pat Yearian of Washington says she gradually came to the realization that she could change the up-at-night syndrome. After all, a mother's reactions to the interrupted sleep is up to her. Pat writes:

> If you resent the interruptions to your sleep—and haven't we all come to believe we need a full night's rest?—you will face each day more frustrated and trying harder and harder to fit the baby into your sleep pattern. On the other hand, if you can adjust your mental attitude to one of greater acceptance, you will find yourself able to enjoy those quiet moments in the night with your infant who needs to be held and nursed, or with your toddler who just needs to be with someone. Acceptance of interrupted sleep doesn't come right away. In fact, for many of us it has taken a baby or two to fully appreciate their needs. When you begin to notice that your sleep can be interrupted many times a night, and yet you are able to face the next day with a smile, your attitudes are changing.

Dr. Gregory White once commented on the subject of sleep in a talk he gave to parents:

> A lot of people are so square as to think they are entitled to a night's sleep. Nobody's entitled to a full night's sleep, and very few mothers get one. Many people do at one time or another during their lives, and I'm all for it. But no one's entitled to it, whether she's a mother or not, if

someone needs her. If a lazy, self-indulgent, old man like me can get out in the middle of the night to help people he hardly knows, certainly a mother can do this for her own child.

Rather than try to change their children's needs, many families have decided to change sleeping arrangements. After all, what babies and young children are seeking is not all that outlandish—they just want to be closer to those who love them.

THE FAMILY BED

What the family table is to dining, the family bed is to sleeping—it brings dear ones together. The custom of mother, father, and young child sleeping together at night is "an age old concept in childrearing which has been practiced throughout the ages, throughout the world," Tine Thevenin writes in her book, *The Family Bed.* She addresses the fears and questions that parents in our part of the world commonly have on the subject, and she probably touches the heart of the matter when she comments, "I have been asked numerous times if it is not bothersome to have our children sleep with us. To this I reply that it is no more bothersome than their presence in our family."

Dr. Herbert Ratner, editor of *Child and Family* and longtime Professional Advisor for La Leche League, has encouraged the use of the family bed for a long time. And Dr. Hugh Jolly of London says, "Psychoanalysts may be firm in their advice that parents must never allow their children into their beds, but those who have practiced it know better and have not had any dire consequences to face—just the opposite."

The beauty of bedding down as a family is that it can be customized to suit each individual family's needs. Some mothers choose to return the baby to his own bed once he is fed and settled. In other households, the crib and separate room for the baby are abandoned, and an all-night family bed is adopted. Sleeping arrangements are as varied as families, and we share only a few of the many experiences of couples who have tried this innovation.

Ann Parker's story is rather typical. This Indiana mother explains that for the first six months after birth, baby Bryan slept in his parents' room, but in his own bed. Ann writes:

> I kept going back and forth every few hours to nurse him, and one time I caught myself asleep, sitting on the side of the bed, with baby in arms. I could have dropped him, and that really scared me! From then on I nursed him in bed lying down, but as soon as he stopped nursing, I would take him back to his bed. That plan didn't work all the time, since I kept falling asleep while he was nursing. But in the morning, I felt better. I had slept longer and without as many interruptions. My husband's sleep wasn't disturbed either, and so Bryan began sleeping with us.

Ann adds that her husband works during the day and goes to school at night. "He doesn't get to see Bryan very much, but this way he can see a lot more of him. A lot of times he enjoys just watching Bryan while he is still asleep."

Another Indiana mother, Joanne White, also found that night nursings in bed can offer some unexpected rewards. Joanne writes:

> So where in my busy day do I come up with eight more hours just to cuddle and touch? Simple, during the night! I'm not going to pretend that I arrived at this conclusion one afternoon, while contemplating. It's been a long learning experience, aided by three lovely little girls, who showed me it was much nicer to nurse in bed at night, snuggled next to their sweet bodies, than to stay awake for hours in a rocking chair and finally return them to their own cribs. I've made some very interesting discoveries along the way. Among them: sleeping together can create strong bonds; I've never had the happiness of having my husband with me for the birth of a child, yet we really notice a special bond between him and this last child, who has been in our bed from the day she came home from the hospital—they are like special cohorts.

Quite often one parent is enthusiastic about bringing the new baby into the big bed, but the other has reservations. When the Lackeys of California were expecting their third child after a wait of eleven years, Mada attended LLL meetings and shared her new found information about

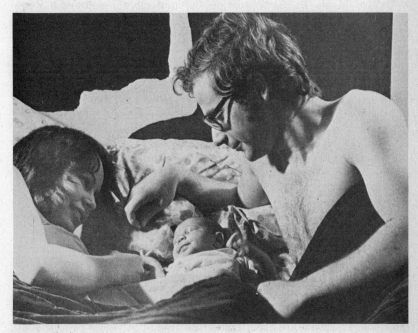

There are almost as many kinds of family beds as there are families. Bonnie and Jerry Hellman enjoy watching three-week-old Melissa as she sleeps between them in their family bed.

breastfeeding and mothering with her husband. Jim Lackey writes that he "agreed with almost every point, except that there would be no baby in our bed, period, end of statement!" He goes on to relate: "One particular night Kellee was nursed to sleep in her mom's arms and then placed in her little bed next to ours. Mada went off to fold diapers. Kellee began to fuss and since I knew how tired her mommy was, I reached over, picked up my daughter, and cuddled her close to me. Imagine my wife's surprise and delight when she came in a few minutes later and found Kellee and her papa asleep together in 'our' bed. Kellee has been there every night since, and at eighteen months, we laugh and say this king-size bed is Kellee's and she lets us sleep in it, too!"

In the Zavari household in Michigan, husband Hassan was born in the Middle East, where a baby sleeping with his parents is a natural part of life. Joan Zavari tells of her reaction to some of the ideas:

> When Hassan suggested nursing, I didn't hesitate. Natural childbirth was even considered and agreed upon. However, being of a conservative nature, I had put my foot down when he suggested putting two beds together and sleeping family style. How would I make the beds? I found lots of excuses. When Stevie was born, I soon found out that some babies wake up five or six times a night. Hassan didn't even say, "I told you so," when I suggested putting two beds together.

Another family, the Gebhardts of Michigan, have developed a "semi-family bed" arrangement. The children all have their own beds and start out the night sleeping in them, but they are always welcome into the parent's bed if they wake up later on. Mary Ann Gebhardt explains:

> When my husband and I go to bed, we have at least one hour, sometimes two, alone. We are then joined by nine-month-old Matthew who usually wakes to nurse about three times a night. His bed is next to ours, and when he is finished, if I'm awake, I return him to his bed. Four-year-old Kim still comes in every night. I'm not sure when (as I never hear her), but she is always there in the morning and I suspect she has been there for a while. In the wee hours of the morning six-year-old Tami usually finds her way in, and once in a great while eight-year-old Teresa joins us for the last hour of the morning. Two years ago she was also a nightly visitor.
>
> This is a pattern all of our older children have followed and as you can see, as they get older, their need to be near us diminishes. When I'm asked if our children sleep with us, I always answer, "not really." After all, they all do have their own beds and start the night there, and upon rare occasion stay there. Mama and daddy have all the time alone together we want and from there welcome lonely, cold wanderers of the night.

By age two or so, many youngsters will proudly take to a conventional bed of their own, although it will be easier for short legs to reach if the spring and mattress are placed directly on the floor. With a twin size bed, you can lie down next to your little one if he wakes up. It's less disturbing for you to then move back to your bed than it would be to move him. For the child who is ready for his own bed, but still wants to be near you once in a while, a sleeping bag or air mattress and blanket can be stowed under your bed and pulled out to make a cozy spot.

Building a Family Bed

An Ohio mother of seven, Martha Pugacz sagely commented a number of years ago: "It's not wall-to-wall carpeting that families need—it's wall-to-wall beds!"

Many couples find that they can accommodate a baby and, perhaps, other little night visitors in the ready-made spaciousness of a king-size or queen-size bed. Those who do not have such a large bed create one by fastening two twin-size beds or a double and a twin together with heavy-duty cord or wire. The space between the two mattresses is filled in with a blanket.

With the family bed, once the baby is moving well on his own, there is the fear that he may fall off. Taking the spring and mattress off of the frame and placing them directly on the floor reduces the height. One Indiana couple went a step further and, without pounding a nail, constructed a guard rail to keep their active baby from going overboard. Letitia Hoffman and her husband, Rick, had moved a spare bed into their room to make their family bed the width of two full-size beds. Parts of the baby's bed were used to baby-proof it. Letitia tells us:

> Rick and I dismantled the long-abandoned crib. We put the two crib ends and one railing at the foot of the family bed. They are held upright between the mattress and the end boards. The other railing goes up the side of the bed and is secured with heavy string to the bed frame and end rail. The opposite side of the bed is against the wall. This leaves about a

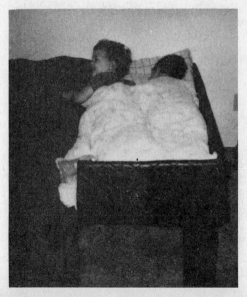

Sherry Bonelli and her husband designed and built a special extension for their bed to provide a special place for Michael after little Danny was born.

two-foot opening to get in and out of bed, which is easily blocked by pillows or a body.

If you have a standard double bed and a crib, you may want to try the solution used by a Wisconsin family. Judy Haugen describes:

> At the point of investing in a king-size bed or building a trundle, we came upon what we feel is a better method of enlarging our sleeping area.
>
> We have an adjustable crib. By raising its mattress to dressing-table height, flipping the side rail down, and lowering the legs to playpen level, we can make it the same height as our bed. When the crack between beds is covered with an extra blanket, we have the perfect bed for our one-year-old who needs early morning snacks and pats.
>
> Since the beds are separate, we do not disturb him, and most of the time he does not disturb us. If he whimpers during the night I only need to reach out and rock his crib (the casters have been replaced by springs) without even opening my eyes. If he is hungry I can pull him to me and, after nursing him, push him back to his bed without sitting up. Lately he has been crawling over to me and helping himself or pulling my hair or tweaking my nose until I accommodate him.

Ruth and Robert Thomas of New Zealand adapted a similar arrangement after Ruth strained a muscle in her shoulder and found that resting the baby on her arm for a long period of time was painful. This "bed and a half" proved to be comfortable for mother and baby. "I had read in the La Leche League NEWS an account by a mother who took the dropside off the baby's cot, placing the cot near the bed. This Robert did, and what a marvelous difference it made. Instead of Rhiannon remaining asleep on the crook of my arm all night, I was able to feed her in her cot, then move over to a comfortable position. It also ensured Rhiannon was covered by her own blankets, and I did not have to worry that some time during the night she would be uncovered or, for that matter, overcovered."

When the big bed seems crowded (even though it may be almost the size of the room) because everyone is huddled over in one spot (yours), you may wonder if this time of intense togetherness will ever come to an end. It does, and your reaction at the time may not be what you thought it would be. Ann Backhurst of Michigan tells of her experience:

> Amy, age four, sleeps alone willingly all night. When Emily was about eighteen months old, she indicated an interest in sleeping in the Jenny Lind crib standing unused in a corner. She now sleeps all night in it.
>
> Ken and I have our queen-size bed to ourselves again; to my surprise, I find that I really miss having the little girls sleep with us. While living through a difficult time with sleeping arrangements, I thought we would never see the end of this "family bed"—I couldn't wait! Now that it's over, we have cherished memories of a little person snuggling up on a cold winter night, or reaching out and putting an arm around and knowing that all was secure.

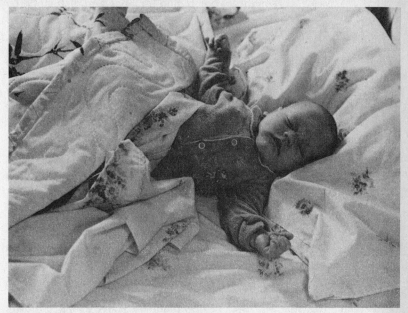

Six-week-old Adam Nelson, dreaming on contentedly after mom and dad are up for the day, gives eloquent testimony in favor of the benefits of the family bed.

BABIES, BEDS, AND SEX

You may be wondering—with baby in your bed, what happens to your marriage? Is there a survival plan for new parents?

We can offer some suggestions, but in the final analysis you and your husband are your own best authorities on what is the most loving, satisfying sexual relationship for you. Sex, like breastfeeding, is ninety percent mental attitude and ten percent technique. Both sex and breastfeeding flourish on the power of positive thinking. Needless worries can be counter-productive. The joy that you experience with the arrival of your baby will spill over into other areas of your life, and you will want to make the most of it. We hope to dispel some of the common myths surrounding sex and breastfeeding by answering some commonly asked questions.

With the baby nursing so often and possibly sleeping in our bed, will there be any time for my husband and me to be alone together? Absolutely. We have all found opportunities! You will have to outwit the baby, but there are two of you. Consider a change of time and place. Where there is a will, there is a way.

Babies usually have one fairly long period of deep sleep. Take advantage of it whenever you can. If your baby is easily disturbed, leave your bed (carefully) for the spare bedroom or the floor in the living room.

If baby is awake, you might try combining romance and distraction by lining up an array of lighted candles. Little babies are fascinated by the flickering lights. Some soft music is another possibility.

Few married couples can expect complete freedom all of the time, without interruptions, to make love. There are the everyday outside demands from a job and from others who have needs. Restrictions do not go away as the children grow older and leave the parental bed. Ask any couple with teenagers. Mom and dad are ready for sleep long before the kids go to bed. But you have a lifetime together to share your love. Tomorrow can be better yet than today.

My breasts are tender, and it's uncomfortable when my husband touches them. Also, I'm concerned. Can sexual foreplay affect the milk? No. Your milk will be fine. Don't worry about passing germs from your husband to the baby on the nipples. Your baby is already exposed to family germs. Nursing does not make your breasts off limits to your husband. The feeling of fullness and tenderness comes mostly in the early days of nursing and is temporary. You will notice it less if you nurse the baby just prior to making love. Your breasts will not be as full, and the baby will be more apt to sleep. But as one husband says, "Engorgement is gorgeous!"

At the time of a sexual climax, some women also have a milk let-down. The husband is often as surprised as his wife the first time it occurs, since the milk literally sprays out. Not all women experience this at a climax, and it lessens as the let-down reflex is better established. The hormones that produce the let-down are also present at the time of an orgasm. Keep a towel nearby for drying off.

When breastfeeding, a woman has a greater interest in sex; OR: When breastfeeding, a woman feels less desire for sexual relations. The response to both of the above is "yes" some of the time and "no" at other times. There are no pat answers.

After childbirth one woman may enjoy a feeling of great responsiveness. Giving milk and making love are very natural and exciting parts of her life. Another woman may notice the opposite. Her desire for sexual relations could better be described as understated, although she loves her husband as much as ever and wants to be close to him; in fact, she needs the reassurance of his affection. Such different reactions are not unusual or abnormal. All men and women have highs and lows in sexual desire at different times in life.

As a breastfeeding mother, it can probably be said that you feel good about being a woman and are at ease with the way your body functions. Breastfeeding is the completion of a woman's sexual cycle. There are marked similarities in the way a woman's body responds during breastfeeding and intercourse. It is a fulfilling time in a woman's life.

Fatigue, it must be said, is probably the greatest deterrent to sex for any new mother. Fit in a nap after dinner, if you can. Sometimes, even when you're feeling more tired than sexy, an extra output of loving effort on your part at the right moment could produce results that are a delight to both you and your husband.

What about feeling "touched out"? A mother once wrote to us, "After having my baby or toddler in my arms most of the day, I feel as though I don't want one more person touching me. I'm annoyed when my husband approaches me. Is this unusual? Can you help me?" You aren't alone in this. Many a mother, after spending a good part of the day holding the baby and having little hands cling and pat, finds herself thinking that the last thing she needs is more body contact. She's "touched out."

Our cultural heritage probably shapes this response at least to some extent. The person who grows up in a society where people maintain a certain physical distance from each other, and even family members seldom hug, may find the almost constant contact with a baby a new experience, one that takes some getting used to. Add to this the fatigue that comes at the end of the day for most mothers of young children, and there may not be the energy or inclination to feel romantic.

This brings us back to the basic relationship. Loving husbands and wives want to please each other. They each try to respond to cues from the other. On one occasion, the wife puts forth an extra effort to respond to her husband's embrace, and on another, he puts her feelings and needs ahead of his own.

There's a time to give, and a time to take. With mutual good will and good humor, it all works out. One word of caution: don't keep score. Once you do, you're sure to lose.

The low estrogen level present during breastfeeding is often the cause of vaginal dryness. This is more myth than fact. Estrogen is low when breastfeeding, but the sex drive in women isn't dependent on estrogen. Vaginal dryness or tenderness, which is sometimes attributed to low estrogen, usually results from having had an episiotomy when the baby was born. An episiotomy can also cause painful intercourse, sometimes for many months. The solution to dryness is simple enough — a little more lovemaking ahead of time, supplemented, if need be, by a little lubrication such as KY jelly.

You were a wife before you were a mother, so your husband should come before the children. Misleading! It isn't fair to put the husband and children in competition with each other for your time and affection. Whoever has the greatest need for love and attention at the time receives it. With maturity, gratification of want can be postponed for a time. Adults who are hungry can wait a while or find something to eat on their own. Babies cannot. With a little understanding, there needn't be a conflict. There is more than enough love to go around.

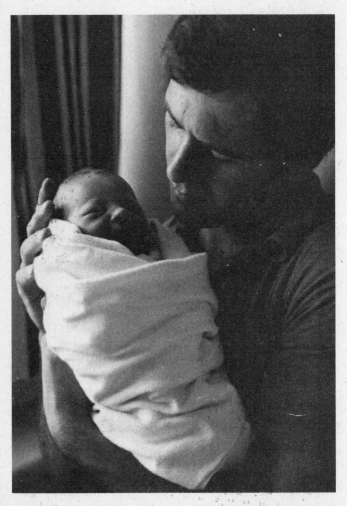

Fathers provide their babies with a special kind of nurturing. Bruce Ross seems eager to begin sharing an abundance of love with his newborn son, Ryan.

Chapter VI

The Manly Art
of Fathering

To the best of our knowledge, no one knows when the art of fathering was first recognized as the wonderful thing that it is. But from what we can find out (and admittedly, records are scarce), the one who undoubtedly made the discovery, the first to appreciate good fathering, was none other than a nursing mother!

In all seriousness, it can be said that present-day breastfeeding mothers have great respect for the father's invaluable contribution to the nursing endeavor. Certainly, this book would be incomplete if it did not consider the father's very special place in the family.

Young men today are breaking away from the stereotyped image of the father in the waiting room of the hospital, pacing the floor, while his wife delivers their baby surrounded by strangers. Dr. L. Joseph Butterfield of Colorado recently made the observation, "I used to call dad the missing American. As soon as the baby was born, he used to take off for the nearest bar and hand out cigars. But now he's back in the family. He's learning that it's no less macho to show tenderness."

Today, a husband is more often next to his wife during childbirth, supporting her and sharing with her the unforgettable emotions of this time. From the moment of birth, father and baby begin to get acquainted. The more a man can participate in the birth of his son or daughter, the more powerful and meaningful the event is to him. Just ask a new father who was at the birth of his child and be prepared to listen!

Beginning with the conception of their child, the roles of father and mother complement each other. It has never ceased to impress and reassure us to see how the unique abilities of one parent balance out and complete those of the other. A child may relate strongly to one parent at a certain stage of life, and then later, the other parent is better able to meet his needs. Mothers and fathers both nurture their children, but they do not provide the same kind of nurturing.

Understanding and respecting these differences is an important part of parenting. At a La Leche League conference in San Francisco, a Colorado father, Tom Kerwin, spoke to this issue.

> There are psychological and emotional differences between men and women which are more than simply accidents and which are not the result of discrimination or cultural emphasis. I suggest that we make

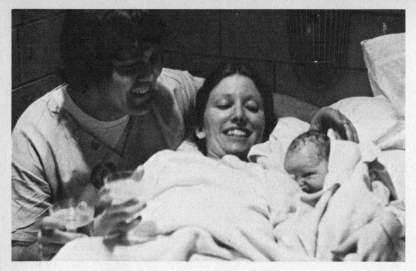

Couples like the Taylors, shown here at the birth of their daughter, Jocelyn, find that sharing the joy of the birth experience bonds them to their new baby in a special way.

better husbands and fathers if we learn something about these differences—if we appreciate the beautiful mystery of them and know better what to expect of our wives and ourselves. On the other hand, I think our wives make better wives and mothers if they help us to learn the differences and to look for the clues since we men are nowhere near as observant of these things.

Little girls and little boys both need a father as well as a mother around—not to teach in any formal sense, but to be there, to be natural, to show the children what men and women are like and how they get along together.

When writing in the La Leche League NEWS, Richard Lawrence of Ohio made the distinction, "Any concept of equality that does not take into account abilities and aptitudes is unrealistic and headed for trouble."

A director of Harvard Medical School's Infant Follow-Up Center, Dr. James Herzog, believes that parental roles are not interchangeable. "When it comes to raising children," he said, "we need to aim for a 'separate but equal' policy." With the current emphasis on equality between the sexes, Dr. Herzog noted that such a view may not be popular but "it may be critical in child rearing." When mothering is part-time, the child is deprived of an important experience. To this we would add, so is his mother.

In Due Time

The metamorphosis that makes a man a father does not happen overnight. He usually acquires the title "father" much more quickly than he captures the spirit of fathering. In fact, men can't even count on the natural assistance of hormones, which aid the mother. It has been said that when a baby is born, so is a mother. Fathers emerge more gradually. Bill Rogers, from California, recalls his own experience:

> When my wife, Roberta, started with the League, I thought it was kind of dumb, but she was pregnant, and I went along with her because I didn't want to upset her. Why did she have to go to a club to find out about breastfeeding? Then the natural childbirth classes came up—you know, my being there and so on—and at first I thought it would be kind of interesting, but I didn't want to seem enthused about it because nobody at work had ever done it, or at least talked about it, and my parents thought it was outrageous. But it meant a lot to her, so I went, and by the time the baby came it meant a lot to me, too.
> I didn't really realize the difference it made until the baby was about eight or nine months old and I started listening to the fellows at work talking about their children, for instance telling about their crabby kid who cried at night, and how they felt like hauling off and hitting him. I found out that none of them changed diapers—that was women's work. Same thing with giving the baby a bath. I started thinking, "Hey, buddy, you're missing a lot. How are you going to get to know your kids?" Well, they said, when they get older, then we'll talk to them, then we'll go out and play ball or go fishing. But the guys who had older children weren't doing those things—all they talked about was how the kids were asking for money or new bikes, or getting into trouble. When I mentioned that when my wife got up with the baby I got up, too, and that most of the time he was in bed with us, they couldn't believe it. "You gotta be out of your tree!" But gradually they stopped putting me down, and now some of them are coming to me to ask, "Where can *my* wife get this information?"

In a charming manner, Elaine McShane describes the growth of her husband in understanding the ways of the breastfed child.

> As I sat nursing our four-month-old daughter, my husband, trained and influenced by the Ontario medical schools, glanced up from his book and commented, "You know, I don't really see much point in nursing past four months."
> And I, who was enjoying this relationship immensely, looked down at our healthy contented baby and wondered aloud how one could say mother's milk was beneficial up to a definite period in time, while the next day the benefits ended.
> As I sat nursing our six-month-old daughter, my husband glanced up from his book and commented that he couldn't see much point in nursing past the age of six months.
> And I, who had planned to avoid all the fuss and mess of bottles stated quite emphatically that if I were going to participate in night-feeding bottles, then so was he.
> "Well," he added, "but I don't really see much point in nursing past the age of one."

When Heather was one and we were still a happy nursing couple, my husband confided, "I don't really see much point in nursing past the age of two."

And I, who found nursing to be such a handy tool for mothering, said that it seemed to be a relationship that we were gradually growing out of.

When Heather was two and nursing, my husband said, "You know, I don't really see the point in nursing past the age of five."

And I, who looked up and saw the twinkle in his eye, just grinned widely and said nothing. After all, there really wasn't much point.

Getting Involved

While more and more men are recognizing that breastfeeding is the natural and ideal way to feed the baby, many first-time fathers don't realize how much they can be involved during the breastfeeding period.

After the birth, the intimate relationship between mother and baby continues. They are still a unit, and for some time mother will be the baby's sole source of nourishment and his main source of comfort. In language that is irrefutable, biology makes it clear that the mother-baby relationship is primary and should not be set aside. But at the same time,

Four-month-old Lauren Brohawn discovers the fun of the great outdoors with her father, Michael. (Photo by Mary Loewenstein-Anderson.)

Fathers Get Involved!

Charles De Falco reads to his daughter, Amelia.

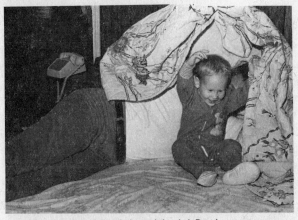

Adam Nelson frolics with his dad, David.

Steve Stern and his daughter Tzipporah, enjoy a stroll. (Photo by Sharon Honig.)

opportunities abound for the father and other family members to establish close rapport with the new baby.

Unfortunately, one piece of advice commonly offered is, "Of course, the father should give an occasional bottle." It is assumed that father must feed the baby in order for the baby to form an attachment to him. After hearing this sentiment a number of times, Geni Wixson says she "rebelled." Her own husband, she points out, amply demonstrates how a father can relate to his breastfed children from early on without relying on a baby bottle. This Maryland mother writes:

> My husband has always had a special time each day with the baby. He whistles to newborns—and our latest "whistled" back (puckered his lips) the day he was born. He plays touching skin-to-skin games. He says "Aaaahh" to the baby, and repeats any sound the baby makes. As soon as the baby sits at all, dad plays some form of rolling and catching a ball.
>
> Taking his lead, our older children hold the baby, talk to him, stroke him, sing him songs (who but a five-year-old can sing "Head, Shoulders, Knees, and Toes" five hundred times—the repetition a baby loves!), and they have contests to see who can get him to smile.

Geni believes that the father teaches the older children the important lesson that there are many other ways to show love to the baby than by giving a bottle.

Another family, the Likens of Illinois, worked out a compatible division of parenting effort to fit the needs of their growing family. Mary Jane tells of life with a baby and older children in the household:

> My husband, Tom, feels that tiny nursing babies are always happier with their mother and so extends his care more to the older children. Even after our three children, he still looks at me when our baby starts crying, with that "she needs you" expression. I think he also enjoys more of the rough and tumble with the older children.
> I strongly feel that the father is not an addendum to the mothering role. The father is a body for baby to feel and explore, a mind to discover, and a person to share a unique relationship with. He develops his own individual role during the breastfeeding period that grows and changes as the mother-child relationship does.

Though mother is the only one who can nurse the baby, there are a number of things that no one else can do quite as well as a loving daddy. Have you ever watched a mother try to soothe a fussy baby by nursing and rocking and patting, and just about anything else she can think of, and then watched in amazement as daddy lifts the little one out of her arms, hoists him onto his shoulder, and promptly puts the baby to sleep! It is a trade secret known only to fathers, whether it is the broad shoulders, the large, strong hands, or that deep baritone voice that does the trick. But no matter—we know that it works, and clever nursing mothers are the first to take advantage of it.

Dads seem to have a special way when it comes to soothing a fussy little one. Chuck Rickert (on the left) and Landon Ortiz have both dropped peacefully off to sleep.

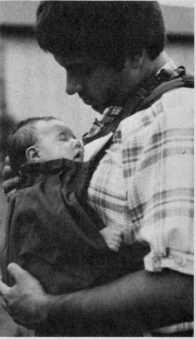

In many a household, father is affectionately known as "the six o'clock savior." Babies are often their fussiest late in the day, mother is tired after a full day of baby care, and there is the added pressure of preparing dinner.

When dad arrives home, even though he may have had a hard day at work, he can often approach the baby in a far more calm relaxed way than the mother can by that point in the day. Many fathers take advantage of the pre-dinner hour to give their wives a break and to establish their own special relationship with their babies.

What do fathers most enjoy doing with their babies? There are probably almost as many answers as there are fathers, but over the years we have observed that fathers seem to have a special gift for playing with even young babies. While mother is often preoccupied with cuddling and feeding, dad is likely to tickle baby under his chin, hoist him into the air, or bounce him on his knee. This kind of physical play is important to the baby's overall development. Babies thrive when provided with both gentle nurturing and lively activity.

Fathers often do the most improbable things with their babies. They have been known to enthrall little ones with step-by-step explanations as they install a new dishwasher or repair a leaky faucet. More than one father has settled into a big rocking chair with his little one to enjoy an afternoon of football on TV. As often as not, they will both be found stretched out on the sofa, sound asleep, a short time later! Dads and babies make a great twosome!

THE FATHER'S ROLE—OTHER DIMENSIONS

As important as it is, the bond between the father and his child is only one aspect of the picture. The father's role has many dimensions. He frequently stands as the main provider. At times, he is a protector. He's a helpmate when needed, and always, he is a companion to his wife.

Father as Provider and Protector

During that period when you will devote your time to home and baby, your husband will step to the forefront as the main provider for the family. It is no small step, especially as the economy is increasingly geared to the two-income family. But just looking at his happy wife and contented baby is constant reassurance that this is the right decision for most families.

There are times when a nursing mother is especially grateful for her husband's loving protection. "Protection?" you ask. "Isn't that a little quaint?" In a sense, yes. It has been a long time since young women trembled by the wayside (if they ever did) waiting for a knight in shining armor to come to their rescue. We can't imagine returning to such an age or attitude. Yet your husband is a protector. You will be especially appreciative of his support when he takes his position next to you in protecting your baby's right to mother's milk. Your husband can field any negative comments or interferences, which may be particularly welcome when such comments come from his side of the family. And two are better than one at slaying the dragons of doubt, which may, at times, shake the confidence of even an experienced breastfeeding mother.

Perhaps you have nursed the baby a number of times and he continues to cry. Someone remarks, "You can't just let the child starve!" No knight in armor ever looked as good as the husband who states in a positive tone that babies cry for reasons other than hunger and suggests that, instead of giving the baby a bottle of formula, "someone" could prepare a refreshing drink for mother.

An Iowa mother, Dixie Lundquist, knows how anxious such a situation can be. "Jason was an extremely sleepy baby for the first few weeks," she writes. "We had a hard time waking him up to nurse much at all. Then all of a sudden, it seemed things changed, and Jason was nursing every two hours for forty minutes at a time. My sister, bottle feeding her infant, was horrified that I was nursing this often. Other friends and family members wondered if I could possibly have enough milk." Of her husband, Rich, Dixie says, "He never doubted me! Jason did gain weight and was contented and happy."

In a talk in support of breastfeeding, Lewis Coffin III, MD, author of a guide to good nutrition for the growing child, said, "The father can be more clear-sighted than the mother about minor problems that arise, because she is so personally involved she may not be able to see the forest from the trees."

Kathleen White of Indiana remembered the early difficulties of breast-feeding and her husband's role in her decision to continue:"Jennifer was about two weeks old and I had sore nipples,"she writes. "One morning as she was nursing and I was getting desperate, I said to David, my husband, 'Would you be terribly disappointed if I put Jennifer on the bottle?' He said, 'Yes, I would. Call your League Leader and find out what to do.' Well, I did, and her advice kept me going." Kathleen added, "When I think of all the things I would have missed if my husband had not encouraged me to continue, I can hardly name them all. How terrible it would have been to miss the deep close feelings I have developed for my daughter through breastfeeding and the true love I have seen intensify between my husband and me since the birth of our child."

Father as Helpmate

A husband and wife are a team—each has an important and unique function in running their household. They trust each other, respect each other's unique role, and help each other out in times of distress.

Most men today are willing to help with work around the house. If they have any misgivings about the subject, it's usually because they don't know what is expected of them. You can avoid a great deal of misunderstanding if you're direct and clear about the kind of help you need. Nonverbal signals have a way of being missed. It may seem obvious to you that the dirty dishes piling up in the sink need to be washed, but your husband may not give them a second thought until there isn't a clean plate on the shelf.

While talking with other young mothers, Martha Hartzell of Georgia found that communication between husband and wife about what is important to each can go a long way toward improving their relationship. "One mother with a new baby was struggling to fix a nice dinner each night," Martha relates. "She was surprised to learn that her husband would rather fix dinner and have her greet him at the door dressed and with makeup on. Another husband was comfortable with his wife in a robe and didn't mind cooking dinner himself, as long as he had a fresh towel hanging in the bathroom each morning!"

Companions

• The most important thing you and your husband can do for your baby is to love one another.

• The couple that enjoys each other's company in little things does not drift apart.

• A parent needs three hugs to make it through the average day. Double that amount for parents with a newborn.

• Mothers and fathers are the world's greatest lovers.

Volumes could be written on the husband/father-wife/mother relationship. We only touch briefly on the subject, looking at it mainly from the

Communicating your feelings both before and after the baby is born will ease your transition into parenthood. (Photo by Pat Crosby.)

perspective of first-time parents with a nursing infant. The baby is growing well and is the delight of his parents' hearts, but he takes up quite a bit of his mother's time, wakes up at all hours of the night, and has found a cozy spot in bed with her. The fact is that babies both expand horizons and rock boats. Your marriage will never again be the same. But it can be even more loving and need never be dull. The silver and gold of future anniversaries are waiting. A prerequisite to attaining the treasure is putting your heads together now to chart your course.

There's a need to talk through the feelings that come with any important junction in life. We have referred to the emotions that a new mother often experiences, and it is just as reasonable to expect the father to react emotionally to his new responsiblities. A father and pediatrician, Jerald Davitz of California, tells fathers: "A very difficult feeling that most fathers have shortly after the new baby arrives home from the hospital is the unsettling sensation, 'Am I sure this is really what I want?' or 'Things were better before.' You need to understand you've got some reason to feel jealous and threatened at first, but that you'll get over it."

Edwina Froehlich recalls a letter LLLI received from a young father who shared the feelings he had that are common to so many men:

My wife is a wonderful mother and I am proud of her. But I went through some real suffering within myself after our first baby was born. I was an only child and my mother doted on me. When I was married, Judy pampered me in much the same way. Then our son, Bud, was born, and it seemed as though all that attention was transferred from me to the baby. I know this was right—Judy was just being a good mother. Even so, I was jealous, also ashamed to discover that I had such a feeling. Eventually I was able to tell Judy how I felt. She was very understanding and reassured me that she still loved me very much. This was what I desperately needed to hear, and we gradually worked things out. Judy tried to give some thought to my needs and I worked on trying to need less.

One day at a League get-together, I talked with some other fathers and discovered that my feelings had not been all that unusual. If I had understood this sooner, I feel sure I could have overcome these feelings more easily, and would have been a much easier guy to live with.

Our second baby is now two months old. This time I was prepared for my wife's total involvement. In fact, I welcomed it. And I realized that our firstborn needed me now more than ever. Actually it has been a beautiful two months for us.

Psychiatrist Lucy Waletzky of Georgetown University, Washington, D.C., found that husbands often experience some jealousy because of the closeness of the nursing mother and baby. She advises: "Effective communication between husband and wife should be encouraged before, during, and after the birth." Motherhood and fatherhood are new roles that need to be talked over and learned together. Time spent together during the first few weeks after the baby's birth can add a new dimension to a husband and wife's love for each other.

And Mary Ann Kerwin adds:

It's of primary importance that couples find special times to spend together. This often requires some creativity and innovation as well as a sense of humor, but this usually enhances the time together. Who ever said that challenges are disastrous? Not us—we keep trying to grow as we meet one challenge after another. Those "stolen" moments together add a delightful dimension to a couple's personal relationship.

Communicate Your Feelings

Many women find themselves totally immersed in nurturing and caring for their tiny baby. Some women have described their feelings about having a newborn as "like falling in love all over again." As one mother recalled, "I found myself head over heels in love with my baby. I found everything about her endlessly exciting and fascinating. I could hardly think about anything else. My feelings were so intense for several weeks that there seemed to be little room in my life for anything else."

Such a new and powerful emotion could well upset the equilibrium in a marriage. A husband may find himself feeling like a jilted lover and, to make matters worse, his wife is too preoccupied with the baby to even notice!

Here is where our old friend, time and its faithful companion, patience, can save the day. It helps to remember that today's intense involvement will become tomorrow's comfortable, easygoing relationship. A baby must be loved and cared for in order to survive, and this initial intense involvement between mother and baby is designed to assure that the baby's needs will be met. With plenty of time, and ongoing communication about their needs and feelings, mother, father, and baby will eventually settle into a new relationship that is comfortable and satisfying for all.

First-time parents are often preoccupied with their new responsibilities. Both husband and wife are putting out a tremendous effort. They must be careful not to let their concentration on their responsibilities isolate them from each other.

Beware of "the grass is always greener on the other side of the fence" syndrome. Recalls one young father:

> I remember kissing my wife good-bye as she was lying in bed nursing our baby. The traffic was particularly snarled on the way to work, and I no sooner walked onto the job than the boss called about a new part that was not up to specifications. Trying to meet a deadline, I grabbed a quick lunch at my desk. At the end of the day, after inching along in traffic, I finally arrived home to find my wife had made it to the chair. The house was untouched, the dishes unwashed, and she was still nursing the baby.

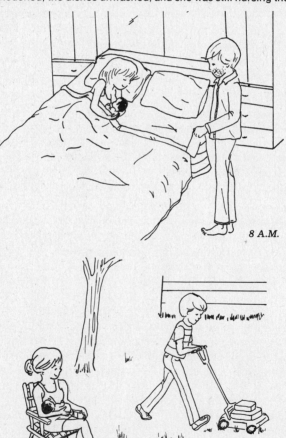

8 A.M.

1 P.M.

On that same day, this young man's wife had planned to quickly straighten the house, start supper, and cut out the dress she was making for the coming holiday season. But the baby was unusually fussy, and devoting herself to their six-week-old left no time for the housework, let alone the sewing project. As she picked up the baby to comfort him yet one more time, the spaghetti sauce that was cooking on the stove boiled over. Looking at the mess, she spent some moments envying her husband's role. In her mind, the morning drive carried him into the bustle and excitement of the city. As an experienced worker, he approached his job with confidence. His work day was challenging, but went smoothly. A leisurely lunch was eaten with friends, and the drive home was a quiet interlude.

This couple was experiencing some of the misunderstandings that can lead to problems if they are not shared and discussed. You'll find there is much to talk over as parental roles develop. Sometimes, expectations and reality are poles apart.

6 P.M.

11 P.M.

Does he ever come up for air?

The Rewards Are Great

In bringing this chapter on fathering to a close, we'd like to share with you some thoughts from Dave Stewart which were included in an article he wrote for LLL NEWS on the importance of fatherhood:

> Parenting is not easy. It can try us to the point of frustration. But this frustration can be productive because it is the symptom of growth and expansion. I sometimes think that nature gives us children to force us to grow up ourselves....Parenting is the finest of arts, and its refinement requires a lot of conscious, unselfish effort. But the rewards are without bound....
>
> Parenting is the greatest opportunity we normally receive to make good in this world. Your job may be important. Your volunteer activities may be important. But few of us do anything so important as to make much difference in society a hundred years from now. But the way you treat your children will matter a hundred years from now. The attitudes you pass on to them will be passed on to their children, who will pass them on to theirs....

The silver and gold of future anniversaries await the couple who grow together. Joe and Marsha Hardin take a moment to reflect on their shared joys as parents. (Photo by Richard Ebbitt.)

> Parenthood works in two directions: Good parenting makes for happy children; but it also makes for happy, fulfilled parents. It is not possible to give happiness without receiving it....
>
> Family ties, when properly established, are among the few things you can count on in this world....If you build your family upon the permanent bonds of birth and maintain an active fathering role throughout your children's growth, your family will never let you down....
>
> Ever uncertain, ever unreliable, ever unpredictable—most of life's offerings are fickle. Fatherhood is forever.

Chapter VII

Gradually, with Love

One of the bigger and more obvious changes with which we are concerned in infancy is the transition from breastfeeding to eating adult foods. The other dramatic changes—growing in stature, walking, talking—go on more or less automatically; but we mothers have a great deal to do with what and how our children eat, and it is our responsibility to learn the best ways of handling this. It is not really such a big chore—it is actually quite easy and fun, too, if done at the right time.

The beginning of this chapter, then, is concerned with when and how to introduce foods other than breast milk, and when and how breastfeeding begins to take a less important role in your child's life. We then look ahead a little and indicate how the same philosophy that guides us in these matters, expressed in the title of this chapter, "Gradually, with Love," applies also to some of the other events of early childhood.

INTRODUCING OTHER FOODS

First, a word about vitamin supplements. If the nursing mother gets an adequate supply of vitamins from her diet, her milk will have an adequate supply of vitamins, in just the right proportions for her baby. Research continues to bear this out. So if your physician considers vitamin supplementation necessary, he or she may prefer to give you the supplements, rather than the baby, especially if you suggest it. As you perhaps may realize, vitamin supplements for babies got their impetus as a supplement to formula, which is still not the perfect food for your baby. As long as your baby is thriving on your milk alone, he has no need for additional vitamins, iron, fluoride, or other supplements.

Other Foods—When?

Hand in hand with bottle feeding of babies, the fashion of feeding solids earlier and earlier developed and took hold in the United States. One of the factors in this was a spirit of rivalry and competition among mothers (and sometimes doctors) to have the biggest baby who ate the most foods in the largest quantity at the earliest possible age. This trend was promoted and encouraged by the baby food industry. Mothers were given the impression that there was an advantage in giving solids early.

Today medical scientists have verified that young babies do best with-out the addition of solids to their diet. Breast milk gives the best assurance of proper nourishment because it is nature's complete food for the baby. It is the perfect food for at least the first six months for the healthy, full term infant, and therefore there is usually no reason for adding any foods to the breastfed baby's diet before that time.

By and large, babies should develop at the pace nature intended. If they are pushed, all sorts of problems may ensue, starting with a refusal to eat at all or, on the other hand, a preoccupation with food that can lead to obesity later in life.

There are at least two very good additional reasons for waiting. First, you want to maintain your milk supply, and the more solids the baby takes, the less milk he will want; the less he takes from the breast, the less milk there will be. It is the mother who starts solids early who will quite likely find that her milk supply is gone soon thereafter. She has substituted an inferior food for a superior food by adding solids to the baby's diet before he needs them.

The second reason for waiting is that the younger the baby, the more likely it is that any foods other than breast milk will cause food allergies. No one food will necessarily do this; but you can't tell until you try. Cow's milk, used in most formulas, (and added to many prepared baby foods) is the most common allergen there is. Many other foods as well are poorly digested and may cause an unpleasant reaction in a two-month-old, but are readily assimilated by the same child if they are delayed until he is six months or older.

It is both kind and wise to give the baby the benefit of a few extra months of the food that nature has devoted millions of years to perfecting for him, until his immature digestive system develops to the point where it can utilize other foods without upsets.

Some babies with a tendency to allergies will refuse solids even at six or eight months, yet will accept them readily at nine months or so. This could be nature's way of protecting that baby from foods that will cause him problems. Such babies can continue to do well on breast milk alone until their systems are ready to tolerate other foods.

The increases in appetite that occur periodically—most often at about six weeks and again at three months—are best met by stepping up the breastfeeding to increase the supply of breast milk; the baby is not ready, physiologically or emotionally, to start solid foods at these times. (See "Frequency Days—Growth Spurts.") At some point around six or seven months, however, when most babies start to teethe, your baby's natural urge to chew and bite begins to develop. His mouth and tongue are ready for the new skills. His digestive system is now ready to handle new foods. When his needs, capacities, and abilities make it logical, we mothers begin to introduce other foods.

Your baby will probably let you know when he is ready; watch him, not the calendar. If he suddenly increases his demand to be fed at some time around six months of age, and this increased demand continues for four or five days in spite of more frequent nursings, you can assume the time

Pamela, I really don't think he's ready for solids yet.

has come to start him on solids. If he is much younger than six months, however, don't get excited at these first signs and rush the start of solids, because his behavior might be due to other causes. A cold coming on might make him want the solace of nursing more often. If he is ill, this is surely no time to begin new foods. In hot weather he may simply be thirstier. Stepped-up activity on your part may be making you feel rushed and tense, and he is calling for needed attention. If he is fussy for some reason other than hunger, he will have enough to cope with without introducing new foods as an added complication in his life. So play it safe and go along with his increased demands at the breast for a few days to make sure it is hunger that is responsible.

Other Foods—How?

As he does with walking and talking, your baby will figure out for himself just how to go about the business of eating as long as you let him proceed at his own pace. After all, he took to nursing, didn't he? By the time most babies are ready for solids, they are also ready and able to sit up alone in a high chair and can handle finger foods fairly well—they just naturally put everything in their mouths. The simplest way to begin solids then is to sit baby in his chair or, if he prefers, on your lap, and let him experiment with a tiny taste or so of his first food.

Since he has probably already joined the rest of the family at the table for meals, maybe even from birth, either comfortably nursing in mommy's arms or tucked up on daddy's lap, it won't be a big change for him. Probably the hardest trick as he gets more active is to keep the food on your plate away from him. Many an unsuspecting little one has inadvertently "started solids" when his mother dropped a bit of mashed potato on him as she struggled to eat her own dinner while coping with a wriggly baby on her lap. At any rate, before you know it, he'll be old enough to reach out and grab his own tasty bits, convey them more or

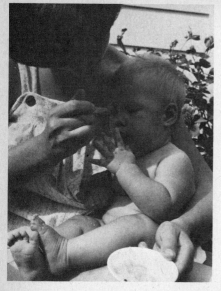

Easy does it with baby's first mealtimes. Mary Thoele offers six-month-old Michele just a taste of food from the end of a spoon.

less in the direction of his mouth, and pop them in. Just see to it that you limit what he gets at first, and gradually he'll be on his own.

These first feedings of solid food usually go more smoothly if you nurse your baby first, to take the edge off his appetite. Otherwise he will be in no mood to try out something new. Then, with practice and patience on your part, he will catch on readily. These first few attempts are merely to introduce the idea of solids to him, not to fill him up. At first, use a small spoon and place just a small amount of food on it, about one-fourth of a teaspoonful. If you have an independent baby who balks at spoon feeding, provide him with finger food. By the time he is a year old, he will probably be feeding himself beautifully.

Now is not the time to worry about neatness. Don't try to keep either baby's face or his high chair scrubbed and shining until you're sure he is all finished with his meal. A hungry baby is easily frustrated when instead of another tasty bite of food he is suddenly attacked by a wet washcloth. You'll take all the fun out of eating if you scrub his face between bites. Squelch your tidy impulses for the time being, and everyone will be happier. A little mess never hurt anybody. Your baby is just learning the basics of eating and isn't ready for lessons in manners yet. Put a big bib on him and move his chair off the rug or put a sheet of plastic under it. (A hungry dog is handy for cleaning up under the high chair!)

You will save some messes, though, and make the learning process easier for him, if you have only one thing at a time on his tray — *one* piece of the finger food, later *one* unbreakable dish with a not-too-large serving of *one* food, and (not at the same time) a small unbreakable cup, half full. Keep servings small. Learning to grasp small finger foods like cooked peas or beans will help him gain finger control and coordination.

New foods should be introduced one at a time. This means a single

Six-month-old Brian Hallam is not too sure about the taste of banana being offered to him by his father, Richard. (Photo by Pat Crosby.)

food, not a mixed food like stew or soup, or even a mixed-grain cereal. The reason for this precaution is that although the baby at six or seven months is not nearly so likely to have an allergic reaction as a younger child, it is still possible. If you introduce foods one at a time and he should develop a rash or a sore bottom, which could be indications of allergy, you will know what the most likely cause is and can eliminate the food temporarily.

It is a good plan to allow a week between each new food introduced. There is no advantage to be gained by striving for the widest variety of foods in the shortest time possible. Rather it is good for the baby to be given the opportunity to experience each new food thoroughly before going on to another. Start with about a quarter-teaspoon of a new food once the first day. Increase the amount little by little until by the end of a week he is getting as much as he wants two or three times a day. He will probably let you know when he has had enough by turning his head, clamping his mouth shut, spitting the food back out, or some such unmistakable gesture. Take his word for it. *Don't start feeding problems now or ever by coaxing, pushing, or forcing.* Give him only as much as he wants, not what you think he should have.

Babies have likes and dislikes about foods, as we all do. So if your baby turns away from any particular food, don't panic. Just skip it and try something else. Even if he has happily consumed three bananas a day for a week, and suddenly he won't look at one, go along with him. He's not sick—just sick of bananas. So when that latest bunch of bananas goes untouched, make your husband happy with a lovely loaf of banana bread for supper, and offer baby something else.

Once a food has been started, try to keep at least a bit of it on his menu once a week or so thereafter, to avoid the possibility of an allergic reaction on its reintroduction after a lapse of some time. This precaution should be kept up during the baby's first year.

Other Foods—What?

Most of us find it unnecessary to use the commercial baby foods at all. They are relatively expensive, and some varieties contain undesirable fillers such as sugar, white flour, or excessive amounts of salt and other preservatives. If you do use commercial foods, read the labels. Sometimes a doctor may suggest these rather than the rest of the family's food if he or she feels the baby is running the risk of getting a poor diet due to the mother's ignorance of proper food values. For instance, if a baby would be fed a diet consisting mainly of starchy, sugary, or highly spiced foods, such as spaghetti, noodles, white bread, and sweets, then certainly such a baby would be better off with a more nutritious variety of strained jar foods. However, if you understand good nutrition, and your family's eating habits are pretty good, then the food from your table will be fine for your baby, too. This also makes the transition to family meals easier. (See "Nutritional Know-How.")

For most babies, starting with table foods is easiest and best. For your convenience we include here a suggested order of introducing foods, which works well for most babies.

Raw, mashed banana. This is a good food to start with, since it is fresh and wholesome and contains more food value than cereals. Babies usually love the smooth consistency of ripe banana. After you've given your baby a small taste the first time and gradually increased the amount, you can offer the baby a whole piece of banana to handle himself, thus quickly eliminating one mashed food as well as pleasing the baby who likes to feed himself, and mash it himself, too . . . between his fingers!

If your baby doesn't care for banana, sweet potato (or yam) is a good alternative. It is preferable to bake it whole to better preserve all the nutrients. Sweet potato has a fine flavor and maximum food value. Most babies love it.

Meat. Meat is introduced early among solid foods because of its high iron and protein content. It is not difficult to reduce table meats to a consistency right for baby. Roasts and chops are not handled too easily at first, but chopped beef, stew meats, or tender pieces of chicken can easily be cut up into small pieces or mashed with a fork. Better yet, scrape across a piece of raw meat with a knife. Tough connecting fibers will remain behind while the tender portions can be gently cooked for baby to eat.

When baby has had a week on one meat, try handing him a good-sized bone with no splinters or sharp corners, but with a few fragments of meat still on it. A chicken drumstick is good, and just about the right size for his grasp. (Be sure to first remove the needle thin splint bone.) Chances are he will chomp away on the bone with great relish, especially if he has the urge to chew and bite. He'll be developing muscle coordination in the process, too.

To make sure you have on hand the kind of meat your baby can handle, keep individual portions of cooked, chopped, or scraped beef or chicken, wrapped and frozen. When you have meat at the table that might be too difficult for the baby, put the frozen meat into a saucepan over low heat, tightly covered or still in its aluminum foil wrapper. The moisture from the frozen meat will steam it nicely in a few minutes.

Fish is another excellent protein food. It is entirely suitable for baby and rich in valuable nutrients, so if your family menu includes fish frequently, you can introduce baby to it, too. Watch out for bones. Check each piece between your fingers before giving it to baby. And wait until baby is older to introduce smoked and pickled fish.

Whole-Grain Breads and Cereals. Finger-sized pieces of dried or toasted whole-wheat bread are good chewing foods for your baby and handy to offer him, perhaps between meals or while you are preparing dinner. Whole-wheat bread is the type most commonly available, but other whole-grain breads (not made with white flour) are also good. At first, more bread may land on the floor than in baby's mouth, but he'll catch on gradually, and there's no rush about it. If you regularly serve a cooked whole-grain cereal you might want to introduce this; but be sure there is no sugar or other sweetener added, and cook it with water, not milk. Baby cereals do not have quite as much food value as your own freshly cooked whole-grain cereals and are an additional expense as well. If your baby likes whole-wheat bread, you don't have to bother with cereal at all unless it is convenient for you.

Another nice thing about whole-wheat toast (or a day-old heel of the

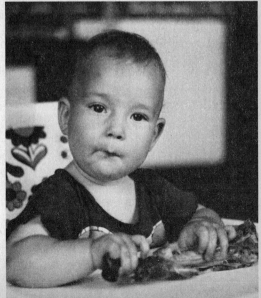

Justin Hammang finds a turkey leg lots of fun, and pretty tasty, too!

loaf) is that it's good for spreading things on. Peanut butter, for instance, is a most popular spread, and it's very nutritious. Be sure to buy the natural variety, without added sweeteners and preservatives. Babies love it. Later on cheese and homemade nutritious spreads can be added to the menu. Pass up the teething biscuits and crackers, as they nearly always have sugar, salt, and other undesirable things added to them. Your baby can teethe very nicely on crusts of whole-wheat bread, a beef or lamb bone, a chicken drumstick, or a stalk of celery.

Now is the time to be a label reader. It's surprising how much sugar there is, for instance, in such "salty" foods as pretzels and crackers.

Potato. Sweet potato, as we suggested before, and white potato are both good. Baking them is easy, and retains the most food value.

Fresh Fruits. Raw, peeled apple can be grated, or scraped with the edge of a spoon, and put in a little mound on baby's high-chair tray to experiment with. It won't be long before you hand him a piece of peeled apple, or ripe pear or peach to munch on. Apricots, plums, and melons are good, too. If baby is eight months or older, other fresh fruits in season may be offered, but with caution. Some berries have seeds that babies are not old enough to handle well. Some may also cause a rash when introduced at an early age.

Frozen blueberries make wonderful finger food; baby will love the cold, crunchy taste, especially if he's teething. Citrus fruits can cause allergy when given early in infancy, so wait with those until baby is about a year. When baby is old enough, tangerine segments are good to start with, but be sure to take the seeds out.

Avoid canned fruits if possible. Many contain sugar, which is not good for the baby, and they have less food value than the fresh variety. On the other hand, unsweetened canned fruits are better than no fruit at all. Unsweetened fruit juices, such as apple juice, may also be added, but in limited amounts. A small glass or two a day is plenty. Dried fruits such as raisins, dates, or figs should not be given before the first couple of years, and then only on a limited basis. They are very sweet and tend to stick between the teeth, causing cavities.

Vegetables. Finely grated carrot mixed with scraped or grated apple goes down easily; or grated carrot may be offered alone or mixed with some of the other foods baby is getting. It is especially good because of its high calcium content. But don't give raw carrots to a young child under three or so, unless they are grated. Small chunks which are not chewed properly can cause problems if they are inhaled rather than swallowed. Cooked vegetables may be offered from your table (one at a time, just as you do with any new food). Raw vegetables have more food value, but for the new eater most raw vegetables are too stringy and generally hard to chew and digest. Fresh green beans, sugar snap peas, or celery sticks are fine for teethers, but be sure your little one is not given anything while he is in bed lying down, as he might choke on it. (Most babies have an excellent gag reflex and manage to get up anything that goes down the wrong way. But keep an eye on them anyway.)

Don't be concerned if, in the beginning, you find little bits of vegetable, virtually unchanged, in the diaper. Even cooked vegetables are harder to digest than many other foods, so there's no hurry about including them on baby's menu.

Eggs. Since eggs, especially the whites, seem to be one of the more common causes of allergies, most of us wait until baby is at least a year old before introducing them. At first the egg should be hard-boiled. Place the egg in water and bring to a boil. Remove from heat, cover, and let stand twenty minutes. Peel under cold water. Presto, a lovely hard-boiled egg. Feed baby only the yolk, mashed and moistened to suit his preferences. Start with no more than a quarter-teaspoon and increase gradually, a quarter-teaspoon at a time. (You may be eating lots of egg salad for a while.) After baby has been eating eggs well for a month or two you can give him scrambled eggs, made without milk. Babies usually love to eat them as a finger food. Or cook an egg in with his cereal for extra nutrition.

Cow's milk. Don't be in a rush about this. If there is a history of allergy in the family, or baby has already shown signs of it, avoid cow's milk entirely. The only milk your baby needs is yours, of course, until he weans, and even then, contrary to popular belief, milk is not an essential food. The human being is the only mammal who continues to drink milk beyond the age of natural weaning. In some parts of the world, adults do not drink milk at all, but eat well otherwise, and the people are healthy and well-nourished.

At about a year you may start offering your baby milk or water from a cup once a day at mealtime or in between, whichever suits you best. (Avoid cow's milk at bedtime, however, as it tends to coat the mouth and teeth and contributes to dental problems. Naturally that admonition does not apply to breastfeeding, day or night, as nursing your baby won't cause cavities.) Don't rush the drinking from a cup. For some time most of it will go down the chin. A tip on getting the baby started with a cup comes from Betty Wagner, and we find it works beautifully: let him drink through a short straw. (The bendable kind works well.) The sucking comes easily to him, and it's neater too—no drips or dribbles. Or, try the kind of plastic cup that comes with a tight-fitting lid and a spout, and doesn't tip over.

If your baby doesn't like cow's milk, forget it, and don't force it on him. He'll get his nourishment from other sources and from foods cooked with milk. Furthermore, cow's milk in large doses can displace more important foods by lessening the child's appetite for them.

By a year, then, baby's beverages should consist mainly of your milk, water, homemade soups (most canned soups contain a lot of salt and many preservatives), and, occasionally, unsweetened fruit or vegetable juice. (Remember to check the label on the juice can.) No soft drinks please, carbonated or uncarbonated—these are heavy on sugar or sugar substitutes and sometimes caffeine, and are lacking in anything worthwhile. There is still no substitute for a good drink of water.

As to other foods, after milk is introduced, you can add butter almost anywhere along the line. Do use it sparingly at the beginning and don't rush it; the baby will enjoy his bread without butter, and until he gets a bit older it will be much less messy if he eats it dry. Cottage cheese and other natural cheeses (not processed cheese food) can be started, too—they are good protein foods.

Hold off on condiments—catsup, mustard, pepper, horseradish and so on. Some of these are heavily seasoned, and some, such as catsup, are highly sugared. (Did you know that some catsup is about 30 percent sugar?) When your little eater begins to demand what he sees others having, he will probably be willing to settle for a lot of fanfare and a minute speck of the condiment.

Skip the sweetened desserts such as puddings, cakes, and cookies. Your baby's sweet tooth is better served with a nice piece of fresh fruit.

Yes, mom. He's eating "food" now.

You can now consider your baby well started on solids, and you will no longer have to think too much about introducing new foods, just about keeping enough food in the house to satisfy his growing appetite. The whole process may have taken three to six months, depending upon how eagerly the baby takes to solids. Notice that from the beginning, if you follow these suggestions, baby is eating as a full-fledged member of the family, from the table. You have given him good nourishment, avoided the expense of special baby foods, and there is no painful transition from strained foods to chopped foods.

As you are getting your little tiger well launched in the eating department, don't forget to read the chapter, "Nutritional Know-How," and look into LLLI's cookbooks—MOTHER'S IN THE KITCHEN and WHOLE FOODS FOR THE WHOLE FAMILY. These will give you good suggestions for keeping baby, and everyone else in the family, deliciously well-fed.

WEANING—WHEN, WHY, AND HOW

"When shall I wean my baby? How shall I go about it? How long will it take?" Some mothers begin to worry about weaning when their infant is only a few weeks old.

Mary White recalls, somewhat ruefully, the rather desperate question she addressed to her husband, Greg, when their oldest child was only six weeks old. "How long am I going to be nursing this baby?" she queried. Her good husband, with all the sagacity of youth and inexperience, replied, "Oh, about six months." Mary recalls that she was horrified by this prospect. Six months! That seemed like forever!

Why do mothers begin worrying about ending breastfeeding almost as soon as they've started? No doubt there are many reasons, but we suspect that not least among them is the fact that society often expects babies to be weaned early. In a bottle-feeding culture, a newborn at the breast may be accepted; an older baby or a toddler, rarely. We mothers are uneasy about the thought that our babies might still be nursing after the accepted period. This can be true even though it is a common sight to see a two- or three-year-old with a bottle. In our eagerness to show the world how quickly our babies are growing up we become anxious that others will judge them less mature if they are still at the breast. Let's take another look at this attitude.

More Than Milk

If we consider nursing only as a means of nourishing the infant, then we can readily see why it might be feasible to bring nursing to an end at an early date. There would be no reason why this could not be as early as the baby could handle a variety of solid foods and milk from a cup—surely well before his first birthday. Of course your milk continues to provide special benefits for your baby as long as you nurse him. It doesn't lose its goodness with the passing of time.

It is when we view the nursing experience as a whole, when we understand that the baby has emotional needs, which for many months can best be satisfied through the closeness of breastfeeding, that it is hard to understand why we must set a specific time for ending this important, intimate relationship. If we do not satisfy these needs when our children are little, they will be as undernourished emotionally as they would be nutritionally when deprived of an important nutrient in their diet.

"I was one of those mothers who planned to nurse only two or three months. By the time my baby was born I'd decided we'd go at least six or seven months until he was on solid food, imagining he would then wean himself at eight or nine months. Little did I know." So said Mary Beard of California. "Six months slipped by, and nursing was going so well by then and was so pleasant for all of us that I guess I forgot about my original intentions. At ten months, Elliott's nursings were still frequent but quite short. When he was eighteen months, I began trying to encourage him to wean by substituting a cup of juice and a story or some other activity when he asked to nurse; but he'd say, 'juice, then nurse,' so that attempt wasn't too successful and I dropped it. He had good motor coordination and walked well by nine months, and maybe being mobile so early made him need extra recharging. In any case, I knew it was right to let him set his own pace."

Emotional Needs

This is how we look at it: the breastfeeding mother and her baby build up a relationship based on their mutual needs, and the relationship changes gradually as the needs change. One of the most urgent needs of the tiny baby is food, and during this period of infancy the mother's physical need is to be relieved of the milk that fills her breasts for the sake of the baby. However, the mother and baby depend upon each other for many other things. The baby needs affection, and the mother enjoys responding to this need. The mother has a strong desire to be truly needed by this tiny one. But at some point, usually gradually, sometimes in a rush, other times almost imperceptibly, the baby's dependence on mother lessens. He begins to broaden his horizons, to try his wings. But nursing is still important, for it is still a secure haven in a sometimes difficult world.

Marilyn Grimes of Arizona expressed some of the feelings common to the mother of an "older" nursing baby when she wrote:

> As I sit rocking Michael to sleep, so peaceful with him at my breast, I realize he's nearing the end of his first year of life. How can that be? It seemed only yesterday I brought him home, a newborn baby in my arms. What a pleasurable experience this past year has been, with the joys and worries of becoming a mother for the first time, and the pride in watching my husband turn into a devoted father. The special times when we both stood looking at our sleeping babe could never be replaced....Michael's asleep now and I put him to bed, his brow still wet with perspiration from nursing. He really has grown so much; I just haven't noticed it, I guess. Our nursing times are so special to me now that they are fewer than before. I keep hoping there will be many more to come, but I know the nursing relationship lasts too short a time.

Increasingly, mothers are finding support for their motherly instincts from the medical profession. "Many professional medical people," says Dr. James Good of Ohio, "feel strongly that the infant should be the one to lead in deciding when weaning should take place. Other cultures are quite comfortable with the nursing child at age three, four, or five years, realizing there is a greater need for psychological support in these years than for nutrition alone."

And really, what is there to be gained by abruptly putting an end to this wonderful relationship?

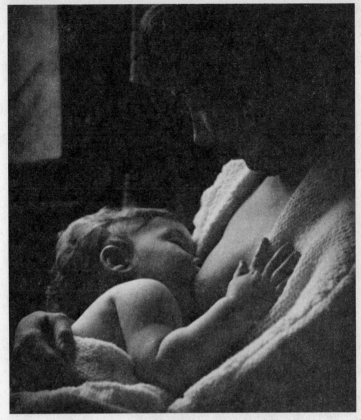

Ian Upton finds comfort and peace at his mother's breast. Why hurry to end this wonderful relationship? (Photo by Richard Ebbitt.)

Too Dependent?

But, you may ask, will continuing to nurse make the baby more dependent on me? This is the fear many mothers have when baby does not wean at the infant stage. Yet what makes us think the child won't grow out of this particular need unless we force him to? Why wouldn't children who have the love and understanding of their mothers and live under normal family circumstances stop nursing sooner or later? It has been our experience that they do just that. Some have the need to continue the nursing relationship longer than others, but they do grow out of it eventually, some at eighteen months, some at two or three, some even older. League mothers have many times over been reassured on this point because we have observed firsthand dozens of babies considered "late weaners." Independence, not dependence, is one outstanding trait they have in common as two- and three-year-olds.

Remember, too, that as he gets older, your baby will probably not be nursing as often as he was at two weeks or six months. The toddler who is "still nursing" may be only enjoying a bedtime snack or a "pick-me-up."

Back To Home Base

A toddler is like a yo-yo. One minute he's off and running in all directions, without a look back. The next he's racing back, charging into your lap, clutching at your skirts, desperately needing you for whatever reason he may have, no matter how mysterious or unexplainable it may seem to you. Don't look for reasons and don't expect him to know why he acts as he does. He may be tired or something may have frightened him; it doesn't matter. Scoop him up and follow his lead. Touching base this way may also mean a reassuring nursing. It may be only a few minutes, but that's all he needs to recharge his batteries and build up his confidence. Then he's off again to tackle the big outside world, confident that you'll be there should he need you again.

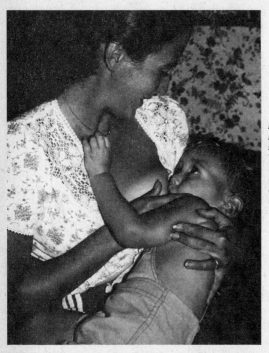

It's hard to say what made Matthew Zimmerman need the solace of a few minutes of nursing. The only important thing is that mother was there, ready and willing to provide this special comfort for her little one. (Photo by Donna Harris.)

What Do You Do When There's Nothing To Do?

Sometimes the older baby or toddler will want to nurse simply because he has nothing more interesting to do, or because it is the only way to get mother's attention. Now that the "baby" is able to run about and entertain himself, there's a temptation to get involved with other things, to the point where we find ourselves too busy with housework or our favorite hobby. But as our little one is growing out of the infant stage, his need for mommy does not really lessen. It changes, certainly, and mothering a toddler requires a great deal of ingenuity and even physical dexterity. His whole being is growing. His mind as well as his body needs stimulation. He needs conversation, and a companion to explore and experience all the new and exciting things his broadening horizons have brought into focus. You can't do these things with him if your mind is elsewhere.

If mommy is engrossed in a phone conversation or TV program, and little Timmy needs some attention, he'll go to great lengths to get it. Some youngsters are satisfied with a nursing (easy to do and you can keep on talking or watching TV), but is that what they really want? Or is it just a stopgap? Better than no notice at all, of course, and he's fortunate that you're willing to nurse him, but might not both of you put the time to better use reading a story or taking a walk in the park?

No one can better share these things with him than you, his very own teacher, guide, protector, and special person. No one knows his "language" as well as you do, nor understands so well his interests and needs. No one else is quite so understanding about changing that perfectly awful diaper, or mopping up the mess he's "accidentally" made around the high chair. You know best when he's hungry and needs a snack to tide him over until dinner time. You know when he's over-tired and needs winding down in your arms, with a song and a rock.

And very important still to this busy, growing, little person is that special time when he can run to you for a little "nursing break." After all, grown-ups need to "take ten" once in a while too, and if we need our coffee break, surely he's entitled to his special thing too.

Special Times

Of course, if a child is ill or has hurt himself, nursing is not only a wonderful comfort to him but a godsend to his mother. Many a wakeful night of floor walking has been averted because a feverish, unhappy toddler has been taken in with mommy and nursed back to sleep. Any or all of the usual disturbances that plague the toddler—the immunizations, teething, and little ills that may befall him may increase his need to nurse, especially at night.

Why not let the baby grow out of this stage of his development gradually and naturally just as he does out of other stages? Toddlers at a certain age, for instance, cling to their mothers' skirts—they feel secure only in her presence and are often timid with visitors unless they are in her arms. We don't push them away from us in an attempt to force them out of this stage of their growth. We accept it as part of their particular age and are glad we are there to comfort and give them security to smile at company and venture away from mother on their own.

"As life goes on and you watch the same child deliver the eighth grade commencement address," Vi Lennon recalls, "you know your small skirt-hider has grown up after all."

The Walkie-Talkie

When your toddler learns to communicate with you verbally, even just barely, it becomes much easier to explain things to him. His demands to nurse in the grocery store can be countered with a scintillating discussion of the colorful display of cans along the aisle, the cute little baby who was

Mmhm, Mama, mmhm?

just wheeled by, or the fire trucks you're going to see as soon as you get through shopping. Buy or bring along something he can snack on, or pull a favorite toy out of your purse. Tune in to his signals of fatigue or boredom and keep the shopping to a minimum. Better three short trips than one long one. (And besides, you won't have so many groceries to carry into the house all at one time. Benefits abound!)

A mother once took rather strong exception to our philosophy of baby-led weaning: "I just can't see nursing a walking, talking toddler," she protested. Right, we agree. Take him up on your lap first, and teach him not to talk with his mouth full.

Night (H)Owls?

Some little ones continue to want to nurse several times a night as well as during the day. That's all right, too, and no reason for concern. When your little one wakes up during the night, pick him up, cuddle him, take him into bed with you, and nurse him if he wants it. Then, if he's willing, put him back into his own bed. However, he may sleep better and wake less often if you keep him in bed with you. It's kind of cold and unfriendly sleeping alone!

Are there other children in the family? If your little one has an older brother or sister, consider some night pairing—two sharing one bed. Young children have probably slept together throughout time, and the arrangement has been beneficial, not harmful. Before establishing the little one in the older one's bed, discuss the prospect with each, stressing the positive aspects of having a night buddy. Then make the move with great fanfare. On more than one night, you'll probably find your two youngsters soundly sleeping, like little puppies, a tangle of arms and legs. They don't mind in the least. Is there reason to worry about how you'll eventually discontinue the arrangement when the children grow older? Not really. They manage this on their own when they no longer need—or want—the companionship. Usually one unceremoniously moves the other out of the bed, but by that time, they are older and quite ready to be on their own. It just means you'll have to get another bed.

Often after solids are started, the baby's need to nurse to satisfy his hunger decreases, but unless mother understands that he still needs the loving and the cuddling, he may miss the closeness those nursing times during the day afforded. Many one-year-olds have erratic eating habits and may wake up really hungry during the night. If you think that this could be the reason your toddler is waking at night, set out nutritious foods frequently during the day (particularly the things he likes) and offer a good bedtime snack. Perhaps he is thirsty. Offer your toddler water often, especially in warm weather.

The older baby or toddler who wakes a number of times at night may be bothered by teething. Even though there doesn't seem to be much of a problem during the day, his gums may hurt more at night when he isn't distracted by a busy daytime world. Have you ever had a mild toothache that started throbbing madly just as you were dropping off to sleep? A toddler cannot express what he is feeling in words, but since frequent waking during the night is so common in children during their second year, teething might have something to do with it.

Fatigue or achy muscles might cause a busy toddler to be wakeful. There are other possibilities. Is he getting enough fresh air and exercise? Was there tension during the day caused by such things as long shopping trips or visiting? A frightening experience? Were there enough hugs and kisses? Too many restrictions? If your answers to these questions satisfy you, and your toddler is still waking at night, blame it on whatever you like and remember that it will pass. Whatever the reason, nursing does seem to soothe a baby-child. (Which is he at this point? It's hard to say.)

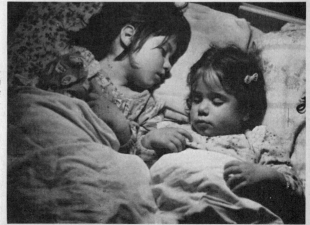

Sara and Tania Adessa find that sharing a bed is the perfect cure for nighttime loneliness.

This brings to mind a very wise statement from Dr. Ratner, who tells us it is an old Jewish proverb: "It is far better," he says, "to lose sleep over your child when he is little than to spend sleepless nights worrying about him when he is older."

Pregnant And Nursing?

You may not be "coping" with only a toddler for long. What happens when you become pregnant again? Surely you can't continue to nurse him then? Of course you can. The modern mother knows that another pregnancy need not require weaning of the older baby. Of course one of the bonuses of breastfeeding is that for many mothers (because of the natural spacing nursing affords) the next pregnancy doesn't occur until your older baby is a year and a half or maybe even older. By that time he's already cut down on his nursing somewhat, and continuing to satisfy his needs during your pregnancy isn't all that hard.

But if you're pregnant, you ask, won't your nursing toddler "take too much out of you"? What about all those valuable nutrients your unborn baby needs? Well, if you're taking proper care of yourself, eating well (See "Nutritional Know-How"), and getting enough rest, even in brief snatches, you won't hurt either baby. Many mothers, ourselves included, have nursed quite happily through pregnancies and given birth to fine, healthy babies.

But, you say, your doctor told you you might miscarry if you kept on nursing. There is no evidence that breastfeeding through a pregnancy

Many mothers, like Peggy Dowd, have nursed a toddler through a pregnancy and given birth to fine, healthy babies. (Photo by Richard Ebbitt.)

will result in a miscarriage. Some mothers who have had several miscarriages at other times have not done so while nursing their older baby. The hormones that cause uterine contractions during the early days of breastfeeding, and which are so helpful in preventing hemorrhaging after birth, have long since gone inactive. So don't worry about that.

In early pregnancy though, mothers often just don't feel very energetic, and you may find that the combination of extra fatigue (caused by the pregnancy, not breastfeeding) and tender breasts is something of a strain. Here's where large doses of "other-mothering" come in handy.

Other-Mothering

What on earth is "other-mothering?" you ask. It just represents the other loving things a mother does besides breastfeeding. We mention this frequently in this chapter, and this is just one occasion when you can put it to good use. You may find that now is the time to distract your older nursing person in ways other than nursing. You can look at a picture book or devise some judicious water play, for example. Of course, he'll only go along with these substitutes for nursing if he's ready for it. And only the two of you can really decide that. But frequently the two-year-old or an older child will be enthralled by mother's sudden lively interest in entertaining him, taking him on walks, or going to the playground. A new puzzle or book can be lots of fun, produced at the appropriate moment, and a set of washable colored markers with big sheets of newspaper to decorate open up a whole new world. Dad can certainly lend a hand here, too, by providing other activities when a young one's thoughts turn to nursing.

The fact that pregnant mothers do well with small frequent meals is, coincidentally, a great way to keep tasty things to nibble on within reach of your little one as well. By frequently offering him drinks of water or, occasionally, unsweetened juice, during the day, his thirst will also be quenched, often before he even realizes he's thirsty. Chunks of fresh fruit are good, too—oranges, melons, or peaches—and they are more nutritious than juice.

But with all this effort going into expanding his concept of mothering, remember that he is still only a little fellow, and that while he may be weaning himself away from the breast, it's at his pace and not yours. You are only supplying him with other things to help him grow. He'll take them or leave them, depending on his readiness to do so, and also on the way in which they are presented to him. As we said with solid foods, don't push, don't force, and don't make an issue of "doing this" instead of "doing that."

Tandem Nursing

(No, that doesn't mean nursing on a bicycle!)

"What if Jimmy is still nursing when the new baby is born? I'd hate to wean him suddenly at that time." He'd have pretty unhappy recollections of little sister's arrival if you did that, and chances are he'd take it out on

"Other mothering" provides the opportunity to enjoy your little person in a variety of new ways. Cecelia Harris finds that sharing a book with her daughter is great fun for both of them. (Photo by Richard Ebbitt.)

her one way or another. If nursing is still an important part of his life, let him continue. There is no need to cut him off. Just be sure little sister gets to nurse first, particularly in the early days, because the colostrum is especially important for her as a newborn.

It's probably better, too, not to let Jimmy stake out one side as *his* and the other as *hers*. Changing off is better for babies, especially with regard to eye development.

There are other fringe benefits to nursing two. The older baby keeps down the engorgement when the milk first comes in, and it keeps the milk in good supply as time goes on. For more on this, and all aspects of nursing the older toddler, read a wonderful book by La Leche League Leader Norma Jane Bumgarner, called *Mothering Your Nursing Toddler*.

Occasionally, after apparently completely weaning himself, a toddler might suddenly ask to nurse again. (This sometimes happens when the new baby arrives.) Don't be afraid to let him try it. Most likely, instead of nursing he will giggle and slide off your lap, reassured by your willingness to go along with his request. Mary Beard recalls:

After Julian was born, Elliott asked once if he could nurse. I said, "Yes," and he said, "Oh," and walked away. Apparently he only wanted to make sure he *could*. Once he was reassured, we never heard anything more about it. Now at age four he's in a different world—one of playmates, swimming lessons, and being a big brother—and nursing is for babies.

He's still a sensitive, affectionate child and seems so happy and grown-up that we know we were right to let him savor his babyhood as long as he needed to.

If, on the other hand, your toddler reacts with enthusiasm and delight at the discovery of this bounty, relax and let him nurse. The more ambivalent your feelings about it, the less sure he is that you still love him, or even want him around. Many eighteen-month- or two-year-olds still need lots of this kind of reassurance. A three-year-old could probably be persuaded to check the refrigerator instead, if you would really rather he do so.

Jan Wilcke of Kansas writes about her experience:

When Ardith was twenty-eight months old, Carrie was born and I weaned Ardith. The weaning would have been too abrupt by itself without the added burden of a new sister contending for mommy's affections. Ardith seemed more tense, and I was unhappy about the situation. So, after two months Ardith began nursing again.

For about six months after that, Ardith nursed twice a day. We were truly a nursing trio for a while! Ardith gradually cut down on her nursing (with some help from mommy). She now nurses once every few weeks. I believe this occasional nursing is important to her in a way different than it is for Carrie. Her need to nurse occurs quite often when she's had a bad morning and we're both "nearing the end of our rope." It's as if she's asking, "Do you love me as much as Carrie? Do you love me enough to let me nurse?" I think tandem nursing, while difficult at times, is a wonderful way to reassure a toddler when a new sibling arrives. And a warm lap with some mommy's milk is a safe—healthy—retreat for the child when the demands of his enlarging world are too much for him. Too, I have enjoyed this special way of loving Ardith and Carrie.

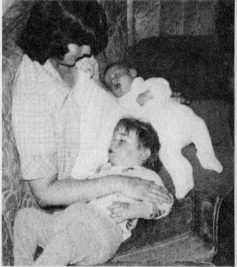

Jean Collier, shown here with three-month-old Sarah and eighteen-month-old Aaron, is one of many mothers who have found that tandem nursing helps to satisfy the emotional needs of the ex-baby.

What If I Must Wean?

Before you decide that circumstances will force you to wean your baby at a particular time, think over all possible alternatives. Illness, medications, surgery for you or him do not necessarily mean that you must wean your baby, even temporarily. Often elective surgery or dental work can easily and safely be postponed. Medications you may be taking that are unsafe for the baby (and these are few indeed) can often be changed to something else with little or no risk. Talk these things over with your doctor. Seek alternatives first of all and keep nursing if you possibly can. There is no way to explain to your little one what has happened when you wean him.

Well, How DO You Wean A Baby?

What if, despite all your best efforts, the decision must be made to wean the baby? The key to how to do it is **gradually and with love,** no matter what. You leave out one nursing at a time, cutting out no more than one a week and never being inflexible about it, especially if the little one is ill or upset for some reason. You'll go out of your way to make the time at which you are omitting the nursing warm and happy in other ways. Your husband can be a tremendous help at this time, by taking the baby out for a stroll or putting him to bed at night, and perhaps by getting up with him if he wakes during the night.

If your baby has still been nursing quite a bit, you will know that sucking is still very important to him. A few older babies or toddlers might do quite well on only the cup, while others, most perhaps, seem to need a great deal of sucking, and you must decide how best to satisfy this need. Consult your doctor before you begin, especially if you think your baby will need to have a bottle. This is a big and serious change in your baby's life, and in yours as well. It should not be undertaken lightly. Whatever you do, proceed slowly and don't try to rush things.

And remember, it's the loving mothering that comes through in all of the many things you do for your baby that's so very important. Your baby will have a hard enough time understanding why he may no longer nurse, so you will need to double up on the cuddling, rocking, hugs, and kisses. He needs the reassurance that you haven't deserted him and are still there when he needs you.

He Outgrows the Need to Nurse

"But when will he wean?" you ask, as your two-year-old holds up his arms to be picked up and nursed again. In his own good time, we have to reply. Actually, he's been weaning himself ever since his first bite of solid food. To wean, says the Concise Oxford Dictionary, is "to teach the sucking child to feed otherwise than from the breast." While most people see weaning as the end of something—a taking away, or deprivation—it's really a positive thing, a beginning, a wider experience. It's a broadening of the child's horizons, an expansion of his universe. It's moving slowly ahead one careful stop at a time. It's full of exciting but sometimes frightening new experiences. It's another step in growing up.

Our culture today has geared us to thinking that all babies should be off the breast at an early age. But this is far from the custom that prevailed in centuries past. In biblical days weaning at age three was often mentioned, and still today in many parts of the world children wean themselves at ages up to three, four, or even older. Niles Newton, PhD, points out that (most) babies in most periods of history and in most parts of the world have been breastfed from two to four years. She also observes that the changes in breastfeeding customs do not seem to have come alone, but in conjunction with a whole body of related customs. "La Leche League's repeated emphasis that breastfeeding is part of a whole philosophy of mothering is borne out by historical trends," she says.

An interesting account of late weaning is found in *The Sun Chief* quoted by Gesell:

> By the time I was six, therefore, I had learned to find my way about the mesa and to avoid graves, shrines, and harmful plants, to size up people and to watch out for witches....My hair was clipped just above my eyes but left long in back and tied in a knot at the nape of my neck....I wore silver earrings, a missionary shirt or one made of a flour sack, and was always bare-legged, except for a blanket in cold weather. When no whites were present, I went naked. I slept out on the housetop in summer and sometimes in the kiva with other boys in winter. I could help plant and weed, went out herding with my father, and was a kiva trader. I owned a dog and a cat, a small bow made by my father, and a few good arrows. Sometimes I carried stolen matches tucked in the hem of my shirt collar. I could ride a tame burro, kill a kangaroo rat, and catch small birds, but I could not make fire with drill and I was not a good runner like the other fellows....But I had made a name for myself by healing people; and I had almost stopped running after my mother for her milk.

Six is a bit older than most of us can imagine as a weaning age. Yet, as we can see, it was perfectly acceptable at another time, and in another place. Yet when asked if a mother can force her child to nurse past the age when he is no longer interested, Dr. James Good says, "There is no way a mother can force a child to nurse beyond the time he wishes. It is an unquestionable fact that all babies will wean themselves sooner or later. There have been no observations or studies to show *any* psychological harm to a person through extended breastfeeding. Contrariwise, it is shown that many problems arise through not breastfeeding, or too early interruption of the mother-child relationship."

now?

"When Michael was approaching twenty months I felt as if he would continue nursing forever," said Anne Allison of Georgia. "It was all too soon, though, that one day without nursing stretched into two and then three. On the fourth day he asked to nurse and I happily obliged. After nursing quietly and steadily for five minutes, he sat up and announced, 'No more, Mommy.' Thus ended our nursing relationship, with Michael weaning himself completely at that moment. There may be times when a mother feels her nursing baby requires a lot of time and attention, but remember to enjoy those special moments of cuddling and nursing your child, because time will pass and before you know it, your baby is an active toddler, then in school, and your relationship as a nursing couple will be only a memory."

Each of us, like all families, must of course find our own particular solutions to things, and these will not always be the same. But recognizing that the needs of babies and young children are often very immediate and very urgent, and being willing to make some adjustments and sacrifices to satisfy these needs will go a long way toward making secure and happy individuals who will make us proud parents as they grow up.

This is also great preparation for the next stage in your life, whatever that stage might entail. The self-discipline learned in "growing up" with our children is invaluable in all future endeavors.

DISCIPLINE—LOVING GUIDANCE

We parents want, perhaps more than anything else, to have the wisdom to guide our child's growth so that his personality develops unstunted and undistorted. We want him to become an independent, mature, loving person, with his talents and abilities developed to their fullest.

We know that our first job is to meet his physical and emotional needs as fully as we can, so that a secure foundation is laid for his advance to maturity. We mothers know that by breastfeeding him we are getting him off to the right start. The breastfeeding relationship itself makes us more sensitive to all his needs, so we are quicker and surer in devising ways of meeting them.

As our child grows, his needs change, and we must progressively let go of him as he assumes the direction of his own life. This process will not be complete until he is fully grown, but it starts in babyhood. This book, therefore, would be incomplete if we did not look into the beginnings of independence and our role in fostering them.

Discipline is an integral part of everything we do for and with our children. Having developed a philosophy of mothering our babies and toddlers through breastfeeding and weaning, we are now ready to go on to develop more deeply other aspects of discipline in the mothering of our young child. "If you have been doing a good job of mothering, you are already doing a good job of disciplining," says Dr. Hugh Riordan, psychiatrist and LLL father.

As your baby enters the toddler years, it becomes important for you and your husband to really share your feelings and ideas about discipline with each other. You might want to read over this chapter together as you begin to develop your own style of parenting.

Discipline is a much maligned word, often associated with punishment and deprivation. Yet this should not be the case. Discipline really refers to the guidance which we as parents lovingly give our children to help them do the right things for the right reasons—to help them grow into secure, happy, and loving persons able to step out into the world with confidence in their own ability to succeed in whatever they set out to do. James Hymes, author of *The Child Under Six,* explains: "Disciplining the young child is the most important job that parents have to do....Discipline sums up our broad goals for the child as a member of society."

The laws of a new baby's growth are operating so strongly that all you can do is cooperate with them or frustrate them; at an early age he can't understand or follow laws imposed from without. If you are patient and cooperative as he follows his own growth and nursing patterns, he can lay a sound foundation for further growth. If you are continually trying to force him into a pattern of your own making, or one imposed on him by others, you will confuse him and perhaps interfere seriously with his emotional development. "Just as the twig is bent, the tree's inclined." the wise old saying goes. Its moral is not to force the child this way or that, but to let him follow his own inner growth patterns in the image of the good values of the parents he learns to love. Then the tree will be straight and tall. Dr. Hymes says:

> We can help our children get off to a good start in learning sound values
> in the years under six, not by what we say to them but through how we
> live with them and let them live. If we treat young children decently, they
> will go on after six continuing to learn as they grow, and to grow as they
> learn.

When we willingly, happily, lovingly nurse our babies, we are sensitive
to their needs and instinctively meet them as fully as we can. A good
beginning! The infant is ready to grow into childhood.

Beyond Infancy

As the baby-child grows, he will need guidance, instruction, and
sometimes correction to learn the ways of our world. If the foundation of
secure love was laid when he was a baby, and if he sees his parents as
kind, polite, and considerate people, he will try to imitate them, because
he wants to act in ways that will please them (most of the time). We still
have to respect his growth patterns and not ask of him more than he is
capable of giving at his stage of development, but we can and should give
some direction to his inexperience. How to do this is where the difficulty
often lies. Before we can successfully begin to discipline our little ones
we must have a clear idea of *why* we are doing what we are doing and *how*
we should go about doing it. There should be no sharp break in our ways
of guiding our child's development. Abrupt weaning and sudden decisions
to "train" the child to do something (as if he were a puppy) are unreasonable
and can be harmful. Punishing young children by spanking and slapping
is ineffective and frequently reflects the impatience and frustrations of
the parent. It is not the kind of behavior we would want our children to
imitate.

Over the years many of us unlearned some of the old wives' tales about
discipline we had been raised with, such as "Train-em-from-day-one-or-
they'll-run-your-life." We learned some give-and-take, some understanding, and tons of patience.

We learned to relax a little, laugh a lot, and be incredibly quick on our
feet. A large part of mothering a toddler is helping him through that
transition from babyhood, when his every wish was a real need, to later
on, when he becomes an outward-looking youngster just starting to
become aware of the needs of others. In the process he needs help in
learning that not all his wishes are needs, and in fact, some of them, if
granted, would most surely not be good for him at all.

While most people tend to respect the growth pattern of the small
infant, the eighteen-month-old or two-year-old toddler is another story.
When little fingers reach for electrical outlets, pennies go into mouths,
and lamps are toppled over, it is all too tempting to give way to our
impulse to clobber the small offender. Of course, we can't permit utter
chaos in our home, or unrestricted freedom. That could be dangerous.
But in handling these situations, we need to recognize that another
growth pattern is showing itself. The toddler is discovering the world
around him, so he (some children more than others) wants to touch, feel,

One way for parents to learn about normal toddler behavior is to spend time with other parents who have little ones. Here Anita Miranda, Stephani Palmer-Bowman, and Kathy Barter share some of the problems and joys of life with toddlers. (Photo by Pat Crosby.)

and take apart what he sees. He is just an inquisitive two-year-old private eye, investigating everything. This is normal behavior for his age, and punishing him is entirely out of place and will only frustrate him. That doesn't mean that you should do nothing at all about it. What's needed here is distraction and firm but gentle steering in another direction, away from the source of temptation. James Hymes explains: "Punishment is only one of the many teaching techniques you can use . . . and the trickiest, hardest-to-use-well technique of all!"

Not all children are alike; with some it is only necessary to caution them a few times about a forbidden object. If the child can learn to respect a few taboos without nagging or scolding from the mother or frustration on his part, then this method is fine. Usually it is wiser to remove dangerous or breakable objects from sight entirely.

If your explorer does find a "forbidden" object, one good way to satisfy his curiosity is to sit down with him and let him touch, feel, and even hold it himself. Show him how the electric hair dryer works, and explain to him in simple language, with lots of gestures, that we must be very careful because it can be dangerous, break, or come apart. Give him plenty of time to explore it with your help. Then change the subject, distract him, and put the forbidden article away—out of sight or reach or, better yet, both. (Remember that toddlers are great climbers.)

An Ounce of Prevention

The time-honored ounce of prevention is most important in avoiding upsets with your busy little toddler. "It only makes good practical sense," says Nancy Stanton of Florida, "to baby-proof your house as much as possible, because otherwise you'd spend your entire day battling with your children. It's hard enough to protect your child against the things you have no direct control over (such as cars on the street), so, especially if you have several preschoolers, keep your home environment as simple as possible. One mother even suspended her kitchen garbage can from the ceiling."

"With very active toddlers, extreme measures are sometimes necessary to preserve your sanity," Nancy says. "Someday you can put the knobs back on your kitchen cabinets. I imagine most of you have already given up at least one lower cupboard to your toddler anyway. Don't forget to fill it with real utensils—an old coffee pot or spatulas."

So keep on your toes, mother, and keep a light touch. If you can hang on to your sense of humor you're way ahead. Laugh a lot (sometimes through your tears!) and you'll all feel better.

In the case of a really dangerous situation such as chewing on an electric cord or running out in the street, mother should allow herself the full emotional expression of her fears; the child will gradually adopt these justifiable fears of real dangers and avoid them. A sudden shriek of alarm, accompanied by some fast footwork gets the message across pretty well when your little one reaches for the electric plug.

Mary White remembers solemnly showing her busy little escape artist a squirrel that had been run over by a car. The squirrel was quite obviously dead, and viewing the sad remains of the "squashed squirrel" left a lasting impression on the young adventurer.

In any case, keep an eye on your toddler, for his own safety. Pediatric experts who have carefully studied accident patterns in the very young child state that it is only when a child has reached the age of approximately three that you can *begin* to teach him how to protect himself. Until that age he can only be protected by the watchful eyes of his elders, and it's up to you to make sure the eyes are there.

To Spank Or Not To Spank?

The time when your child is a toddler is often a more difficult time for mother than for her fast growing child. Outwitting a determined toddler is a much greater challenge than paddling him to "make him mind." His pranks and explorations are to him just innocent fun or healthy curiosity. They may be dangerous, destructive, or just inconvenient, but he doesn't know that. It's our job to teach him (in other words, discipline him) and set limits for him. But we have found that in the long run, spanking a defiant toddler only leads to tears, resentment, and an uncontrollable (and understandable) urge to hit a baby brother or sister. (And later on in life, to hit his own kids as well.) James Hymes explains it this way:

> Discipline means that a child learns right from wrong; good from bad; the decent, the kind, the gentle, the thoughtful from the indecent and cruel and hurting—*and that he acts on what he knows because he believes in it.* These are not simple lessons to teach; not the kind you can beat into a child.

Dr. Herbert Ratner, well-known expert on the family, on being asked, "What do you think of spanking?" replied, "I'm totally against it, for several reasons. First, it gets you nowhere. The more you spank, the more your child will goad you to do it. It becomes a test of wills between parents and child. A child's will should be respected, not broken. Child rearing is not like training animals. The goal should be to make the child a disciple of loving what is right."

Although some parents insist the Bible tells them they must spank, nowhere do we find God exhorting mothers to hit their children. True, fathers are warned that to spare the rod is to spoil the child, but back in Old Testament days sons, for whom this admonition was given, didn't even come under their fathers' jursidiction until they reached the age of twelve, and daughters not at all. Presumably if mother had done a good job with the children in the early years, there wouldn't be much need for dad to get after them with the rod later on.

Another point, we are reminded by Betty Bevember of Illinois, is that the rod really refers to "the shepherd's crook, which was not used to beat the sheep but to gently guide them back on the path, or lift them from dangerous situations." Ross Campbell, author of *How To Really Love Your Child,* raises the question: "If the rod were used for beating, how could we take comfort in Psalm 23, 'Thy rod and thy staff, they comfort me'?"

Untold numbers of parents have raised good, kind, loving, and well-behaved children without hitting them. Nobody said it was easy, and often it isn't, but it's worth the effort. Our children learn by the examples they see, and parents are the ones they most desire to imitate. So we must ask ourselves what kind of example we want to set for them.

Setting Limits

"But," you say, "If I can't hit him, what *do* I do?" My two-year-old gets very angry with me when I tell him he can't have a cookie. If I try to hide them he throws a tantrum."

Your little one needs to know that there are some things he may do or have and others he may not. Parents have to decide what those things are, and then take appropriate action. Mothers and fathers should of course come to an agreement beforehand on such things as values and methods of discipline, and then be as consistent as possible thereafter.

Dr. Hymes points out:

Children want limits.... Discipline brings contentment to children, as well as safety to our world. A youngster who goes along during these early years never knowing what he should do and what he should not has a terrible time. In a literal sense, he is lost....knowing no limits, he is full of fears....The youngster who knows no discipline feels no love.

So hide the cookies, by all means, or don't bring them into the house, and quickly distract your demanding son or daughter with something else. If that doesn't work and the child is having a tantrum, just pick him up, if he'll let you, and give him a soothing hug; or sit quietly nearby if he won't. Don't worry—he'll stop crying pretty soon. It will be sooner if you are not upset by the goings-on. After your child has quieted down, treat him normally—as if nothing had happened, and resume life from there. Don't mention the cookies again—in fact keep them out of sight from that point on. Preschoolers have remarkably short memories, and they surely don't bear grudges. An occasional flare-up like this won't destroy forever the beautiful relationship you've built up between you, and it will in all likelihood make life easier by making clear just what the limits are.

Is This Permissiveness?

Parents sometimes find it difficult to make the changeover from the total giving to the needs of a baby to the more active role of seeing to the needs of a toddler. We are still looking after their needs, but not always with total acquiescence to their demands. Marge O'Sullivan of California gives us some very helpful examples of the difference between *permissiveness, punishment,* and *true discipline*:

Act I A classroom where a group of mothers and their little ones have gathered for a meeting:

Scene I—During the meeting a toddler comes to a sink and begins to play in water. Before long the child, the sink area, and the surrounding carpeting are soaked. Mother watches from nearby. *PERMISSIVENESS.*

Scene II—Another child comes to the sink and begins to play. Mother approaches and turns off the water, takes the child to another area, and offers toys. This child will not be distracted and begins to cry. Mother picks up child sympathetically and leaves the meeting so others won't be disturbed. *DISCIPLINE.*

Act II A private home:

Scene I—Firstborn child, now a toddler, begins to empty desk drawers. Mother (reading) shouts at child to stop several times, finally gets up and slaps the child, then returns to her book, leaving the child sobbing. *PUNISHMENT.*

Scene II—Second child at the same stage. Mother is more relaxed. Says "please stop" several times, then adds, "Oh, well, he has to explore." *PERMISSIVENESS.*

Scene III—Same mother, third child, same stage. Mother has grown more and listened more. All drawers but one are firmly closed, and the one drawer is filled with toys. Child soon loses interest in "his" drawer and begins to check others. Mother takes child to another room to introduce new interest. *DISCIPLINE.*

Act III A house of worship:

Scene I—A two-year-old sits quietly for three to four minutes, then begins to crawl around. Mother sits child down (roughly) several times. Child finally settles for tearing pages from hymnbook as mother watches. *PERMISSIVENESS.*

Scene II—Another family. Mother has several favorite, quiet toys for two-year-old. Spends much time keeping two-year-old occupied. When child's tolerance level is reached, mother takes child to the back of church (or outside). *DISCIPLINE.*

Decisions, Decisions

"It's easy to spank," says Dolores Cuthbertson of Colorado. "It's harder to think. We cannot expect three-, four-, and five-year-olds to know what to do if we don't tell them, nor do we need to be overly concerned that they will not know how to make decisions when they are ten or twelve if we don't let them begin now. We can really do both—tell them when it's major and let them make choices when it isn't." For example, instead of asking your very opinionated two-year-old to select his own clothes every day, give him a simple choice between two outfits that would be acceptable to you and say, "Pick the one you want to wear today." This way he will slowly learn to make decisions and to take responsibility.

Say What You Mean

"Come in the house right now, Kate," you call for the fifth time. Kate, still cheerfully ignoring your summons, goes right on playing. Do you really want her to come in "right now" or don't you care? If you don't care, then don't call her until you do. Then, call her once. Wait a couple of minutes and call again. If she doesn't respond, go out, scoop her up, and carry her cheerfully and speedily into the house. She will soon learn that you mean what you say.

"To a two-year-old child, a call to stop playing and come in for lunch may on certain days be too much," says Edwina Froehlich. "Try going out there ten minutes in advance with a nutritious snack you know he'll like, and when that's finished start the getting-in process."

A reminder to get the toys picked up a half hour before dinner may not be enough. Offer the snacks, then be prepared to help him pick up the toys. Time-consuming? "You bet," Edwina says, "but so are tantrums or crying spells." And this is more fun.

If you have to go to the store right now, don't ask little Hercules if he would like to go to the store. He'll probably say "no," and then will come the argument. Instead say, "Come on Herc, we're off to a big adventure at the grocery store," stuff him into his coat, and be on your way.

"Yes" Today, "No" Tomorrow?

With discipline of any sort, as with the care you've been giving your baby right from the start, consistency is a key word. Say "no" as seldom as possible. (Saying "no" often teaches a child to say "no" more often than "yes," which is not the road to true discipline.) When you do say "no," say it calmly, firmly, and good-naturedly, but let your child know you mean it. It usually works better just to pick him up, with a cheerful hug, and remove him from the source of trouble, drawing his attention casually to some other fascinating object or activity. The younger the child, the more easily he will be distracted. As children get older, you will need more finesse, but an ounce of distraction is still worth a pound of exhorting.

Look to the Cause

When your little one misbehaves, there may be a variety of reasons. Is he tired? Bored? Hungry? Over-stimulated? Sometimes figuring out the cause of misbehavior is a good way to avoid future problems.

Little children (like grown-ups) are often at their worst if they are over-tired or hungry, Nancy Stanton, observes: "Toddlers usually do need some extra sleep in the daytime, but they don't want to miss anything. If your child is really tired, stop everything—close the drapes, turn off the TV, don't do anything yourself—put a pillow on the floor and both of you lie down. At least one of you will drift off."

Or maybe his behavior is a signal to mother, telling her it's time to stop talking on the phone or visiting with the neighbors, or whatever it is she is doing that takes her away from her little one, mentally if not physically. It's time to get back down on his level and notice him.

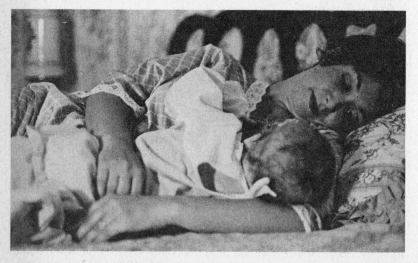

Jill Bohan finds that curling up in bed to nurse a tired thirteen-month-old Natalie provides a refreshing perspective on the rest of the day. (Photo by John Franklin.)

Debbie Johnson of New Jersey tells this story: "Finding a long-awaited pause in the conversation, my four-year-old son, Josh, said to me, 'Mom, now I remember why I used to kick you all the time before I was born....I was trying to get you to stop talking!'"

The Terrible Telly

One nuisance, which many parents do not think of as such, is the television. Your children's TV time should be drastically limited at any time of the day, of course, but especially in the evening, when the more mature shows are on. Parents don't realize the effect these may have on their seemingly oblivious young children. Things that wouldn't frighten us a bit can come back to terrify the two-year-old in the middle of the night, mostly because he doesn't understand them. The noise, the bright colors, the intrusion into what could otherwise be a peaceful family gathering, can be just too much for him. As a matter of fact, it might be a good idea for the entire family to try doing without the TV for a week or so, just to see how nice it is. Some studies have already shown that children who watch a great deal of television have more behavior problems than those who do not.

Sound and Fury

On the subject of toddlers and tantrums, Edwina Froehlich, one of LLL's founders, recalls her own experiences:

Temper tantrums can be devastating to both mother and child. Having had to cope with two children who had tantrums, I did learn a little. I followed the usual suggestions with the first boy—a spank on the bottom made him scream harder, of course; trying to firmly take him to his room was hard on my shins; a stern reprimand couldn't be heard over his screaming. Ignoring him was the best of the lot, since at least it didn't add to the child's hysteria. Still, neither did it solve anything, and it did nothing to prevent future tantrums. As I became better informed about our nutritional needs, I became aware that the timing of the tantrums often coincided with periods of hunger. They seldom occurred immediately after a meal. Once in progress, you can't stop a full-blown tantrum by offering food, but understanding it at least enables you to cope better. Better still, it can perhaps show you the way to help prevent or at least lessen the tantrums.

When our youngest was about two and a half, a friend had come for lunch, and we spent several hours afterwards talking about how to raise children. Peter was for the most part amusing himself, but late in the afternoon, when I told him to stop something he was doing, his tolerance level burst and he had a beaut! I went over and sat on the floor beside him and reached over to pat him gently. At first he rejected my hand and literally threw it back at me. So I just sat by him and waited, whispering, "I love you Petey." He quieted very quickly and rolled himself over to me, burying his face in my lap, and finished sobbing in comfort. When the storm was over he had forgotten what started it and we trotted immediately to the kitchen. This was Peter's first real tantrum, and while I was happy and relieved to know that I now knew how to handle one, I girded myself for repeat performances. To my surprise, he had only two or three more, and they were mild and quickly over.

The tantrum a child throws in public is no harder on *him* than if he were at home, but it is agonizing for the parent. Onlookers are quick to show their disapproval of your "naughty" child.

Embarrassing though it is, the basic approach to handling the tantrum is the same—the parent cannot react in anger, but must remain calm and speak in quiet, soothing tones. Both mother and child are in a state of distress in this situation, but the child is the more helpless of the two. He cannot just turn off his rage on command. If it is at all possible, pick the child up and move to a more secluded spot where he will bother fewer people. But you may have a baby in your arms, or the enraged child may be too heavy or kicking too wildly to permit removal. Any attempt to reason with him in this highly emotional state will be wasted. The only thing you can do is stand by quietly and wait it out.

He'll calm down sooner if you remain calm and nonthreatening—not easy for you when you may really feel like beating him into submission or screaming at him to stop. As soon as the child will permit it, touch him gently and try to lead him away. When the sobbing has stopped you can offer him a nutritious snack if you suspect he is hungry, but be sure it is not a sweet. He may think he is being rewarded for his performance.

If your child has tantrums often, try to determine if there is a pattern. Do the tantrums occur at the same time each day? Only with certain people? What seems to be the source of the frustration? Can you possibly remove the source?

Do what you can to avoid the frustrating situations that cause him to explode. Be sure to distinguish between the person and the act. It's not the child you disapprove of, only what he has done. If you make this clear to both your child and yourself, you won't feel guilty about disciplining him by setting limits. If you keep letting him know the difference, he too will eventually come to understand it.

As Vi Lennon says, "It takes three hugs for an adult to get through the day," so imagine how many hugs your little one needs every day!

Tooth and Claw

What about the child who bites or hits? This seems to be a rather common problem, and a difficult one, especially when other children are around. Norma Jane Bumgarner, author of *Mothering Your Nursing Toddler*, tells this story:

About two years ago (at an LLL meeting), my beautiful, superbly mothered, absolutely perfect toddler was bitten by somebody's rotten,

*Come, darling, let's do something different
like wash our hands and brush our teeth.*

neglected, little monster—or so it appeared to me at the time. As I comforted my baby I shot reproachful glances in the direction of the little culprit's mother, making no attempt to hide the feelings we all have when somebody hurts our child.

As proof that there is justice in the world, our next child turned out to be not only a biter, but the most determined, dangerous biter I have ever seen. This is one of the most difficult things I have ever dealt with in my life, and it was made even harder for me by those few mothers who reacted the way I did two years ago.

Naturally, when we realize this is going to be a problem with our youngster, it behooves us to take immediate action. The mother of the biter must be ever watchful and, as soon as she sees her little werewolf approaching his prey she must intervene by removing him from the scene with great dispatch and firmness. Speed is of the essence. "Yelling, spanking or biting the child back doesn't solve the problem," writes Diane Kramer of New Mexico. "Young children are usually very oral in reaction. They use their mouths to feel, to love, to test, and to argue, and it takes time and maturity for them to realize that not all these reactions are acceptable. Meanwhile, love them, cuddle them, help them through their frustrations, and recognize that this too shall pass."

Toilet Habits or "On The Potty Train"
When will your child have his toilet habits under control? This varies, like everything else, with the individual child. Some children acquire control of the sphincter, or "hold-back" muscles, sooner than others. The timing is a matter of no real importance. Parental intervention is perhaps more likely to delay control than hasten it. Often, enough bowel control to prevent "accidents" most of the time comes toward the end of the second year; the same degree of daytime bladder control, about a year later. "Sleeping dry" is usually last of all. But there is considerable individual variation. Your part is simply to give your child friendly encouragement and let him observe from time to time how older children and adults manage the details. He'll do the rest. In this, as in other aspects of growth, you let him know how pleased and proud you are about his accomplishments; but don't make too big a production of this either, or the inevitable lapses might cause him more concern than they should.

Your young child will naturally become very absorbed in what he is doing from time to time. We usually describe this as playing, but it is really working at learning about the world, about his own abilities, and about other people and his relation to them. He may become so absorbed that he won't let himself be conscious of the growing feeling of bladder fullness, sometimes until it is too late to avoid an "accident." If the situation is one in which this might cause embarrassment or property damage, and you notice his absentminded contortions in time, you might offer a tactful reminder. But taking himself to the bathroom is essentially *his* business. Remember that by sometimes waiting a while and unconsciously letting the accumulating urine stretch his bladder a little, he is tending to the business of growing better than if you interfere. Treat "mistakes," when they occur, with casual sympathy and especially as the child gets older, help him save face by quick and unobtrusive disposal of the evidence.

Of course, it's necessary for a while to lend a hand with such things as wiping and washing hands afterward, but this help can be given casually. You take the same friendly interest in his comfort in this respect as you do in other ways, and you continue to help as needed until he gradually takes over for himself the socially approved routines of toileting, with the same casual attitude he has learned from you.

Bed-wetting

Staying dry all night happens when the child's bladder gets large enough to hold the amount of urine that accumulates during the night. Even after your child is able to start and stop urinating at will when he is awake, his bladder will still empty automatically at night when it becomes over-full—a wise precaution of nature's. One of the things that helps the bladder grow large enough to hold the night urine is the child's occasional holding of the urine somewhat past the time when he first feels the urge to void during his waking hours; this stretches the bladder gently.

You can see then that an over-anxious mother who watches her toddler narrowly and rushes him to the toilet every two hours, or every time he shows signs of needing to urinate, may actually be delaying the time when he is able to sleep dry through the night.

But what about the child who, no matter how well we handle the question of wet beds, still just can't stay dry, even when he's beyond the age of three or four (or much older)? This happens probably more often than most of us realize, and it can be very trying to the parents and a cause of misery to the child. There are some children who just don't have much bladder control when they are little, and it is only with the passing of time, along with the quiet support and encouragement of parents, that the problem solves itself. One suggestion, which works pretty well in some cases when a child is six or seven years old or so, is to encourage the child to wait a bit longer during the day when he feels the need to urinate. Holding it in for an extra ten minutes, or whatever he can, helps to enlarge the bladder capacity. Some doctors suggest that the child measure the amount of urine he passes each time. The bigger the amount, the bigger the bladder capacity, and he should be encouraged by this visible evidence of his maturity over the months.

The Sandman Cometh Not

"That's all very well," writes one mother, "but you haven't been to our house. Bedtime is especially disastrous! There's no end to it, and we usually all end up exhausted and exasperated. What do you suggest we do about that?"

Here again, anticipation is terribly important. While it may not matter in your home whether or not your preschooler goes to bed at a predetermined time every night (since he doesn't have to get up early the next morning), some regularity is a good idea, whether it's early or late. Suit your own schedule, but then be alert and watch for signs of fatigue in your child. You may be so engrossed in what you are doing, or he may be so busy playing, that neither of you realizes that it's been many hours since he last had some sleep. A warm bath with time to play in the tub, a nutritious snack such as an apple, and a quiet story time, when you snuggle together under the covers, all lead to a relaxed little person, ready and willing to go to sleep. He'll want you to stay with him of course, and you should. Perhaps he is still sleeping in your bed, and bedtime is for both of you. Enjoy it. There is no sense in putting him to bed in his own room, with his very own teddy bear, when he'd rather have the loving companionship

of mother or daddy, or even big brother or sister. It's scary all by himself, and he will think up a hundred different reasons to call you back or to appear at the living room door, forlornly hoping that this time you'll let him stay with you. Don't set bedtime too early or he just won't be sleepy. Children can only sleep a certain number of hours, and if your child goes to bed at seven, he may be up bright-eyed at five A.M. "You can't have it both ways," reminds Dr. Ratner.

When he is ready, make bedtime a cozy, quiet time, with no rush or hurry. You'll find that he will sleep better during the night, will wake much less often as he grows older, and the nightmares and leg aches that plague so many preschoolers just aren't happening. Sweet dreams, everyone.

A Look Ahead

As your children get older, the outlook on discipline becomes easier to some degree. But children will keep pressuring you, testing the limits, on into their teens. If they know that you are and always have been firm and consistent and loving, and that you trust them, it will be easier.

As you set limits for your older child you may find that at times he may be really angry with you, but he'll get over it soon as long as he knows that you really love him. Show him you love him by your actions, even when you have to say "no." A friendly backrub, a quick swing around the room with him in your arms, or some special thing you do together will reassure him. Soon the storm clouds will blow over and the sun will shine in your home again.

Nancy Stanton has this to say: "Sometimes mothers get into the kind of box one of them described this way: 'I've tried every kind of punishment I can think of with my son—spanking him, locking him in his room (he tears it apart), but nothing works. He seems to think up terrible things to do on purpose just to upset me.'

"I think in this kind of situation the relationship has gotten out of hand. I'd suggest taking a look at your own life and outside activities. Maybe you're doing too much to take the time to build on some positive encounters with your child. Make a list of the most important things and kinds of behavior you value. Then start the day with a word of praise. Check yourself during the day to see how many positive, neutral, and negative encounters you have with your child. It is not unusual for a child to misbehave because otherwise no one would pay attention to him."

From Generation to Generation

Whatever happens, remember that each child is an individual, and you can't lay down hard and fast rules that will be appropriate for all children. In this matter of discipline, if you have the intimate understanding of your little one that the breastfeeding relationship fosters, and if you are clear in your own mind about the real nature of discipline, you can safely follow your own instincts as parents. "It's not our job as parents simply to take care of our children, but to help them learn how to take care of themselves," says Norma Jane Bumgarner. And later on in life, they may even end up taking care of us. So do a good job now, reap the rewards when you grow old. Jalelah Fraley, a mother from California, once remarked: "Out of all this will come sons and daughters well on the road to meeting the needs of our own grandchildren in a wholesome, happy way—we shall see an era of 'gently nurtured' loving human beings."

The Heart of the Matter

When your child is born, you devote yourself to meeting all of his needs; you nurse him when he is hungry and hold him close as long as he needs and likes it. As he grows, he wants less snuggling and more sociability; you prop him up in the midst of the family from time to time and go about your business—never getting too far away, though, so that when his brief spurt of "independence" has spent itself, you can welcome him back to the haven of mother's arms. As the days and weeks and months go by, he becomes more independent in other ways; he starts eating solid foods and does not nurse so long or so often. Soon he picks up bits of food to bring them to his mouth himself. And one day, he is feeding himself, handling a spoon with dignity and aplomb, albeit with occasional spectacular messes. Now he is drinking from a cup, and as the months speed by, taking no more than a friendly nightcap from the breast, except when he seeks the solace of this familiar comfort. You are still there when he needs you. There is never an abrupt withdrawal of your love as expressed first through the warmth and closeness of nursing and later in other ways. Secure in knowing that he can retreat for a bit into babyhood if he wants to, he ventures further and further into childhood, and finally (all too soon, it seems in retrospect), he isn't a baby anymore; he eats at the family table and enjoys the family meals. Before you know it, he will be on his way to school, with a cheerful wave back as he goes.

He's off to a good start toward independence.

The years go by, and though parenting doesn't get any easier, it is always challenging and interesting. Our children will never stop needing us in one way or another, thank goodness! But we have to learn when to stand back and when to offer our help. And someday, your little boy will be proudly standing over his own wife as she happily nurses their baby, or your daughter, looking so like her mother at that age, will be nursing hers. All the work and worry, the time and the endless patience, have paid off. It's all very much worthwhile.

We hope that in these few pages we have been able to give you our perspective about the way in which we believe the start in life you give your child through breastfeeding can lead to self-discipline, which comes with maturity. We can't give you a blueprint for all the situations you will encounter, but we can tell you that bringing a positive attitude to child rearing will make a tremendous difference in the outcome.

With your understanding guidance, your child will grow from dependence to independence gradually, and always with the love that is his birthright, and the great need of our world.

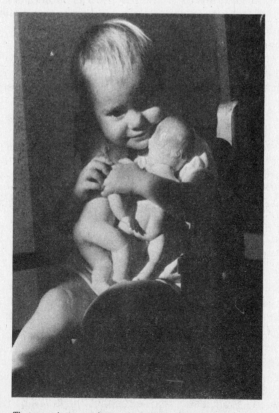

The warm, loving mothering she has received is reflected in the way Hayden Sears mothers her baby dolls.

Chapter VIII

Nutritional Know-How

If your eating habits need improvement, the best time to change them is before you become pregnant, so that your body builds up the proper nutrients in preparation for pregnancy. If you have not gotten around to improving your eating habits but want to do so now that you're pregnant, by all means *begin*. Your investment in your baby's welfare should provide strong motivation that will make it easier for you to change your eating habits.

Your baby will get off to a fine start on your milk, as perfect a food as there is. You will want him to build on this good start by giving him healthful foods when he is ready for them and by teaching him nutritionally sound eating habits that will become lifelong practices. The best way to accomplish this is by being a family in which *everyone* has good eating habits.

In this chapter, we include some general principles of food selection and utilization. We think that a broad understanding of how nature relates to you nutritionally is most important. We believe this understanding will be valuable to you as a guide in choosing the foods you and your family need for good health—more valuable than chemical analyses or detailed food lists (and much simpler!)

Nowhere have we found this sensible approach better stated than by Dr. Herbert Ratner, so we have included his remarks on the principles of good nutrition in the paragraphs that follow. We have also added a few practical suggestions that come out of our experiences with our own families, as well as some special hints for nursing mothers.

THE BASIC APPROACH

Nature is the best manufacturer and supplier of our dietary needs. This can be seen in two ways. First, the living animals and plants are the best sources of food elements needed for optimum life. Second, these sources of food, generally speaking, contain all our nutritional needs (minerals, vitamins, carbohydrates, fats, and protein) in proper balance and proportions. How, then, do you go about selecting foods that are most beneficial?

Eat a Variety of Foods

First, eat a variety of animals and plants. Don't concentrate on four-legged animals, like the cow, to the exclusion of two-legged animals (fowl); or land animals to the exclusion of water animals (fish and other seafood). In the plant kingdom, don't restrict yourself to a few vegetables, to the exclusion of fruits, nuts, legumes, grains, and cereals; or green vegetables to the exclusion of orange vegetables.

People instinctively seek a variety of styles and colors to decorate their bodies. The inner body also thrives on a diversity of foods with a wide range of flavors, colors, even textures—chewy, soft, firm, juicy, crisp. All the different textures, colors, and flavors of food reflect different food elements and values needed for the body.

Secondly, eat a variety of the parts of animals and plants. In animals, don't just concentrate on muscle (for the most part the expensive cuts) such as steaks, chops, and roasts. Don't overlook liver, tongue, sweetbreads, hearts, kidneys, gizzards, soup bones, and the old-fashioned catchall: fresh sausage that you or your butcher make—free of chemicals, preservatives, dyes, and excessive amounts of fat. Remember also milk, cheese, and eggs.

Don't forget that there are different parts of plants, too, that are edible. The parts don't have to belong to the same plant. There are leaves, like the greens that go into a salad, as well as Swiss chard and cabbage. There are roots, like carrots, beets, yams, turnips, and onions. There are stems and tubers, like asparagus and potatoes, and the fruits of the plant, like corn, string beans, and tomatoes, as well as apples, oranges, grapes, bananas, and melons.

There is even a variety obtainable in fats, which are needed in the cooking and preparation of many foods and which also supply large amounts of energy. There are animal fats and vegetable fats. There are solid fats and liquid fats. Animal fats include butter, cream, lard, and chicken fat. There are even fish oils such as those used in cod-liver oil and vitamin A capsules. Modern cookbooks offer many ways to extend our food preparation habits from the use of animal fats to the broader use of the many vegetable oils available to us. However, nutritionists today usually recommend moderate use of fats of any kind, since many of us consume too much fat.

Vary Your Menus

As you are planning your family's meals, you'll want to provide this variety in selecting foods. You can respect your own likes and dislikes as long as your dislikes aren't too numerous and as long as you do not impose your likes and dislikes on the rest of the family. After all, you don't want your children to grow up with restricted eating habits.

If there is a particular food you or other members of your family dislike, there is always a substitute. Cheese and yogurt are good substitutes for milk. Eggs are a good alternative to meat and fish, as are combinations of whole grains, nuts, dried peas, beans and lentils. This demonstrates one

Cooking can be fun, and often becomes a family affair. What better way for little ones to learn about the importance of good food than right in their own kitchen? *(Mary Ellen Lehman shares her kitchen with Becky and Tim.)*

lovely thing about nature. It provides such a variety of foods that every culture in every age on every continent has had a varied selection of foodstuffs available to eat. It has resulted, among other things, in a wondrous variety of national cuisines. Modern transportation and mechanization make possible a varied selection of foods throughout the year by sharing the productive seasons and rich bounty of other parts of the world with all of us.

Everyone doesn't have to eat a uniform diet; you can eat what you want in terms of the culture you're accustomed to or the new cultures you explore. As one mother used to say about her daughter-in-law's "strange" cooking, which she reluctantly enjoyed, "If you put good things into it, why shouldn't it come out tasting good?" There are many, many different ways of achieving good nutrition. For example, healthy adults who come from a culture where a vegetarian diet has been worked out over thousands of years know how to achieve a vegetarian diet that meets all of their nutritional needs. However, if for many years you've relied on animal sources for your protein and then decide to eliminate these sources, we recommend that you thoroughly inform yourself about vegetarianism. To suddenly eliminate meat and dairy products without providing for the nutrients—protein, fats, vitamins (especially vitamin B_{12}, often missing in vegetables), and minerals—found in them can lead to deficiencies that will ultimately result in poor health. Pregnant and nursing mothers and young children can be most seriously affected by an inadequate diet. If you decide to become a vegetarian there are good books available to help you. (See the Book List at the end of this book.)

Eat Natural Foods

Eat foods in as close to their natural state as possible. Generally speaking, the further one gets away from the natural state of a food, the poorer the food is nutritionally. Fresh foods are better than frozen or canned foods. Since cooking is one step removed from the natural state, some foods are better raw than cooked. This is especially true of fruits and vegetables, with a few exceptions. For example, vitamin A is more attainable in cooked carrots. Most protein foods need to be cooked. Under-cooked foods, with due allowance for digestibility, are better than over-cooked foods. The stir-fry method used by the Chinese permits food to be cooked quickly and to retain many of the nutrients and flavor found in uncooked foods.

By partaking of the many digestible parts of the living whole, and by concentrating on natural foods, you will get all of the known nutrient essentials in proper and natural proportions rather than in artificial concentrates. You will get all of the essential nutrients that have been discovered by science, and you should get those that have yet to be discovered; not only the vitamins and minerals of today, but the vitamins and minerals and other nutritional factors still undiscovered. This approach to nutrition is also more economical, and it doesn't require a science course. It will protect you against ill health and at the same time supply you with a variety of choices to please everyone in your family.

What to Avoid

Chemical additives. The fewer the additives the better! Civilization, although it has brought much progress, has also created some real problems in nutrition. In common use today in the food industry are a large number of chemicals that are added to food to enhance its color or prolong its shelf life. Claims have been made that some of the commonly used chemicals are harmful to one's health. Much more study needs to be done to determine just how safe these chemicals are. In the meantime, since some of the chemicals have not been properly tested and their safety is uncertain, it would seem wise to avoid them when possible. Read the labels on bottles, cans, and packages and choose those items that have the fewest chemicals or dyes. Better still, whenever possible, prepare your own food from the best products available.

In addition to trying to avoid additives, there's another major danger that must be emphasized. The appetite, our inborn guide to good nutrition, has been confused by highly refined and unnatural foods—the products of modern food technology. Because of this confusion, poor tastes and poor food habits have been developed, and in many instances, poor nutrition has resulted.

Sugar. One of the chief offenders in confusing our appetites is sugar. Sugar is the principal seducer of the appetite. Used excessively it can dull the palate for the delicate flavors of fresh, natural food. Sugar can be easily misused and is especially bad for infants and young children, primarily because it satisfies hunger needs and displaces healthful, natural foods. Sugar is obvious in many desserts, candies, and soft drinks. But there is also an amazing amount of "hidden" sugar found in many other commonly used packaged and/or bottled foods. For example, when you have fixed a juicy hamburger on a fresh whole-wheat bun, you ought to be able not only to anticipate a tasty item, but also to presume that you're not eating anything sweet. That will be true only if you avoid using the usual accompaniments—catsup or chili sauce, both of which contain a good portion of sugar, and cole slaw, which can be quite sweet. And who would expect that you would be getting sugar when you tackle that steaming platter of spaghetti laden with yummy tomato sauce? Among the ingredients listed on the label of bottled sauce you'll likely find at least one kind of sugar, perhaps dextrose or glucose. Look for the tomato sauce that has the least amount of sugar or make your own. (See LLL's cookbooks—MOTHER'S IN THE KITCHEN and WHOLE FOODS FOR THE WHOLE FAMILY.)

Thirteen-month-old Ellen Wingard finds it hard to decide which she likes best—cooking or eating!

Even some brands of salt have sugar added. Peanut butter, a good nutritious food which is a common staple in the American diet, often contains considerable sugar, syrup, or dextrose. Buy the brand whose only ingredient is peanuts, with or without salt. It is very important to your good health that you acquire the habit of reading the label on every packaged or bottled food item you buy.

Many of the best cooks in La Leche League have learned to cut out sugar entirely or greatly reduce it in as many recipes as they can. They have found that even in dessert recipes a sharp reduction in the amount of sugar called for works equally as well, and does not detract from the flavor. If your family is fond of gelatin desserts, for example, prepare your own using unflavored gelatin. Let ripe fruit be the only sweetener. If your little ones are served fresh fruit gelatin from the beginning, they'll love it. As you and your husband wean yourselves from too much sugar, your taste buds will begin to appreciate the flavor of natural sweetness.

Salt. Salt (sodium chloride) can be another offender in our diet. Like sugar, it is often misused in an attempt to enhance the flavor of our food. This may result in an excess intake of salt, which can be harmful.

1. The body must work extra hard to get rid of the salt it doesn't need.

2. Excess salt can cause retention of abnormal amounts of water, which isn't good for us.

3. Excessive use of salt is linked to high blood pressure in some individuals. (Hypertension can lead to stroke—a leading cause of death in the U.S.)

Salt was originally added to foods as a preservative and to cover up the unpleasant taste of foods that were spoiling because of lack of refrigeration. While salt is inexpensive and convenient, we would be far better off if we reduced the amount we use in cooking. Many excellent cooks have found other ways to enhance flavor; they use lemon and/or a variety of herbs, spices, and other seasonings.

Some mothers have removed the saltshaker from the table. You should also be aware that canned, bottled, frozen and packaged foods can be very high in salt content. Cutting down on salt may result in a few complaints at first, but it's a challenge to your cooking skills to put tasty dishes on the family table. Soon your salt lovers will have changed their ways.

Approximately three grams of salt per day (which is less than a teaspoon) is sufficient to satisfy the salt needs of most adults under average weather conditions. (During hot weather a little more salt is needed.) Many foods naturally contain sodium, so our need for salt is taken care of when we eat a varied diet of good foods. Extra salt should always be used very sparingly.

As for your baby, your milk contains just the right amount of salt for him. By eating solids in as natural a state as possible he will continue to take in only as much salt and other nutrients as he needs. Since he hasn't acquired an unnatural taste for salt, he will continue to eat what's good for him and enjoy it to boot.

In the past, salt was added to most commercial baby foods, not for the sake of the child, who neither needed nor wanted the extra salt, but to make the food taste better to the mother. After this excess salt was found to be harmful to babies, consumer pressure caused the baby food companies to discontinue this practice. If you follow our recommendations for introducing solid foods to your baby, you probably won't be using too many of the commercial baby foods anyway, so you won't need to worry about what is added to them. If you do use them, however, even occasionally, again we would advise you to read the labels.

Highly processed cereals and grains. These products provide another source of confusion to our appetites. Many cereals and grains are converted, in processing, from natural to unnatural foods. This processing robs the cereals and grains of important minerals and vitamins. To correct this problem, an enrichment process was developed. From the public-health point of view, this was the most efficient way to correct the nutritional deficiencies that were occurring because of the preference which people were developing for refined foods—(white instead of yellow or brown, fine instead of coarse, etc.). But *this enrichment is only an enrichment of an inferior product;* it does not make it into a superior product. It bears little resemblance to the original. The original always remains preferred, whether in breast milk for the infant or natural food in general.

Some wonderful originals we have forgotten, and for which we need to re-acquire a taste, are products made from whole grains. Cooking from recipes that use whole-wheat flour, whole rye, rolled oats, brown rice, millet, bulgur, buckwheat, kasha, or cornmeal is less expensive and far more rewarding in both flavor and quality than cooking exclusively with white flour.

Cereals, with which we often start the day, have also been depleted of many nutrients, which have been sparsely restored by so-called enrichment. Pre-sweetened cereals are especially bad since they contain a bare minimum of food value and large amounts of tooth-decaying, appetite-seducing sugar. Whole-grain breakfast cereals, both hot and cold, are delicious, and there's good variety to choose from.

There are many cookbooks available today that offer recipes using whole-grain products. LLL mothers have tested hundreds—look for them in the LLLI cookbooks. Also, one League Leader, Marlene Anne Bumgarner, has written a book called, *The Book Of Whole Grains.*

Read the Labels

We've mentioned before that acquiring the habit of reading the list of ingredients on food packages, cans, and bottles is a most important aspect of shopping. It will help you to avoid foods that contain chemicals and fillers you don't want, or to which you may be allergic.

Another reason it is important to read the list of ingredients is because labels are often misleading. A can labeled "fruit juice drink," for example, is just an artificial fruit-flavored drink. It is *not* pure fruit juice. By calling it a "drink" the company has stayed within acceptable advertising practice. Unfortunately, many novice shoppers buy it thinking they are providing good fruit juice for their families. Another confusing item is "milk drink." Sometimes the company brags about the vitamins they've added, but these "fortified drinks" offer much less food value than real milk.

Since you'll want to eat foods in as close to their natural state as possible, don't be misled be the word "natural" on the label. Marketing specialists have discovered that the word "natural" has great sales appeal, so it is tacked on to all kinds of products that have been processed to a point where they are far removed from the original natural product.

Be aware also that there's a difference between "cheese food," processed cheese, and unprocessed, natural cheese. Only the latter has nothing added and nothing subtracted from the original product, and you'll find more flavor and food value in it than in the other two products. Most grocery stores carry the natural cheese; read the label. If you visit the La Leche League office in Franklin Park at noontime, you'll find the aroma of melted cheese filling the air. A favorite with a number of employees is a thick slice of cheddar, Swiss or Monterey Jack cheese melted over crisp green pepper slices on whole-wheat bread.

If an ingredient is listed on the label as "wheat flour," it refers to white flour. It must say "100% whole wheat" to mean that. You should also know that ingredients are listed in descending order of amounts found in the product. For example, if flour is the first ingredient listed, it means there's more flour in the product than anything else. If the second item is sugar, dextrose, or syrup, that means that next to flour there is more sweetener than anything else, and so on down the line. The chemicals are usually listed last, but some highly processed items may have more chemicals than food: for example, coffee-cream substitutes, some pudding desserts, and some ice creams contain many chemicals.

HOW TO EAT WELL

By following the basic approach we have outlined so far, and adding the art of making foods tasty and attractive, you'll bring the joy of eating to the family table and you and your family will benefit nutritionally. Here are some practical tips to help you and your family to eat well.

Changing Food Habits

Food habits don't change overnight. Introducing new foods requires tact, patience, and imagination. Here are some suggestions that have worked for us during transition periods.

If your family is not accustomed to fish, perhaps you can introduce it by serving thin fillets, completely boned. Broiling is the easiest and quickest way to cook fish fillets, and the shorter the cooking time the more nutrition retained. Fresh fish is by far the tastiest, but when not available use frozen. Spread a thin coating of melted butter or oil on the fillet and broil about five minutes on each side, longer if frozen or if fillet is thick. Before serving the fillets, sprinkle them with dill weed, paprika, curry powder, or whatever herb or spice you prefer, or squeeze on some fresh lemon juice, or accompany with tartar sauce. Once fish has become accepted, try baking a whole fish, stuffed or otherwise. When cooked properly, it is succulent indeed, and some claim it surpasses steak!

Liquid fats such as corn or safflower oil can be worked into the diet in homemade salad dressings, pies, bread, muffins, and pancakes. A change to these oils would be good if you have been using mostly animal fats.

What could be more natural—nursing a baby with the aroma of good home-grown food nearby! (Anna Treder with Monica.)

Whole Grains

Introducing whole grains to your family can be a most enjoyable change because there are hundreds of ways to use them. If your family doesn't like oatmeal for breakfast, try cornmeal, either as a cereal, good old-fashioned fried cornmeal mush, or, when you have time, nice hot corn bread. For the latter, avoid cornmeal muffin mixes that have at least half white flour. Some recipes use a combination of cornmeal and whole-wheat flour, others use cornmeal only. Kasha is an old standby from people whose origins are in the Middle East and Eastern Europe. It is both nutritious and easy to cook. It can be used hot or cold, much like rice. Wholebran is also a good breakfast item, and many whole-grain cookbooks contain recipes using it either hot or cold. The smell of spicy raisin-bran muffins baking will draw people to the table. A hot bran muffin split open and spread with pure creamery butter is hard to resist. What a pleasant way to get your family off to a good, energetic start for the day! Try using granola, too. Granola recipes abound and it's fun to make up your own, since the commercial varieties are often heavy on sweeteners.

Husbands and older children have been known to balk at the introduction of whole-wheat bread. One suggestion is to offer them "half and half" sandwiches for a while—using one slice of whole-wheat bread and one slice of white. Very young children whose tastes have not had time to become conditioned usually like the whole grain bread right away.

If you do a lot of baking, you can introduce whole-wheat flour gradually into your baked goods. Just substitute a small amount of whole-wheat flour for the white flour you usually use in the recipe. This is especially easy to do in homemade breads. Many mothers have found that baking their own bread is great fun and a lot easier than they expected. If you gradually increase the amount of whole-wheat flour to the white flour over a period of months, eventually you'll be making a one hundred percent whole-wheat bread that no longer tastes "strange" to your family. It may even become more desirable than the white bread they used to like, especially when it's hot from the oven!

When you do use less-nutritious white flour in your recipes, be sure to use unbleached flour, since this contains some of the wheat germ. (You'll also avoid the extra chemicals used for bleaching.) For extra nutrition, place one tablespoon of soy flour in each cup of white flour. Soy is high in protein, so it will add to the food value of the baked goods and will not be noticed in the final product. Dried skim-milk powder is also a nutritious supplement if milk allergy is not a problem. A tablespoon or two can be added to various cake, bread, muffin, or pancake recipes without changing texture or flavor.

If your menus include a lot of pasta dishes, you can make your own whole-wheat pasta and pizza crusts. Whole-wheat noodles and spaghetti are also available in many stores. One mother we know is famous for her super apple pies. She makes a whole-wheat crust and avoids using a sweetener of any kind by using the sweet apples known as "Delicious," to which she adds raisins and the family's favorite spices. Concentrated orange juice also adds sweetness and can be substituted for other liquids.

Nuts And Seeds

Plain raw nuts and seeds are too full of goodness to overlook. Even when roasted they are still nutritious, though less so than when raw. If you've used nuts or seeds only for holiday snacks and now would like to work them into your regular menus, we have a few suggestions to offer. You can significantly increase nutrients in your potato salad, or chicken or tuna salad, by adding a tablespoon or two of hulled, raw, unroasted sesame seeds. They are so tiny and bland in flavor that even the pickiest member of your family won't notice them. A sprinkle of raw sunflower or hulled raw sesame seeds over breakfast cereal or yogurt also will increase food value and add both flavor and a bit of crunch to an otherwise soft food. In just about any kind of batter you make, you can add sesame seeds or finely ground nuts, and no one will be the wiser. Nuts and seeds are delicious in waffles, pancakes, and muffins and breads of all kinds. In the United States raw pecans, almonds, walnuts, Brazil nuts, cashews, and peanuts are all readily available. They each have wonderful flavor and specific food value. Nuts and seeds packaged by the ounce and sold in the grocery store are relatively expensive, as well as often stale. Look for one of the new, "old-fashioned" stores where you can scoop nuts, seeds, and dried fruits from big bins and buy them by the pound. These usually offer considerable savings over the packaged variety, and they are likely to be fresher and better flavored. Store them in the freezer to keep them fresh longer.

A caution is needed about giving nuts to children under three or so. The young child may not chew them well and there is a danger of small chunks being inhaled into the lungs instead of going down the throat.

Between-Meal Snacks

Make between-meal snacks nutritious and not just something to fill up on. If you or the children are ravenous and supper isn't ready, try raw vegetables or fresh fruit. If the apple or orange you offer the hungry little one is sliced, peeled, and cut into small portions, even the most finicky little eater is less likely to refuse. An older child can enjoy the whole fruit unsliced and unpeeled. Even if a light eater's appetite is somewhat lessened by the before-meal snack, it really doesn't matter as long as the snack is nutritious. Just consider it part of his meal. Try handing out pieces of raw vegetables as you prepare them for the meal. Many's the nutritious morsel that has been gobbled avidly when handed out beforehand that might have been scorned when it appeared, cooked and decorous, on a dinner plate. This reminds us of a mother who routinely cooks only half of the vegetables for a meal, serving the remainder raw at the table so each child can take his choice. You'll have to be careful of raw carrots, though, for the child under three. The same problem is involved as with small chunks of nuts, which may not be chewed properly, and can be inhaled rather than swallowed. Young children can usually handle other raw vegetables and fruits quite well.

Dried fruits, including raisins, are nutritious, but should not be eaten as a daily snack. They are hard on the teeth because of the high natural

Mommy will let you put the eggs in the water in a minute.
Then we'll put them on the stove to boil.
We're going to make such a nutritious snack!

sugar content. Because of their sticky texture they also tend to stick in the crevices of the teeth, evading the toothbrush and thereby contributing to tooth decay. In addition, many dried fruits have been sulphured, and dipped needlessly in honey or rolled in sugar, which you don't need. If you have access to sun-dried fruits, with no sugar or honey added, they make excellent sweeteners for cakes, cookies, or muffins made from wholegrain flour. Used in this way they are easier on the teeth than in the form of snacks.

Quenching Your Thirst

Unsweetened fruit and vegetable juices can provide food value as well as quenching your thirst. There are many varieties of canned apple, grape, tomato, grapefruit, and pineapple juices which are unsweetened, with no chemical additives. But you have to read the labels and avoid any that are called "fruit drinks." Frozen orange, apple, and grape juice concentrates are also available in unsweetened brands. Freshly squeezed orange or grapefruit juice is a treat when it's available.

If you begin having these juices on hand, chilled and ready, your family will learn to enjoy their natural sweetness. Of course, you'll want to completely avoid buying colas and other soft drinks. If they aren't even in the house, the natural drinks will be more appealing.

We do want to caution you that even unsweetened fruit juices in large quantities can cause problems, especially for toddlers who may fill up on them at the expense of other good foods.

Don't forget water! To really quench one's thirst there is nothing like it! Sometimes when it comes from a jug in the refrigerator it is more appealing to the younger set. Empty fruit-juice bottles can be filled with water and refrigerated. Or buy a pitcher with a lid. Water will seem more attractive poured from a brightly colored container than if it were just "plain old water from the faucet." A slice of fresh lime in a glass of ice water on a hot summer day both looks and tastes refreshing. Because of the pressure to serve soft drinks, parents have to be patient and persistent in resisting, and imaginative in providing substitutes. But you'll do your children a real favor.

GROW IT YOURSELF

One of the best suggestions we can offer is to plant your own vegetable garden. If you have space in your yard, so much the better. If not, see if your local park district offers small plots of land to would-be gardeners. Or see if a friend or neighbor would like to lend you space in return for a few fresh fruits and vegetables.

There is something very special about the smell of a garden growing—the pungent scent of tomatoes, the sweet-sharp smell of carrot tops, and the rich warm smell of good dirt. If necessary, inexpensive wire fencing can be put up to protect the growing fruit from the feet of eager children or playful dogs. (Cats, squirrels, and birds you can't keep out.)

An advantage of growing your own vegetables is that they will be free of the chemicals commercial growers use in the soil, as well as free of the pesticides that are sprayed on the plants during various stages of growth. Unfortunately, some of these chemicals remain on the skin of the fruit or vegetables and cannot be washed off. When you peel the fruit or vegetable to get rid of the suspected chemicals, you also lose some valuable nutrients. With homegrown produce, it's a choice you don't have to make.

Family gardening provides an inexpensive source of wholesome foods, as well as a project in which the entire family can participate. Leslye Korvola checks the vegetables with Hilkka and Katie.

Tomato plants grow and multiply—five scrawny little plants will produce quite a harvest, given enough sun and water. If you use different varieties of plants, even if they are planted at the same time, some will ripen earlier than others and you'll have tomatoes for your entire growing season. Growing tomatoes doesn't have to involve a lot of work, either. Pressed for time one year, Edwina Froehlich dug four shallow holes in the midst of a lush growth of weeds, and dropped a tomato plant into each. She says, "I cleared a small circular area around each plant, and it required only a few minutes each week to keep that area free of weeds. The plants flourished without the aid of chemicals of any kind. The firm, ripe, worm-free fruit was beautiful to behold and as succulent as could be. It worked so well I've been planting tomatoes among the weeds ever since. Given a choice, the bugs and worms seem to prefer the weeds."

Mary White describes the results of her family's gardening efforts one year:

We had lettuce every night, beans served both hot and cold, in salads and with butter. The broccoli, once it got started, just kept on growing well into the fall, and together with the Swiss chard, seemed able to withstand even severe frosts. The spinach fizzled out and went madly to tops early in the season. Our cabbages didn't do well either, nor did the little onion sets. But the tomatoes, bless them, impressed the neighbors, pleased the babies, and made the whole darn thing worthwhile. I made lots of chili with our surplus tomatoes and put it in the freezer.

It's a great way to get the kids outside, and get your mind off the fingerprints on the walls. Everyone gets fresh air and exercise.... Checking on the progress as the plants grow from tiny shoots, then seeing the little blossoms appear and after that the vegetables themselves, is more fun than just reporting on the first robin in the spring. You don't need lots of space, and some things just cheerfully keep growing despite all kinds of adverse conditions.

Edwina and Mary both live in the midwestern United States, and your experience may be different from theirs; but wherever you live, you can grow something that thrives in your kind of climate. Start by obtaining some seed catalogues—they make fascinating reading!

SPECIAL HINTS FOR NURSING MOTHERS

We have remarked earlier that if you have good eating habits, there is no reason for you to make any major changes when you are carrying or nursing a baby. You do have to remember to eat enough to keep yourself in good health. Eating well is part of being a good mother.

A Few Reminders

Nursing mothers just naturally feel the need for extra liquids. A nursing mother needs plenty of water—either "straight" or in the form of fruit and vegetable juices, milk, soup, or other liquids. In the excitement and bustle of caring for a new baby, however, you may not always notice that you are dry and thirsty. Some mothers take a drink of water just before each nursing. If your urine is not concentrated (darker in color and smaller in amount), but is pale yellow in color, and you produce large amounts, you are drinking all you need.

Constipation (hard, dry stools) may be a secondary sign of inadequate fluid. If you get constipated, increase your liquid intake as well as your consumption of fresh fruits and raw vegetables. And be sure you're getting enough whole grains (breads and cereals). Avoid fancy remedies. In fact, it is better to try to prevent the problem by starting during pregnancy to eat the proper foods and to see that you are well stocked with the necessary items to use after baby is born. Many new mothers have found that raw pears are especially effective for keeping bowels loose. Prunes, raw or cooked, and prune juice are also helpful.

Milk, Milk Products, And Other Sources Of Calcium

You don't have to drink milk in order to make milk for your baby. If you are allergic to milk, don't think you have to drink it during pregnancy in order to furnish your expected baby with calcium. Cow's milk is a good source of calcium but it is also a very common allergen. If there is a history of allergy in the family you might want to cut down on milk during your pregnancy as this is when some babies become sensitized to it. The reaction shows up after the baby is born.

Even if you are not sensitive to cow's milk, you may not care for it. It is good to realize there are other products that will provide the calcium you and your baby need. Yogurt, hard cheeses (such as cheddar, Swiss, and parmesan), and cottage cheese are good sources of calcium. Many people with milk allergies can tolerate at least small amounts of these. Tofu, a soybean product becoming more widely available in recent years, is also a good source of calcium. If you eat these products regularly, you will not need to drink milk.

In the fish family, very high calcium is found in canned sardines and canned sockeye red salmon, both of which are normally eaten with bones. These bones, unlike the thin sharp bones found in most fish, are usually round and soft enough to eat. They provide a nice crunch to the softer consistency of the fish.

Vegetarians who eat no dairy products may rely on legumes (especially soybeans), black strap molasses, sesame seeds, and the green vegetables (dandelion greens, mustard greens, collards, and kale) for calcium. Spinach and Swiss chard, though they are green and leafy and full of goodness, contain a form of calcium that is not well absorbed in the human body. Generally, meat and nuts are not good calcium sources but three exceptions worth noting are liver, almonds, and Brazil nuts.

Caffeine And Soft Drinks

Coffee and tea are all right in moderation. If you are getting most of your daily liquids in water, juice, or milk, and the rest in coffee or tea, you can probably consider it a moderate consumption.

Remember that soft drinks contain lots of sugar and no food value. In addition, cola and some other drinks, including cocoa, contain caffeine. *Excessive* caffeine intake by the nursing mother may cause a reaction in her baby. If you drink more than two or three cups of coffee a day and drink cola besides or eat chocolate frequently, you're getting quite a bit of caffeine. If you suspect it may be causing problems in the baby, cut down for a week and see if it helps. Since people do become addicted to caffeine, cutting it out abruptly may give you a headache.

The sugarless soft drinks are not good either. The sugar substitutes may be easier on the teeth but could be hazardous to your health. Remember—if you as a parent consume soft drinks daily, you can be sure your children will want to follow your example.

Supplements

Many people today report good results in preventing or eliminating certain deficiencies by taking vitamin or mineral supplements. Of course they are only supplements—they do not substitute for good food. They are also more expensive and not as much fun as food.

Your doctor may advise supplementary vitamins and minerals for you during pregnancy, particularly iron, to replenish and build up the stores from which your baby is building up his own supply of iron to carry him through his first half year of life. During the nursing period, your doctor, rather than prescribing vitamins or minerals directly for the baby (who does not need them while he is totally nursing), may prefer that you continue taking them.

Many mothers have reported that they get good results from taking brewer's yeast, which is a natural vitamin B-complex concentrate. Some feel that it definitely helps increase their milk supply; others report that it is a remarkable help in combating fatigue, depression, and irritability. Of course, the best way to combat these bugbears of motherhood is by improving your daily diet and getting enough rest. But if you feel you need extra help, brewer's yeast might be right for you. It contains not only the B-complex vitamins (often called the nerve vitamins) but also large amounts of iron and protein. Although the powdered yeast can be bitter, some stores have a palatable powder that mixes easily in juice or milk. Many find this more convenient than taking a number of tablets daily.

There are some mothers who report fussiness in their babies when they take brewer's yeast.

A Word About Dieting

Now is not a good time to go on a reducing diet. A moderate amount of extra weight in the form of stored fat can be quite handy, given the additional energy requirements associated with the increased activity of caring for a baby. Moreover, when breastfeeding you have the opportunity to use up the calories that are naturally stored during pregnancy in anticipation of the nursing period. The mother who does not breastfeed her baby must work off these calories in some other way.

An English mother and author, Margaret Whichelow, wrote in *Medical Opinion:* "My own personal experience was that any conscious effort to lose weight by restricting my calorie intake resulted in a reduction of milk supply before any reduction of my waistline. With an average intake, during lactation, of above 3,000 calories per day, I lost twelve pounds (slowly and steadily) during the nine months in which my baby gained ten pounds."

If by the end of the year you are not back to your original weight, you can check your eating habits again. An honest appraisal and a little common sense will help you to achieve a weight that is healthy for you. If you are a mother with a real weight problem, rather than go on a crash diet when you are nursing a baby, stick to basic foods, but cut down on the portions. Also limit or avoid sweets of all kinds.

Chapter IX

Special Circumstances

Special circumstances for mother or baby may sometimes affect breast-feeding. Special situations require extra knowledge and often, too, more patience and commitment. But take heart. Mothers have continued breast-feeding in almost every situation imaginable, and they have found that when the circumstances surrounding breastfeeding are less than ideal, the special benefits of breastfeeding become even more important.

New babies and mothers struggling with special problems after birth appreciate the emotional closeness and reassurance of their unique breastfeeding relationship. Breastfeeding lets them get to know one another despite the complications. In addition, breast milk's nutritional and immunological benefits are especially important for the baby at risk.

Problems may arise at birth or after breastfeeding is well established. Well-meaning friends and relatives, and occasionally medical people as well, may urge you to give the baby a bottle, arguing that it will be much

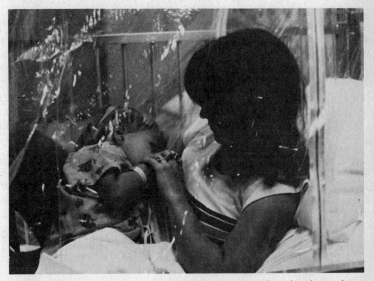

Mothers have used creativity, imagination, and determination to be with and nurse their babies. Pictured here is Kathy Shelling who crawled right into the oxygen tent to nurse her son D.J.

215

easier to manage. Some doctors mistakenly recommend formula feeding for sick babies or when the mother is ill. Artificial feeding, however, carries with it many risks and deficiencies of its own and can make things much more difficult for your baby, especially if there must also be long hours of separation from you, his mother.

In the case of a sick baby, this abrupt desertion can upset him so much that it slows down his recovery. At the very least, sudden weaning and separation may leave baby confused and unhappy. And even a few days of formula feeding exposes your baby to the risks of allergy, as well as the deprivation of important immune benefits found only in mother's milk.

Sudden weaning is hard on you, too. Your breasts may become engorged and painful, and this can lead to a breast infection. Of course, you'd miss the special contact you had with your baby when you nursed him.

The circumstances that might temporarily prevent you from nursing your baby are extremely rare. If you or your baby become ill, make it clear to your physician that you want to nurse your baby in spite of the special circumstances, and ask for his or her cooperation in bringing this about. Your positive attitude toward breastfeeding is a most important factor and one your doctor will take into consideration. Be confident that your milk is best for your baby if he can have any liquid or food by mouth (or even by nasogastric tube inserted through the baby's nose and into his stomach). Not only is breastfeeding safe for the sick baby, it is one of the best medicines for him. Frequently physicians lack confidence in human milk because of their inexperience with breastfeeding and may recommend substitute liquids. Your insistence on continuing to breastfeed whenever possible during a period of medical treatment can make a difference in the type of treatment the doctor may advise.

Your doctor may wish to contact La Leche League; you should encourage him or her to do so. Many doctors and nurses take advantage of the League's information and experience with mothers breastfeeding in unusual situations. Over the years, with the help of professional advisors, the League has compiled one of the best collections of medical and other information dealing with breastfeeding. If your doctor is not familiar with La Leche League and its Professional Advisory Board, you can tell him or her about the League's resources. Give the doctor a few samples of our literature and let him or her know how to get in touch with us. You'll also appreciate the support of your local La Leche League Leader. She may even be able to put you in touch with another League mother who has breastfed in a situation similar to yours. If your doctor is unwilling or unable to take positive steps to keep your baby nursing, feel free to seek other medical advice and assistance. Your baby's welfare comes first.

For additional information about breastfeeding in special circumstances see LLL Leader Pat Brewster's book, *You Can Breastfeed Your Baby . . . Even In Special Situations. (See the Book List.)*

BREASTFEEDING AFTER A CESAREAN BIRTH

Of course you can nurse your baby despite a cesarean birth. You will probably get off to a somewhat slower start, however, as a cesarean section is major abdominal surgery, and it will take time to recover. If you are going to have a planned cesarean, you'll want to find out in advance as much as possible about cesarean births. (See "The Cesarean Question.") Many mothers who have previously had cesarean deliveries have been able to have vaginal deliveries for subsequent births. Often the reasons for the first cesarean do not apply to subsequent births. But if it is necessary for you to deliver your baby by cesarean, or if you are reading this after you've had a cesarean birth, you can be confident that a cesarean birth need not be a deterrent to a happy breastfeeding experience.

Babies born by cesarean tend to be sleepier and more lethargic than those born without the aftereffects of anesthetics. It may take a few days for this sleepiness to wear off, and your baby may temporarily have a weak sucking reflex. Try to discuss the choice of anesthetics with your doctor. While a general anesthetic may be the easiest to administer, it will make you unconscious for the birth and drowsy for some time after. This may postpone your first contact with the baby you have waited so long to hold and nurse. Ask if you can be given a regional or local anesthetic so that you can be conscious for the birth and hold and nurse your baby soon afterwards.

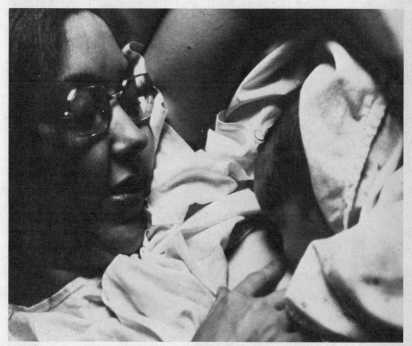

A cesarean birth need not interfere with breastfeeding. Beth Shearer nurses newborn Erin in the recovery room soon after her cesarean birth. (Photo by Ralph Underwood, courtesy of C-Sec.)

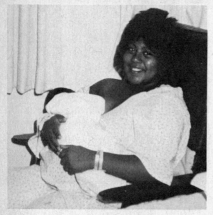
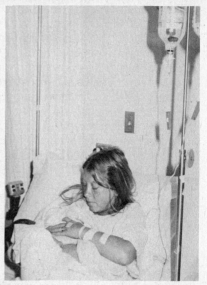

Mothers who have a cesarean birth find they must experiment to find the most comfortable position for breastfeeding. The mother on the left finds she is more comfortable sitting in a chair, while the mother on the right uses a pillow to support the baby for nursing.

Your milk will come in after a cesarean just as it would after a vaginal birth. Remember that breastfeeding is far easier than artificial feeding and will help a great deal to improve things for both you and your baby. Your recovery will be eased because caring for your baby will be easier. Having him close to you and knowing you are able to give him the best start will make you feel better and much less likely to feel blue or inadequate as a mother.

After a cesarean birth some hospitals routinely place the baby in the special-care nursery for twenty-four hours. However, if your baby is healthy and is not having difficulty breathing, your doctor can write orders to circumvent this. You may be able to have your baby with you in the recovery room and, with help, breastfeed the new arrival shortly after birth. Take the pain medication prescribed for you; it will not harm your nursing baby, and it may make you much more comfortable. Ask to have rooming-in, so that you can continue to nurse your baby early and often. Perhaps your husband can spend part of the day with you and help you care for the baby. You will soon find yourself satisfied and confident that your good mothering can meet all your baby's needs.

You will probably need help at first positioning the baby for nursing. Most mothers whose babies are born by cesarean find that nursing while lying down is most comfortable, especially during the first few days. The hospital nurse who brings your baby to you can help you turn on your side and lay the baby on his side at your nipple. Just let your breast touch his cheek, and he will turn and latch on. To feed from the other breast you will need to roll over. First, roll the baby onto your chest and hold him there securely. Then use the side rails on the bed to help you turn over. If you need to burp the baby, rub his back while you hold him on your chest. Sometimes the rolling all by itself will bring up the burp.

Loretta Bailey of West Virginia discovered that she preferred to nurse sitting up after her cesarean birth: "One of the nurses suggested that I sit propped up in bed and lay a pillow in my lap to keep the baby's weight off my incision. This arrangement was much more comfortable for me. After about three feedings Rachelle was doing a good job of sucking, and we seemed to be off to a good start." Other mothers recommend nursing while sitting tailor-fashion (cross-legged), with the baby propped up on pillows on their knees.

Don't worry if you feel awkward or uncomfortable during those first nursings. It takes time for mothers and babies to learn to work together, regardless of the birth experience. Focus on the joy you feel at your baby's safe arrival and look forward to the special days ahead. Concentrate on your own recovery. You will need lots of rest now and after you leave the hospital. Drink plenty of fluids; this will help your recovery and your milk supply, too. You will also want to move about as soon as possible. Hospitals have found that postoperative patients recover more quickly and with fewer complications when they are allowed to get up and walk as soon as possible after surgery.

And don't forget!—frequent feedings are always best, both to help bring in your milk and because the extra close contact and handling of the baby will stimulate him to be more wakeful and to nurse more vigorously.

When you get home remember that you must still rest and take it easy. A mother who has given birth by cesarean needs extra help with the housework, meals, and the other children. Tuck your baby into bed with you with a stack of diapers and a pitcher of juice close by. You and the baby can rest and nurse while you get your strength back and build up your milk supply. Your toddler may want to cuddle up with you too, especially after the long separation he's experienced while you were in the hospital. If you explain to him about your tender abdomen and guide him as he climbs on your lap, you may be able to avoid unintentional but painful knees in the stomach.

In many parts of the United States, mothers who have had cesarean births have organized support groups to share their common problems and experiences. One of the best-known is C-SEC, a support group for women having cesarean births. For further information, see the Appendix of this book. La Leche League can also help you through your local Leader, who can provide suggestions, support, and lots more information for you about breastfeeding and mothering after a cesarean birth. Or write LLLI.

Finally, Ann Hague of Georgia writes:

> Although a cesarean mother and baby may have to be more patient and persistent, the rewards are well worth it. My surgery healed nicely, and my baby and I are experiencing a beautiful relationship through breastfeeding. A cesarean birth can be an apprehensive time, but it should not rob you of the remarkably loving experience of breastfeeding.

IF YOUR BABY IS PREMATURE

Premature babies come in many sizes. Some may weigh two pounds or less; other premies may be fully developed and weigh close to five pounds. Some will be able to nurse soon after birth, but others will have to be kept warm and protected in an isolette and will not have the strength to suck. If your baby is very small, he may have to stay in the hospital longer than full-term infants, perhaps for several weeks. But knowing you can give him your milk will help you overcome the worry and fright you may feel about his condition. Providing *your* milk for *your* baby is something only *you* can do. If your baby is very tiny or sick, nurses at the hospital will feed your expressed milk to your baby through a tube inserted through his nose to his stomach, or they may use a bottle with a special premie nipple. Often, when the baby is ready to take milk from a bottle, he is able to start nursing. Kathie Patten of South Dakota writes:

> It was a good feeling knowing that I was able to do something for my baby. Giving birth prematurely had left me with subtle feelings of guilt, and so even though I could not give our baby the warm, loving feelings of motherly touch and sounds, I knew I was the only one who could provide him with superior nourishment.

Later on, breastfeeding helps make up for the separation you and your baby have experienced. Ann St. Clair of Iowa thought this was the most important reason for breastfeeding her daughter, Danielle, who weighed only two pounds and eleven ounces at birth:

> I finally decided to breastfeed because of the very special bond that exists between a breastfeeding mother and her baby. I felt that with Danielle separated from me for possibly eight weeks, we would lack the bond which normally is established between mother and child from birth. I wanted to make up for the love and security that only a mother can give to her baby. To take her home after being bottle fed by a nurse and then continue bottle feeding—I might just as well be that nurse. How would the baby know the difference?

Your baby benefits in many ways when he receives your milk. Research shows that milk from mothers who deliver prematurely adjusts to meet the special needs of their premature babies. The immunities in your milk protect your baby from illnesses to which premature infants are especially vulnerable. Human milk is easy for your baby to digest; it doesn't place any additional strain on his body as he struggles to adjust to life outside your womb. When you provide your own milk for your baby you are making a critical contribution to his care. Medical technology cannot match this, the perfect food for your baby. (Supplements such as vitamins are not necessary in the fully breastfed premie.)

If your premie is unable to nurse directly from the breast, start expressing your milk as soon as possible. Colostrum is especially important for him.

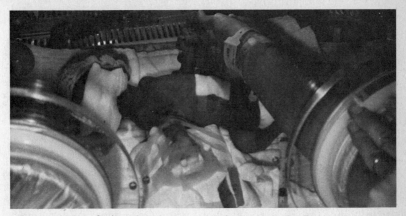

The warmth of a mother's touch is important to even the tiniest baby. Jane Munger reaches into the incubator to comfort her tiny baby Erin.

Remember too, that as soon as he is able to take anything by mouth (or nasogastric tube), your milk is best for him. Very frequent, small feedings (about every hour or two) are best.

Until you can put the baby to your breast, hand-express your milk or use an electric pump. (See "How to Express and Store Breast Milk.") Thinking about the baby, looking at his picture, and calling the hospital for a report on his progress will help bring in more milk. Milk is an emotional secretion, like tears. Don't despair if the supply decreases somewhat as time goes by. Your body doesn't respond to a pump the way it would to a cuddly baby. Your supply will go up again when you begin to nurse your baby directly.

Ideally, your milk should be stored in a refrigerator and fed to your baby within hours of collection without any kind of processing. Heating the milk destroys many of its protective qualities. If your milk cannot be fed immediately to your baby, it should be frozen. This will keep bacteria in the milk from multiplying and will do minimal damage to the milk's other components. And always remember that human milk is far better for the premie than artificial formula, and your own milk is best of all.

Mary Carson, former editor of LLL NEWS, tells this story of her great-granddaughter, Nicole, who weighed one pound, fifteen ounces at birth:

> During those early weeks she was in the isolette hooked up to a lot of life-sustaining and monitoring apparatus, and being stuck so often for the necessary tests. Poor baby! But lucky baby too, because her parents, Janet and Bruce, one or the other or both, were there with her every day, loving her, talking to her, patting her in the isolette, holding her when that became possible. And giving her Janet's good milk when that became possible, through a tube at first. Janet used an electric pump rented from La Leche League to furnish the milk, and to keep up her supply for the happy day which eventually came, when Nicole was able to take her nourishment direct from the breast—weakly and uncertainly for a while, but with increasing strength and obvious delight.

> We are especially thankful, not only for the medical expertise of Nicole's doctors, but for the sympathy and warmth with which these professionals encouraged and helped Janet and Bruce with all this.

Hospitals vary in the amount of support and cooperation they extend to mothers of premature infants. Many supply containers for the milk, make pumps available, and best of all, allow babies to go home early. In the United States some premies are allowed to go home, if they are nursing well of course, weighing as little as three and a half pounds. In other parts of the world even smaller premies are sent home, nursing well.

Unfortunately, not all hospitals or doctors are this understanding. Some even refuse to give the mother's own milk to her baby. If this should happen, ask for a consultation with another doctor, preferably one who is more current in his or her knowledge of the value of mother's milk for premature babies. He or she may be able to enlighten the hospital staff and influence the situation positively. A League Leader may know such a doctor or she may have some other suggestions. Meanwhile, keep up your supply by pumping regularly. You can freeze the milk for later use; you may need it during those first days of breastfeeding when your supply hasn't quite adjusted to the baby's demands.

Be persistent about keeping in touch with the hospital and doctor about the baby's progress. Most professionals are very understanding about the need for parents to know what is happening to their baby. They will also encourage you to come in and give your baby as much personal care and attention as possible. Even when the baby is in an isolette, he needs human contact, and you need to be with him, too. Linda O'Brien of Arkansas traveled forty-five miles to be with her son in an intensive care nursery, even without encouragement.

> No one seemed to understand the need I had for Jeff or the need I knew he had for me. On every hand I had people ordering me to rest—go home—they said—sleep! We can take care of your son. At times I felt maybe they were right and I tried. However, once home I could only weep. So I returned to the hospital prepared to stay. Jeff was crying when I arrived but responded to my voice and stroking. It was very evident he knew his mother even though he was only two days old.

The First Nursing

Finally the time will come to put your baby to the breast for the first time. Stroke your baby gently and talk to him. Express some milk to soften the nipple and to help the baby understand where the milk comes from. He may latch on and suck right away, or he may only half-heartedly suck or lick the nipple at first. Nursing is a new experience for your baby if he has become accustomed to bottle feedings. He may find this new kind of nipple confusing.

Sandy Countryman, from Indiana, tells what happened the first time she tried to nurse her premature baby:

> The doctor suggested that a close member of our family, who is an LLL Leader and experienced with premies, go to the hospital with me to give

me support and encouragement. It had to be someone who *knew this would work.* We went into an unused room with a rocking chair, I was trembling with excitement! I held Melissa close and talked lovingly to her, as I exposed my breast. I'd expected her to latch on immediately and nurse, but she didn't. She looked at me with her big brown eyes and simply enjoyed being held, caressed, talked to. I expressed a little milk and pointed up my nipple with my fingers, but she didn't seem to understand. She would turn to the breast, open her tiny mouth, and lick my nipple. She even tried to take it in her mouth several times, but she didn't know what to do with it after it was there. I tried to be very patient, as I continued to encourage her to nurse.

Then she fell asleep! My friend and I talked about many things, as I continued to hold my sleeping baby and watched the minutes and hours go by. She was so peaceful!

When Melissa woke again, she was hungry and seemed frustrated. She smelled my milk and knew it was there, yet did not know how to draw it out. Again it was gentle guidance and encouragement—again and again— and then she latched on. She nursed! It was only for two or three sucks, but she really did it! She then promptly fell asleep. But after almost four hours of trying, she had finally nursed!

It took a number of days for Melissa to become established solely on the breast. It also took much time and patience on my part, and I needed lots of loving support from my family and friends, but it was worth all our efforts. We have watched her grow into a wonderful little girl, who returns our love a thousand-fold.

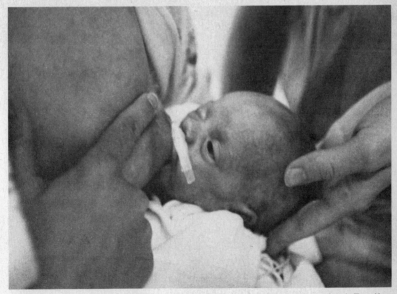

The first nursing for a premature baby requires patience and perhaps a helping hand. Tiny Ken Rudzenski is helped to nurse for the first time at the age of seven weeks weighing three pounds, four ounces. A nasogastric tube is still taped under his nose.

If the premature baby is reluctant to nurse at first, be patient with him. Another mother, Pam De Young writes: "It was important for me to remember that a premature baby is taught to suck from a bottle. A baby doesn't refuse to nurse to be stubborn or to hurt your feelings. Getting a hold on the nipple was a big problem for him."

During those first nursings spend lots of time cuddling and holding your baby. He will learn to know you as his source of love and security, and this is very important. After you bring your premature baby home, he will still need to nurse frequently, about every two hours—occasionally even more often. Switching him back and forth from one side to the other every seven to ten minutes each feeding will do wonders toward building up your milk supply, and the closeness and sucking will do wonders for the baby.

If he has been on supplements, ask your doctor for guidelines on how quickly you can withdraw them. Make it clear that your eventual goal is total breastfeeding. You will know that your baby is getting enough by counting the number of wet diapers. As usual, six to eight good wet diapers per day is a good sign. With lots of close loving care, your premie will gain and thrive beautifully. Fay Clements of Kansas writes:

> Was it worth the extra effort involved? Hand-expression for a month, many trips to the hospital? YES! Who could doubt it? Nathan is nursing right now as I write this. As I look into his happy little fat face, I'm so thankful I am able to nurse him.

For more details on premies write to La Leche League International for "Breastfeeding Your Premature Baby."

IF YOUR BABY IS JAUNDICED

Your baby may be only hours old, but more likely he is two or three days old. The whites of his eyes as well as his skin have a yellow cast. The doctor informs you that the baby is jaundiced and may refer to the bilirubin level in the baby's blood. A few cases of jaundice need treatment. This may include exposing the baby to daylight or bili-lights, or in extreme cases, exchange transfusions.

Jaundice is common in babies during the first weeks after birth, whether they are bottle fed or breastfed. In almost all cases, no treatment is necessary. The jaundice disappears, and the baby is none the worse for the experience. Even when treatment is called for, there are a number of ways to avoid any separation between mother and baby. You may continue to nurse your baby, and both of you can be assured of receiving breastfeeding's ongoing benefits. In fact, nursing your baby soon after he is born and frequently thereafter is an excellent way to keep jaundice from becoming a problem. Some authorities believe that weaning, even temporarily, is never a necessary treatment for jaundice.

Normal (Physiologic) Jaundice

The majority of jaundiced babies have what is known as normal or physiologic jaundice. In the normal course of events, new red blood cells are continually being produced and old cells broken down. The breakdown of the old cells produces—among other things—iron and bilirubin. The iron is stored in the liver to be used later in the manufacture of new red blood cells. Bilirubin, an orange-yellow pigment, is viewed, in the state of our present knowledge, simply as a residual by-product and must be disposed of by the liver. Before birth, this was taken care of by the mother's liver. But after the baby is born, his immature liver cannot always eliminate the bilirubin as fast as it is produced. The excess is temporarily stored in blood and tissues, giving the baby the distinctly yellow look known as jaundice.

In a normal, healthy, full-term baby, physiologic jaundice usually appears on about the second to fourth day and in most cases gradually disappears in about a week. Normal (physiologic) jaundice is not a disease, is harmless and has no aftereffects.

When jaundice is marked, most doctors order laboratory tests to measure the concentration of bilirubin in the baby's blood. It is wise, if the laboratory report shows an unusually elevated bilirubin, to have the test repeated for verification. No problems have been found in the otherwise normal, healthy, full-term baby when the bilirubin level is under 20mg/dl. Some authorities have written that 25mg/dl is a safe level in such babies with non-Rh jaundice.

Breastfeeding Is Important

Frequent nursing right from birth is important. It has been suggested that physiologic jaundice is occasionally increased in breastfed babies as a result of hospital routines that interfere with early and frequent nursing. Jaundice tends to be aggravated when the baby does not have ready access to his source of nourishment, the breast. Colostrum is especially important because of its cathartic effect. Bilirubin in the blood is picked up by the liver and passed into the bile, which goes into the intestine. The meconium (the baby's first bowel movements) contains large amounts of bilirubin. If it is not moved out it can be reabsorbed into circulation. Because the colostrum helps the baby to pass the meconium, it helps to prevent this reabsorption.

Giving the baby bottles of water "to flush out the jaundice" is not a good solution. Regarding this practice, Dr. Lawrence Gartner, who has done extensive research on jaundice in the newborn, reports: "Water or supplements given to newborns in the first four days do not affect the degree of jaundice." And, of course, water feedings often leave the baby less interested in the breast. Anything that interferes with nursing your baby soon after birth and about every two hours thereafter can increase jaundice in the breastfed baby. Frequent nursing is one of the best ways of helping the baby get rid of the bilirubin.

Kernicterus

The reason doctors are concerned about high levels of bilirubin is because of the risk of kernicterus. Kernicterus is a staining by bilirubin of certain brain nuclei, associated with some degree of irreversible brain damage. Kernicterus is rare, and is of greatest concern in the premature or sick baby with pathologic jaundice. In the otherwise healthy, full-term (non-Rh) baby, it has not been reported to occur at levels of bilirubin below 20mg/dl. Some authorities have placed this figure at 25mg/dl.

Pathologic Jaundice

In the newborn, pathologic (abnormal) jaundice is most commonly caused by Rh or ABO blood incompatibilities (hemolytic jaundice). While Rh incompatibility is becoming relatively rare, ABO incompatibility, a much milder condition, is still quite common. Your doctor will know whether or not to watch for either of these conditions by checking your blood type before your baby is born. In the healthy, full-term baby with Rh incompatibility, a serum bilirubin of 20mg/dl is the critical level. Above this level, there is danger of kernicterus. Various infections, congenital defects, or drugs given to the infant may also cause abnormal jaundice. In contrast to physiologic jaundice, abnormal jaundice is often visible at birth or within the first twenty-four hours, and the bilirubin level may rise quite rapidly. It is caused by an abnormal breakdown of red blood cells.

Babies with pathologic jaundice can and should continue to be breastfed, even with Rh or ABO incompatibility, for the same reasons given above.

Breast Milk Jaundice

An unusual form of jaundice, known as breast milk jaundice, usually develops five to seven days after birth and may last up to ten weeks or so. It is thought to be due to an unidentified factor in the milk of some few mothers. Physiologic jaundice is often confused with breast milk jaundice in breastfed babies. Since physiologic jaundice is usually diminishing by the time breast milk jaundice begins to appear, the effect is not additive to a significant degree.

In the first week, the critical level of bilirubin is the same as with physiologic jaundice, and light therapy can usually prevent it reaching this level. If the level rises early and rapidly toward 20-25mg/dl, it might be advisable to put the baby under the bilirubin lights sooner. This situation is most commonly seen when the baby has not had the benefits of early and frequent nursing. In fact, Dr. Marianne Neifert of Colorado observed that "no-breast-milk jaundice" is a more apt name for the condition. Mother's colostrum and milk are far better than water and/or formula.

The fact that your healthy baby is still somewhat jaundiced after several weeks or that the level fluctuates a few milligrams is no cause for alarm. By all means continue nursing him. Some authorities believe there is no reason for even temporary weaning on this account. The older the baby, the better able he is to process and excrete the bilirubin. With breast milk jaundice, as with physiologic jaundice, no known cases of severe or mild kernicterus have ever been reported in the otherwise healthy, full-term newborn with a bilirubin of 20mg/dl or less. Again, some authorities would set a limit of 25mg/dl.

Therapy—A Little Light on the Subject

Exposing the baby to light is a common form of treatment for jaundice. This can be natural daylight or daylight fluorescent tubes. (To be effective, the tubes must be new.) The light helps to speed up the elimination of bilirubin and, by keeping the bilirubin from approaching critical levels, may decrease the need for exchange transfusions in the infant at risk. When used for the treatment of jaundice, such lights are referred to as bili-lights.

The baby is placed under the lights—about sixteen inches away—with protective patches taped over his eyes. Bili-lights should be used only when necessary. In many hospitals the use of bili-lights involves routines which unnecessarily increase the periods of separation between mother and baby and cut down the baby's free access to the breast.

When there is no Rh incompatibility, the routine use of bili-lights in healthy, full-term babies when the bilirubin level is only in the 8-12 mg/dl range imposes a hardship on both baby and mother and should be avoided. Besides, at these levels, the lights are not very effective.

The earlier and more rapid the rise in the bilirubin level, however, the sooner light therapy is justified. In pathologic jaundice, light therapy is started at a lower level. The same is true for the sick or premature infant.

If your jaundiced baby must spend time under bili-lights, remember to insist on continuing to nurse at least every two hours, waking the baby if necessary. Light therapy does not have to be continuous to be effective. When you nurse the baby, remove his eye covers, cuddle him close, and look into his eyes. Holding and stroking him even while he is under the lights will provide needed stimulation and comfort him as well. You don't want him to tire himself out by crying, either.

You may even be able to have the bili-lights "room-in" with you and your baby. Anita Stanley, whose first two children were kept in the nursery under bilirubin lights, anticipated the problem with her third child.

"When the jaundice did develop, the baby stayed with me in my room, from early morning to late at night, despite the fact that he was under the bilirubin lights. We finally got to know the joys of meeting the baby's needs ourselves during those first few crucial days, with lots of nursing, cuddling, and touching. Rooming-in and early extended contact proved a real joy."

Home Treatment

Mothers are sometimes told that a jaundiced baby must stay in the hospital after the mother is ready to go home to "keep him under the lights" and to test his blood. However, if jaundice is the only problem in your otherwise healthy baby, assure the doctor that you will bring the baby back to the hospital for the tests and that he can be kept under the lights at home. Home is the best place for both of you whenever possible, and there is no need to delay your baby's homecoming for these reasons. Another mother, Linda Hoffman of California writes: "On the third day after his birth, we discovered Randy was jaundiced. His bilirubin count was 13 mg/dl. Our pediatrician wanted to hospitalize Randy and put him under the bilirubin lights. I could visit him only ten minutes every hour. The doctor had no understanding of our need to be together at this time. He also felt I should stop nursing Randy."

The Hoffmans believed that such drastic measures would disrupt the establishment of breastfeeding and the developing mother-child relationship. Linda and her husband consulted another pediatrician. She explains: "He allowed us to keep Randy at home, providing we would take him to the hospital for blood tests to keep track of his bilirubin count. To help bring down the bilirubin level, I nursed Randy every two hours and put him in daylight. This works about as well as the hospital lights. His count reached a high of 17.8 on the eighth day and from then on it began to decline until it was normal."

For natural light therapy, undress the baby, and place him in daylight. A nice bright room will do. There is no need to even open the window. **Do not put your baby in direct sunlight.** This is not necessary and could be dangerous. Babies have tender skin and burn easily. your baby must be protected from overheating and chilling as well as sunburn.

If there is no bright daylight, you can set up bili-lights at home. Use new, ordinary fluorescent daylight tubes such as those often used in kitchens. With such a setup, you and your baby can be happily together at home.

Premies and Jaundice

Up to now we have been talking about full-term babies. In the case of premature babies, especially if they are very small or if there are complicating factors such as severe illness, operative delivery, or a baby compromised by drugs or anoxia, intervention is advisable at lower concentrations of bilirubin. In a sick two-pounder, for example, a bilirubin of 9mg/dl could cause damage; on the other hand, a healthy five-pounder would be able to handle bilirubin almost as well as a six-pound full-term baby. In any event, **keep nursing,** or at least supplying him with your milk. If your baby is jaundiced, you can receive further help with breastfeeding by contacting a La Leche League Leader or La Leche League International.

MULTIPLE BIRTHS—MULTIPLE BLESSINGS

Can you nurse twins? Triplets? Yes! The League knows of thousands of mothers who have breastfed their twins. While there are fewer triplet mothers, a number of these admirable women nurse their trio. One surprised but determined mother of three said she could see no reason

Chris Rouse is delighted to have an armful of babies—Adam, Kelly, and Matt, breastfed triplets, are four months old.

why three newborns had less need for mother's milk than one baby, and so she proceeded accordingly. With triplets, the babies may need supplemental feedings in the beginning (preferably with breast milk supplied by other mothers), but eventually, many triplet mothers are able to satisfy their babies themselves.

All of the doubly blessed mothers agree that having enough milk is no problem. The tried and true maxim for breastfeeding holds for multiples as well as one baby—the more you nurse, the more your milk supply builds up. A mother who lived in Illinois, Lee Mueller, had twins who each weighed eight pounds at birth, yet she found no need to resort to supplementary bottles or to start solids earlier than usual. A Wisconsin mother of twins, Judy Latka, commented, "I've taken breastfeeding a baby so for granted that it surprises me when people are amazed at the twins nursing. That part is easy—it's the extra set of loving arms that I need." Judy was aware of the importance of nursing the babies soon and often, and she explains, "I had discussed my desires many times with my doctors, and it was well worth the effort. My hospital stay was brief. I went home when the babies were twenty-eight hours old."

Because twins often come in smaller packages, they need the protection of mother's milk even more than single babies. This thought encouraged several mothers to start nursing their twins even though they had bottle fed their older children. One mother breastfed twins after her nursing efforts with her previous six children had been short-lived. She says, "Can you imagine my finding the answer to relaxed mothering with my twins, when I never seemed able to nurse the other six?"

In planning for two or more (and we hope you have prior notice so you *can* plan), take the hints for easy housekeeping and mothering and multiply them to fit your needs. Cut your work to a minimum. Getting enough sleep will be your problem, not getting enough milk. However, your babies need the same relaxed loving attention that every baby deserves, and a tired mother is hard pressed to give this. If you possibly can, get some help with the house for the first few months. Your spare minutes should be spent resting and relaxing the way you like.

With two babies on the way, a Massachusetts couple, Marge and Jon Saphier, outlined a plan of action. Marge explains:

> We decided to try to relieve me as much as possible from the housework so I could dedicate my time to the twins and our four-year-old daughter. Fortunately, we were able to have a graduate student live with us. She was given room and board for making two meals a day, cleaning up the kitchen, and cleaning up the general clutter of the house. We also decided to buy food in bulk; our cellar now looks like a supermarket. I only had to buy fresh produce weekly. This not only cut down on my time in the supermarket but also reduced our food bill.

Marge offers the following five hints for functioning effectively as a nursing mother of twins: "(1) Get as much rest as possible. (2) Drink plenty of liquids. (3) Eat good, nutritious meals and snacks. (4) Have help with meals and household tasks. (5) Last, but certainly not least, contact LLL. Although I am a League Leader, I cannot tell you how much I needed and appreciated the support everyone in the League gave me."

Before her twin sons were born, Marge paid a visit to several mothers of twins "to see them in action and to determine if my planning was suited to our family." She says that "after each visit, I found my confidence and excitement increasing."

A question that was uppermost in Paula Johnson's mind as a new mother of twins was how to feed both babies when they decided to nurse at the same time. This Missouri mother tells of her experience:

> The first try was hilarious! If you're holding a baby in each arm, what do you do when a newborn loses the nipple? Wish for a third hand, that's what! I soon discovered pillows, and we've got the system down pat now. For a couple of frantic weeks, they refused to nurse at the same time. But with practice and the aid of pillows we finally discovered a lying-down position that is comfortable for all three of us. The nicest part is that now I can doze off while nursing, whereas before I sat upright until both were finished. That made for short nights!
>
> Looking back now, I realize I did little else but nurse the babies in those first couple of months. But now, here we are at four and a half months, the girls are both completely nursed, and believe it or not, things are going pretty smoothly for us (well, most of the time). I have a fantastic husband who helps by preparing breakfast and by accepting my relaxed

housekeeping. You can't be too hung up on those little details when there are twins to nurse. Our older son, Aaron, who is two and a half, gets in on the act by finding a vacant place around me and just snuggling in. He sometimes gets out his babies to nurse while I'm nursing mine. He's sure babies only come in twos!

Feedings at the breast are sometimes delayed for mothers of twins or triplets because a baby must be in an isolette. This was the case when Judy Blauch delivered her triplets in Capetown, South Africa. Judy and her husband, Paul, had been reassured that the boys were in fine condition though it would be weeks before they would be sucking well. Judy began expressing her milk at regular intervals while in the hospital. She tells of her feelings:

> Very, very little milk was coming out and I was becoming a bit apprehensive. There was an inpatient clinic in the mornings where the mothers would bring their newborns for the morning feed. The nurses were there to help provide support and information in a casual, friendly atmosphere. The mothers would sit in an informal circle while feeding, and I was part of this circle although I used the breast pump since my babies were still in incubators.

> At times, I would wonder if the supply would ever pick up to meet normal demands, let alone those of three babies. What kept me going was believing that once the boys were nursing full-time the supply would build up to meet their needs.

> Jason and Jeremy were three weeks old when they came home, and Justin was discharged ten days later. After Justin was home, breastfeeding all three went very well. I had a splendid supply for all three infants. I nursed two at a time and then, while one was being winded, I'd put the third one to the breast.

Yvonne Price of Illinois, whose triplets, Perry, Yvonne, and Alex, are now fourteen years old, was the League's first "triplet mother." Yvonne's helpful suggestions encouraged Shirley Bedeski, then living in Massachusetts, to breastfeed her expected triplets. Shirley and Jack Bedeski already had twins, who had been bottle fed. Shirley breastfed John, Jr., who arrived after the twins and after Shirley became acquainted with the League. She and her husband "often thought how wonderful it would be to have a second chance with twins." When the opportunity presented itself with the triplets, Shirley was asked, "How do you expect to breastfeed three babies with only two breasts?" Her reply—"One at a time."

Madeline, Daniel, and Jacqueline Bedeski were delivered by cesarean section. Mother and babies left the hospital after ten days. Shirley had arranged for help and devoted herself to these newest challenges in mothering:

> I had a woman from Child and Family Services come in and help care for the other children while the babies and I concentrated on rest and

recuperation and building up the milk supply. At the end of her two weeks, two of the babies were totally breastfed, and I only needed four to eight ounces of supplement a day for the third. By the time they were two months old, all three were on their mother's milk only.

From Texas, Patti Lemberg notes that the question she is asked most often is how she positions her twins for simultaneous nursings. She describes the system that worked well for her:

When they were tiny, each rested in the crook of an arm, bottom at my hand, legs extended along my thigh. If one wiggled out of place I caught the back of the diaper and pulled him back. In fact, I still use this position if they both want to rock and nurse at the same time. Another good position is sitting on the couch with heads in lap and bodies extended under my arms onto the couch. This one is great because both hands are free to hold a book and sip a beverage. When they are still tiny it's best to put a pillow under each for height and comfort. These days, we prefer to nurse lying down on their bed (a mattress on the floor), with David on the left in the standard nursing position for lying down and Alan on the right across my chest. That may sound awkward, but any position that is comfortable to all is fine. You need to work with the furniture and pillows until you find what's best for you.

The most valuable piece of furniture I owned during the first six months was a big overstuffed rocking chair my dad bought at a garage sale.

Patti also reflected on the trying times and the rewards she found in breastfeeding two:

They nursed about every two hours for twenty minutes at a time and slept one four- or five-hour stretch a day. The hardest time for me was the six-week growth spurt when each of them nursed every forty-five minutes. It was a bit much, but I just took the same attitude I had taken during the last weeks of pregnancy: "Next year this time they'll be toddling around, so cute—I won't even remember this day." I did have sore nipples, but I used lanolin and put the least hungry on the most sore breast. It only hurt for about two minutes while they were just getting started, and my nipples healed soon.

The most important advantage I have gleaned from the whole nursing experience is confidence. I know my way of mothering is good, and that makes me happy, which in turn relaxes me into a patient frame of mind, which can't help but increase my intuitiveness, which induces loving guidance rather than instant hysteria, fostering positive results which breed pride and confidence! It's a lovely merry-go-round. Now, with two toddlers running in and out, complete with sand and soil, it only takes me about three hours to clean house—including stops for getting drinks, kissing bumps, and loads of "help." When you're on the confidence-patience-relaxation-pride merry-go-round, it all seems simple!

The Lembergs pass on a simple and practical hint for new parents of twins. "A large oval laundry basket with a king-size pillow inside makes a dandy duo caddy at first."

A New York mother, Patricia Berg, considers her twins "Happy baby times two!" Pat and her husband, Ted, worked as a team in keeping their lively production going.

Ted took time off work when I returned home from the hospital. We spent a wonderfully peaceful vacation with our children. We didn't hire someone to come in after Ted returned to work. In retrospect I think it would have been helpful to have a high school girl come for a few hours a day to help with my two older children (then five and three) and do light housework. Those first weeks were tiring, but a patient husband who was willing to rock and soothe a fussy baby made it much easier.

Four little eyes gazing up at her tell a twin mother how much she is loved. Below: Michele McKinney nurses her twins, Joré and Sienna, by placing one on the other one's lap. (Photo by Harriette Hartigan.)

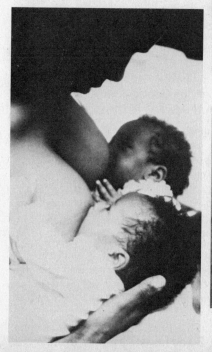

Alexa Navamore finds that pillows help her to position Peter and Meredith.

Sheila Jobe shows how to achieve the football hold with babies' legs under her arms. Emily and Elizabeth don't seem to mind a bit!

I got to know baby Megan very quickly since she slept little and needed a great deal of nursing and contact. My relationship with Joelle was a little slower in forming as she was quieter and it seemed we had less time together in the beginning. I realize now that I often hesitated to nurse the girls simultaneously during those early weeks. However, when I did nurse them together (their feet toward my back, heads on a pillow) I found that the rush of good feelings so familiar to the nursing mother came even more easily. There's just something about four little eyes looking up at you so absorbingly! I also found that nursing the babies together would bring on a very strong let-down whenever I felt my supply a little low, usually in the afternoon.

Whether to nurse the babies singly or two at once is one of those things that mothers work out quickly to suit themselves and their babies. Another League Leader and twin mother, Carolyn Johnson of Illinois, described her method of satisfying two hungry babies in a letter she wrote as an LLL correspondent to another mother of twins:

When time was a factor, I nursed the twins together, sitting in a rocker, with Jill on Judy's lap. Otherwise, I found it much easier to nurse the babies separately. I would awaken one about half an hour before the other was "due" to get up so as to avoid nursing them together. I also used a pacifier in case a half-hour nursing didn't supply enough sucking. Of course, I alternated the twins so that one wouldn't always have "first pickings."

If one was still hungry after nursing on one side, I would offer the other breast. Then the next one would begin on the breast last nursed by the other. Usually, the last to be nursed would be the first to wake up hungry. There were times when they would want to nurse again after only 1½ to 2 hours, which is to be expected, and this only served to increase my milk supply to meet their demands. Usually it would take two days of very frequent nursing and they would again be satisfied with an easier schedule.

I always made sure the twins were nursed at least every three hours and would awaken them if necessary. At night I didn't watch the clock, but kept them alongside our bed in a bassinet and buggy, and all I had to do was scoop the hungry one into bed, doze and nurse until the other one awakened, and then switch. This was a marvelous system for me because it gave me the sleep I needed. I also didn't change them at night unless they had soaked through their plastic pants. They never got diaper rash and didn't seem to mind not being changed at night.

For the first six weeks, I had a high school girl drop in from 3:30 until 5:30 P.M. to bathe our older children, ages 5, 4, and 2, and play with them while the twins and I "retired" to my bedroom for two hours of rest each day. My husband was a great help to me also.

Almost all mothers who nurse more than one baby comment on their hearty appetite and increased thirst. Some make a practice of eating an

One down, one to go! Germaine Weaver nurses Raina as Rhiannon sleeps peacefully in her daddy's arms.

extra meal before going to bed. Carolyn Johnson says;

> I noticed my appetite and thirst increased quite a bit during the first few weeks (I think I ate about six times a day), which is probably nature's way of providing the extra fluid and food for nursing two. I lost twenty pounds when they were born and an additional seven pounds in the next two weeks, which put me a little underweight. However, these pounds gradually came back so that by the time the twins were six weeks old we were all in fine shape.

Regarding the work of managing more than one baby, one mother of twins commented, "The rewards are great, but during the first three months you won't have time to think about it."

Another experienced nursing mother of twins maintains, "The problems of breastfed twins are twin problems, not breastfeeding problems."

With more than one baby, your attention is focused on the babies in a special way. Just watching them—noticing their differences, their uneven growth pattern, their inherent temperamental leanings—is an ever-interesting, ever-changing spectacular. It can give you insights and knowledge that add greatly to your competence as a mother, as well as to your enjoyment of your babies. As one of our twin mothers puts it, "I'm afraid having one baby will be rather dull after watching two bloom and grow!" Quads anyone?

For more information about breastfeeding and mothering twins or triplets, see LLLI's booklet *Mothering Multiples*.

SPECIAL BABIES

The baby born with a handicap or a special problem needs breastfeeding even more than normal babies do. The special baby benefits particularly from the special love, attention, and reassurance that go with nursing at the breast. If your baby has a special problem, contact La Leche League for information and help with breastfeeding.

Down's Syndrome

For the baby with Down's Syndrome, a loving home environment, with maximum interaction between baby and the rest of the family, will help to develop his capabilities to the fullest.

Breastfeeding, with its enhanced interpersonal relationship, demonstrates to your baby your love and affection in a very special way. Breastfeeding is especially important for Down's Syndrome babies because they have a greater susceptibility to infections than do normal infants, so the immunity factors found in colostrum and breast milk are especially valuable. And mother will find the same joy and delight in nursing a Down's Syndrome baby as she would any other baby.

The majority of Down's Syndrome babies are happy and playful. Though he is mentally retarded, the Down's Syndrome baby responds readily to love and returns it enthusiastically to those around him. He is usually a delight to the whole family.

Lucille Clancy wrote of her Down's Syndrome baby, "My heart said 'I love him,' my head said 'I wish it didn't have to be this way,' but soon Chad's big, happy smile thanked me a million times for the extra love I had given him."

Many mothers have said how important the emotional support they received from their husbands was in helping them adjust to having a handicapped baby. As Louise Wills put it, "I cannot underestimate my

Six-month-old Chad Clancy. "His big, happy smiles thanked me a million times for the extra love I had given him."

husband's help with Erika. Because of him, I have been more able to think of Erika *first* as a child, and *second* as a child with a disability." Remember that by drawing on each other for support and understanding, you and your husband will both grow stronger in the process.

A Down's Syndrome baby is often sleepy and may have a poor sucking reflex, so extra help and patience with breastfeeding is in order. Be calm and patient as he learns to suck and swallow. The rewards of nursing your baby are well worth the extra effort, so don't be discouraged if you encounter problems. With your loving help the baby will catch on.

Down's Syndrome babies sometimes have health problems that complicate nursing, but breastfeeding is nearly always possible and should be encouraged. For additional help be sure to contact your La Leche League Leader and obtain a copy of our booklet, *Breastfeeding the Down's Syndrome Baby.*

Above all, remember that this special baby who has been placed in your care will give as much as he receives. As Lucille Clancy put it, "Loving Chad is a continually growing·experience which teaches us love, acceptance, patience, and humor. There is a sadness in knowing that something is missing, like a piece of a puzzle, but there is joy, too. The added dimension that Chad has given our family will continue to enrich us as we live and grow together."

Cleft Lip/Cleft Palate

These two conditions often occur together, although a cleft palate is somewhat more common. The baby with a cleft lip can nurse at the breast even before surgery to close the cleft. With a cleft palate, an opening in the baby's palate (top of his mouth) makes it difficult for him to maintain the suction that helps him nurse. But unless the cleft is extremely severe, you and your baby can probably discover a way for him to breastfeed.

This does not mean breastfeeding will always be easy. It may in some cases be very difficult, and in a few, impossible. But even if your baby is unable to nurse at the breast, your milk is still very important to him. By holding him close to your breast as you feed him, you will be able to give him even more of the warm closeness of the breastfeeding relationship.

One mother used an electric pump for eight months to express the milk for her eighth child, giving it to her in a special bottle. As a result, the baby was in the best of health before undergoing the necessary surgery, and her recovery was quick.

Edith Grady found that if she held her breast in baby Andrea's mouth, Andrea, who had a cleft of the soft palate, could "milk" the breast with her gums and tongue. Edith later saw a study on breastfeeding that showed that suction plays a very *minor* part in extracting milk from the breast. Rather it is the jaws, tongue, cheeks, and gums that actually press the milk from the breast. Suction mostly serves to keep the nipple in the baby's mouth. This can be done for the baby with a cleft palate by his mother when she holds the nipple in his mouth and keeps his head close to her breast throughout the entire feeding. This was certainly true for

Edith, who writes, "Baby Andrea is nursing without suction. She even learned to grab hold of my breast and push it into her mouth herself."

If the baby is bothered by milk running into his nose during nursing you may have to stop from time to time for a breathing spell. These babies often nurse better sitting up, or lying on a particular side. Experiment in your first weeks of nursing with different positions. Be patient with this special baby of yours, as it will probably take him longer to learn to nurse.

Your baby will probably undergo some type of repair surgery while he is still nursing. Lip-repair surgery is usually performed while the baby is still quite young and receiving only breast milk. As Tammy Shaw discovered, a talk with your surgeon about breastfeeding and its importance to your baby's well-being can convince him to let you nurse again soon after lip-repair surgery:

> My husband and I showed Dr. Johnson the information about nursing. He enthusiastically agreed to try it "my way." He believes in the mother-child bond, and therefore understood my wish to nurse Peter after surgery. He assured me that if any stitches pulled out after nursing, it would not harm Peter in any way to quickly replace a stitch. He agreed it was important that Peter be comforted. After the surgery when Dr. Johnson appeared and saw that Peter was nursing happily, he commented that it was nice to see him calm and not crying so soon after surgery.

Cleft palate repair usually comes between one and two years of age. Your nursing toddler may not want to suck immediately after the operation because the roof of his mouth will be sore. He may want to lie at your breast or simply hold your nipple in his mouth without actually nursing. But as he recovers—in a week or so—he'll return to nursing, maybe with more enthusiasm than ever since the surgery has made it so much easier.

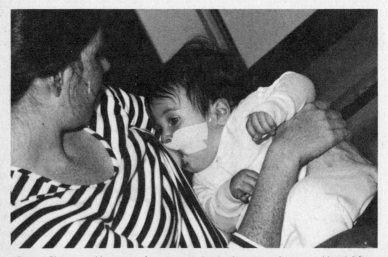

Tammy Shaw was able to nurse her son immediately after surgery for repair of his cleft lip.

Cystic Fibrosis And Other Malabsorption Diseases

Babies with cystic fibrosis, celiac disease, or other malabsorption problems do very well on mother's milk. In fact, such malabsorption diseases are often delayed if baby is breastfed. Later, when baby is older and the disease does begin to manifest itself, it is far easier to treat and manage.

Kathleen Winterer's son, Ben, gained weight steadily on breast milk despite cystic fibrosis; Ben was much healthier because he was breast-fed:

> At the time of Ben's hospitalization we were told we could expect one or two pneumonias his first year, and I am very happy to say Ben just turned two last month and hasn't had any yet. Of course, I like to think that colostrum's benefits in the beginning helped him through that first crucial year.

Whatever the baby's problem, it would be rare indeed if he were unable to nurse. It is still important to remember that if your baby is able to take anything by mouth, your milk is best for him. La Leche League has a great deal of helpful information about these and other special problems, so be sure to get in touch with LLL if the need arises.

IF YOUR NIPPLES GET SORE

Even though sore or cracked nipples can be very uncomfortable, they are certainly no reason to miss out on the advantages and pleasures of breastfeeding your baby. Sore nipples often get better in a few days even if you do nothing at all about them. Still, it's a good idea to give even slightly sore nipples some special attention to guard against their getting worse. You'll enjoy nursing your baby more if you're comfortable.

Length Of Nursing Time

Sometimes mothers are advised to nurse less often or for very short periods of time to prevent sore nipples. Actually, the opposite is true. After the first few minutes of nursing, when the milk lets down, the pain subsides. Taking the baby off the breast after only two or three minutes (before the let-down) makes nipples worse, not better, and frustrates the baby. Nursing about ten minutes on each side, as often as every two hours, is actually easier on nipples that are tender than nursing less frequently. The breasts don't get too full, and the baby isn't so hungry that he chews or nurses frantically on the sore nipple.

Use Of Ice

Many mothers have found that applying ice eases nipple pain immediately and also helps bring out soft, small nipples or the nipple on an engorged breast. Ice applied right before nursing will make those first few minutes easier for both you and baby. Simply crush the ice, wrap it in a wet washcloth, and apply it to the sore area. Or dampen gauze squares, put them into the freezer, and apply as needed.

Least Sore Side First

Always start a nursing on the least sore side. After ten minutes or so, after the let-down has occurred, switch the baby to the other side. If both nipples are sore, try to hand-express milk until you have a let-down, and then put the baby to the breast. (See "How to Express and Store Breast Milk.") Use whatever method you have found helpful to relax before nursing.

Nursing Positions

Change positions from one feeding to the next to distribute the sucking pressure to different parts of the nipple. Sit up for one feeding, lie down for another. Check how the baby is positioned at the breast. Does he take in some of the areola (dark area) as well as the nipple? If he has only the nipple in his mouth, he will have to chew and exert continuous pressure just to hang on. Hold the baby with his body turned toward you, and bring the baby to the breast so he isn't pulling on the nipple. Many cases of sore nipples improve dramatically with better positioning of the baby at the breast.

Use Of Pain Relievers, Pacifier

Some doctors recommend a mild pain reliever and vitamin C with lots of fluids during the time your nipples are painfully tender. Consult your doctor, and if this is not enough, he or she may prescribe a stronger pain-relieving medication.

Ten minutes a side may not satisfy all of the baby's sucking needs, especially if he likes to nurse for longer periods. After ten minutes of nursing on each side, if baby still wants to suck, try the pacifier. Think of it as a *temporary* measure. It is no substitute for mother. Continue to hold your baby while he has the pacifier. That way you can satisfy both his sucking need and his need for you. Remember, the pacifier is only for very sore nipples, and only for short-term use. As to the choice of pacifier, our only suggestion is to use a one-piece pacifier so there will be no danger of its separating, with the horrid possibility of baby's swallowing a piece.

Treating Sore Nipples

Between nursings, expose your nipples to the air. Leave the flap down on your bra, or, if you are comfortable without one, do not wear a bra during the period of soreness. A soft, loose blouse or T-shirt will let air through to your nipples.

It is possible that your sore nipples are caused by an allergic reaction to something you may be using, such as laundry detergent. Try changing detergents or using disposable nursing pads. Avoid pads coated or lined with plastic; they can cause trouble, especially in hot weather, by holding moisture in and keeping air out.

A mild ointment prescribed by your doctor may help heal the nipples. While most preparations do not contain ingredients harmful to the baby, be sure to read the label for instructions about removing the substance before putting the baby to breast. Vaseline or pure lanolin are usually safe, although lanolin can cause problems if mother or baby is sensitive to wool. Apply the ointment *very sparingly*. Too much keeps out the air that is necessary for healing and makes the nipple slippery and difficult for baby to grasp properly.

You will get better results if you apply a thin coat frequently throughout the day (after nursings), rather than if you put a lot on all at once. If nipples are cracked, apply a light coating of vaseline to the crack before nursing. It will soften the edges so they don't pop open while baby nurses. Gentle application of plain warm water is equally effective.

Avoid using alcohol, ointments containing alcohol, tincture of benzoin, soap, and other drying agents on your nipples. These only irritate the skin further. Be careful, too, not to get cologne, deodorant, hair spray, or powder anywhere near the nipples.

A Sunlamp May Help

Sun or ultraviolet light will also help to heal sore nipples. In tropical cultures where the breasts are customarily exposed to sun and air, mothers don't seem to have sore nipples as often. Direct sun, not through glass, has wonderful healing properties. You can also achieve this effect with careful use of an ultraviolet sunlamp.

Sitting three feet from the lamp, expose yourself twice a day for no more than one minute at a time the first day, two minutes the second and third days, and three minutes the fourth and fifth days.

If there is no indication of skin redness you may increase by one minute every fourth day and continue doing this twice a day until the soreness is gone.

If you do notice a redness stop adding minutes but continue at the same level for several days.

Then try gradually increasing, one half minute at a time, to see if you can tolerate a longer period.

If not, keep it at the level that is best for you.

Be very careful when you use the sunlamp. Keep baby out of the room. Cover your eyes with a towel or your hand. Time yourself exactly with a clock or oven timer. Don't guess. Handle the bulb with care; it gets very hot even after a short period of time. Read all directions carefully. And above all, be careful not to get a sunburn; that will aggravate your sore nipples rather than heal them. At the first sign of pinkness on the rest of the breast, do not increase the time. If you know that you are sensitive to the sun, you will want to be extra careful with the use of the sunlamp.

Thrush

If sore nipples persist or if you suddenly get sore nipples after several weeks or months of comfortable nursing, you and/or your baby may have contracted thrush. If your nipples get itchy and the area around them is tender, or if the skin becomes pink and flaky, you may have thrush. Thrush is a fungus infection that thrives on milk. It's not really serious, although it is a nuisance for you. It rarely bothers the baby at all. It may appear as white spots on the inside of your baby's cheeks, or his gums. Your baby may also have a persistent diaper rash in connection with thrush, and you may have a vaginal yeast infection. Thrush can be related to taking oral contraceptive pills or an antibiotic. It is more common in warm, humid climates. You may have it on your nipples even when there is no sign of it in baby's mouth.

Thrush may take several weeks to cure, but there is no reason to discontinue nursing. Your doctor may prescribe medication to be used in the baby's mouth and on your nipples. Or you may try this simple procedure recommended by one of our medical advisors: Dissolve a level teaspoon of baking soda in a full cup of water. Using a fresh cotton swab, thoroughly wipe the baby's mouth, especially the tongue, insides of cheeks, and gums, with this solution after every nursing. Be sure to use a clean swab each time and make a fresh glass of solution daily. Stir it before applying. At the same time, bathe your nipples after nursing with a vinegar solution—one tablespoon of vinegar to one cup of water.

Wash your hands thoroughly after using the bathroom, as this will help keep thrush from spreading. You must be persistent about treating thrush. Continue to nurse and use the soda and vinegar solutions diligently. If there is no improvement after a few days, consult your doctor.

Extreme Cases

Even with nipples that are cracked and bleeding you can continue to nurse. Don't be alarmed if you see blood in the baby's mouth. It won't hurt him, and the bleeding will stop soon. Only in very rare cases of extremely sore nipples should nursing be stopped for a day or two. You can hand-express your milk during that time and give it to the baby with a spoon. (See above section on use of a pacifier to satisfy baby's sucking needs.) When the nipples start to respond to treatment, resume nursing as soon as possible.

The best treatment by far for sore nipples or any other problem that may befall you is, of course, plenty of rest and a good diet. None of these should be too difficult to manage, and with their help, your natural warm loving feelings toward your baby will go a long way toward making you feel better, and healing whatever is hurting.

BREAST PROBLEMS

Plugged Ducts

It sometimes happens that a nursing mother notices a very tender spot or a sore lump in her breast. The first thing to consider is a plugged milk duct. (The milk is unable to flow through the duct.) Frequently this difficulty arises from inadequate or irregular emptying of some of the milk ducts. The baby may suddenly decide to sleep through the night or, if he's a little older, nurse sporadically throughout the day. Another possibility to consider is that a tight bra is causing a plugged milk duct by pressing on a milk gland. This keeps the baby from getting all the milk out.

Rest is essential at the first sign of trouble—often *lack* of rest triggered the trouble to begin with. Mothers sometimes just get too busy or lose track of time, and skip a nursing. Slow down, spend more time with the baby, and don't let too long a period of time go by without nursing.

Sometimes all that is called for is the removal of the dried secretions that are covering the particular nipple openings; this can be done by soaking with plain water. Soak the breast in warm water as you lean over a basin for ten minutes or so three times a day. (Try to nurse the baby or hand-express some milk right after the soaking.) Applying heat in other ways can also help, such as using a heating pad or well-wrapped hot water bottle. Some mothers are fortunate enough to have a baby-size hot water bottle that they can tuck into their bra over the sore spot.

Always be sure to let the baby nurse often and long, especially if the breast is lumpy or you notice any hard areas. An ounce of prevention is particularly worthwhile here, to avoid a breast infection from developing. Keeping the breast fairly empty and the milk flowing is the best way to improve the situation.

Breast Infections

The sooner you start to treat a breast infection, the better off you will be. If you should notice the type of soreness described above, accompanied by a fever or a flu-like "sick" feeling, you probably have a breast infection and should start the following treatment immediately. There are three basic rules to follow: **Apply heat** (see the suggestions above), **get plenty of rest**, and **keep the breast empty** by frequent nursing.

Your doctor may not realize that it is all right to nurse on an infected breast. Studies show that the baby is not harmed in any way by continuing to nurse. Antibodies are formed in your milk that protect the baby from the bacteria causing your infection. Sudden weaning is an emotional and physical shock, to both you and your baby; and the breast engorgement that would follow sudden weaning would only make the infection worse. According to a study of many mothers, continued nursing helps clear the infection much faster. An empty breast heals faster, and nothing empties your breast so well as your baby's nursing. If your doctor advises you to discontinue breastfeeding, let him or her know that you feel very strongly

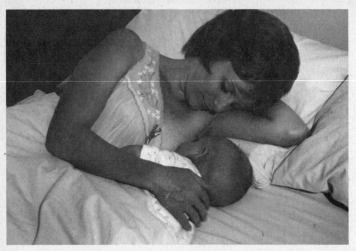

Rest is essential for a mother with a plugged duct or breast infection.

about continuing. Your firm convictions may change the doctor's mind. If not, get another opinion from a doctor who is knowledgeable and supportive of breastfeeding.

Be sure to get lots of rest. Go to bed if possible, with baby tucked in beside you. It's the tired, rundown mother who is trying to do too much who is most susceptible to breast infections. Take time out to relax. (Lying in bed worrying about the housework that isn't getting done does not count as time spent resting.) Eat well—small, nutritious snacks if you don't feel like big meals—and be sure to drink plenty of liquids. Being rested and well-nourished will also help prevent breast infections. You will want to change nursing positions from time to time. Until the infection clears up, let the baby nurse first on the sore breast at each feeding to be sure it does not get too full.

Loosen any constricting clothing around your chest and sleep without a bra. Send out a call for help to your husband or others to lend a hand with housework and such. Let everything go except the absolute essentials, and let some of them go, too.

Your doctor may prescribe antibiotics for a more serious infection. If he or she does, take the complete course of medicine prescribed. Too many people stop taking antibiotics as soon as they start to feel better, only to have the infection come back a few days later. Of course, antibiotics aren't always necessary. Used repeatedly, they may discourage our bodies from building up their own antibodies. If the doctor doesn't think you need a prescription, so much the better. Some doctors prescribe vitamin C (one thousand mg. four times a day) for a week or so, taken with plenty of fruit juice or water. This, together with the prenatal vitamins and iron your doctor may have already prescribed, should help a great deal.

On rare occasions an infection may worsen and develop into an abscess. (If you have caught the infection in time and treated it carefully as described above, this rarely happens.) The doctor may decide to open the abscess and drain it surgically either in his office or at the hospital as an outpatient. Even with an abscess you should keep nursing if possible. You may have to stop nursing on the abscessed side for a few days if the wound is very near the nipple, but you should continue to hand-express the milk from that side to keep the breast empty and promote healing. Do keep nursing the baby on the other breast, and within a few days return to nursing on both sides. For more details on sore breasts and breast infections, read LLLI information sheet *Sore Breast—What, Why, and What to Do?*

Breast Lumps

Most lumps in the nursing mother are inflammatory, due to plugged ducts or a breast infection. Some are due to benign tumors (fibromas) and only in the very rarest of cases are they due to cancer.

If you have a lump that does not go away in a week with you treating the breast carefully for a plugged duct or infection, we suggest that you consult a physician. Weaning is not necessary either for diagnosis or treatment (including removal if needed) of breast lumps. To empty the breast, nurse the baby immediately prior to examination and/or whatever procedure the doctor may want to undertake. Nursing may be resumed again right afterwards, except after a radioactive Gallium breast scan.

Jean Hart, from New York, tells about her experience of having a lump removed from her breast:

> I had chosen to have an in-and-out procedure under local anesthesia in the emergency room. My older daughter stayed home with Bill, my nursing toddler. I drove myself to the hospital. The lump was removed and the wound was stitched and bandaged. After an hour, I drove home.
>
> Bill wanted to nurse right away and I was thankful I had him to keep my mind busy while I awaited the news of the biopsy report. Because of the bandage on my left breast, he was willing to nurse only on the right side. The doctor told me not to nurse on the left side at least until the stitches were removed—about ten days—to avoid infection. *(Note: Depending on the location of the incision, some mothers are able to continue nursing on the affected side without interruption.)*
>
> So I hand-expressed from the left side once a day for about ten days. I was thankful to receive the good news that the tissue was benign.
>
> About twelve days after surgery, I nursed Bill on the left side when he was almost asleep. For two to three days it was slightly painful, mostly due to the low milk supply. As of this writing, seven weeks later, the milk supply is adequate in both breasts—so of course, Bill is nursing more often.
>
> What started out to be a traumatic and fearful medical emergency was turned into a calm and easily handled situation. I made sure that the surgeon included in his report to my gynecologist (who first found the

lump during my annual checkup) that I continued to nurse the child after surgery with no adverse effects or need to wean.

Other Breast Surgery

Previous breast surgery usually need not stop a mother from nursing her baby even if she has had a breast removed because of cancer. Breastfeeding will not expose the mother to any greater risk of malignancy, nor will it harm the baby. And since milk production works on the basis of supply and demand, one breast will supply plenty of milk for baby.

Mothers who have undergone breast augmentation surgery also are able to nurse their babies. However, in some cases of breast reduction surgery (depending on the type done and on how extensive it was), breastfeeding may not be possible. If the nipple area has been displaced and reattached, the ducts may have been cut through, and nursing would be impossible.

HOW TO EXPRESS AND STORE BREAST MILK

Feeding your baby breast milk from a bottle is not as good for the baby as breastfeeding, and in almost all circumstances you will be able to nurse your baby directly. But if you do find that you need to express a quantity of breast milk, a few suggestions will prove helpful.

Any effort to remove milk from the breast must attempt to duplicate what takes place when baby is nursing at the breast. Thinking about your baby, or, if possible, holding and/or nursing him while you pump will help stimulate the let-down. A warm shower or moist heat on your breasts will help you relax and let down your milk.

Hand-Expression

Hand-expressing your milk is convenient, economical, and clean—and not at all difficult once you get the hang of it. Don't worry if nothing comes out the first few times. You will soon get the knack. Watching someone else do it may help you understand how to hand-express, but you will eventually learn on your own exactly what technique works best for you.

Wash your hands before expressing your milk. Have a clean, sterilized container ready—preferably one that is not too large. Use a plastic one, since important immunological components of the milk can stick to the sides of a glass container and are thus lost to the baby. Cup the breast in your hand with your fingers just back of the areola (dark area), thumb on top and other fingers underneath, supporting the breast. Squeeze your fingers together rhythmically while pushing back towards the chest wall. Don't slide your fingers along the skin. Rotate your hand around the breast in order to get at all the milk ducts that radiate out from the nipple. After you have worked on one side for three to five minutes, repeat the process with the other breast; then do each side once more. This changing back and forth gives the milk more of a chance to come down

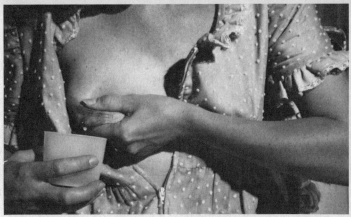

There is a knack to hand-expressing, but a little practice will get the desired results.

the ducts, and you will be able to get a bit more each time, just as you do when baby "switch nurses" at the breast. Hold the container just under your nipple with your free hand to collect the milk.

You will probably want to express your milk about as often as you would nurse the baby, every two or three hours.

Rosalyn Kalmar, from California, developed a unique method of hand-expressing for her premature baby. She describes it:

> After some trial and error, I arrived at a simple two-handed method which worked well for me. If you want to try it, you will need two small containers to collect the milk. Place them on a fairly low table; sit in a chair that is high enough so that your breasts will be about an inch above the containers; use pillows if necessary. Bend forward so that the nipples point straight *downward* into the containers. Cup the entire palm and fingers of each hand under each breast, placing thumb on top of the breast just above the areola. Squeeze the hand together, at the same time pushing the breast slightly upward; gradually increase speed and pressure as the milk begins to come. Rotate the position of the hands slightly from time to time to avoid excess pressure on one spot and to be sure that all the milk ducts are emptied.

The "Juice Jar" Method

This method of expressing milk gets its name from the type of jar that is used—the one-and-a-half quart bottle in which cranberry juice is often sold. You can make do with any jar of about this size, but be sure to pay special attention to the size of the mouth of the jar. It should be about two inches across—wide enough to cover the areola area but not much wider. When the suction is created, you don't want too much of the breast to be pulled into the opening of the jar.

Many mothers have found this method of expression to be helpful since no skill is necessary, as is the case with hand-expression. Also, since it can be set up with materials you can obtain easily, it is readily available and less expensive than other pumps. The milk is drawn out by suction, so it can be a particularly effective method when there is engorgement. A word of caution is in order, however—extreme care should be used (especially if there is a toddler in the house) since you will be working with a glass container and hot water.

Follow this procedure:

Thoroughly wash and rinse the jar.

Heat (almost to boiling) enough water to fill the jar.

At the sink, pour a small amount of the hot water into the jar. Wait a few seconds, then slowly fill the jar with hot water. After a few minutes, empty the jar. (Protect your hands; the jar will become very hot.)

Place the jar on a table. When the rim is comfortable to the touch (use your wrist for the final test), lean over and place your breast into the jar. To insure a good seal, wet your breast before placing it in the jar. (The mouth of the jar will cool faster if you wipe it quickly several times with a cold, damp washcloth. The interior of the jar should remain hot.)

With your breast in the jar, wipe around the base of the jar with the damp washcloth. The slowly cooling air creates the suction, and milk will begin to drip. To encourage the flow of milk, gently massage around the breast. Often the milk will come out in a spray. Once milk is no longer coming out, you can break the suction by inserting a finger between your breast and the jar.

If you plan to save the milk, pour it immediately into a sterile container for storing and place in the refrigerator or freezer.

Using A Breast Pump

Breast pumps are not as convenient or economical as hand-expression, but if you must maintain a milk supply for a long time without nursing your baby, a pump might be the answer for you. There are several kinds on the market—both electric and hand-operated pumps. Of the many types of hand breast pumps available, the least effective and least comfortable is the type with the little glass jar and a rubber bulb which you must squeeze. These are widely available, but we do not recommend them.

Several of the hand breast pumps are quite effective and convenient. A cylindrical hand pump designed in Japan is one of the most efficient. This is distributed in the United States by Happy Family Products. (See Appendix for information about obtaining these and other pumps.) Another effective hand breast pump is the Loyd B Pump, designed and distributed by a League father. It is hand-operated with a trigger action which you squeeze, similar to that found on spray attachments sold for some household cleaning products. The Ora Lac pump operates by suction obtained by a tube the mother puts into her mouth. The milk goes directly into a collection bottle. This pump is also effective.

There are several types of electric breast pumps available. You can usually rent one for the length of time you'll need it as they are quite expensive to purchase. Some La Leche League groups have electric breast pumps available for rent to mothers who need them in an emergency situation. Drugstores, hospitals, and medical supply houses may also have breast pumps for rent.

The most efficient and most comfortable electric breast pumps are the ones which closely imitate the pull and release of the baby's sucking action. This type of pump was originally designed in Sweden and is now sold under the brand names of Egnell and Medela. Other types of electric pumps, such as Gomco and Whittlestone, are also effective.

When using any breast pump, carefully follow the directions for cleaning and use that come with the pump. A little gentle breast massage is helpful before you begin, and even while you are pumping. Stroke the hand down the breast, from the outside toward the nipple, moving around the breast. Alternate breasts with the pump as you would with hand-expression. With an electric pump, you can do a little hand-expression on the other breast as the pump begins to work. This helps let down the milk.

Remember that breast pumps work by suction, so you must be careful since this pulling can irritate nipples and make them sore. With an electric pump, set the pressure on the lowest level. At first, limit the time you spend pumping to five minutes or less on each breast, about every three hours or so. Then increase the time gradually.

Storing Milk

If you are expressing milk for a premie or a sick baby in the hospital, you must be scrupulously clean. At least once a day you should sterilize anything that comes in contact with the milk—containers, covers, parts of the breast pump—by boiling in water for twenty minutes. Use small containers, preferably plastic ones.

Wash your hands with hot soapy water before each session and rinse thoroughly. If you are using a breast pump, wash the parts of the pump which come in contact with the milk. You might also want to rinse your nipples and the surrounding area with plain sterile water. (Anything stronger will dry and irritate the nipples.) After expressing your milk into a clean, plastic receptacle, pour the milk into a sterile container (also plastic), cover it, and if the milk will be given to the baby within twenty-four hours, store it in the refrigerator. Giving fresh milk is best, as both freezing and heating (sterilizing) can destroy valuable immunities. If you must keep the milk longer before feeding it to your baby, it should be frozen. If you want to store milk more than a week or two, it must be quick-frozen and kept at 0° Fahrenheit. (Unless your refrigerator has a dual temperature control, the freezer section will probably not be that cold. In that case, you should store the milk in a separate freezer.) If you are taking the milk to the hospital, transport it in an ice chest stocked with ice so that it doesn't thaw.

It's a good idea to freeze your milk in small amounts. You can always thaw more milk if your baby needs it, but you must discard any that is not used after it's been thawed. Once thawed, breast milk should never be refrozen. You can't save that milk for a later feeding. Do not let milk stand at room temperature to thaw. Instead, thaw it quickly by putting the container under running water, first cold, then gradually getting warmer until the milk has liquefied. You can then warm it in the container in a pan of water on the stove until the milk reaches body temperature. (It should feel slightly cool, not warm, on your skin.)

To Express Milk for Another Baby or for a Milk Bank

Because breast milk has been found to be so important for sick or premature babies, nursing mothers are sometimes asked to donate their extra milk for these babies. In many hospitals, special milk banks have been established for this purpose. If you are asked to donate your milk, you will naturally consider your own baby's needs first, and you will probably pump or hand-express milk to donate only after feedings. If your baby is a little older, you might be able to express milk from one breast while the baby nurses at the other. This is less time-consuming, but can usually be done only if you are using an electric breast pump. Other methods usually require two hands.

The milk bank will probably have its own set of instructions and may even provide you with an electric breast pump to use. If you are donating your milk for a sick or premature baby, you must be scrupulously clean in your techniques for expressing and storing your milk. If you, your baby, or any other member of your household has been ill, you should not donate milk until everyone has been well for twenty-four hours. For further information about donating milk, contact your La Leche League Leader.

When the time comes that you are no longer donating milk, cut down gradually on the pumping. You have built up a milk supply much greater than your own baby needs, and the sudden drop in demand might cause engorgement, just as sudden weaning would. Taper off gradually, simply by pumping out some of the milk whenever your breasts feel overly full and uncomfortable. Or, see if your baby will help out with an extra nursing. He'll probably be happy to oblige.

"LOSING YOUR MILK?"

Many nursing mothers at one time or another worry that their milk supply is too low—that they may be "losing their milk." They may notice that the baby is less interested in the breast, or perhaps he is fussing a lot and just doesn't seem to be satisfied after he has been nursed. Happily enough, there are a number of things that can be done to reverse this downhill trend and re-establish a good milk supply.

Once you have the following highlights in mind, you'll find it helpful to read the other related sections of this book for more information on the points we briefly cover here. We hope, too, that you can be in touch with another nursing mother, someone who is knowledgeable and supportive. You are always welcome to contact the League.

Many mothers worry needlessly about "losing their milk." Just remember, the more you nurse, the more milk you will have. Kathleen Wilkening and her son Peter seem content to do just that.

But first, a word of caution: many nursing mothers are fooled into thinking that they are losing their milk, when in fact there is no problem at all with their milk supply. These "false alarms" may be caused by a number of things that many people (particularly an unsure breastfeeding mother) are quick to blame on not enough milk. The following questions will help you determine if your situation is a "false alarm," or one that requires some positive steps toward increasing your milk supply.

• **Do your breasts suddenly seem quite soft, compared to the very full feeling you have had until now?** This in itself is no cause for concern. it may only indicate that the initial engorgement has decreased and that your body has settled into a more comfortable milk-making pattern.

• **Has the let-down feeling become less intense or perhaps disappeared altogether?** This is normal for some mothers. Some women will continue to have a strong let-down sensation for many months, others never notice this tingling sensation, and there are some who find that it subsides, or disappears completely, after the first few weeks.

• **Is the baby nursing more often, perhaps even wanting to nurse on and off all day long?** This is a common occurrence in the early weeks following birth, particularly those first few days home from the hospital. If the baby spent a good deal of the first week or so sleeping, he may just now be waking up and needing the nourishment that is so important to his well-being. The comfort of frequent nursing (and lots of body contact) also helps him adjust to his new world.

Then, too, some babies have a strong sucking need and don't seem to be happy anyplace but at mother's breast. If you have such a baby, by all means nurse him as often as he seems to need it. As he gets a little older this need will become less intense, but in the meantime you can feel good knowing that breastfeeding brings your baby such comfort and security. And remember the more you nurse, the more milk there will be.

• **Is baby nursing only five to ten minutes on a side, instead of the fifteen minutes or longer that he used to nurse?** At this point he may simply have become a more proficient nurser, able to get the milk he needs more quickly than he did as a newborn. If he is gaining well, this is no cause for worry.

• **Are you leaking less milk than you were, or not leaking at all?** Some women leak during or between feedings for many months, while others leak only in the early weeks or never at all. This is an individual variation from mother to mother, and is no indicator of a good milk supply or the lack of it.

• **Does the baby seem to be extra fussy?** Most people are quick to assume that a fussy baby is a hungry baby, but this is not necessarily the case. Some babies are simply unsettled during the early weeks and fuss a good deal. (It is comforting to note, though, that breastfed babies on the whole tend to be contented as long as there are frequent nursings and plenty of body contact.) Lots of patience and tender loving care until this period passes is the best remedy for such a baby.

Most babies experience a growth spurt at about six weeks, and again at about three months, although your baby's growth spurts may come somewhat earlier or later. If it is a growth spurt that is causing your baby to fuss and seem dissatisfied after nursing, a couple of days of more frequent nursings will bring your milk supply up to meet his increased demands.

If your baby has six to eight wet diapers a day, he is getting plenty of milk. (This is not a reliable guide if baby is getting bottles of water.) If baby continues to be fussy for no apparent reason, take a quick inventory of your diet. Occasionally a baby will be sensitive to something the mother is eating, making him irritable and restless.

When The Milk Supply Is Down: A Quick Checklist
If you decide that your milk supply is indeed low, it is a fairly simple matter to increase it. Plan on spending a couple of days at home relaxing, doing little else except nursing the baby every two hours or so for about ten minutes on each side, with perhaps one longer stretch between feedings during the night. "Switch nursing" can be very helpful to increase the milk supply. This means nursing from each side at least twice at each feeding, switching back and forth.

Remember the golden rule of breastfeeding: the more often you nurse, the more milk you will have. Within forty-eight hours of your stepped-up nursing, you should notice an increase in your milk supply.

It is important for you to know what caused your milk supply to taper off in the first place, so that the problem doesn't repeat itself. Mostly, you need to be aware of what helps and what hinders your efforts. By answering the following questions, you will probably find a clue to why you are having difficulty. This list is based on one compiled by a La Leche League Leader in Colorado, who designed it to quickly help the mother whose first call to the League begins with the anxious remarks: "I don't have enough milk! I'm drying up! I'm losing my milk!"

- **Are you giving both breasts at each feeding?** Nursing at least every two to three hours?
- **Are you letting your baby nurse as long as he seems interested, allowing him to pause and rest, without watching the clock?**
- **Are you drinking plenty of liquids?**
- **Are you eating well and regularly?**
- **Do you understand "supply and demand"?** This means that the more milk your baby takes from you, the more milk your body wil produce.
- **Is your baby getting solids too soon, before about six months of age?**
- **Do you know that babies have "frequency days" when they nurse more often than usual to bring in more milk for their expanding needs?**
- **Is your baby getting bottles of water or juice, or sucking a lot on a pacifier?** Any of these things may make him less interested in breastfeeding.
- **Are you comparing your breastfed baby with a bottle-fed baby?** Their daily feeding schedules will be dissimilar because breast milk digests more quickly, so while the breastfed baby benefits more from his mother's milk, he is hungry sooner than the bottle-fed baby next door.
- **Are you taking birth control pills?** The Food and Drug Administration has warned that they should not be taken by breastfeeding mothers. One of their many side effects is a reduction in the milk supply.
- **Are you doing too much as a new mother?** Newborn babies leave their mothers with little time or energy for other demanding activities.
- **Have there been any upsetting incidents in your life, or a situation that is causing you to feel tense?** Soon after such an incident, your milk may be slower to let down, but this is a temporary situation.
- **Are you getting rest and relaxation, and doing something that you really enjoy?** A happy, relaxed mother produces more milk than one who is tense and upset, and she has a more content baby to boot!

Just keep remembering—with frequent nursings your milk supply will increase to meet your baby's needs, even though you may have only a little milk now. A confident attitude and improved nursing know-how will have a remarkable effect on your milk production in a very short time—a day or two, or maybe three. So read on, relax, nurse, and enjoy your baby!

RELACTATION

In the usual course of events, a mother's body is prepared for lactation during pregnancy, and the birth of the baby signals the mother's breasts to begin producing milk. With the baby's eager sucking, the milk continues to be produced. If the baby is not put to the breast after birth, or if breastfeeding ceases soon afterward, the milk "dries up." Relactation is the process by which a mother is able to re-establish her milk supply several weeks or months after lactation has stopped. It is a difficult and time-consuming process, but it can be done. This is possible because the sucking of the baby stimulates milk production. In fact, in certain very special circumstances, some mothers have been able to establish a milk supply for a baby without the impetus of pregnancy and birth.

Often mothers who have attempted relactation have been those whose babies could not tolerate any artificial formula and needed breast milk to survive. One of the first mothers helped to do this by La Leche League was Lorraine Bormet. Her story is included under the section titled "Allergies."

Beth Roberson from Tennessee tells of her experience with relactation:

I started breastfeeding my son Zachary in the hospital. My pediatrician was not supportive of breastfeeding and told me I should give it up (it would be best for the baby!). I followed his advice and quit breastfeeding after only seven days. I felt miserable about it but thought that the doctor must know what was *best*.

When Zachary was seven weeks old, he developed severe diarrhea and diaper rash. After almost four weeks of trying different formulas, Pedialyte, and medicines, his new doctor, an excellent, supportive pediatrician, said we had gone as far as we could go with different formulas and suggested that relactation was probably the only solution.

I contacted Marty Wilson of La Leche League, and she assured me it could be done, but would require time and patience. She also arranged for donors to give us their milk until mine came in. I used a Lact-Aid Nursing Supplementer to give Zac the donated milk.

The first day I gave Zac the donor milk the diarrhea stopped entirely. It was a miracle! During the second week I began to express a few drops of milk and was delighted. By the end of the second week Carol Blanton, another Leader, thought the baby was getting too much donor milk. She suggested I try cutting off the donor milk entirely for a day or two, with permission from the baby's doctor, to see if my milk increased. The doctor agreed. The next few days were rough going, to say the least, but things began to improve daily. By the next week Zac had gained seven ounces, and at the end of the week the doctor had me stop all supplements. I was finally on my own!

Relactation was a difficult process, harder than I had anticipated. I got discouraged many times, but the Leaders, the mothers who donated their milk, and Dr. Gomez, Zac's pediatrician, gave me so much moral support that I did make it at last.

Audrey Brellisford was able to nurse her adopted son, Finn, even though she had never been pregnant.

Zac is now thriving and gaining weight and is quite a happy and contented baby. We are both very grateful to La Leche League and everyone involved in helping us.

After hearing stories of mothers who had successfully re-established milk supplies for their allergic babies, mothers who were planning to adopt babies began to wonder if they could also provide breast milk for their adopted babies. The first few adoptive mothers who were in touch with LLL were nursing their toddlers when they adopted their new babies. By putting the young baby to their breast often, they were able to increase their milk supply to fully meet the infant's needs.

Carol Marino from Connecticut tells us about her experience when she adopted a baby girl from Korea:

When Carol Ann Ree Ja, just four months old, arrived to join her homemade sister, Judea Vera, she was tired and hungry. I put her to my breast in the car, and she nursed beautifully all the way home from New York airport to Waterbury. It was surprising to me that she took to nursing so readily, since she had been bottle fed from the time she was born until she came home to us.

Sister Judea, seventeen months when Carol Ann Ree Ja arrived, had been gradually weaning herself and was only nursing occasionally—maybe once every week or so. I realized before her new sister arrived that I'd have to build up my milk supply, and I started pumping a month ahead of time—five minutes on each breast four times a day the first week, eight times a day the second week, and from then on each hour during the day, until the last three days, when I pumped five minutes on each breast every two hours around the clock. So there was plenty of milk when Carol Ann Ree Ja arrived.

Judea stepped up her nursing when the baby came home, and during the first month I often nursed two children at the same time, one on each breast. Finally one day Judea pointed authoritatively to my breast and announced, "Baby's!" She never nursed again.

Encouraged by these success stories, other mothers planning to adopt babies became interested in nursing them. It was found that even mothers who had never been pregnant were able to establish at least a partial milk supply so that their babies were receiving some breast milk even though they also received some formula or other supplements.

Jo Young, from England, describes her experience:

My introduction to La Leche League was both sudden and intense. I spent every moment of the first two weeks of my endeavor to breastfeed Peter, our adopted three-week-old baby, with two of the Leaders here in Britain, Suzanne Mudge and Sally Nilsen.

With great effort and sacrifice from a small handful of people I succeeded in my effort to induce lactation, and incredibly, Peter was completely nourished and sustained at my breast by the time he was three and a half months old. He remained solely breastfed from then until he began to experiment with solids at about six months. During the early months when he was basically dependent on formula, Peter looked rather fragile and unwell, suffering from constant colds. I am convinced that the breast milk he has had is responsible for the marvelous changes in his looks. His skin has cleared and he is now a large, bouncy, blooming, typical breastfed baby.

I can never hope to convey totally the depth of my gratitude to the friends who helped us. I think they realize the wealth of the gift they have given Peter and me.

Apparently Peter is the first adopted baby in Britain to be completely breastfed. I hope he will be the first of many more.

The practice of nursing adopted babies has become so well accepted that some adoption agencies hold meetings for the mothers who plan to breastfeed. Mothers report that the extra effort required in building a milk supply for their adopted babies is well worth it. The closeness and intimacy of the breastfeeding relationship is extremely important to these adoptive mothers. From Arizona, Anne Sanger writes:

Lisa is one year old this month. It seems like such a short time since we took her from an adoption agency into our family. She was four days old then and seemed so small. Now she is a happy, beautiful one-year-old.

I was able to nurse Lisa with the help of the Lact-Aid Nursing Supplementer. I did a lot of preparation prior to her arrival. Seven days after nursing her using the Lact-Aid, my milk came in. When Lisa was ten months old, we were able to discontinue using the supplementer. We are still a happy nursing couple.

It is difficult for me to explain what it means to me to be able to nurse Lisa.

I wanted to give her the gift of love and the wonderful way of communicating that the nursing relationship opens to mothers.

As I look back on this last year, I know that breastfeeding my adopted child was not the easiest thing I ever did in my life, but it has been one of the most rewarding. We feel very fortunate to be the parents of such a happy child.

The Basic Technique

If you are a mother who is interested in relactating, you can't do better than to learn as much as possible ahead of time—both from printed material and through a knowledgeable nursing mother. The information here is intended only as a brief explanation of the process. The basic technique for relactation is to encourage the baby to nurse as often as possible. This is how you stimulate the breasts to produce milk. Adoptive mothers can often begin establishing a milk supply before they have their babies. It helps, of course, to know when you'll get your baby. Use hand-expression for three to five minutes on each breast several times a day, gradually increasing the number of times per day. If this is kept up faithfully, the breast will begin to produce milk—usually in two to six weeks. It may only be a few drops at first, but if there is some milk, there will soon be more.

One of the most difficult aspects of relactation is getting the baby interested in sucking at the breast if he has been used to bottles for several weeks or months. This requires a great deal of patience and determination. The mother who is attempting to relactate needs a generous amount of support and encouragement. It's a good idea to be in touch with a La Leche League Leader who can provide further information.

You will need to give the baby some formula or donated breast milk in the beginning. You should nurse the baby first, for as long as he is willing, before you offer the supplement. Many mothers eliminate bottles completely and give the supplement with a spoon or eyedropper. The eyedropper can be slipped into the baby's mouth as he nurses to keep him interested in sucking at the breast. There is also a nursing supplementer, called the Lact-Aid, which allows the baby to receive his supplement as he nurses at the breast. (See the Appendix.)

If you use a bottle for the supplement, you'll want to avoid the standard bottle nipple with large holes. Find a nipple that more closely resembles the "real thing," and be sure the holes are not too large.

In addition to putting the baby to the breast as often as possible and giving the supplemental milk (either donated breast milk or formula) only after a feeding (or in small amounts during a feeding with an eyedropper or the Lact-Aid Nursing Supplementer), you will gradually be able to cut back on the total amount of supplement you give the baby in a day. You want him to be hungry enough so he will continue to keep taking the breast. It is a delicate balancing act—you want him to be somewhat hungry, but you do not want him to lose weight.

While you are establishing a milk supply, it is very important to check the baby's weight on a weekly basis to be sure he continues to gain, even if only a small amount.

The mother who is relactating finds that for a time she is working almost around the clock feeding her baby as often as she can. Of course, the more often the baby nurses, the more he benefits from his mother's milk, and the more milk there will be waiting for him the next time. The early weeks can be very trying, but from then on, you coast!

For more detailed information about establishing a milk supply for an allergic or adopted baby, contact your local La Leche League Leader or write to LLLI.

SLOW WEIGHT GAIN

Baby Pamela weighed seven pounds at birth. On leaving the hospital when four days old, she weighed only six and a half pounds. Pam added ounces slowly, very slowly. When she was placed on the scale at seven weeks, the indicator only showed seven pounds, two ounces.

Such a slow weight gain is a warning signal. It calls for a close look at baby, mother, and the nursing routine. If you find yourself in this situation, don't rush to replace the real thing, breastfeeding, with an artificial substitute. Adjustments can be made, and nursing, with its long-term benefits, can continue.

Why does a baby gain so slowly? There may be one simple explanation or a combination of reasons for such a state of affairs. Could illness be causing the problem? Often, the baby who is not feeling well does not nurse well. Of course, the baby's doctor will check him over thoroughly to be assured that an illness is not the cause of the problem. And if the baby *is* sick, nursing is of even more value. An all-out effort to maintain breastfeeding, along with appropriate treatment for the illness, will speed recovery.

Is there a pacifier in the picture? It is *not* mother's—or baby's—"best friend." A pacifier will quiet a baby, but the nourishment factor is nil. (See "About the Pacifier.") Is the baby getting water between feedings? Bottles of water reduce the amount of time at the breast. One mother's first three babies all lost weight the first month of breastfeeding, yet when she eliminated water with her fourth child, there was no weight loss. Supplemental bottles can also cause nipple confusion causing the baby to suck less vigorously at the breast.

Time at the Breast

How often is the baby being nursed? Not nursing often enough is probably the most common cause of low weight gain. Breast milk is quickly digested, and frequent nursings are easier for the baby and provide him with a steady supply of nutrients. If slow weight gain is a problem, it's important that you nurse every two hours, with perhaps one longer stretch of about four hours at night. If a feeding begins at eight o'clock, put the baby to the breast again at ten, regardless of how long the eight o'clock nursing lasted. Plan to nurse the baby ten to twelve times in each twenty-four-hour period.

"Switch Nursing"

If your baby is not gaining well, always nurse on both breasts at each feeding, and change breasts several times during the course of a feeding. This means that you'll nurse on one side for ten minutes or a little longer (if baby is nursing steadily), then switch to the other side. After ten minutes or so on the second side, go back to the first side, and repeat the process. Mothers find that such "switch nursing" is an excellent way to keep baby interested in nursing longer.

The Extra-Placid Baby

Every once in a while, the slow gainer is a placid baby, a quiet little soul who regularly sleeps for four or five hours at a time. Some of these "storybook babies" gain beautifully, and there is nothing to worry about. But often this little sleeper isn't gaining well because he just isn't nursing as much as he should be. If your baby is one who sleeps a lot, you may be thinking, "Such a good baby." But if he seems even more quiet as time goes on, don't be lulled by such placidness. Keep a careful check on the number of wet diapers. You should be getting at least six to eight really wet diapers a day. As for weight gain, a pound a month is acceptable; less demands your attention.

No one knows for sure why some little ones are so placid—too undemanding, really, for their own good. It may be related to the birth experience, or perhaps it is the aftermath of a delay in starting breast-feeding. What we do know is that such a downhill slide can be reversed. Mother takes the initiative and actively encourages her baby to nurse more often. With a sleeper, you have to become a clock-watcher. For a few days or weeks, you are the gentle prod encouraging your baby to nurse more often. Handling baby and nursing him often helps to rouse him. He needs this stimulation as much as he needs your good breast milk. It all works together to get him going.

Encouraging the Sleepy Baby

At first, baby may be inclined to sleep rather than nurse when you pick him up for a feeding. (See "Sleeping or Screaming?" for some hints on rousing the napping infant.) To keep baby actively nursing, strip him down to a diaper and hold him, skin-to-skin, next to you. (If you are chilly, throw a blanket loosely around the two of you.) Rub his back or feet. Joggle him a bit if he dozes. Talk or sing to him. One mother of a sleeper said that every time her baby opened his eyes during a nursing, she'd say loudly, "Yes! Good! You can do it!" Each time he responded to her words or the sound by nursing well for another minute or so. Whether it was mother's pep talks or her all-around attentive mothering we can't say, but baby's thinness was soon replaced by dimpled elbows and chunky legs.

If baby is disinterested in nursing, try whetting his appetite by expressing some milk directly into his mouth. If need be, fill an eyedropper with milk that you have already expressed and drop some into the corner of his mouth to spur him on.

An Illinois mother, Ruth Ann Hladish, had nursed all her other children and had been a La Leche League Leader for years when she personally experienced a slow gaining baby with son Tommy's arrival. Tommy had had a complete blood exchange at birth, and breastfeeding had been suspended for a few days, so mother and newborn had less than an ideal start. "Tommy no longer had the rooting instinct," Ruth Ann said. "He was content to sleep with my nipple in his mouth. For a number of days, I devoted myself to getting Tommy to nurse. There was no question in my mind of giving up, but I did talk to myself a lot. I kept repeating all of those things I had been saying for years to other mothers who called for help. And it worked. Tommy is now fifteen months old, still breastfeeding, healthy, and a joy to all of us."

Tiny and Fussy

Occasionally, a baby is wakeful—fussy even—and spends a considerable amount of time at the breast, but still lags in the weight department. The question then is—how well is the baby nursing? Is he taking the nipple well? He should be getting at least some of the areola, the dark area surrounding the nipple, into his mouth. The baby who sucks in a fluttery manner on the end of the nipple will get the milk that has already collected in the breast, but he will not bring on the additional milk that comes when he draws the nipple further into his mouth and nurses vigorously. He isn't getting as much milk as he should, nor is it the richest milk, that with the highest fat content.

If you suspect that your baby has such a sucking habit, look carefully at how he is nursing. Most of the time, a mother need not give a second thought to position and such things once past the first few nursings, but when there is a concern about the baby's weight gain, the extra attention to these details can be most worthwhile.

When nursing, position baby so that he is facing the breast and does not have to turn his head in order to take the nipple. (See "A Nursing Session in Slow Motion.") Hold his body close to you, making sure that his nose is clear so that he can breathe easily. Be sure to press a little more firmly with the finger above the nipple in order to make it point upward when you give it to him.

Be patient with him. He'll soon be nursing with the best of them. Many suggestions for the sleepy baby work well here, too—lots of skin contact, frequent nursings, and switch nursing.

Checklist For Mother

If your baby is slow to put on weight, we suggest that you weigh him about once a week to assure yourself that he is gaining, even though slowly and perhaps unevenly. Four to seven ounces a week is considered a good weight gain. And be sure to check for linear growth (length) as this is just as important as weight gain in determining the baby's well-being.

Also, you'll want to take good care of yourself. Are you doing too much and not getting enough rest? One pediatrician's prescription for slow gainers is to put mother and baby to bed together for a few days. Try to reduce outside stress in your life. Make your baby your main concern for the time being.

Are you eating well? Think now—what did you have for breakfast today? Was lunch "on the run?" Are you drinking enough water or juice? Your liquid intake can include some coffee and cola, but keep in mind that excessive amounts of beverages containing caffeine have been known to adversely affect the weight gain of some babies. The same is true of smoking, especially if the mother is a heavy smoker.

Are you taking birth control pills? These should not be taken by a breastfeeding mother as they can affect both the quantity and the quality of mother's milk. Could it be that you are anemic? It is known, too, that an underactive thyroid in the mother may result in a slow gaining baby. Both of these conditions can be easily corrected.

When the baby is not gaining as well as he should be, there is bound to be concern. But taking him off the breast is seldom, if ever, the answer to the problem. There is always the possibility that it will introduce a whole new set of problems.

DIARRHEA

It is good to know that if your baby is otherwise well and thriving, it really doesn't matter how loose his bowel movements are. As the mother of every breastfed baby knows, not all loose stools constitute diarrhea. In the breastfed infant it is quite normal for baby to have very loose, runny bowel movements. Many breastfed babies, especially in the early weeks, have as many as six or eight stools a day; later on, as they get a bit older, they may have only one a week or even fewer. All this is well within the realm of normalcy. Just keep plenty of diapers on hand and you will have no problem. Even the occasional green, watery stool in an otherwise healthy baby is nothing to worry about.

However, if your baby is having twelve or sixteen stools a day, or if they have an offensive odor or contain mucus or flecks of blood, you can be reasonably sure this is diarrhea. Even the completely breastfed baby may on occasion have diarrhea, usually related to a cold or other illness. Perhaps, if he is older, it is caused by an allergic reaction to a food he is eating. If your baby is not his usual happy self, acts ill, or runs a fever, these are symptoms that all is not well with him. Check with the doctor if baby is ill, as he or she may want to prescribe something for the baby. The doctor may also tell you not to give baby anything by mouth except your milk. **Breast milk is the best food there is for the sick baby, and as long as**

he can take anything by mouth it should be your milk. If baby is not ill, try to determine if there are possible causes of his unusual stools. Even the occasional bottle of formula can trigger diarrhea in the sensitive baby. And in a few rare cases, if there is a history of allergy in the family, the baby may be reacting to cow's milk in his *mother's* diet. If this is the case, try eliminating milk and all milk products from your diet for a week. Then resume drinking it and see what happens.

Has baby been given a new food lately? Try cutting it from his diet for a week or so. Is he taking vitamins or fluoride? These (especially the fluoride) can sometimes cause gastrointestinal upsets, including diarrhea. Remember, there is no need for additional vitamins, fluoride, iron, or other supplements in the completely breastfed baby.

Meanwhile, remember that as long as baby continues to thrive, it really doesn't matter how loose his bowel movements are.

Lactose Intolerance

Occasionally, when a baby has very frequent, loose stools it may be suggested that he has something called lactose intolerance, and you may be told to take the baby off the breast. There is no need to do that. True lactose intolerance is virtually unknown in babies and young children under weaning age. As children grow beyond weaning age, the enzyme lactase, with which they were all born and which is necessary to convert milk sugar (lactose), begins to disappear from their systems. This occurs because after weaning, milk is no longer a necessary part of the human diet.

Lactose intolerance is not a problem for the totally breastfed baby. On the other hand, cow's milk allergy (sensitivity to the protein in cow's milk), is frequently confused with lactose intolerance, and should be ruled out as a possible cause of baby's diarrhea.

If baby is ill or has been given certain medications, such as antibiotics, he may develop something called "secondary lactose intolerance," which shows up as diarrhea. The best thing to do in such situations is to take baby off everything by mouth **except your milk**. For the toddler who has been on lots of solids and other liquids, you may need to give water by cup also, as your milk supply may not be enough for him. As the effects of the illness or the medication wear off, his stools will return to normal. In the meantime, because of the special closeness and comfort he derives from the breastfeeding relationship, as well as the physical benefits of your milk, he will recover much faster.

Regardless of the age of your nursling, whether he is a little newborn or a sturdy toddler, remember that if he develops diarrhea, don't panic. And whatever else you do, keep nursing.

Vomiting

Sometimes when baby is ill, along with diarrhea he may be unable to keep down his dinner. The miserable feelings of nausea that accompany an upset stomach may cause him to want to nurse even more than usual, since of course he doesn't realize that putting more food into his rebellious stomach means that it's just more to come back up again. What to do? Certainly the child who is vomiting must be taken off all solid foods for the duration. And giving him big drinks of water, milk, ginger ale, or sweet drinks will probably be more than his sick stomach can handle. A certain amount of vomiting for a day won't hurt him and may help clean out his tummy. If you let him nurse on a fairly empty breast after he has vomited, he may not be so likely to lose it all again. (If he does, there's no harm done.) Just hand-express most of the milk before you nurse him. If he is still having at least two or three wet diapers a day during his illness, he is not in danger of dehydration; with calm gentle mothering and lots of little nursings, he will weather the storm. Often in little ones, an illness manifests itself first with vomiting and later with diarrhea. In any event, **don't wean**.

For the baby who is six months or older, or the toddler who is begging for something because he is thirsty, perhaps a few ice chips or water from a teaspoon will satisfy him for a while. The advantage of ice is that it goes down slowly and is an interesting distraction to boot. If you can hold him off with something like that, fine. If not, let him nurse on the emptied breast but don't give him anything else. If a baby has been vomiting often for more than a day or so, check with your doctor; he or she may want to prescribe something to help stop the nausea and vomiting. If oral medication won't stay down, the doctor may want you to give it rectally. But again, nursing for comfort, if not for food, is important to your little sick one, so don't deprive him of that.

NURSING STRIKE

Occasionally a baby refuses to nurse for a period of several days. This can be a real puzzle, especially if the baby is under two and not likely to be ready to wean. You will have to use your motherly ingenuity to figure out what the exact problem is.

Consider the following possibilities: Is your baby teething? Does he have a cold or a stuffy nose that prevents him from nursing easily? Does he have an earache that makes it painful to nurse? Are you anxious or upset about something? Babies respond to their mothers' feelings.

Has nursing become a stressful time, possibly because of older children or too many outside interruptions or distractions? Have you been deciding when the baby should nurse and when he should stop, instead of letting him lead the way? Has the baby become dependent on a pacifier or his thumb, so that he routinely sucks quite a bit on either?

Has some recent change in your nursing pattern confused the baby? Has he had bottles? Been left with a sitter? Been repeatedly put off when he cries to nurse? Have you gone back to work, or are you worrying about what will happen when and if you do have to leave the baby?

Sometimes a nursing strike happens after baby bites mother a time or two, and your understandable reaction has upset him. He bites, you jump or let out a startled cry. Baby is frightened, cries, and won't resume nursing for fear of another jolt or yell.

Sometimes the unexpected can cause a baby to refuse to nurse. Mary Shumeyko of New Jersey writes:

> The other day our twenty-month-old, Jonathan, bumped his chin. His mouth seemed to be bleeding a bit, so we wiped it off, I nursed him, and he continued playing. I went back to what I was doing, thinking, "What an advantage to be nursing a toddler and soothe the hurt so easily."
>
> Several hours later, after happily nursing to sleep, Jonathan awoke crying in obvious pain. I offered him my breast. He tried to nurse, then drew away, crying harder. This continued all night, with Jonathan waking every half hour or so, and my husband or I walking the floor with him since he wouldn't nurse.
>
> The next morning he seemed to feel better and tentatively asked to "nit-nit." When he opened his mouth I discovered the problem: he had cut his tongue when he bumped his chin, and (after the initial numbness wore off) nursing obviously had been quite painful. My heart went out to him. Not only had he injured himself, but his standard "cure-all" hurt even more. Fortunately the mouth heals quickly, and he's once again nursing regularly. The episode was a good reinforcement for me, though. After one night of not nursing, I'm more aware than ever of how precious this beautiful relationship is.

Even if you are not sure why the baby has gone on a nursing strike, you will want to help him get back to regular nursing as soon and easily as possible. Try nursing him when he is very sleepy, or already asleep. Many babies who refuse to nurse while awake will nurse when they are drowsy or asleep. You can still offer the breast when baby is awake, but don't force it. Some babies are more likely to nurse if mother is walking about rather than sitting still. In any case, plan to devote yourself almost entirely to the baby for a few days. Lots of cuddling and stroking and maybe some relaxing time spent just with mom away from the hubbub of the rest of the family will calm the baby and encourage him to start nursing again. Rethink your priorities, and decide to let the spring housecleaning go until fall. Put off joining the club, going back to work, or taking that sculpture course for a few more months. You will both be better off and happier when things get back to normal again.

Carol Strait, an Iowa mother, sheds some light on why some babies may refuse to nurse:

> When my two-and-a-half-month-old baby girl began refusing the breast, a thousand thoughts ran through my mind—I was eating the wrong foods, she was teething, I was too nervous (what nursing mother wouldn't be nervous when her new baby suddenly refused to nurse?), she was weaning herself—and even the fearful thought that she didn't like me! Quite by accident I discovered the answer to our problem. My first clue was that Christie always seemed fussier and wouldn't nurse when we went somewhere. This was because I had just showered and applied spray deodorant. I'm not sure what ingredients in the spray were

responsible. My big problem was easily solved by simply switching from a spray to a solid stick deodorant. Now my little girl and I are a happy nursing couple again.

Another disruption in the normal course of nursing that sometimes catches mothers by surprise is the "holiday weaning syndrome." It occurs when holidays or other especially hectic times, such as moving, result in our getting so busy that we overlook our baby's needs. It's easy to put off that nice quiet moment of nursing, because we're just too busy with other things. In the midst of cooking, entertaining, shopping, and such, the leisurely closeness of the nursing relationship is temporarily or even permanently lost. Solids or bottles may be tried to tide baby over, or perhaps he's "good" and consents to wait—and wait—for nursing time to come around. And then suddenly, no one knows quite how, baby is weaned. Toni Pepe from Connecticut describes holiday weaning:

> A unique season in the private life of the baby has been cut short, and later, in the long days at home, come the regrets. Guard against holiday weaning. In the seasons of the world, these days of celebration return again and again—but the special season of nursing comes only once in the life of a child.

WHEN MOTHER IS ILL

"How can I take care of my baby if I get sick?" This is a common question of anxious mothers. Of course, caring for an active, healthy baby is a demanding job at any time, but when mother is ill it can be a real chore and a worry. One reassuring thing is the fact that nursing your baby makes caring for him so much easier. For minor illnesses like a cold or the flu, you wouldn't even consider stopping nursing. For one thing, the germs are not transmitted through the milk, and the baby has no doubt been exposed to the illness for at least as long as you have, and certainly before you knew you had it. To stop nursing would only make matters worse and would be very hard on both you and your baby. You need the extra rest afforded by nursing, and the baby still needs all the benefits of breastfeeding, including the immunities in your milk. So keep nursing as usual, and don't worry about giving anything to the baby through your milk. He may not get sick at all, and if he is still nursing and does get sick, he will probably have only a mild case.

If your illness is more serious—for example, if you have pneumonia, hepatitis, or even tuberculosis—doctors on our Professional Advisory Board still advise continued breastfeeding. Again, it is the least effort for you, affording the most rest, and your milk provides special protection for your baby against the virus or bacteria that's causing your own illness. (See "Breast Milk: An Arsenal Against Illness.")

If you become seriously ill and your doctor suggests weaning the baby, explain how important breastfeeding is to you and your baby. If your

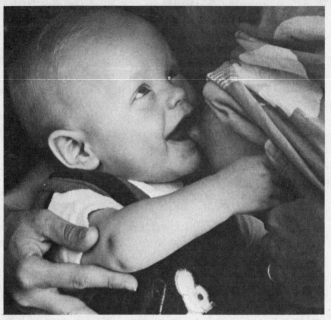

✎ *Illness on the part of mother or baby need not put an end to the joys of breast-feeding. Five-month-old Colin Anderson lets his mother know just how special nursing is to him. (Photo by Martha Schulte.)*

doctor still insists that weaning is necessary, remember that you are always free to consult another doctor before making a decision as serious as weaning your baby. Also check with your local League Leader or LLLI to determine what other mothers have done and what other doctors recommend in similar situations.

Hospitalization

If you can remain at home during your illness, so much the better. Get help with the necessary housework, laundry, and meals, and to take care of the older children. Tuck your little baby in bed with you, where he will be close by all the time and able to nurse whenever he wants.

If a serious illness or an accident puts you in the hospital, you will have to make some special arrangements to have your baby kept with you, or at least brought to you. Nursing mothers have found all kinds of ingenious ways to avoid being separated from their babies during hospital stays. Discuss your needs and those of your baby with your husband and your doctor. Your condition, the hospital's facilities, and your baby's age and usual nursing pattern will all influence the situation.

Sometimes minor surgery can be performed on an outpatient basis under local anesthesia. (Removing breast lumps is one example.) You can then return home to rest and nurse your baby without any prolonged separation. Procedures such as dental work can nearly always be carried out without interruption of breastfeeding. When the potential surgery is elective, your doctor may be willing to postpone it until the baby is older.

If you must stay in the hospital overnight or for several days, your husband or a friend or relative can bring the baby in to visit you and nurse. Some hospitals may even be willing to admit the baby and allow him to room-in with you. If your nursling is an active toddler you will want someone else there with him to help keep him out of trouble.

Be flexible and polite as you talk over your wishes with the doctors and hospital. If you are willing to cooperate with hospital personnel, they will return the favor. Let them see how much it means to you to keep your baby with you if at all possible.

If it's major surgery that's called for, remember that mothers have been able to successfully nurse following cesareans, and by the same token you will be able to nurse soon after your surgery, too. Many of the medications used at times like this are harmless to the nursing baby.

One mother from Illinois needed surgery for the removal of her gallbladder. By the time her baby was four months old, surgery couldn't be postponed any longer. The mother went into the hospital on the morning of her surgery. She nursed the baby, and he then went off with his aunt (who was nursing her own one-year-old) for the remainder of the day. The other three children stayed with their grandmother. A few hours after surgery, the baby was brought to the hospital where he stayed by his mother's side, nursing on and off through the night, with dad there to lend a hand. The next day mother and baby were back home with the rest of the family, where she continued to convalesce. Family and friends took turns bringing in meals and entertaining the children, and the mother had a peaceful recovery.

Even when doctors and hospitals aren't quite so cooperative, nursing need not be abandoned entirely. Merrelyn Mastro of Florida tells of her experience:

> When Frances was a year old, I had to have a hysterectomy. I hope my story will convince an undecided mother not to give up the idea of nursing even though circumstances warrant an absence. The surgery was successful. There were no postoperative complications, and my husband was allowed to bring the girls in to see me four days later. Frances was allowed to nurse (with a pillow under her to protect my stitches) for the first time in four and a half days. I had used a breast pump to relieve myself and to keep up my milk supply. Pete said that after that short period of nursing, Franny seemed relieved and slept better that night than she had during any of those while I was away.
>
> My doctor discharged me the next day and I came home and resumed the womanly art of breastfeeding and otherwise mothering my family.
> I thought "complete hysterectomy" was the end of the joys of nursing, and it was very depressing and frightening. As my daughter suckled her milk supply back to her satisfaction I came to realize how important motherhood and nursing had become to me. I'm glad my doctor hadn't convinced me to wean Franny completely because I need her closeness now almost as much as she needs me.

Medications for the Nursing Mother

Be sure to check with your doctor before taking any medication while nursing, even a drug like aspirin that is available without a prescription. Usually the amount of the drug found in mother's milk is so small that it won't affect the baby at all, but you still want to avoid unnecessary drugs for your own sake while you are nursing your baby.

If you must take medication, chances are your doctor can prescribe a drug that is known to be safe for nursing babies. Ask him or her specifically about this and be sure the doctor knows how important nursing is for both you and the baby. Abrupt weaning will only complicate things for both of you. You may develop sore breasts or even a breast infection, and baby will be most unhappy at being suddenly deprived of this special kind of mothering. For some babies, too, the risks of artificial feeding are considerable. The baby is deprived of the immunities in his mother's milk (which may be of special importance when mother is ill), or he may be allergic to the formula. All in all, weighing the pros and cons, it is nearly always best to keep nursing and seek alternatives to any treatment that calls for weaning the baby.

If your doctor insists on a particular medication and weaning as well, seek another opinion. It may be possible to alter the treatment or postpone it until the baby is older. Some drugs that may affect a newborn won't present any difficulties with an older, more mature infant. While a few drugs are contraindicated while nursing, alternative choices are almost always available. There is much information available about medications and breastfeeding. A comprehensive report, "Breastfeeding and Drugs in Human Milk," was published as a supplement to the *Journal of Veterinary and Human Toxicology* in 1980. LLLI carries a reprint of it.

Questions regarding the appropriateness of a particular drug during lactation can be addressed to the League's Professional Advisory Board through a La Leche League Leader or sent directly to LLLI. Suzanne Gerwick of Georgia found peace of mind by calling the League when her doctor prescribed an antibiotic for her, and she could not locate her son's pediatrician to make certain that she could continue nursing while taking the drug.

At this point I decided to call a La Leche League Leader. She passed along to me the references from the LLLI Professional Advisory Board. To my relief I learned that other mothers had taken this same medication and continued to nurse. Their babies were not affected. When I finally was able to reach my pediatrician, he also agreed that I should continue nursing, but I was grateful for the peace of mind La Leche League's information had given me until his return. I am thankful for his support as Jack and I continue our nursing relationship.

Nursing mothers should not take birth control pills, not even the mini-pill. These alter both the composition of the milk and the milk supply itself. No one knows as yet how they affect the baby. Don't forget that breastfeeding itself delays ovulation and pregnancy for a good many months in most women. (See "Breastfeeding and Your Reproductive Cycle.")

Immunizations

If your blood is Rh-negative and your baby's is Rh-positive, you will probably receive an injection of Rh antibodies (RhoGAM) very soon after you deliver. RhoGAM is used widely to prevent Rh complications, and it is not harmful to your nursing infant.

Along with RhoGAM, many other vaccines do not affect the breastfed baby through his mother's milk. According to the Center for Disease Control of the United States Public Health Service: "Most vaccines can be given safely to the mother of the nursing infant." Acceptable vaccines include: smallpox, typhus, typhoid, yellow fever, oral polio, tetanus, diphtheria, pertussis, rabies, measles, rubella, cholera, and influenza.

The smallpox vaccination is rarely used anymore, but if you must have it, rest assured that it will not harm the baby through your milk. However, the U.S. Public Health Service considers smallpox vaccination inadvisable for the mother of any infant under one year of age, nursing or not. The intimate contact between mother and child makes possible transmission of the smallpox vaccine virus from the site of the mother's vaccination to her baby, and such accidental inoculation of the baby could cause complications. If for some reason you must receive the smallpox vaccine, there is no advantage to weaning. Rather, care must be taken to avoid accidental inoculation of your baby through contact with your vaccination.

A word of caution is also in order regarding the rubella (German measles) vaccination, not because the vaccine itself may affect your baby (there is no indication that the rubella vaccine will in any way harm the nursing baby), but because there will be certain restrictions on you following its use. The woman receiving this vaccine is regularly cautioned to avoid becoming pregnant for at least two months following the vaccination. We mention this because taking the birth control pill to avoid pregnancy can be harmful to your baby. (See "Breastfeeding and Your Reproductive Cycle.")

The mother who is fully breastfeeding (giving no supplements or solids) rarely ovulates before ten weeks, so if vaccination is necessary, it is safest to be vaccinated shortly after delivery. (You can easily be tested for immunity first.) You should also know that the side effects accompanying the vaccine are sometimes painful and may last for several weeks. These can usually be alleviated with aspirin, if prescribed by your physician, and should not be considered reason for weaning.

With regard to immunizations for your baby, the same schedule is followed for the breastfed baby as for bottle-fed infants. There is no need to refrain from nursing the baby before or after administration of any vaccine, including the oral polio vaccine.

MOTHERS WITH SPECIAL PROBLEMS

Even mothers with unusual problems or handicaps can breastfeed. This shouldn't come as a surprise since you know that breastfeeding is much more convenient than bottle feeding. Imagine how much easier it is for a blind mother or one confined to a wheelchair to breastfeed than to prepare bottles and artificial formula. If you are a mother with a handicap or an unusual medical situation, be sure to contact La Leche League. Many LLL publications are available on tape or in Braille for use by handicapped parents. The League can also put you in touch with other mothers and doctors who are familiar with breastfeeding under conditions similar to yours.

Diabetes

In recent years medical science has made pregnancy and childbirth safer for diabetic women, and more and more of them are deciding to nurse their new babies. Many diabetic mothers find that nursing improves their condition. The easier transition from pregnancy to nursing makes for less of an adjustment, since your body just goes right on supporting both your baby and yourself.

A diabetic mother will have to make adjustments in her diet depending on how often her baby nurses from day to day. If she takes insulin, she will have to regulate the dosage as carefully as she did while she was pregnant, in order to keep her diabetes under control while nursing. The insulin itself will not hurt the baby.

Epilepsy

Mothers with epilepsy benefit from the nursing hormones and the relaxation engendered by natural mothering. If the mother must take medication to control her epilepsy, she should check with her doctor about the drugs' effects on her nursing. Most drugs prescribed for epilepsy won't harm the nursing baby. Some mothers have been on them for years with no effects on their babies either while nursing or later in life. If your doctor is uncertain about the effects of a particular drug, perhaps one that is so new little is known about it, he or she may be able to prescribe another drug instead. One other caution: mothers with epilepsy must take special precautions for their children's safety in the event of a sudden seizure. You'll always need a safe place nearby to put the baby down.

Other Problems

We have known all kinds of mothers who have nursed their babies despite handicaps. They write and say that breastfeeding is much easier for them than bottle feeding. This is true of mothers with multiple sclerosis, mothers who are deaf, mothers with injuries, mothers recovering from major surgery, and on and on. Nursing is one thing they *can* do. Gail Stutler, while recovering from brain surgery, "couldn't even name a diaper," when she gave birth to her second child. "But," she writes, "the most beautiful thing I *could* do. I could scoop up a tiny bundle, put her to my breast, and nurse her close to my heart. I could satisfy at least one of the desperate needs I had when deprived of all my capabilities."

BREASTFEEDING AND WORKING

You're in a dilemma. You find that you must go back to work and you cannot take your baby with you. Will you still be able to breastfeed? Yes! By all means plan to nurse your baby, or, if you are already nursing, look forward with confidence to continuing. You may be able to furnish your baby with all of the milk he needs, but even if you can't, some breast milk is better than none. Besides, you don't want to wean suddenly, for your baby's sake as well as your own.

You may be thinking, "All right, but isn't breastfeeding difficult when a mother has to miss feedings?" It does take some extra effort, and it requires that you plan ahead, but the same is true of most worthwhile things in life. You have to be convinced that the advantages outweigh the disadvantages. For your baby, there are all of breast milk's health-giving qualities. For yourself, you will find that when you return home from work, nursing your baby will probably be one of the most restful and enjoyable times in the day. As one mother said, "If you must work, nursing your child will help both of you over the rough spots." Another working and nursing mother observed, "I love being able to make the shift from the workaday world to the world of family with the closeness of breastfeeding." To this, another mother added, "I wish I could tell all working mothers how much easier, special, and joyful it is to breastfeed. I am surprised to find that some people seem sorry for me and others think it is so courageous to do the perfectly natural thing."

The greatest difficulty for you and your baby is the separation from each other that working entails. Being away from mother is a serious disruption in a young child's life. Our plea to any mother who is thinking about taking an outside job is, "If at all possible, don't." Please consider all alternatives before making the decision to leave your baby. You may find some helpful suggestions in the chapter, "Are You Thinking of Going Back to Work?"

You may decide, however, all things considered that getting an outside job is your only recourse. Your best move then is to minimize the amount of time you will be away from your baby. An eight-hour workday presents more than twice the problems of a four-hour one. Your baby's need for you compounds itself as time goes on, even when he is cared for by someone as familiar to him and as loving as his dad. Two or three half days a week is a far better way to break into the new routine than the usual forty hour workweek. Even if your employer does not usually hire part-time employees, ask about the possibility. You have nothing to lose and much to gain.

Investigate the possibility that you and another mother can share one job, thus giving yourselves more flexibility and freedom. Sharing a job means that two people divide the hours and responsibilities of a position usually filled by one person. While serving in the Virgin Islands, Linda Murphy found that she and another RN, "who was the other half of my position," accomplished "*more* than the work of one and a half persons" by splitting the work load. "And we had less absenteeism," she adds.

Postpone Working

You'll want to stay home with your baby as long as you can after he is born. A mother and baby have a great need for each other at this time. Princess Grace of Monaco, who breastfed all three of her children, explained her views at a La Leche League Conference in 1971:

> I have many duties and obligations of State, but my family comes first. I would have liked to have breastfed my children for a much longer period than I did. But, at the beginning, when they first needed me and I them, State had to wait upon mother.

Bargain for as long a maternity leave as you can possibly manage. Rosemary Cogan, a nursing mother-physician from Texas, advises, "Beg, borrow, ask the grandparents for money presents if necessary, but arrange not to return to work for at least six to eight weeks after baby is born." Three months at home with your baby is better yet. If you can stretch the time to six months, you will probably have seen him to the time when he begins to take other foods. Then, when necessary, the sitter can feed the baby solids rather than give cow's milk, which is more likely to cause an allergy. Of course, the longer you can stay home with your baby, the longer both of you will enjoy the benefits of being together.

How-To

The key to being able to breastfeed and work is learning how to express your milk. The milk you collect at work can be given to your baby by the sitter, and, of course, no other milk or formula is as good as yours for your baby. Expressing milk also keeps your breasts from becoming overly full. By regularly taking milk out, you'll maintain your milk supply, as well as your poise while you're on the job. (Overfull breasts might tend to leak when you least expect it!)

Another thing to be careful about is the possibility of a breast infection. You are—at least for a while—in a much more susceptible situation in that regard. The added stress of working, and the uneven nursing schedule make it more likely that you'll get a breast infection if you don't take really good care of yourself. Keeping the breasts emptied regularly will help to avoid this problem. Extra rest is also essential, and so is a good diet.

How, When, Where

Hand-expression is probably the simplest method to use, once you master the technique. Small hand pumps are also available, but they vary considerably in efficiency and comfort. See "How to Express and Store Breast Milk" for details about hand-expressing as well as recommended pumps.

Most mothers take advantage of their breaks at work to express milk. If you make it a point to nurse the baby just before you leave home, the

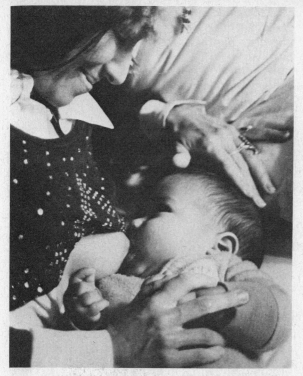

Of course you can breastfeed your baby even if you return to work. Folk singer Buffy Sainte-Marie continued her career after her baby Dakota Starblanket was born, yet they still enjoyed the closeness of breastfeeding.

chances are the baby will not be hungry again for a while, and your breasts will not be overly full before your break. But anytime your breasts are getting uncomfortably full, take a few minutes off and express just enough milk to relieve the fullness. Under the circumstances, you may not be able to save the milk, but your first concern is to avoid a plugged milk duct.

To make things easy for yourself, be sure to wear the proper clothing. Two-piece outfits are always a good choice. Save the dresses that open in the back for some other time.

For your regular milk-collection session, try to locate a spot where you can relax and have privacy. An office you can commandeer for fifteen minutes is ideal, or perhaps you'll find an unused room—a storeroom, for instance. At first you may not be able to express a great deal of milk, but the amount usually increases quickly as you become more adept with the procedure.

Any sterile container can be used to hold your milk, although those made of hard plastic are considered better than glass bottles. The sterile plastic bags that fit into nursing bottles are convenient since they're ready to use, and it's a simple matter to take a fresh one each time you express milk. Mothers find that small amounts are convenient at feeding time. There is less waste, since the sitter can tailor the amount given to the baby more easily. If you are due back from work shortly, but the baby is hungry at the moment, the sitter can warm one or two small packets of milk (by holding them under hot running water) to take the edge off baby's hunger. The smaller amount will not spoil his appetite for the milk he'll soon get "straight from mom."

Each little bag or other container of milk must be closed securely. If the bottle liners are used, they should be placed into a rigid container such as a jar or heavy plastic cup for added protection when you place them in the refrigerator or freezer.

The milk that you express must be kept cold at all times. Many places of business have a refrigerator on the premises. Wouldn't the manager of the cafeteria agree to donate the use of a small spot on a shelf in the refrigerator for your unusual but most worthy cause? If no refrigeration is available, you can do as many other resourceful working mothers do and bring a large thermos jug filled with ice from home in which to store your containers of milk. For the trip home, you will need ice or an insulated bucket or chest to keep the milk at a safe, cool temperature, ready for the sitter to give to the baby the next day.

A Word About Sitters

The most important task you will face before you go back to work is finding the best person possible to care for your baby while you are gone. Can you arrange for a family member to take over this responsibility? Your husband comes to mind as the first choice, if he is available. He is already familiar to the baby, and the element of change for the baby will not be quite so great. A loving grandmother or an aunt who truly enjoys babies and who is already familiar to the baby are also high on the list of choices. A motherly neighbor may enjoy caring for a little one for a short period during the day.

Most people, though, are not so lucky as to have a family member or friendly neighbor available as a sitter and must look further. They must also be more concerned with references and interviews. If the sitter is new to the baby, by all means have her come to the house a few times so the two of them can get acquainted before you begin working. You can then also tell her that you are nursing and explain in detail how you want the baby fed, what his likes and dislikes are, what his sleeping pattern is, and, very important, the fact that you do not want your baby to be left to cry.

When choosing a sitter, you are looking for someone who will give your baby as nearly as possible the same single-minded devotion and care that you would give him yourself—someone who knows babies—who understands their needs. Will she sing to him? Talk to him? Rock him gently to sleep? Keep him dry and comfortable and always close by?

If the sitter comes to your home, baby will be in familiar surroundings, which is good. If you have a two-, three-, or four-year-old that you were thinking of sending to nursery school, consider instead leaving both children with the sitter. They'll be company for each other, and you'll find that big brother or sister will be so reassuring and protective to the baby that it will warm your heart. The sitter may do some light housekeeping or meal preparation for you, which will be a help, but remind her that this is always secondary to baby's needs.

Preparations Ahead Of Time

Mothers sometimes worry that the baby will not accept the rubber nipple after he has only had the breast. They are warned that they must give the baby at least a bottle a day "to get him used to it." A more valid worry is that the baby will take the rubber nipple and reject mother. If this happens, you are then struggling to get him back to where he was supposed to be in the first place.

In the early weeks, particularly, bottle-feeding methods are anathema to breastfeeding. In those first months when you and your baby are together, live the life of a breastfeeding mother to the fullest. These are the days to dawdle, to relax and enjoy. Plans and arrangements for work schedules, baby-sitters, and feedings when you are away may have to be considered later, but for now put them on the shelf. The most important need right now is getting as much rest as you can. A happy, relaxed mother and unlimited time at the breast are the basics for giving baby a good start. A Houston mother advises, "Nurse as baby wants, with no schedules and without worry about going back to work." In between times of nursing and enjoying the baby, you'll be treating yourself to good nutritious things to eat and drink.

Judy Hayes, an Oklahoma mother, advises, "Do not make elaborate separation plans other than arranging for good baby care. Do not try to imitate your being away by avoiding nursings in advance or by trying to substitute bottle feeding a time or two during the day. Mothers who have tried such tactics find that they just don't work. The baby will adjust better and be less confused if all circumstances are generated by reality rather than by pretense."

Feedings While You're Away

Mothers usually instruct the sitter to give the baby breast milk if it is available and supplement, if needed, with whatever the doctor has prescribed, only after the supply of mother's milk is gone. You'll be better off if the sitter gives the fewest number of bottles possible. Juice, when it is introduced, can be given by spoon or cup. As much as possible, you'll want to satisfy baby's sucking needs at the breast.

If your baby is three or four months old, or older, you might want to consider asking your doctor if you could start some mashed banana instead of introducing formula.

Is there a chance that you can nurse the baby during your lunch hour? Some mothers are able to go to the baby, while in other instances the sitter brings baby to mother. It can be a most refreshing break for both. Anthea Fraser with the Singapore Breastfeeding Mothers Group was usually, but not always, able to come home for lunch, which was then lunch for herself and her nursing baby. She advises the mother who may sometimes be delayed to "keep your own private milk bank, if you have a freezer compartment in your fridge. Immediately before leaving for work, I used to express any surplus milk into sterilized containers for freezing. This was given to my daughter on a spoon when I was unable to return at lunchtime."

Don't be surprised if you find yourself calling from work frequently to find out how your little one is doing. It's good for all of you to stay in touch, so phone as often as you can. Perhaps the sitter has a question that you can quickly answer.

When You're At Home

If you and baby are separated for a considerable length of time, give special attention to your homecoming. Starting a new job, or even taking up where you left off in the old one, is a very tiring thing for a new mother. You may find yourself absolutely undone by the end of the day. Meal preparation or household chores are best kept to a minimum for the first hour or so after you get home. Barbara Van Horn of Pennsylvania, suggests, "If mother doesn't get home until suppertime, she can try to prepare part of the meal in advance, since this will be the time baby wants to nurse and cuddle. She (as well as the baby) may need to nurse. This is a potentially hazardous time if hungry husband and perhaps older children press for a meal. The baby *may* be asleep, of course, but then that hardly ever happens the hour before supper, whether mother is working or not!"

Time will be a most precious commodity in your life. When a woman combines mothering and working, she must be a miser with her time. Don't overlook the trusty baby carrier to help you catch up with household work and keep the baby close to you. It has proved a blessing to all of us at times. And don't be surprised if your baby becomes something of a "night owl," wide awake, bright-eyed and busy in the center of family activities, where, naturally, he is the center of attention. Some working mothers tell us that they deliberately encourage an up-at-night, down-during-the-day sleeping pattern for the baby. The family enjoys the baby's company, and the baby sleeps for longer periods for the sitter.

For many working mothers who must miss feedings during the day, night feedings are welcome. The baby benefits nutritionally, and the extra nursings stimulate the production of milk. No pump or hand-expression is as efficient as a baby at the breast in keeping up the milk supply.

When there is change in the routine, a mother's breast responds accordingly. Gail Saxton of Utah recalls her return to work when her baby, David, was ten months old:

> The week before my first workday came and David was still nursing several times each day and a couple of times during the night, with both of us really loving it. As the time neared, I realized that we would not be able to end this relationship. I felt that we would be able to handle it, since my husband would be with David and his three sisters most of the time. At the end of the first day, one very top-heavy mother and her baby

nursed all evening and all night long. My milk supply soon adjusted to the increased stimulation at night.

When breastfeeding is firmly established, and the time for you to go back to work cannot be postponed any longer, then introduce the bottle (filled with your milk, of course). But don't give it to the baby yourself. Logical little person that he is, he may not accept mother's milk from a bottle when mother herself is right there. Ask your husband or the sitter to give it to baby. You don't want to try this at a time when he is really hungry, but you don't want to try it soon after a nursing, either. If all else fails (meaning the baby refuses the bottle), the sitter can give the milk to baby with a spoon. This is all the more reason why you'll want to keep those early days back to work short. There are a great many adjustments involved for both baby and you.

Try to locate a League group in your area. As a new mother, you're bound to have questions. If possible, practice hand-expression or use the pump for a while before the time when you must return to work. Ann Lindsay of New Jersey tells of her experience:

> When we learned that my husband would be laid off at the end of the current academic year and I would have to return to work full-time, I contacted Carol White of the Cranford League, to whom I shall be eternally grateful. My husband would be caring for eighteen-month-old Tomek and five-month-old Merrillek during the day and teaching at night. The fact that Daddy was there—not just a baby-sitter—made the difference in the success of our role-switching venture.
>
> I had mistakenly thought that because I had always had more than enough breast milk for Merrillek, I would have no problem pumping. But, as I discovered, there is quite a method to it. When I first started pumping, three weeks before returning to work, I could get an ounce or two. Three weeks later I could get eight ounces by using a pump for fifteen minutes before I nursed the baby first thing in the morning. I nursed him at 6:00 A.M. while he was still asleep and again at 8:00 A.M. I pumped at 12:00 and 4:00 and got eight more ounces, which I put in a jar in the refrigerator at work and then into a thermos for the trip home. At home I immediately put the milk in the fridge, then nursed and cuddled the baby.

When you have a day off work, nurse your baby on demand. Many mothers tell us that it is "only mother" on weekends—no bottles or supplements, even though these may be used when mother is at work. A great deal depends on the baby's age, the length of time the mother has been working, and the extent to which milk, juice, or solids replace breast milk at other times. Some mothers feel that they can regulate their milk supply to some extent by the amount of fluids they drink. They increase their intake of nutritious beverages as the workweek comes to an end and then continue to drink as much as they can while at home. On the afternoon or evening of the day before they again go back to work, they cut back on fluids. They claim that when they are drinking more, they have more milk, and the supply lessens as their intake of fluids lessens. Whatever you do, do *not* let yourself become too full nor too tired. Take your baby to bed, nap, and nurse. Enjoy being with your baby.

Is It Worth It?

In telling her story, one mother from South Dakota, Kate Hanlon, answers this question best:

> I have been able to work full-time and continue nursing my baby daughter, Erin, without too many problems. I learned to master the breast pump and have had no sore nipples or plugged ducts, and my daughter is fed the best. At work, I usually express my milk midway through the morning and afternoon. It helps to relieve some fullness and stimulates my breasts so my milk supply doesn't diminish. My babysitter is a veteran nursing mother of four, and she offered a lot of encouragement.
>
> I do get discouraged at times. I am always running late; we eat hurry-up meals of peanut butter or fried egg sandwiches. I am tired all the time, my house is a mess, and half my garden vegetables go to waste before I can get to them. However, each Friday at five o'clock I am so relieved that another week has gone by and Erin is still my nursing baby. The things that don't get done don't seem worth it anyway, and we get by.
>
> I am grateful to my sister, Frances Mach, who is a La Leche League Leader. She has been all my support and has provided me with brewer's yeast, a breast pump, fabric nursing pads, and countless fact sheets and books in addition to encouraging advice and phone calls. If it hadn't been for Fran, Erin would not have been breastfed, and she and I would have missed out on a great beginning.

Another mother, Cissy Zigler of Georgia, worked as a flight attendant while she continued nursing her baby. She explains:

> Because my husband and I were divorced during my third month of pregnancy, I was determined to "make it" on my own with my baby. Although many doubted me, my family and LLL gave me tremendous support and encouragement.
>
> Adam was born by cesarean. Nursing him was so peaceful, relaxing, and easy after having had surgery. But no sooner had we settled in at home than I had to start planning for my return to work as an airline flight attendant—I had only ninety days leave after his birth. Luckily I only had to make three trips a week. I always chose night trips so I would miss only one or two feedings.
>
> Until Adam started solids at six months, I used a breast pump every three or four hours while away. I would put my milk in plastic disposable nursing bags and pack them in ice until I got home, when they would go into the freezer to be used while I was on my next flight.
>
> Everyone has wanted to know how I've done it and "Isn't that hard?" I just tell them—loving my baby so and giving of myself in this special way is the most beautiful, wonderful, and rewarding thing I've ever done. Nothing is too difficult when love is the guiding force.

PART TWO

NICE TO KNOW

Photo by Richard Ebbitt

Breast milk is the superior food for the human infant, a fact that twelve-week-old Elliott Smith would gladly endorse. (Photo by Martha Schulte.)

Chapter X

Breast Milk: The Superior Infant Food

For the most part, milk is thought of as a food, since that is its most obvious role. While breast milk has long been recognized as the superior food for the infant, in the last decade it has been found that human milk also contains living cells that actively protect the baby against illness. We take up that advantage in a later section, "Breast Milk—An Arsenal Against Illness." For now, let's consider your milk as the source of the elements your baby needs to grow and develop.

The comment, "My, how that baby has grown," is music to a mother's ears. Your baby's rate of growth during the early months is far greater than at any other period of his life after birth. The human brain is one-third its adult size at birth and reaches the two-third mark by age one. Your baby's head grows about four and one-half inches during his first year to allow for the tremendous growth of his brain. The bony portions of his skull do not knit together, you'll notice, until this growth has been accomplished.

Good muscle development and an increase in length are other significant signs of progress, more significant even than a specific weight gain, though adding pounds is important, too. The fat pads in your baby's cheeks are a distinguishing mark of the young baby, and they're a sign, too, of his well-being. Getting bigger is serious business for a baby, and milk is the means.

Since milk is intended as the sole food for the baby for a critical period of time, the first requirement is that it be a complete food—one that supplies all that is necessary in ideal proportions. No formula can make the claim that it meets this exacting criterion. In his book, *Breastfeeding, the Biological Option,* G. J. Ebrahim points out that with artificial infant feeding, "Any inadequacy in the milk will be translated into an altered composition of body tissue being formed at the time." As with any building process, the finished product will be under par when the components used in construction are not according to specifications.

Secondly, if a food for the infant is to do no harm, it should also agree with his still developing digestive system. Again artificial infant feeding falls short. The means for digesting any food other than mother's milk, including the ingredients which make up formula, have not yet fully developed in the infant. What is more, the first food passing through this newly operating system influences how the system develops.

Milk is not simply acted upon in the body processes; it acts on its own to bring about changes in body chemistry. With techniques advancing to where scientists can observe the microscopic world within the body, we will probably soon find that the breastfed baby looks drastically different on the inside than his counterpart who is formula-fed. His mother's milk conditions his stomach and intestines for their lifetime of work. Researchers studying ulcerative colitis in adult patients concluded that very early artificial feeding increases the predisposition to this disease as age advances. The study, which was reported in the *British Medical Journal* in 1960, also suggested the possibility that artificial feeding in the first two weeks after birth may influence the development of a number of diseases occurring in later life.

Today many babies are fed one of the soybean formulas in the hope of averting some of the allergy problems associated with cow's milk. This "vegetable soup," as one doctor calls it, is nutritionally inferior in many ways and has been found to be almost as apt to cause allergies in the very sensitive baby as cow's-milk formulas are. Other substitutes such as meat-based formula, which are used only as a last resort, are also acknowledged to be far less acceptable in many ways.

Human milk, being custom-made for the human baby's digestive system, is more readily assimilated than cow's milk. The addition of other foods to the diet of the young baby only interferes with the finely tuned balance between breast and baby. Your milk is truly compatible to your baby's nutritional makeup. Breast milk will sustain, strengthen, protect, fill out, and put a recognizable bloom on your baby's skin. It is all he will need until he is ready for solid foods at about the age of six months, if he is full-term and healthy when born. A baby who has special problems or is born prematurely may have special needs, but when milk is called for, breast milk is always superior and the food of choice for the human infant. This remains true, too, for the baby who is sick or is gaining slowly. A highly respected researcher, the late Dr. Paul György said: "Human milk should be considered superior to cow's milk as the initial physiologic food for the human infant....Breastfeeding reduces both morbidity and mortality rates, especially the latter....Human milk is for the human infant, cow's milk is for the calf."

A LOOK AT MILK—BOVINE AND BREAST

A look at the composition of milk in its many forms can be both fascinating and illuminating. We offer merely an overview here of this complex commodity. All milk, it can be said, is formed in a "mold" in the mother's mammary glands, corresponding to her biological makeup. Milk differs from species to species just as the other cells in a mother's body are unlike those of other species. Monkeys do not look or act like mice; they are different—and the same holds true for their milk. While it is obvious that milk is milk, just as blood is blood (with each performing a similar function in mouse, human, or whale), it is also readily apparent that there are important differences between the milk of different species.

Human milk and cow's milk, like the milk of all mammals, consist mainly of water, protein, fat, lactose (a sugar), and a generous dash of vitamins, minerals, and salts, as well as traces of hormones. While both of these milks weigh in with the same caloric value—an average of twenty calories to an ounce—the proportions of the different components are different. In the preparation of infant formula, cow's milk is diluted with about an equal amount of water, and sugar must be added to recoup the lost calories. Both milks are the expected white color, although mother's milk may sometimes look thin and blue compared to artificial homogenized formulas. What you cannot see is how perfectly your milk adapts to your baby's digestive system and nutritional needs. As J. Ross Snyder wrote in *The Journal of the American Medical Association* as long ago as 1908: "The deft manipulation of cow's milk to duplicate breast milk is not unlike the claim that by clipping its tail and ears one can so modify the calf that it can be substituted for a baby."

When comparing breast milk to cow's milk or any other artificial formula as a food for the baby, the similarities fade and the differences are pronounced. After all, human breast milk is the only food uniquely made by nature for the human baby.

Proteins

Of all the substances that make up living things, proteins are the most distinctive, the most characteristic of the species. Certain key proteins in your milk are as different from those in cow's milk as you are from a cow.

As you would expect, proteins are stellar performers on the nutritional stage. They are active in a number of roles, and when substitutions are made, as happens when the baby is given cow's milk or formula, there will be multiple changes in a number of nutritional functions. In their most notable function, proteins break down into amino acids, the building blocks of body tissue. Since your milk comes from your body, it contains all of the essential amino acids in the proper proportions that your baby needs.

Some proteins also double as enzymes, agents that may act on food to promote digestion. Naturally, those in cow's milk are ideal for the calf's multi-stomach digestive system. The large amount of casein protein in cow's milk forms large, tough, rubbery curds, that are difficult for the human baby to digest. This explains why the formula-fed baby remains "full" longer than the breastfed baby. However, casein protein does not have as high a nutritive value as whey protein, which is more plentiful in mother's milk.

Other specific proteins in milk are capable of destroying harmful bacteria or protecting the young against infections that may enter the blood stream. Those in cow's milk furnish protection against diseases in the cow. Your milk protects your baby against threats to him from his environment. Additionally, when proteins are heated much above body temperature, as is true in the preparation of formula, these special properties (such as the ability to serve as digestive enzymes, transport minerals, or protect against infection) are usually destroyed. However, heating does not impair their nutritional qualities.

Cow's milk has more than three times as much protein as human milk. This disparity makes sense when the goals of bovine and human growth are examined. The calf is on his feet within hours of birth, and his prime bodily needs are muscle and bone. In less than two months, the calf is expected to double his weight, adding an average of 65 pounds. In contrast to the calf, the infant need not add such bulk and generally doesn't double his weight until five or six months of age. He won't walk until close to a year. Of crucial importance to the human infant during the early months is having the right nutrients for the continued development of his brain and the rest of the nervous system. As Jelliffe and Jelliffe state in *Human Milk in the Modern World,* "In the case of the human neonate, rapid brain growth is *the* characteristic of the species."

New brain cells continue to be added until your baby is about nine months old—a process that is never again repeated. Another important development is the ongoing insulation of the nerves from one another, which makes motor coordination possible. For good reason, weight gain is not the best indication of the baby's bodily development.

When cow's milk is used as the base for a formula, the over-supply of protein must be reduced. The young infant just cannot handle the excess amounts of protein and salt found in cow's milk. The addition of water to the milk is still not sufficient to permit the infant's kidneys to rid the system of excess. To ease the strain on the kidneys and to correct an imbalance of bodily fluids, bottle-feeding mothers are advised to regularly give their babies extra water. Should the weather be hot or the baby develop a fever, further depletion of fluids occurs, and the infant is at an increased risk of dehydration. In contrast, your breastfed baby will do very well on your milk alone, because of its perfect balance of nutrients and fluids.

With the dilution of cow's milk in the formula, other problems surface. All of the other components of the milk are also halved, for better or worse. Examples of this are two amino acids that bear sulphur—methionine and cystine. Methionine, plentiful in cow's milk, is not well-utilized by the infant, while cystine, which the baby can readily use, is already in short supply in cow's milk before dilution. Mother's milk has cystine in just the right amount.

The essentials for growth, the amino acids, must be present in certain amounts and proportions if they are to work well individually and collectively. When there is an excess of some amino acids and a depletion of others, the baby must work to get rid of the excess and suffers from a depletion about which he can do nothing. The discordant consequences of such a condition are not yet fully known. What is well-known is that harmony prevails when the baby is breastfed. All the amino acids in breast milk are used by the baby; none end up in the diaper or barge around the system confusing the metabolic processes.

The specific proteins in cow's milk, most of which are foreign to the human body, can interfere with your infant's immune system and may adversely affect the proper development of the brain, cause anemia, and produce allergies. And when some of the other components of the milk, such as the fats and sugars, are also strangers to the human baby, there are further metabolic distortions in the unfolding of the play. The utilization of foodstuff by the body no longer proceeds according to the original script, and the risks to the baby may be serious.

Fats

The fat in milk, playing the role of the "heavy" in our pageant, readily illustrates the tailoring of milk to the species. It varies in amount in different mammals by almost thirty-fold. In particular, the young of sea mammals must acquire a layer of blubber to protect them quickly against icy waters, and this need is reflected in the high percentage of fat in the milk of the seal.

For your baby, the fat in your milk means high energy in the form of calories to grow on and to lay down as a reserve store of fuel. The resulting layer of fat tissue blankets his frame against heat loss. Along with his soft skin, it makes him especially nice to cuddle.

On an average, human milk has close to four percent fat, which accounts for over forty percent of the total calories in the milk. Mothers who are severely undernourished and have no fat reserves of their own to draw on, tend to produce milk that is somewhat lower in fat than that of well-nourished mothers, though the protein and lactose content of their milk is still within the acceptable norm.

Unlike the predetermined fat content in a bottle of formula, the amount of fat in mother's milk varies from feeding to feeding and from week to week, but over a period of time it meets the needs of the infant. The practice of having a mother express a sample of milk, which is then allowed to stand in order to examine it for the level of fat, may be an interesting way to see how cream rises to the top of unhomogenized milk, but it is useless for determining if the milk is "too rich" or "not rich enough."

The kind of body fat an infant develops depends on the kind of fat in his diet. The infant on cow's milk or formula has fat deposits of a different composition than those of the infant on mother's milk. This is significant because fats break down into fatty acids, the only way in which fat can be used, and the various fatty acids are differently absorbed by the body.

Certain fat products are optimum in the development of the brain and nervous system, and it is of concern that some fats in formula are biologically inappropriate and less than optimum for the infant.

If fat cannot be absorbed, it is useless to the baby. Fat that is not absorbed may even act as a bandit, robbing the baby of calcium, since fat and calcium can form an insoluble "soap" which passes right through the baby's digestive system.

The fat of human milk, in contrast to the other animal and vegetable fats, is absorbed and utilized by the baby with remarkable efficiency. Such a harmonious state comes about because a fat-digesting enzyme, lipase, is in the mother's milk. This maternal lipase, another gift from the mother's breast, complements and augments the infant's lipase. It is activated in the baby's intestine and aids in the digestion of the infant-tailored fats or lipids in that same milk.

In order to increase fat absorption in formula feeding, the butterfat in cow's milk is replaced with linoleic acid, a vegetable oil. The move looked good in theory when it was first introduced, but as is too frequently the case, formula manufacturers cannot equal the complexity, subtlety, and wisdom of nature. Disastrous effects occurred in certain infants before adjustments were made. What had not originally been realized was that additional vitamin E was needed to offset the linoleic acid in order to protect the infant against a serious form of anemia.

The changeover to vegetable oils in formula also loads a baby with a greater amount of unsaturated fats and a decreased supply of cholesterol. High cholesterol levels of a particular type may be a problem for some adults, and attention has focused in recent years on reducing the amount of cholesterol in the diet—but a baby in the first year of life needs cholesterol. Certain fats are utilized in the covering—or myelination—of nerves which, in turn, permits muscular coordination. Your baby will sit, crawl, and then walk as the process of myelination is completed.

Some authorities feel that the seemingly high cholesterol content of human milk may be the means by which the infant's system is adapted for handling these fats in later life. The implications of introducing a fat of a different nature, which produces different effects on the infant's cardiovascular and nervous systems, have not gone unnoticed by researchers in their efforts to prevent the alarming increase in diseases of the heart and blood vessels. Giving our babies a physiologically sound start in life still seems to be the best insurance against future disease.

Lactose

Sharing top nutritional billing with protein and fat is the sugar lactose. It is found only in milk and is frequently referred to as milk sugar. Among sugars, lactose has remarkable properties that benefit the newborn. In the familiar role of a carbohydrate, it is a source of quick energy, but that is only one of its functions. Lactose may contribute to the optimum

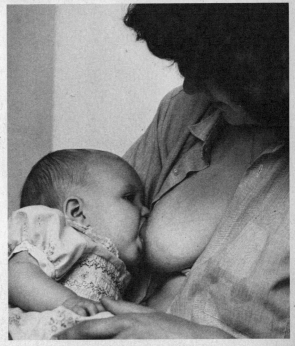

Six-month-old Claire Postlewaite seems convinced of the value of breast milk and is determined to get her share.

development of your baby's brain and central nervous system. In general, the bigger the brain the higher the percentage of lactose in the milk of the species. Lactose also enhances the absorption of certain minerals, calcium in particular, which is necessary for good bone and tooth development. It also determines to a great extent the kind of environment in your newborn's heretofore sterile gut, or intestinal tract.

Mother's milk contains half again as much lactose as is found in cow's milk—a fact that is readily verified by the sweet taste of breast milk to the adult palate. The sugar content of cow's milk must be increased for use in infant feeding, and in many instances table sugar, sucrose, is used. A "spoonful of sugar" does help the formula go down, especially so since the baby's taste for sweetness is present at birth and, in fact, is the first taste acquired. Since sucrose is sweeter than lactose, it seduces the baby away from breast milk just as chocolate milk and other sweetened milks seduce the older child from regular cow's milk.

Taste aside, sucrose and other substitute sugars are not the equal of the lactose in mother's milk. Lactose breaks down and releases its energy at a slow, steady pace, thus avoiding the highs and lows in blood sugar that are characteristic when cane sugar, sucrose, is the dominant sugar in the artificial formula. Compared to the baby fed a sweetened formula, the baby nourished on his mother's milk has firmer flesh, is more solid, and is more resistant to infection.

This high level of lactose in mother's milk is related to a correspondingly low level of minerals and salts in the milk, an arrangement that is ideal for the human infant. It is the nature of milk, as it is of blood, that it has a balance of solids to liquids that benefits the organism. In milk, the determining factors are lactose, salts, and minerals. When lactose is high, as it is in human milk, the level of minerals and salts is low. In cow's milk, this ratio is reversed, and there is a carry-over into cow's milk-based formula of unnecessary minerals and salts. These may sometimes overwhelm the baby's kidneys and result in a less than desirable balance of fluids in the baby. Your milk comes from your body, and your body adjusts the lactose, minerals, and salts to meet your baby's need throughout the period of nursing.

Of all the sugars, that in milk is ideal for the baby because of its special effect on the microinhabitants of the intestines. Milk sugar promotes the growth of a select group of bacteria, mainly *Lactobacillus bifidus*, which thwart the development of the undesirable bacteria that are responsible for severe diarrhea in the young. Aiding the growth of these good bacteria is a substance called the bifidus factor. Mother's milk contains much more bifidus factor than does cow's milk or formula. Evidence of its effectiveness may be recognized by anyone who changes a breastfed baby's diaper. The bowel movements of the totally breastfed baby have a distinct, not unpleasant, buttermilk-like smell caused by the fermentative bacteria. It's proof that the small world within is populated by a preponderance of beneficial, "good guy" bacteria. The formula-fed baby's stools have a strong, adult-type odor—very unbecoming to the baby.

Until your infant's own immune defenses are more fully developed, your milk not only provides superior nourishment, it is also a major safeguard against infantile diarrhea.

Vitamins, Minerals, and Other Good Things

Vitamins and minerals, living and nonliving products respectively, are bit players with important roles in nutrition. They are essential to growth and health. Since some are continually being used or passed out of the body, supplies must be replenished daily, and breast milk is the best and most balanced source for infants. Dropping a supplemental dose of vitamins or minerals into your baby's mouth "just in case" is not a sure way to avoid problems. The need for iron is a case in point.

Iron. In reference to an infant's need for iron, Dr. Frank Oski stated that babies "should not see, smell, or touch any cow's milk in the first year." The professor and chairman of the Department of Pediatrics, State University of New York Medical Center, made that statement at a pediatrics symposium in Ohio in 1981.

It has long been known that babies taking quantities of cow's milk are prone to iron deficiency anemia. While mother's milk contains somewhat more iron than cow's milk, the assumption was often arbitrarily made that the baby receiving only his mother's milk was just as much in danger of becoming anemic as the bottle-fed baby. The truth is that when iron supplements are given, the baby's delicately balanced use of iron may unwittingly be put in jeopardy.

Two specialized proteins in mother's milk, lactoferrin and transferrin, pick up and bind iron from the infant's intestinal tract. In scooping up this iron, they stop harmful bacteria in their tracks. The bacteria, including the potentially dangerous E coli, which may cause diarrhea, are deprived of the iron they need for growth. When iron supplements are given to the breastfed baby, the iron-binding abilities of the two guards, lactoferrin and transferrin, are overwhelmed, and the bacteria, lolling in the excess iron, thrive.

The iron in mother's milk, while sometimes thought to be low in quantity, is just enough, since the baby can absorb it extremely well. Up to fifty percent of the iron in breast milk is absorbed, as compared to four percent iron absorption when fortified infant formula is given. As he grows older, the iron that your full-term, breastfed baby receives from your milk is meant to be naturally supplemented by the iron reserves he acquired at birth.

This store of iron comes about in good part as a result of the blood flowing to the baby from the umbilical cord following birth. Your baby receives his full quota of blood if the cord is not clamped or cut until it changes from being thick and blue to being a thinner, white cord, about five to ten minutes after the baby is born. With this procedure, your newborn receives several ounces of additional blood, about a thirty percent increase in blood volume. The extra blood carries additional oxygen to your baby's newly operating systems. When the blood cells are broken down, the leftover iron is stored for future use. In this way, the full-term baby's supply of iron will be adequate well into the second half of his first year.

Calcium, Phosphorus, and Vitamin D. Calcium and phosphorus are two major minerals found in milk and are generally thought of in tandem. Calcium, in particular, is well-known for its role in the formation of strong bones and teeth. Cow's milk has high levels of calcium and phosphorus— much higher than those in human milk. This is necessary in cow's milk because the calf starts walking from birth. Despite this large supply of calcium in cow's milk, rickets, a disease of young children caused by lack of calcium, was rampant in the United States in the early 1900's as populations shifted to the cities and artificial infant feeding replaced breastfeeding. The sight of older children with abnormally bowed legs was all too common until it was learned that a high concentration of calcium in the blood means nothing if there isn't sufficient vitamin D to activate it. Better late than never, the essential vitamin D was added to the cow's milk sold for human consumption.

Breast milk seems to have low levels of vitamin D. Earlier reports of a special, water-soluble form of vitamin D in human milk have not been confirmed by more recent research. Yet rickets is rarely found in fully breastfed infants. This is true even in northern climates where there is less exposure to sunlight, which activates the formation of vitamin D.

A recent study comparing breastfed babies who received vitamin D supplements with those who didn't showed no difference in growth or bone mineralization between the two groups. Apparently breastfed babies do just fine on whatever amount of vitamin D there is in mother's milk.

Of course, you will want to take your baby outdoors, weather permitting, so that he benefits from the natural sunlight. A few minutes a day of the sun on your baby's cheeks is all that is needed. Babies were meant to have mother's milk and also enjoy the outdoor world.

The story of calcium also revolves around its neighbors, phosphate and fat. If the concentrations of calcium and phosphate are not in the right proportions, the usefulness of these minerals to the infant is impaired. Again scientists had to tinker with the amounts of these two minerals in cow's milk to bring them in line with mother's milk. As mentioned before (see "Fats"), unused fat reacts with calcium in the baby's system and—zip!—out goes the calcium. In the breastfed infant, fat is well absorbed, and calcium and phosphate are in good balance. The comparatively low levels of calcium in your milk notwithstanding, the retention of this mineral in your breastfed infant is still generally higher than that found in infants on formula, and the supply is adequate for your baby's needs.

Zinc. Your breast milk contains less zinc than cow's milk, but what is present is better absorbed by your baby. In fact, breast milk is a specific treatment for a rare, inherited metabolic disease called acrodermatitis enteropathica. Infants with this condition suffer a zinc deficiency brought about by a reduced ability to absorb zinc. Whereas babies prone to AE develop the disease on cow's milk, which has more zinc, babies with AE who are switched from cow's milk to breast milk, with less zinc, are cured. This special property of zinc in breast milk was only discovered in 1978. It is now understandable why AE is a disease that increased in incidence as breastfeeding declined.

Taurine. Bile acids, which are aids to digestion, react differently when the baby is breastfed than if he were bottle fed. In the breastfed infant, bile acids join with taurine, an amino acid found in research to be important to brain development in rat pups. The human infant is unable to manufacture taurine, and so is completely dependent on his food supply for this nutrient. In the infant's natural food, mother's milk, taurine is plentiful, but it is virtually nonexistent in cow's milk. This recently discovered fact is of concern to formula manufacturers and is perhaps a forerunner of the many new facts that have yet to be discovered about the amino acid composition of human milk. The work in this area is only just beginning.

Vitamin B$_6$ and Friends. A pioneer in breastfeeding research, the late Dr. Paul György is renowned as the discoverer of riboflavin and vitamin B$_6$. Prior to his work, no one knew that babies needed vitamin B$_6$. This lack of information was reflected in the preparation of infant formula at the time, and some infants on a well-known formula inexplicably developed convulsions. The problem cleared with the addition of vitamin B$_6$, a substance that was in mother's milk long before it was identified and listed in the medical books.

Scientists now also know that a certain protein in mother's milk has the capacity to bind B_{12}. The protein is, in a sense, a strong security agent, keeping the vitamin B_{12} under lock and key for the baby's use and making it unavailable to any threatening pathogens. This binding action, as with that of lactoferrin, deprives the problem bacteria in the baby's gut of the resources to grow, and so stops a potential problem before it can start.

Fluoride. Fluoride is currently receiving a great deal of attention, linked as it is to sound teeth and decreased dental caries. Mother's milk contains fluoride, and while the amount is less than some believe it should be, it seems to be perfectly suited to the baby's need, a fact that many experts recognize. Even so, there's often pressure on parents to give their babies fluoride drops. A supplement may be potentially dangerous since the *toxic* dose of fluoride is only a little more than double the *preventive* dose. In any case, there are no data to show that totally breastfed babies benefit from supplemented fluorides. Again, that old but new adage still holds—more is not necessarily better.

Vitamin C. The milk of an adequately nourished mother contains all the vitamin C her baby needs. Scurvy, a disease caused by lack of vitamin C, is virtually never seen in the breastfed infant. The vitamin C in cow's milk, about half that in human milk, is destroyed through processing, and it has become customary, mandatory really, to give vitamin C supplements to bottle-fed babies.

Keep in mind that this important vitamin is not stored in the body and therefore must be replenished each day, more or less, by the breastfeeding mother. This is seldom a problem since a wide variety of fruits and vegetables contain vitamin C. (See "Nutritional Know-How.") Giving vitamin C supplements directly to the baby is inadvisable. If there is a question of vitamin C adequacy, a supplemental dose can be given to the mother. She not only benefits herself, but through her milk, she dispenses the vitamin in the proper form and amount to her baby.

Contaminants

Who has not heard of DDT, PCBs, and PBBs, to mention just a few of the man-made, toxic chemicals known by their abbreviated names? Once highly acclaimed and used widely in industry and agriculture, these and other such substances have since gained the unattractive reputation of being stubborn contaminants—waste products littering our environment. We mention them here because traces of such contaminants are found in milk, both human milk and cow's milk. The situation can become intensely personal for a breastfeeding mother when large amounts of a chemical are discovered in the area in which she lives. What are the implications for her and her baby?

Our advice is to take any panic rhetoric with a grain of salt and use common sense. Put the matter of contaminants in perspective. First of all, there is no evidence to date of any harm coming to a breastfed baby because of the presence of these substances in his mother's milk. They are found only in minimal amounts. Even when mothers were suddenly exposed to high levels of pollution, such as resulted from the accidental contamination of livestock feed with PBBs in Michigan in 1973, breastfed babies did not show signs of toxicity. When the United States Senate Subcommittee on Health and Scientific Research held a hearing on environmental toxins and breastfeeding in 1977, one of the participants, Dr. Mark Thoman, editor of *Veterinary and Human Toxicology* and a member of LLLI's Professional Advisory Board, testified: "On the basis of the research to date, no risks to the human infant from contaminants in human milk have been demonstrated, and no official group that has studied this matter has recommended the blanket discontinuance of breastfeeding." In a policy statement, the American Academy of Pediatrics affirmed: "There are no known effects in children at levels found in people in the United States." As chairman of the Academy's Environmental Hazards Committee, Dr. Robert Miller said, "For the health of their babies, we strongly encourage mothers to breastfeed their babies."

Contaminants are not to be taken lightly, of course. They pose a risk to all of us, and research should continue to determine the overall extent of this risk. But when attention focuses almost daily on the amounts of contaminants in breast milk, there's a tendency to lose sight of what is happening at other periods in the baby's life, before birth for instance. As Dr. Thoman points out, "The chemical insult from any toxin is more crucial in the first six to eight weeks of pregnancy than it is during the months of lactation."

By giving some serious thought to what you eat and the products you use in your home, you can help sweep your immediate environment clean and thus lower the amount of contamination you, your baby, and the rest of the family receive.

We suggest that you discontinue the use of pesticides and other sprays in your own home. According to Dr. Thoman, "Certain chemicals are considered safe, but when introduced near young babies, they are not. I have found so-called nontoxic sprays can be hazardous." You can also avoid laundry products containing chemicals. Clothing treated to resist weather, moths, or wrinkling may also be suspect. Permanently mothproofed garments may contain dieldrin, which is absorbed through the skin.

As much as possible, try to avoid eating foods with pesticide residues. Fruits and vegetables should be peeled or thoroughly washed under running water. When you are pregnant and nursing, freshwater fish from waters that are known to be contaminated should be avoided. Fat can be cut from meat, since most of the noxious substances are concentrated in the fat. As a protective mechanism, the body stores such contaminants in body fat, which explains why it is unwise for a nursing or pregnant mother to go on a crash diet. The sudden loss of weight releases some of these accumulated chemicals and increased amounts may cross the placenta or enter the milk supply.

Periodically, it is suggested that breastfeeding mothers have their milk tested for contaminants. When mother's milk is analyzed, it is not unusual to find levels of one or more of the contaminants that exceed the currently established limit for commercial foods. It does little to clarify the situation. Dr. Edward Kendrick of the University of Wisconsin spoke to the issue in *Pediatrics,* 1980: "It should be clear to all that risk/benefit analysis leads to different conclusions for commercial milk as compared to human milk. The analysis leads to different conclusions because the alternatives in the two cases are so markedly different. The application of particular contaminant limits to commercial cow's milk does not lead to the use of a substitute food but rather to the use of cow's milk with a lower contaminant level. However, the application of these limits to human milk leads to the use of a substitute and possibly inadequate food for the infant, namely infant formulas."

We would add, too, that the baby being nourished on a formula is exposed to other contaminants peculiar to artificial feeding, such as lead and contaminants in the water used to prepare the formula. Furthermore, analysis of human milk shows variability on a day-to-day and even a morning-to-evening basis, so a single test would be inconclusive. A study in Norway on insecticides in human milk showed a dramatic variance in the same mother's milk at different times. In most cases, the repeated testing and careful analysis required to give meaningful results is time-consuming and expensive.

Dr. Kendrick speaks for many other authorities when he explains: "To ask mothers to have their milk sampled voluntarily when neither the experts nor local physicians can decipher the results not only wastes health-care dollars but generates maternal anxiety with no useful outcome. We must await the clear demonstration of risks associated with breastfeeding before making such suggestions. At present, it is a balance of potential risks against known benefits, and the known benefits must take precedence."

Even in the chemically prolific twentieth century, mother's milk still provides the greatest protection against the broadest array of insults to the infant.

BREAST MILK—AN ARSENAL AGAINST ILLNESS

Mothers who breastfeed their babies have often noticed that when the rest of the family comes down with a cold or flu, the baby remains free of it or has only a mild case. But until recently, a mother's conviction that breastfeeding protects her baby in a special way could be substantiated only by comparative studies of breastfed and bottle-fed babies. The studies, which go back to the turn of the century, show that nursing the baby definitely prolongs the period of natural immunity to many viral diseases, including mumps, measles, polio, herpes, hepatitis, some kinds of pneumonia, and other respiratory infections. They also show that nursing protects against a number of bacterial diseases. And it has long been known that breastfed babies have fewer problems with diarrhea than artificially fed infants.

With the advent of the 1970's, scientists developed more sophisticated techniques for examining milk, and new information came to light. Thus researchers now know some of the scientific reasons for what the early studies indicated and what many breastfeeding mothers believed all along. The story that is unfolding is more amazing than had ever been imagined. The protective makeup of breast milk reads as though it were taken from a scientist's dream list. Dr. John W. Gerrard, a Canadian researcher, wrote in *Pediatrics* in 1974, "We presumed that the function of breast milk was little more than the provision of nourishment. We now know that breast milk also provides effective protection, more effective than antibiotics, against certain common enteric pathogens, and that it can also be expected to provide relative freedom in infancy from allergic disease, a growing problem of modern feeding habits."

Dr. Herbert Ratner coined a phrase that aptly describes breast milk's unique qualities—"nature's vaccine for the newborn." What the new research also revealed, and what was somewhat of a surprise to many, is that this unique protection starts in high gear, with your baby's first feeding of your colostrum.

"Nature's Vaccine"—Starting with Colostrum

The first milk from your breast, which is called colostrum, is low in fat and carbohydrates, and high in protein. It is exceptionally easy to digest and is a superb "pick-me-up" for the newborn. In a few days, the thick, creamy-looking colostrum begins to change into thinner, mature milk.

Colostrum had been a wallflower in infant nutrition for a time, virtually ignored by many. During the 1970's, researchers began to notice some of its sterling qualities. They found it is loaded with living cells that can go to the newborn's defense against a number of potentially harmful agents. Mother's breast, it is now recognized, takes over where the placenta leaves off in protecting the baby.

From early research, it was known that your infant arrives in the world with a supply of antibodies—protective proteins. These come to him from your blood via the placenta. The antibodies, which are also known as immunoglobulins, have been manufactured by your immune system in response to infections that you have been exposed to. These include some of the common contagious diseases of childhood. While the immunity you have to these diseases is lifelong, that which is passed on to your unborn baby gives him temporary protection until his own immune system begins to develop.

In addition, protective antibodies to germs that you have come into contact with in the course of daily living in your home environment also cross over to your baby while he is in the womb. These immunoglobulins permit your baby, when he is born, to enjoy the same immunity as you when he enters the familiar environment of home. Until recently, scientists believed that the full extent of a mother's gift of antibodies to her baby

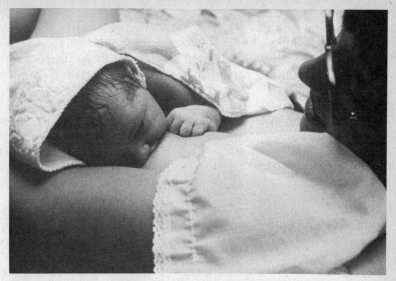

The concentration of immunities in colostrum is at its highest within the first hours after birth. Andrea Frigault is happy to provide a full supply of those benefits to newborn Samuel. (Photo by Harriette Hartigan.)

came by way of the placenta. What misled the scientists was information derived from studies on the cow, a highly researched animal because of its importance as food.

Research had shown that the calf, unlike the baby, receives no antibodies before birth. Its full, and only, allotment of protective cells comes in the first feeds from the mother cow within hours after birth. As every dairyman knows, the calf that is deprived of colostrum is soon a dead calf. It was also learned that the predominant antibody in this lifesaving colostrum is the immunoglobulin G (IgG). When the scientists turned their attention to the baby, it was found that the primary antibody in the baby's cache when he is born is the same antibody, IgG.

The conclusions drawn from these early studies, while not unreasonable, were not quite right either. It was assumed that the transfer of antibodies from mother to baby is a one-time occurrence. Since the important IgG is already present when the baby is born, it was thought that human colostrum was of little importance in the fight against infection.

Then along came the advanced technology and suddenly, colostrum the dispensable became colostrum the star. It abounds in immunities. Scientists found them in concentrated forms and in new modes that even surpass those acquired by your baby through the placenta.

In their laboratories, scientists made the surprising discovery that colostrum has an abundance of an antibody that is new to the baby, secretory immunoglobulin A (IgA). It comes about because colostrum in particular (but the later milk as well) is alive with protective white cells—leukocytes. These white cells, which are also found in blood, are the body's chief defense against infections. They have the ability to destroy or thwart the bacteria and viruses that can cause serious disease.

The presence of live white cells in milk means that milk is a living tissue, like blood. With the exception of red blood cells, breast milk is very much like blood. Even before scientists knew about these live white cells, breast milk was referred to by some doctors as "white blood," precisely because it has the life-giving properties associated with blood.

What caused a stir of excitement among scientists was the finding that there are about as many leukocytes in breast milk as in blood. White cells come in a variety of forms, each with unique properties. Some of those in breast milk produce the important secretory IgA.

The Protective Shield—How It Works

As its name implies, secretory IgA is secreted, which allows it to act as a first line of defense in the body. Whereas IgG, the main antibody coming to the baby through the placenta, is a blood circulating or humoral antibody, IgA exerts its protective effect directly at those points where germs are most likely to arrive on the scene, at the portals of entry to the body, such as the throat, lungs, and intestines. These areas are covered by mucous membranes, which act as barriers against pathogens, and it is here that IgA is employed in the battle against infection. The leukocytes migrate to the baby's intestinal tract, for instance, and continue to manufacture IgA. This antibody's somewhat different construction from its relative in the blood also allows it to resist the processes of digestion. The immunoglobulins stand as sentries along the frontier that is the lining of the gastrointestinal tract. When a threat presents itself, they bind to it and help guard the intestinal wall from being penetrated by germs or foreign proteins that are capable of causing allergies.

A leading specialist in the protective roster is the macrophage, or "big mac." A type of leukocyte, the "macs" are capable of engulfing troublesome organisms. They swallow the germs, and with the help of a protein enzyme, lysozyme, destroy them. (Lysozyme, it was found, is also in good supply in mother's milk.) Once the offender is destroyed, the macrophages move on to the next challenge.

The concentration of these antibodies in your colostrum is at its highest in the first hours after the birth of your baby, which provides yet another reason for putting baby to your breast as soon as possible. Starting breastfeeding within the first half hour or so following birth is in keeping with the infant's own inclination to nurse at that time. It is also an important step in promoting mother-infant bonding. There are multiple reasons for not postponing the first feedings. And no other fluid—glucose, water, tea, formula—comes close to being as good for your baby as colostrum.

As the weeks of breastfeeding go by, and the colostrum gives way to the mature milk, the concentration of antibodies in your milk decreases. But while fewer of these immunities are found in each ounce, the amount of milk your baby takes is increasing. In this way, he continues to receive ongoing protection against many organisms, both viral and bacterial. Under the protective umbrella produced by mother's milk, the infant makes the smooth transition from dependence on the limited antibodies he received at birth to the time when he can actively manufacture his own.

In Hong Kong recently, researchers discovered that certain leukocytes in mother's milk react to the presence of a virus by producing interferon, a protein that warns the surrounding cells of the impending danger. The interferon manufactured by the breast milk leukocytes closely resembles that produced by blood leukocytes and is added protection for the infant against a variety of viral diseases.

Another fascinating finding was the discovery that the breast can deliver a particular antibody in response to a new threat to the baby. Even when the needed immunoglobulin had not been previously present in the mother's blood, a chain of events begins when the fully breastfed baby is beset by a new germ. He, of course, continues to nurse, perhaps even more often than usual, and the offending organism is passed from baby to mother. In ways not yet fully understood, the breast produces a matching immunoglobulin on site, locally, and sends the protective element along to the baby in the milk. It's a system of "specialized programming," with the nursing mother making antibodies on demand to germs that challenge her baby. The baby places the order, and mother programs the cells and delivers the appropriate antibody.

The discovery of breastfeeding's direct, dynamic role in preventing illness helps to explain how babies, as long as they are breastfed, can survive in a highly infected environment. It is an advantage that, unfortunately, is most apparent in its absence, a fact that came home to the world in modern times following the introduction of bottle feeding in underdeveloped countries.

Some Studies—New and Old

A World Health Organization study in rural Chile in 1970 showed an alarmingly high number of deaths among infants. On examining the data, researchers found a strong correlation between the method of feeding the baby and the baby's well-being. Those infants who received formula or cow's milk before the age of three months were at a three times greater risk of dying than babies on breast milk alone. It was also found that any amount of formula upset the favorable condition produced by breast milk alone. Young babies who were partially formula fed fared little better than those who were completely on artificial feedings. Sadly, when the family income rose, mothers were more apt to give bottles and so, unknowingly, increase the amount of risk to their babies. Breast milk, it was concluded, provides a remarkable safeguard against infection for the young child, but this impressive shield will be weakened by the introduction of the supplemental bottle of formula or cow's milk.

With the rising interest in breastfeeding, researchers again checked old studies. One of the best known is the Grulee study of over 20,000 babies in Chicago in the 1920's and 30's. Mothers regularly brought the babies to the Chicago Infant Welfare Society for checkups, and the youngsters in the study were followed for at least nine months. Grulee and his associates divided the babies into three groups based on how they were fed: breastfed, almost half of the babies, 9,747; those who were partially breastfed, 8,605 babies; and totally artificially fed, 1,707 babies. A record was kept of deaths from all causes and illnesses due to infections.

Many of the medical advances that we take for granted were still in the future, so the babies were on their own, basically. A profile emerges from Grulee's figures of how breastfeeding or bottle feeding affects the health of the child.

In all of the babies, respiratory infections were by far the most common cause of illness. A noticeable difference in the three groups was found in the ages at which the babies came down with respiratory illness. Once past five months, only a small number of breastfed babies developed respiratory infections, while such illness among the artificially fed group remained high. An even more telling difference among the three groups was the number of deaths from respiratory infections—four of the more than 9,700 breastfed babies, 44 of the 8,600 partially breastfed babies, and 82 of the 1,700 babies of the artificially fed group died of respiratory illness. Deaths from respiratory infections in bottlefed infants were 120 times greater than among breastfed babies.

Obviously the breastfed babies had an accelerated or additional protective mechanism against respiratory infections that carried over into the latter half of the first year and longer. How this comes about is not completely understood, but it is probably associated with the distinctive immunoglobulin of breast milk—IgA—which fortifies the body's mucous membrane barriers against infections.

The second biggest problem for the babies was gastrointestinal infections such as diarrheal diseases. The breastfeeding babies had far fewer intestinal infections compared with both partially breastfed and artificially fed babies, fewer even than respiratory problems. When figures were compiled on the total number of deaths from infections of all kinds, it was found that in all, 129 of the artificially fed babies and 75 of the partially breastfed group died of infections. If the rate of deaths among the totally artificially fed infants were applied to the completely breastfed group in the study, it could be expected that there would be over 730 deaths in this large number of infants. But as the records of fifty years ago show only 13 of the over 9,700 breastfed babies died from infection. The breastfed baby had a forty times greater chance of surviving than his bottle-fed friend. Even in the light of today's modern medical advances, the low mortality rate in breastfed infants as recorded by Grulee from the Infant Welfare Society reports stands out as an enviable record.

More recent studies in Britain in 1951 and in Sweden in 1954 also attest to the fact that breastfed babies have fewer fevers, stomach upsets, colds, and earaches. Infections in the bottle-fed babies tend to be of longer duration, and again, the number of deaths was notably greater.

An updated comparison of illness among breastfed and bottle-fed infants was made in 1977 in the United States. The babies in the study were from middle-class families who enjoyed a high level of medical care, education, and housing. Dr. Allan S. Cunningham found that episodes of significant illness in the 164 breastfed babies were uncommon, and when there was illness, it occurred at a later age than in their artificially fed counterparts.

A recent study cited in the *American Family Physician* magazine looked at illnesses in babies as measured by visits to the doctor. Records were compared on 66 bottle-fed and 40 breastfed babies. Only 25 percent of the breastfed babies had to be seen by the doctor even once in their first six months because of illness. For the bottle-fed babies, this figure was 97 percent. By the age of a year, the breastfed babies who did come down with a sickness required from one to five visits, while the bottle-fed babies who were sick made up to sixteen visits to the doctor.

With today's ever expanding knowledge, it is very unlikely that such large numbers of babies would again be lost to diarrhea, at least not in the technically developed countries. Modern advances in medicine are a godsend in many ways, yet our first hope always, as parents, is that antibiotics and hospitalization will not be needed. We pray that our children do not become ill in the first place. The admonition of a grandparent to "keep the baby's feet warm," or "tie the bonnet snug," may or may not be relevant, but it is part of the concern we all have to keep the littlest ones in the family healthy. Antibiotics are of no use in combatting most viral diseases, and harmful side effects from their use do sometimes occur. Also, some kinds of germs that once succumbed quickly are now becoming increasingly resistant to most antibiotics. While it is reassuring to know that medical help is available, we would rather not have to test the cure, however powerful it is said to be.

The resistance to infectious disease that human milk affords the baby cannot be duplicated in any other way. Your milk is indispensable to your baby. As Dr. James Baggott, a biochemist who is well-versed in the study of human milk, has observed, "The preventive powers of breast milk should be used to their maximum."

Human milk is in a class by itself, the standard against which all other infant foods are measured. None can match it, and the reasons why are becoming more apparent all the time. Modern scientific research on breastfeeding is considered a Cinderella story, with the familiar item, mother's milk, looking better all the time.

MOTHER'S MILK CANNOT BE DUPLICATED

Mother's milk is a unique and unmatched commodity. In their definitive book on breast milk, *Human Milk In The Modern World*, Jelliffe and Jelliffe state, "There is no possibility of cow's milk being humanized biologically. The two products are much too complex and dissimilar."

There are components of breast milk that still have not been identified. A researcher in the field, Dr. W. Allan Walker of Massachusetts General Hospital, has stated: "What we now know about human milk is just the tip of the iceberg....We'll discover a lot more factors in milk that enhance its protective and nutritive value."

Your milk is not an inert combination of ingredients that can be identified, measured, and fairly well-duplicated. Mother's milk could be likened to a living garden, a plot of pink roses, for instance, blue forget-me-nots, and baby's breath (of course!). There is the continually changing and mysterious interaction of plants with each other, with the soil they're growing in, and with a host of other organisms. A formula could be compared to a bouquet of cut flowers, removed from the field that gives them life. What is more, rather than pink roses, there is a somewhat similar flower in the formula-bouquet. The forget-me-nots may be blue, but there aren't as many. And the baby's breath is missing (of course!).

Even if it were possible to incorporate all the unique proteins of human milk into a formula, they would subsequently be inactivated in the processing needed to make the formula safe. Any commercial product would need to be sterilized or pasteurized. The president of a well-known formula manufacturing company summed up the contribution of industry to infant nutrition by saying, "We're second best to the breast."

Mother's milk cannot be duplicated because, in reality, no two mothers' milks are the same. Even the milk of an individual mother varies from day to day and during different times of the day—just as other fluids and systems in our bodies fluctuate. The colostrum your baby receives in the first day of his life is quite different from the colostrum on day two or three; as different as your baby is when one hour old, then twenty-four, and then a comfortable forty-eight hours old. Even the taste of the milk changes with the diet of the mother. You could say that your milk is programming your baby's taste buds for the coming fare on the dinner table. During a nursing, your milk varies from skim to creamy, permitting your breastfed baby to enjoy a change of tastes that could be compared to a multi-course meal.

Breast milk is recognized as the superior food for the infant, but there seems to be no end to the promotions aimed at a mother to persuade her that her breastfed baby needs something in addition to her milk. The "something," it seems, is always for a price. Glossy advertisements will congratulate you on nursing your baby and then smoothly slip in a statement to the effect that some vitamin or other popular and important-sounding item is "borderline" in mother's milk. The ready solution, we are to believe, is giving the baby the commercial product. But what is "borderline" is the scientific background for such ads.

In a paper presented at La Leche League International's Breastfeeding Seminar for Physicians in California in 1976, Dr. W.G. Whittlestone of New Zealand, international authority on lactation, stated, "Milk is in effect a source of biological information which carries on those processes started in the placenta and completed with weaning and the total independence of the growing young."

We can confidently say that the baby ingesting his natural food, his mother's milk, is on the right track, nutritionally speaking. Mother's milk is a known production. There is a certain predictability that no longer holds true when the script has been changed. The newborn receiving a foreign food is in an uncharted situation. When the course has been altered at the beginning, no one really knows what might be the outcome next month, next year, or fifty years hence.

To quote Dr. Herbert Ratner: "The script of nature gives rise to the prescription, and what wise nature inscribes is the perfect prescription. Art, however, is only imitative of nature, and like any imitation, only approximates but never matches nature's product. That is why the best of formulas, artificial as they are, will always fall short of nature's formulation— human milk, perfected as it was through time."

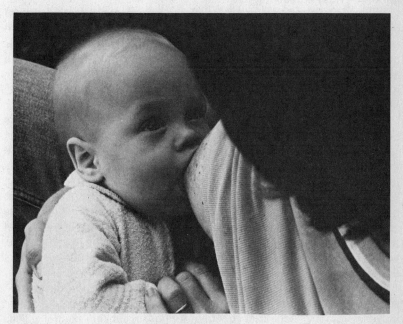

Mother's milk cannot be duplicated and neither can the loving gazes of breastfed babies like five-month-old Colin Anderson. (Photo by Martha Schulte.)

HOW THE BREAST GIVES MILK
(Magnificently, of Course!)

A mother's breast is a superior food source. The way in which it supplies milk for the baby is as remarkable as the milk itself. But in a bottle-feeding culture, a person may unconsciously think of the breast in terms of a bottle and so transfer some characteristics of the bottle to the breast. Mothers are told to wait until the breast feels full before offering it to the baby, just as a bottle is filled before giving it to the baby. The thought has been expressed that "the breast must fill before the milk will flow."

Not so. Your breast may feel empty, but as your baby nurses, milk comes in. While a nursing bottle is a container and nothing more, a nursing mother's breast is the manufacturing site. It is never totally empty and is always capable of producing more milk. Breast and bottle have little in common.

Your baby's eager sucking is the key to milk production. While the giving of milk is usually associated with the birth of a baby, there have been instances throughout history of women bringing in a milk supply for a baby other than their own simply by encouraging the baby to suck frequently at the breast. A member of the League tells of having been breastfed by her grandmother following the death of her own mother. Her grandmother had nursed all of her children and felt that this was the least she could do for her motherless granddaughter.

A picture of the inner structure of the breast could remind one of branches of a tree radiating from the nipple. The top branches are deep in the breast, coming together at the trunk, leading to the nipple. Small buds represent the milk-producing cells, known as the alveoli, which select the nutrients and protective agents needed to make the milk. Droplets of milk pass through the small ducts and are stored in reservoirs just behind the nipple.

There is a continuous build-up of milk that collects in these reservoirs between feedings. Over a period of time, this supply can make the breast feel quite full, but it is only a fraction of the milk the baby receives. The milk that collects between feedings, known as the "foremilk," usually accounts for about one-third of a baby's intake at a feeding. The remainder and greater portion of milk comes directly "off the production line" as your baby nurses. This process begins as his strong sucking action makes contact with the nerves in your nipple. Impulses from these nerves travel to the pituitary, the master gland in the brain, by way of the hypothalamus, which is near the pleasure center in the brain. Nature intends for mothers to enjoy breastfeeding their babies.

Two powerful hormones, prolactin and oxytocin, are then released in sequence. Milk is secreted under the influence of prolactin, while oxytocin moves it from the ducts. With your baby's vigorous sucking, band-like cells around the alveoli constrict and squeeze out larger, more concentrated fatty globules and proteins than are found in the foremilk. Baby is then

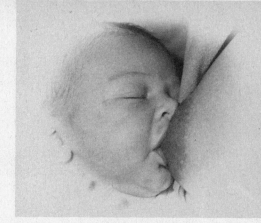

A mother's breast is a superior food source as well as a haven of comfort to a tiny baby. (Photo of Lineé Henning by Harriette Hartigan.)

getting the "hindmilk." It is a tasty reward for his continued nursing and for your patience in keeping him at the breast.

This outpouring of milk is known as the let-down reflex. At the onset of the let-down, some mothers feel a tingling or pins-and-needles sensation in their breasts. A few women may find this feeling intense enough to make them catch their breath. It is an obvious sign that the milk is coming in, but it is not something to wait for anxiously and worry over. Other equally bountiful mothers do not have this sensation, or they notice it only on occasion. Frequently, a let-down occurs more than once during a feeding without a mother's being aware of it.

Whether you feel the let-down or not is not important. It's there in operation. If it is a little slow in the early days of breastfeeding, it may be because you are somewhat nervous and your body is still adjusting to this new experience. This is not uncommon, and with perseverance, it won't be long before mother, milk, and baby are in tune with each other. You may then find that your milk lets down at the first sound of a baby crying—your own baby or any other baby!

Fright, or a sudden shock, may temporarily hold back the let-down, especially in the early days of nursing, giving a mother the impression that she has "lost" her milk. Milk is still there, and more will come, once mother and baby relax. Scientists believe that this interesting phenomenon in milk letting down developed in the early periods of the human race. It is theorized that when a wild creature or some other danger threatened a mother and her baby, her milk would not let down as a protective measure. It was time for mother and baby to flee, not sit and nurse.

There are no longer wild animals at our doors, so even when you feel anxious, snuggle down with your baby and imagine your milk pouring out to him in all of the profusion of a glorious Milky Way. A sixteenth century artist, Tintoretto, portrayed what has been identified as the milk let-down in a painting, appropriately titled, "The Origin of the Milky Way." It shows Hercules nursing at Juno's breast as her milk ejects in a spray of stars.

Wendy Davis seems to be delighted with the benefits of breastfeeding her baby, one-week-old Ashley.

$\mathscr{A}dvantages\ to$

$\mathscr{M}other\ and\ \mathscr{B}aby$

ALLERGIES

Protection against allergy is one of the many advantages a baby receives from his mother's milk. Your baby will not be allergic to your milk; you can count on this with certainty. It is a fact, a law of nature, that infants never become sensitized to their natural food. It would be just as strange for a baby to become sensitized to his mother's milk as for a chick in the egg to become sensitized to its egg yolk.

Proteins make the critical difference. The protein in your milk is totally compatible with your baby. The proteins in cow's milk and in formulas based on cow's milk are potential troublemakers for the human infant. Some babies, when exposed to these foreign proteins, become sensitized. When again fed cow's milk or cow's milk formula, they react with a variety of symptoms, depending on the part of the body that is sensitized. An allergic reaction can mimic a respiratory or intestinal infection by producing the same kinds of severe symptoms. As anyone who has an allergy knows, it is not to be sneezed at!

For the infant, breastfeeding serves as both a preventive measure and a cure for such allergic disease. One of the most dramatic cases of an extremely ill baby getting well on breast milk came early in La Leche League's history. Lorraine and Emil Bormet's two-and-one-half-month-old David, bottle fed since birth, had been suffering from almost continuous diarrhea, breathing difficulties, and eczema. Different formulas were tried, including soybean and meat-based varieties, with no improvement in David's condition. Almost as a last resort, the doctor suggested that breast milk was probably the only thing that David could tolerate.

Lorraine located a nursing mother several miles from their Illinois farm home, and the mother agreed to help. Following David's first feeding of breast milk late one evening, his astonished mother reported that, "he fell asleep and slept through the night for the first time in his life."

Convinced of the value of breast milk, the Bormets dared to hope that Lorraine could bring in her own milk, even though it had been a period of months since the baby's birth. She contacted La Leche League for advice. Milk production, we could assure her, is stimulated by the baby's sucking, and so she began the painstaking work of encouraging David to take the breast. Lorraine stayed in close touch with Marian Tompson, one of La Leche League's founders, and David continued to receive breast milk from generous donor mothers. Eight days after she began her efforts to breastfeed, drops of milk appeared. Some weeks later, Lorraine Bormet was completely nursing her baby, who by then was symptom-free, healthy, and content.

In the years since the Bormet story unfolded, numerous other mothers with similarly allergic babies have contacted the League, and many have found that, despite a late start, they can breastfeed. A more detailed explanation of how breast milk can be re-established is given in the section "Relactation."

Other equally enthusiastic accounts come from parents who had problems with cow's milk allergies with an older child and decided to go with mother's milk when expecting a new baby. They comprise a large group and are probably among the strongest advocates of breastfeeding. Kathy Driskell of Illinois tells the story of Michael, the Driskell's second child:

> Michael is our second child, and immediately prior to his birth I still could not come to a decision as to the best feeding method. We had experienced a series of problems with our first child, Jennifer, who was bottle fed. She had an immature digestive tract and vomited after almost every feeding, until she was nearly six months old. This was followed by chronic diarrhea until she was past two. Her pediatrician changed the formula numerous times, but to no avail. He finally concluded that it was an inherited allergy.
>
> Needless to say, I was eager to avoid this nightmare with Michael. Some of my friends had tried to encourage me to breastfeed, but frankly, it scared me to death. Coming from a large, close-knit, strictly bottle-feeding family, I had visions of my relatives shaking their heads in pity at my poor starving baby. Finally, after much debate, my husband, Ed, and I decided the best thing for Michael would be to give breastfeeding a try for a week or two. Now, fourteen months later, I have to look back and laugh,for Michael turned out to be the chubbiest, healthiest child I could have imagined. Totally breastfed for five months, he was lovingly nicknamed "Porker" by daddy and grandparents because of his rapid weight gain. Needless to say the digestive problems were nonexistent (he rarely even spit up), and his nickname still fits quite well at fourteen months. Nursing my son has been an experience I wouldn't have missed for anything.

Freedom from allergies is high on Brenda Bane's list of the advantages of breastfeeding. Brenda writes:

> We have three lovely children; Stephen is seven, Brian is six, and Sara is now thirteen months. Both of my sons were bottle fed. I would like to share the advantages I have experienced first hand of the breastfed first year as compared to the bottle-fed first year.

During their first year, both boys went to the doctor at least once a month, mostly with bronchitis and tonsillitis. Sara has been there only twice in her life. Both boys were allergic to formula, while Sara adjusted to my milk perfectly and thrived. Both boys are still allergic; Stephen's allergies are quite severe. To date, Sara has no known allergies.

As babies, the boys had colic very badly; Sara had none. The boys averaged only five hours of sleep per night at age one, while Sara enjoys about eleven hours. She is such a happy baby; the boys cried all the time, making me nervous and naturally tired and grumpy quite often.

Last but not least, let us not forget the cost of hypo-allergenic formula, cereal, baby food, bottles, sterilizers, and vitamins as compared to only mother's milk for most of the first year, then on to finger foods from the table. As for me, I eat better, am much healthier, and have really enjoyed relaxing along with my daughter.

Jani Howd of South Dakota was not thinking of allergies when she began breastfeeding, but later she wrote:

Avoiding allergies was not one of my primary reasons in deciding to breastfeed our first child. I can recall feeling fortunate that we had no serious allergies in our family. Now, two years later, I definitely know that it is an advantage that should not be taken lightly.

During her first year, Angie was a perfect example of a contented, healthy breastfed baby. Her only problem seemed to be a supersensitive skin. When I began introducing table food to her at about five and a half months, she ate willingly with a good appetite. At twelve months any attempt to feed Angie cow's milk or eggs resulted in a reaction. By eighteen months, eggs were no longer a problem, and at twenty-one months she seemed to tolerate milk.

Shortly after this, Angie developed eczema. We immediately took cow's milk away, but the eczema never disappeared completely until I put Angie on a strict elimination diet. The fading eczema wasn't the only change noticeable in Angie. Starting about the age of eighteen months, temper tantrums and sleepless nights were a matter of course, along with a loss of appetite. John and I attributed it to her growing independence and tried to handle her with love and patience.

Now that she is eating foods that agree with her, it is a rare sight for her to have a temper tantrum. She is our happy, contented, breastfed toddler. Her appetite has returned and the change in her disposition is almost unbelievable. Breastfeeding certainly does not entirely prevent allergies from ever occurring, especially with a very allergic individual like Angie, but it was reassuring to hear her dermatologist tell me that had she not been breastfed, her allergies would be more severe, in greater number, and she would have had food-related skin problems sooner, and have kept them longer.

From the scientific world, John W. Gerrard, MD, wrote in *Pediatric Annals* in October 1974:

> The evidence that breastfeeding prevents allergic disease is based on five factors. First, allergists such as Glaser, who practiced when breastfeeding was common, noted a greater prevalence of allergies in infants brought up on formula than in those brought up on the breast. Second, breastfed babies, after developing allergies when given supplemental foods, recover from their allergies when these foods are avoided. Third, babies on the breast alone may develop allergies that subside as soon as the food to which the baby is sensitive is eliminated from the mother's diet. Fourth, some babies—approximately 20 percent in our experience—grow out of their cow's milk allergy by the age of twelve months. (Such babies, if brought up on breast milk and not given cow's milk until the age of twelve months, would not be expected to develop cow's milk allergy.) Finally, it has been our experience . . . that babies with gastroenteritis due to cow's milk allergy often develop normal gastrointestinal function when given breast milk alone.

Dr. E. Robbins Kimball, a pediatrician and member of La Leche League's Professional Advisory Board, found in a study of 1378 children that the incidence of allergies is closely related to the length of time a baby is breastfed. Babies who were bottle fed from birth, or breastfed four days or less, developed the highest percentage of allergies. Nursing the baby for six months or longer provided the greatest protection from allergies. Of the 528 babies in the study who were breastfed, or as Dr. Kimball says, "had only mother" for six months, none developed an allergy when there was no family history of allergies.

A baby may react to foods other than cow's milk, of course—early solids, for instance, or perhaps vitamins or fluoride drops—so you'll do your baby a favor if you're careful to limit what goes into his tummy to what is compatible to his young system. Your milk only is your best bet for about six months. While your baby remains on breast milk, his intestinal tract is protected and is given time to mature. Potentially allergenic foods, which he may eat later on, such as egg white, citrus fruits, corn and wheat, will be less likely to cause problems. If your baby shows signs of a reaction to a new food or if there is a history of allergy in the family, you may want to postpone giving solids longer. Be sure to read the chapter on starting solids before introducing your baby to other foods. (See "Introducing Other Foods.").

If there is a history of allergies in your family it is generally a good idea to avoid eating an excessive amount of any food during pregnancy. There is evidence that a baby can become sensitized before birth to a food that his mother eats. A quart of milk a day would be considered excessive. Uncooked foods, such as raw nuts and fruit, are also usually more of a problem in this regard.

Can Baby React To Something Mother Eats?

In rare instances, a food that a breastfeeding mother eats will cause a reaction in her baby. Again, proteins figure in the picture. The protein from cow's milk, eggs, or some other food in the mother's diet may penetrate her gastrointestinal tract. These "stray" proteins in her blood can find their way into her milk. If her baby reacts to these "strays," it's an indication of a pronounced sensitivity to that food, and very likely the baby has a strong tendency toward developing allergies. In such a case, the answer is to exclude from the mother's diet the food containing the specific protein. Mother's milk itself is fine; the stray protein riding along is all that needs to be eliminated. Switching the baby to an artificial infant food would bombard him with a large dose of a possible allergen and make the problem worse—jumping from the frying pan into the fire.

When looking for the reasons why a baby is unusually fussy, has a rash or diarrhea, or develops other allergic-like symptoms, it's important to remember that the cause could be something quite simple, so consider the most common possibilities first. Is the baby receiving any supplemental bottles of formula or juice? Vitamin or fluoride drops? He may be crying because he's coming down with an illness. A baby who is nursing very frequently may be going through a growth spurt. Consider you own situation. If you're continually tired or rushed, make life easier for yourself and your baby by slowing down. Are you taking any medication? This could be the problem. Something that the baby comes in contact with could be causing a rash. A few common possibilities include detergents, soaps, fabric softeners, dyes (colored sheets), wool, feathers, lotions and hair sprays (place a towel around your shoulders when you spray your hair). Common diaper rash has been mistakenly diagnosed as an allergy more times than we can begin to recall. A change in laundering methods and the use of an ointment usually clears up the problem in short order, with the baby still happily nursing.

If the rash, fussiness, or whatever persists, your totally breastfed baby may be reacting to something you are eating. Fortunately, there is a relatively simple and cost-free method of finding out if your diet is involved. Start by eliminating a particular food for a week and see if there's a difference in the baby. Since cow's milk is one of the most troublesome foods in this regard, you might want to try eliminating milk first. Be sure to also exclude other dairy products and all foods that are made with milk. Other common problem foods are eggs, wheat, fish, chicken, citrus fruits, oats, corn, chocolate and nuts. Try eliminating one at a time and see if your baby's symptoms disappear.

Occasionally, a mother can eat a small portion of a food as part of a meal with no reaction on the baby's part, but a large amount taken alone at one time will spell trouble. If you have a highly allergic child, a little detective work may be necessary on your part, but you're already ahead of the situation by breastfeeding.

This section wouldn't be complete if we didn't add that changing your diet may not end the fussiness. If the symptoms are mild or come and go, and your baby is otherwise thriving, you may not be able to pinpoint the cause of your little one's complaint. Look over the section, "Why Is He Crying?" for suggestions to help you and baby through such a period. In mothering, the occasional squall is like the weather; we learn to live with it.

BONDING

Important questions are being asked about the bond, or strong attachment, that a mother has with her baby. How does it develop? Doesn't it just happen naturally? In a sense it does but, as with breastfeeding, an unfavorable climate can thwart the best efforts of nature, and of mothers and babies. Years after her baby was born, one mother recalled the emotional emptiness she experienced as a new mother: "I can still remember the disorientation I felt after the birth of my first child. I saw her momentarily in the delivery room. I would have been capable of holding her, but she was taken to the nursery and I was wheeled to my room. While the nurses spoke of the baby, and I knew she existed, I did not feel like her mother. Obviously, I was no longer important to my daughter's well-being. In the days which followed. I felt increasingly incompetent. Elizabeth had little interest in nursing, and I had little milk for her. I became very depressed."

Following a less than ideal beginning, most of us gather up our motherly feelings, loose ends and all, and manage to find our way in mothering. We do well enough in our new role in spite of a rough start. Yet the mother-child relationship is too important to be slighted for even a short period. This is especially true, as science is discovering, in the very sensitive period immediately after the birth of the baby.

Researchers in various parts of the world are finding that contact—early and extended contact between a mother and her baby—is the precious ingredient that promotes maternal attachment. Not surprisingly, many of the hospital routines and procedures that suppress a mother's milk have a like effect on the affectional ties she has with her infant. And as you would surmise, the principles that support breastfeeding also encourage healthy maternal-infant attachment.

Doctors Marshall Klaus and John Kennell of Case Western Reserve University School of Medicine, the researchers who are usually associated with the term "maternal-infant bonding," conducted a comparative study in 1972 based on the length of time mothers and their babies were together in the first few days after birth. The mothers in one group enjoyed an uninterrupted hour with their babies before the newborns were two hours old, and mother and baby were also together for five hours during each of the next three days in the hospital. The mothers and babies in the second group experienced what is too often the usual routine in hospitals: a glimpse of the baby at birth, a brief contact for identification at six to eight

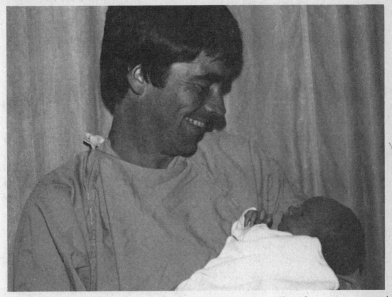

The bond between a father and his newborn child is also important. Kevin Long seems intrigued by his father's happy smile.

hours, and then visits of twenty to thirty minutes for feedings every four hours. When the babies were a month old, and again at age one year, the researchers monitored how the mothers in both groups responded to their children. Even allowing for the fact that no two groups of mothers and babies can be perfectly matched for purposes of a study, the differences were significant.

Those in the extended-contact group caressed their babies more often, and the interaction between mother and baby involved greater eye contact, suggesting a more personal response on the part of the mother to her baby. When their babies were upset, these mothers picked them up and comforted them more readily. Breastfeeding progressed more easily and continued longer. At two years, differences were noted in the way the mothers spoke to their children. The extended-contact mothers used a more descriptive vocabulary and asked more questions, whereas the mothers in the other group issued twice as many commands.

Such differences, it is becoming clear, may have a long-term effect on the child's development. When a mother is closely attuned to her baby, she is more ready to accept the busyness of the toddler years, a prime time for learning. As M. M. Alderman observed in a collection of articles on the young infant in 1975, "Since increased maternal attentiveness facilitates later exploratory behavior and early development of cognitive behavior in infants, early contact between the mother and baby can have a potent influence on the later development of the infant."

It has also been recognized that separation can take various forms, yet its disruptive influence is the same. From Cambridge, England, Dr. Martin Richards and colleagues point to what they term "psychological separation." Mother and infant are together, but the baby is listless and therefore unresponsive to his mother's efforts to coax him into opening his eyes or in some way communicating with her. "The clearest case of psychological separation," the researchers report, "occurs when the mothers receive an analgesic drug during labour." They conclude, "Changed patterns of mother-infant interaction are set up which may persist for many months, if not longer."

Dr. Michael Daly, Chairman of Obstetrics and Gynecology at Temple University Health and Sciences Center, Philadelphia, commented at a seminar in New Jersey in 1976, that delivery-room routine and hospital design tend to preclude necessary mother-infant interaction during the crucial first two hours of the child's life. He noted that babies who remain with their mothers for at least forty minutes within the first two hours of life feed and gain weight more satisfactorily, speak at an earlier age, and have a larger vocabulary at age two than babies who are separated from their mothers after delivery. He warned: "Our practice is separation. We'd best change the way we build our obstetric, neonatal, and intensive-care units. The physical and emotional interaction during that sensitive period does matter."

Studies also show that no matter when the extra contact between a mother and her baby takes place during the first few days, there is a difference in the mother's response to her baby—a finding that is encouraging to mothers who must experience some separation but who make every effort possible to be with their babies as much as possible. While a surgical delivery or the birth of a premature infant may not permit a mother to be with her baby as much as she would like, she can take heart in knowing that there is more interest than ever before in helping her to find ways to minimize separation. Many doctors and hospitals are breaking rank with old traditions and are welcoming parents into the exclusive world of the premie nursery. And many husbands are with their wives, supporting them emotionally, during a cesarean birth. Mothers who are conscious during their cesarean surgery are encouraged to touch their babies as soon as possible, even when they are not able to hold them, and to breastfeed soon afterward.

Nor is the value of early contact limited to mother and baby. When the father can hold and speak to his new son or daughter soon after birth, the beautiful bonding sequence is replayed. Rael Wienburg of Ontario, Canada, put his thoughts in writing following the cesarean birth of his daughter:

> Our twin sons were born six years ago via the "general anesthetic" cesarean and what a traumatic experience it was! I was kept out of the picture altogether and, as a couple, we saw the boys for the first time a day and a half after birth. Bottle feeding followed and, before you knew it, six months of tedious, non-ending, sleepless nights!

But not this time! With the help of London LLL Leader (and close friend) Cathy Wirick, we approached this birth well prepared. Our daughter Kate was born by cesarean, yet with an epidural and my presence, the experience will remain with us for the rest of our lives. Even though I'm squeamish when it comes to operations, I was not at all upset, and while the doctor worked, I chatted with my wife and the friendly anesthetist. Margie felt fine throughout, with no discomfort. I doubt whether ten minutes had passed before the baby's cry filled the air. Within seconds she was handed to me to be held. I immediately placed her cheek-to-cheek with Margie. By now the tears were flowing and the three of us were one.

Margie began breastfeeding as soon as she got to the recovery room. Her determination enabled her to breastfeed, as Kate would not latch on and it literally took three to four days of coaxing and persuading to succeed. Once again, LLL (via Cathy) helped considerably. We have found that demand feeding has been easy for both of us. (We often have her in our bed.) Margie gets the nursing periods to relax, hold, and just adore our little daughter. The months since Kate's birth have been relaxed and beautiful.

When other family members are also present for the welcoming ritual, or can visit soon afterward, they, too, become a part of the bond. Kathy Replogle of Alabama described the closeness experienced by the whole family on the birth, at home, of their third child:

We noticed a deep bond between the boys and their new sister, not just at first, but even now at several months of age. They always want to look her right in the eyes, touch her, and sing to her. I recognize that they have almost "motherly" feelings about her. In their sister, Juliana, we notice a calmness and contentment that we attribute to her peaceful, love-filled entry into the world. As a family, we have shared the miracle of birth, and we will always treasure those moments.

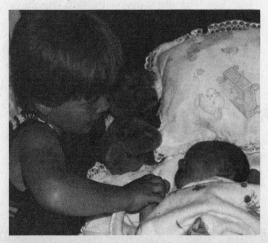

Siblings bond to their new brother or sister, too. Robert Bauchiero reaches lovingly for his ten-hour-old sister, Sandra.

Miles away, another mother, Joyce Reis of Kentucky, reflects on the interaction of her toddler, suddenly a "big brother," and the new baby sister in the family, who was greeted at birth by mother, father, and the older children:

> Jeremy and Heather have a fascinating relationship—completely the opposite of that which many would anticipate between a toddler and usurping newborn. I believe the tenderness and concern he shows toward her, and the fascination with which she looks into his eyes, can be partially attributed to their bonding at birth. Jeremy loves to hold and stroke her and never objects to sharing his "milky" with her. They even sleep together in a bed attached to our bed. Medical science has finally begun to recognize the importance of mother-father-baby bonding at birth. It may be years before they accept the significance of sibling bonding, something that is being experienced in many LLL families.

With the extensive attention now focused on maternal attachments—as deserving as it is—there is the danger that a mother may pick up the notion that mother-baby bonding takes place only during the first hour or so following birth, and after that, nevermore.

An astute grandmother, Mary Carson of Illinois, who was the editor of LLL NEWS from 1971 to 1978, saw signs of such an overzealous emphasis and commented in the NEWS:

> It's true that the earlier you have your baby with you, and the more opportunity you have for uninterrupted, loving contact with him, the easier it is for the relationship between you to flower beautifully. The same thing is true of breastfeeding—it leads naturally and happily to the kind of good mothering that provides fertile soil for your baby's growth, and your growth as loving, responsive human beings. But anywhere along the line, however unpropitious the beginning, change is possible in the marvelously complex human baby—or human adult.
>
> So bond away to your heart's content, taking things a day at a time and not looking back regretfully at what you did, or didn't do, yesterday. All is not lost, ever. There are always boundless possibilities ahead for you to make the most of in the light of what you now know, what you now desire.

JAW, TEETH, AND SPEECH DEVELOPMENT

The body-building enthusiast working out in a gym and the little one at your breast—his fists tightly closed, drops of perspiration on his brow, and his jaws working vigorously—are both engaged in body shaping routines. The gymnast's exercise may result in developing big muscles; your baby's exercise in eating will affect the shape of his face, his smile, and his ability to speak clearly.

Of course heredity lays the foundation for facial structure and has a role in the shape of things to come. A square jaw or a narrow chin, for example, may be a family trait. But whatever your child's potential, it is enhanced by the simple, repeated motion of sucking at mother's breast. Breastfeeding encourages proper facial development and may indeed spare your child dental or speech problems in future years.

It is easier for a baby to take a bottle than to nurse at his mother's breast, but such easy living isn't in baby's best interest. The long, hard artificial nipple used in bottle feeding may promote underdeveloped facial structure. It may also encourage baby's tongue to thrust forward, causing a deviate swallowing habit. If this habit persists beyond bottle-feeding days, there's the possibility that the alignment of permanent teeth will be affected. A rubber nipple, a pacifier, or baby's thumb may press against the roof of his mouth, narrowing the upper dental arch and limiting the amount of room for the teeth. Of such are orthodontic problems made. One mother who had both bottle-fed and (later on) breastfed babies found that only the bottle-fed ones needed to have their teeth straightened. The babies who were breastfed grew up with beautiful, even teeth and far fewer cavities.

In the late 1970's, it was suggested that breastfeeding caused dental caries in children, especially when nursing continued beyond early infancy or when the baby was allowed to fall asleep at the breast. Dr. Otto Schaefer, Director of the Northern Medical Research Unit of the Canadian Department of Health and Welfare, for one, refuted the report, explaining that it "is contradicted not only by my own experience in several thousand Eskimo children breastfed traditionally more than two and up to three-and-one-half years, but by the experience of approximately one-half of mankind, and for all of mankind until the turn of the century, having been breastfed for more than one year without ever seeing rampant decay in children." Once our children are eating other foods, there is an increased possibility of tooth decay, depending on the diet, but continued breastfeeding never hinders, only helps, the formation of straight, strong teeth.

When your baby nurses at your breast, your nipple responds by shaping itself to his mouth in a way that no artificial nipple can. A mother's nipple is soft and flexible. Your baby moves your nipple back into his mouth and up against the hard palate with his tongue, elongating the nipple and bringing his gums and lips around some or all of the areola (dark area). His cheek muscles are extremely active, enhancing facial development.

Through honest labor, baby earns his dinner and prepares his tongue and mouth to make the complex adjustments needed to form the sounds used to speak clearly. This extra "speech training" through breastfeeding is especially important to our sons, for boys are generally less mature at birth than their sisters and seem to need speech therapy twice as often as girls do when they reach school age.

Two speech surveys in New Zealand, one in 1971 and the other in 1973, tested whether "factors influencing the development of the sucking response could have an effect on improving the muscles required for speech." Frances E. Broad, who conducted the survey, looked for "any differences in speech between breast and bottle-fed children." She also examined "influences likely to affect early reading ability," because, she explained, "it has always been thought amongst speech teachers that if a child could speak clearly he had a very good chance of being able to read well." Her study covered 319 children, ages five and six. Dr. Broad writes, "The Putaruru and West Coast surveys show that improved speech and reading ability coincide with breastfeeding and that the improvement is dramatically seen in the case of the male child."

Clear speech also depends on good hearing, and repeated ear infections early in life can make it difficult for a young child to hear the fine differences in sounds. Breastfeeding's protection against infection is an added bonus. Ear infections can occur in bottle-fed babies who are given their bottles while lying down. The pressure created by sucking on a bottle can force milk into the middle ear, causing irritation and sometimes infection. Nursing at the breast does not require this kind of suction, so a breastfeeding mother can nurse her baby lying down and not worry that this practice will cause an ear infection.

The good effect breastfeeding has on baby's ability to speak is, of course, enhanced when his mother, father, and all of the family talk to him and coax the first "coos" from the budding linguist.

BREASTFEEDING AND YOUR REPRODUCTIVE CYCLE

As breastfeeding begins, your reproductive cycle moves into a rest period. If your baby nurses often, as babies usually want to do, you probably won't have menstrual periods for some time, usually for seven to fifteen or more months after delivery. The time when you can again conceive is almost always postponed until after that first period. While you may be able to become pregnant while still nursing, it will not be as soon as you would if you were a nonbreastfeeding mother.

Almost all mothers who are totally breastfeeding their babies are free of menstrual periods for the first six months and do not become pregnant during that time. Many of these mothers find that their periods do not return until the baby is a year old or older. By this time, he is more independent and is eating a variety of foods, although he may still be nursing. Dr. Herbert Ratner notes: "It is the baby's sucking that controls the mother's ovulation. The more the baby has a need to suck, the less ready he is to be displaced by another. The less the baby has a need to suck, the more ready and able he is to cope with a new sister or brother." In many cultures where breastfeeding is still the norm, where babies nurse freely for food and comfort and mothers use no other form of birth control, births are usually two or more years apart.

This rest period in your reproductive cycle comes about because your baby's frequent nursing stimulates the release of hormones that hold back the monthly preparations for a new pregnancy. Ovulation, the release of an egg, usually does not take place, and you do not have menstrual periods. A state of natural and healthy amenorrhea is produced.

We keep referring to "total breastfeeding" simply to distinguish it from the partial or "token" breastfeeding that is often seen in predominantly bottle-feeding societies. Total breastfeeding is the baby's complete reliance on mother for nourishment and all of his sucking needs. Studies show that it is the frequency of nursings that holds back ovulation. In a study of the !Kung mothers of Africa, it was found that births were spaced on an average of forty-four months apart due to breastfeeding. These mothers put the baby to the breast for a brief period several times an hour. They keep their babies with them most of the time, at night as well as during the day, and the frequent, short feedings are no bother. Mother is the baby's only source of sustenance for the first half year or so, and breastfeeding continues well into the second year.

If the baby's time at the breast is restricted, the mother's "time of grace," the space without periods or the chance of a new pregnancy, will be shortened. Nursing according to a rigid schedule, using bottles or a pacifier, or giving solid foods early all reduce the amount of stimulation from breast to hormone centers. The same is true when the number of feedings is curtailed— during the night or when the mother is away from her baby.

A marked increase in short intervals between births—a baby every year—is regularly seen in cultures that give up total breastfeeding for artificial infant feeding. This is not the way nature programmed a woman's body.

Numerous studies over many years have confirmed the effect of breastfeeding on fertility. We know this, too, from personal experience, our own and the experience of the thousands of breastfeeding mothers who have been associated with the League. John and Sheila Kippley gathered data on American women who practiced total breastfeeding and found there was an average of 14.6 months without periods following childbirth. LLL Leader Sheila Kippley writes in her book, *Breastfeeding and Natural Child Spacing,* "This is only an average. Some, an exceptional few, will experience a return before 6.0 months postpartum. Others will go as long as 2.5 years without menses while nursing."

While there are many factors still to be identified in the relationship between breastfeeding and ovulation, breastfeeding does lengthen the time before menstrual periods resume and naturally postpones the possibility of another pregnancy.

Variations in Cycles

While some nursing mothers go for two years or longer without menstrual periods, other women who are totally breastfeeding have early menstrual periods following childbirth.

Total breastfeeding will always delay ovulation for a time, but the resumption of regular periods is usually an indication that ovulation is occurring. For most women, the first one or two menstrual periods occur without previous ovulation. But a mother who has regular periods should consider herself able to conceive again. When menstruation does return, there is no reason to stop nursing the baby. Breastfeeding can and should continue. Drinking lots of water before the time of a period will help to ease premenstrual tension and keep you relaxed.

In reference to early periods, we also want you to know that the bleeding some women have at about six weeks is rarely a true menstrual period but rather withdrawal bleeding caused by changing hormone patterns.

Most women, by far the majority, do not ovulate without having a prior menstrual period that is sterile, one that is not preceded by ovulation. Put another way, pregnancy does not usually take place (in the completely breastfeeding mother) without having at least one period to first herald the coming change. But occasionally, there is no sterile period first to alert the mother, and ovulation occurs and conception may take place before menstruation resumes. This is the exception, and the still nursing baby is usually older and eating a variety of other foods. It can be something of a surprise if a mother finds out she is pregnant several months into a pregnancy. "I was kind of in shock at first," one mother explained, when such a turn of events occurred in her life, "but once we got used to the idea, I had to admit it was the shortest pregnancy I ever experienced."

Early periods may also be more irregular than what you were used to before you became pregnant, since it takes a while for your cycle to settle into a more predictable schedule after a birth, whether breastfeeding or not. You can find a more detailed and thorough explanation of the physical changes in your reproductive cycle while breastfeeding, and how you can become more aware of them, in Sheila Kippley's book *Breastfeeding and Natural Child Spacing.*

Forms of Contraception and Their Effects on Your Nursing Baby

If you're planning to use other forms of contraception in addition to breastfeeding, you should be aware of the effects on your nursing baby of two often prescribed methods—the birth control pill and certain forms of the IUD. The pill—old, new, or mini—may seriously affect both the quality and quantity of your milk. In a series, *Population Reports*, Robert Buchanan wrote, "Nearly all studies report that combined oral contraceptives appeared to decrease the volume of milk produced or to shorten the duration of lactation in some women....Some women using orals have produced milk containing decreased protein, fat, lactose, calcium, and phosphorus. Many questions remain to be answered." And the general advice on oral contraceptives given in the *Journal of the American Medical Association* holds for the mini-pill as well: "It is neither wise nor advisable to prescribe oral contraceptives to nursing mothers."

The chemically treated IUD may contain some of the same ingredients as the birth control pill, and is not recommended for the breastfeeding mother for the reasons mentioned above. The use of either of these contraceptive measures can change the perfect infant food, mother's milk, into a food that is less than perfect and may even be harmful.

A Nice Extra

When your reproductive cycle is in this resting state, lactation amenorrhea, you are less likely to have problems with anemia and the fatigue that goes with it, since there is no monthly loss of blood. Also, the tension or other mood swings that often precede menstruation couldn't be missed less. It's a more tranquil time, heightened, no doubt, by the "mothering" hormones that bathe away lesser anxieties—a natural tranquilizer, if you will. A mother's attention is more with her baby and the ones she loves than on many of the concerns that used to seem so important. One husband added a personal advantage for breastfeeding when he noticed that "living was easy" with a nursing wife. She didn't seem to pay as much attention as previously to such things as the house trim that he hadn't gotten around to painting or the loose hinge on the gate he's been meaning to fix.

BREAST CANCER

Are women who breastfeed their babies less likely to develop breast cancer than those who do not? The answer to this question is still being sought, and the search is complicated by the fact that other factors can, and probably do, influence the rate of cancer in a population. Yet researchers keep coming back to breastfeeding as an important consideration in the prevention of breast cancer. Dan H. Moore, PhD, American Cancer Society Research Professor at Hahnemann Medical College and Hospital in Pennsylvania, noted at a symposium on breastfeeding at the University of Pittsburgh in 1979: "In populations throughout the world where breastfeeding is practiced most, the incidence of breast cancer is relatively low."

Among the Eskimos in Canada, only one case of breast cancer was found in the fifteen year period from 1954 to 1969, even though the population had grown from 9,000 to 13,000. As the traditional Eskimos were assimilated into Western culture and the length of time that a mother nursed her baby decreased (or the bottle replaced the breast altogether), the incidence of breast cancer increased. Dr. Otto Schaefer, Director of the Northern Medical Research Unit of Canada, comments, "We have noted remarkable changes in regional breast cancer epidemiology in Eskimos and other people, which appear to be directly related to the local duration of lactation. In both Alaska and Greenland, breast cancer has been found only recently among native people. It was not seen in earlier times." A predominantly bottle-feeding society, the United States has had a mortality rate from breast cancer of 23 per 100,000 women for the past forty-five years. "In contrast to the relatively high mortality rate in the United States," Vorherr and Messer wrote in the *American Journal of Obstetrics and Gynecology* in 1978, "The breast cancer mortality rates in Thailand, El Salvador, Egypt, and Japan are only 0.9, 1.4, 3.0, and 4.4 per 100,000 respectively." In these countries, breastfeeding is still a common way to feed babies.

A possible explanation of breastfeeding's protective role has to do with the hormonal state found in the woman who is totally breastfeeding, which differs from that of a woman who nurses little or not at all. In support of this thinking is the fact that sexually active women who have no children have one of the highest incidences of breast cancer.

One factor that may be related to the low incidence of breast cancer in nursing mothers is the total number of anovulatory months during the reproductive years. Among the Canadian Eskimos studied by Dr. Schaefer, the Eskimo mothers commonly breastfed their babies for three years or longer. Another pregnancy followed, with more years of nursing. Pregnancy and nursing continued over a prolonged number of years.

A study in New York in 1964 by M. Levin and Associates points to the length of nursing time as an important factor in the protection against breast cancer. There was a decreased risk of breast cancer among women with a history of seventeen or more cumulative months of breastfeeding. A total of thirty-six months or longer of breastfeeding was associated with a "marked decline" in the incidence of this cancer.

Of unusual interest is the recent finding among women in the fishing villages of South China. Among the Tanka, the women who live and work on fishing boats traditionally nurse their babies on the right breast only. Researchers found that almost *eighty* percent of the breast cancer in older women developed in the left breast, which had not been nursed.

Breast cancer and breastfeeding were also in the news some time ago with the widespread reporting of research linking a cancer-virus in the milk of a mother mouse with breast cancer in her female offspring. Subsequent research disproved the theory that such a cancer-virus, transmitted in the milk, plays a role in human breast cancer.

GIFT OF TIME, MONEY, AND PEACE OF MIND

"As a mother who has done both, I can tell you that nothing is more convenient than breastfeeding," Katie Hartsell of Kansas wrote in response to a statement made on a TV show regarding the ease of bottle feeding. "When the baby begins to cry, the mother has a readily available supply of milk at the right temperature. There is no waiting for the bottle to be warmed. There is quite a savings to the family budget and no waste."

The cost advantage of breastfeeding is considerable, especially compared to premixed formulas and disposable bottles. One young couple, trying to

The convenience of breastfeeding can be clearly seen as Heidi Holmes pauses for a snack high in the Alps.

budget for their new baby and their first apartment were shocked by the "substantial jump" in their weekly food bill with the regular purchase of formula. Viola Lennon calculates that a six-month supply of formula and baby food equals the price of a major appliance or cleaning help for that length of time. A check of prices in Los Angeles in the mid-1970's found the popular, ready-to-eat formulas were three times as expensive as the extra food required by a nursing mother, all of which can be low-cost.

Beyond money, breastfeeding offers a gift of time; it represents hours that you do not spend shopping for, preparing, sterilizing, warming, or cooling bottles for the baby—the last is a special boon in the middle of the night. A student-mother wrote that she and her husband decided to use bottles with their first baby so her husband could also feed the baby, but more than once "it would be time for a feeding and there were no clean bottles." With the second baby, mother breastfed.

A father from New Zealand, Harry Parke of Cambridge, offered some personal, practical thoughts on the economy and convenience of breastfeeding to a group of fathers. "My wife and I figured that by nursing our first son, Christopher, we saved considerably in the first year by not using formulas, sterilizers, early solids, electricity, birth control means, etc. Raewyn immediately decided that the money saved was to be a deposit on a freezer, and it now stands in the hall!" Harry added: "Another advantage of breastfeeding to husbands is not having to get up in the dead of night to heat that early morning bottle. As a shearer who frequently crawls out of bed at 4:00 A.M. to go to work, I can't stress this point firmly enough. To get up at 2:00 A.M. to heat a bottle would be real cruelty!"

As a nursing mother, you will have complete freedom of movement with your baby. You can take off on short notice for a family excursion, a long trip, or that full-day picnic when formula can spoil. You can make your plans and pack your bags without worrying about having an adequate supply of formula for the baby—a formula that may not be available everywhere. You won't even have to be concerned that a strange water supply can make your baby ill, since a breastfed baby does not need extra water.

Wherever you and baby are, so is your milk. It's a most reassuring thought, particularly in the rare, but always stressful time when the usual, normal supplies of food are cut off. This doesn't happen too often, but we do hear from mothers who have had such experiences and are most grateful that their little ones were spared the brunt of this disturbing situation.

In the Midwest, an unexpected and severe snowstorm stranded a family in their car, and while the husband went for help, his wife snuggled the baby under her coat, keeping them both warm, and the baby nursed and slept. This young mother found the feeling of normalcy associated with feeding the baby helped to keep her own fears in check until the rescue crew came for them.

Another family unexpectedly spent a night in the mountains. The four Walkers of Ohio—mom, dad, five-year-old Scott, and one-year-old Adam, in a backpack atop his father's shoulders—set out for an afternoon's hike and didn't make it back to their camper for twenty-one hours. "We had hiked these trails so often we thought we knew them all thoroughly," Judy Walker wrote. But when the Walkers started down the trail they thought led back to their car, they inadvertently went down another trail, which they learned later, "went right off the map." The night spent in the isolated area was cold, rainy, and so dark "we couldn't see each other." Judy concludes her story: "My husband kept scooping leaves over us trying to keep us dry, and all night, at least once an hour, Adam woke, hungry, wet, screaming. Each time I nursed him, as it was the only thing that calmed him. I thank God that throughout that cold, wet night I had warm milk to fill my baby's tummy and to comfort him."

Kay Troisi from Alabama tells of her family's experience:

A hurrricane came roaring through our community with little advance warning of its nearness or intensity. A lot of damage resulted, including many fallen wires, and snapped pine trees perilously perched on power lines. Consequently, we were without electricity for two and a half days. During this time, I realized even more what an advantage breastfeeding is. Our daughter, Tamara, was only three weeks old and not having to worry about how to feed her was an immense relief. There was no concern over preparing formula, not to mention sterilizing, storing, or heating it without electricity. Not only did I have ready nutrition and reassurance for Tamara, but baby *and* mother were also consoled by our nursing session during the worst of the storm. We could be in our own little world while nursing, oblivious to the external ragings. After the storm, continuous closeness ensured a peaceful baby, contented mother, and overall a happier family, during a time when perhaps other families would be in chaos.

Chapter XII

Trends in Infant Feeding

Haven't you wondered, "Why was the practical art of breastfeeding all but lost to mothers in much of the western world?" After all, nature has long been a solicitous provider for the young, and we humans would not have survived to the dawning of the modern age without mother's milk. Long before the invention of the microscope and the discovery of germs, the breast was disarming microscopic invaders and passing the protection on to the nursing infant. True, throughout history some mothers have chosen not to feed their babies themselves, but have enlisted the aid of wet nurses. Yet almost suddenly, in the span of a generation, there was an almost total changeover from breastfeeding to bottles and formula. Why did so many mothers forsake breastfeeding?

As we know from our own experiences with our first babies, the woman in the middle of this century who wanted to breastfeed seldom got beyond the early adjustment days in nursing. A common explanation was that a modern woman was "too nervous" and could not produce enough milk. Or her milk was too rich or not rich enough. There were multiple problems. Feeding the baby became a frustrating and anxious experience for mother and child. In contrast, the nursing mother of antiquity, who is portrayed in art with her baby at her breast, is the picture of serenity. What did she know that the well-educated woman of the twentieth century did not know? Certainly, there was no La Leche League to call for help!

Then And Now

In many ways the birth and feeding of a child were simpler and easier in centuries past than what you may experience today. No sedatives were administered at the time of labor and delivery to depress the baby's eagerness to nurse. With few exceptions, putting the baby immediately to the breast was the expected culmination to giving birth. Mother and baby were not separated and so not deprived of the opportunity to rest and nurse, nurse and rest, balancing supply with demand. It was taken for granted that there would be milk, just as it was taken for granted that, at the proper time, the child would walk.

No well-meaning (but not too well informed) relative questioned a mother's decision to nourish her infant at the breast. It could probably be said that the mother of old did not make a conscious decision to suckle her baby. It was what was done, like embracing a loved one. For the majority of women, there was no practical alternative to breastfeeding. And there was none of the uncertainty that a modern mother may have on choosing the right method of infant feeding for herself and her baby. The mother shown in the classic pose on canvas and the mother we can imagine nursing her newborn in a simple bed in a cottage were at peace with themselves.

The Motherless Babe

Admittedly, this positive picture was offset by the occasional tragic case of a baby without a mother. Deprived of breast milk, an infant's chances for survival were poor. Often another nursing mother in the community literally took the little one to her bosom. When such bountiful service was not available, the only hope was to subsitute the milk of another animal, the goat or the ass, or give the baby a "pap," a bland mixture of uncertain nutritional value. The mother of one of the League's founders could recall as a child stirring a large pot of barley gruel for hours. It served as the "milk" for a tiny cousin whose mother had died shortly after birth.

Eventually cow's milk was altered to the extent that, more often than not, it was accepted by the orphaned infant. A bit of rubber shaped into a facsimile of a mother's nipple replaced the clumsy cow's horn or other apparatus that had been put into service to feed the baby. Artificial infant feeding became feasible and more readily available than ever before, and for the exceptional case of the motherless baby, it was truly a blessing.

But by all logic, formula and the baby bottle should have remained an acknowledged second choice, to be used only in emergency situations. That's not what happened, of course, and there's no simple explanation of why it didn't. In retrospect, we can see that certain newfound skills and ideas converged and, for a time, captured people's attention and suspended their logic.

The Machine Age

Synthetic infant food came into a world that was riding the crest of high hopes for technology's wizardry. Through human ingenuity, the previously accepted natural order of things was changing. The "lighter than air" machine defied gravity and conquered the skies. The awesome power of electricity had been harnessed, and machines were taking the drudgery out of life.

No longer did man need to earn his bread solely by the sweat of his brow, and it didn't seem all that farfetched for science and technology to free woman of the demands of feeding the baby. It was a tantalizing possibility. Deep down in just about all of us there's the yearning to set aside—if only temporarily—the responsibilities of parenthood. To the mother of a demanding baby, the nursing bottle can seem very attractive, detached as it is from mother herself.

In the meantime, refrigeration and sterilization helped to make artificial infant feeding safer. Advanced technology made possible the mass production and distribution of the new products. It's hard to say whether technology was responding to the need or creating it, but the result was a snowballing effect. The same industrial revolution that brought modern artificial infant feeding into existence also spurred a demand for it, as women left their homes to work in factories. But along the way, there were some disquieting footnotes to the brave new story of artificial feeding.

Problems

From the early part of the century, studies showed that there was a greater incidence of illness and death among artificially fed infants than among breastfed babies. The author of several volumes on children's diseases, J.P. Crozer Griffith, wrote in the *Journal of the American Medical Association* in 1912, "Roughly speaking, we may say that the breastfed baby has at least five times the chance of living than the bottle-fed possesses." In some of the cases reported, up to fifty percent of the bottle-fed babies died in the first year, compared to about fourteen percent of those who were breastfed. According to the pediatrician's "bible" of that day, *Carr's Pediatrics*, only two to three percent of all babies suffering from summer diarrhea (then a life-threatening problem) were totally breastfed. The problems of artificial feeding were recognized at the time, but the understanding of cause and effect was hazy.

The reason for such a marked difference in the health of the two groups of babies, it was thought, had to do with the preparation and delivery of formula. Breast milk, after all, goes directly from the producer to the consumer and does not become contaminated and infect the child. So attention focused on upgrading sterilization techniques and general hygiene in artificial feeding techniques. Expectations were high at the time that once these problems were overcome, bottle feeding would be on a par with breastfeeding.

With this in mind, programs were launched to instruct mothers who were bottle feeding in ways of sterilizing the milk mixtures and the nursing bottles. While the usual manner of preparing and storing food in a household sufficed for the other members of the family, it would not do for the baby. These campaigns did result in safer artificial infant feeding, but they did not close the gap in the total amount of illness and death between breastfed and artificially fed infants. It was some time before this fact was realized, and meanwhile, the message on infant feeding that mothers were hearing was emphasizing bottle feeding. Even today, in many parts of the world the increased prevalence of artificial feeding is producing the same tragic results.

The Medical Profession

With the arrival on the scene of newfangled ways to feed the baby, someone with specialized training was needed to advise mothers. The old expert, an experienced granny or auntie, was knowledgeable in a way of mothering that suddenly seemed as old-fashioned as the horse and buggy. In the new science of infant feeding, the medical doctor fell heir to the role. Traditionally, medicine has dealt with the baby who is having difficulties, and so the medical schools were soon devoting more and more attention to training young doctors in the intricacies of adjusting formula mixtures to the bottle-fed baby with a problem. Nursing mothers, it was assumed, were doing what came naturally and didn't need the physician's help. Almost without notice, the subject of breastfeeding in the curriculum for medical students all but dried up.

Along the way, something more was lost, namely an appreciation of breast milk's protective nature. When most babies were "brought up" on mother's milk, a doctor learned of the value of breastfeeding mainly from personal observation. For the most part, the nursing baby did not come down with the variety of illnesses that required the doctor's skills. Explanations of how breastfeeding protects the child from illnesses were scanty in the medical literature of the time, and understandably so. The means for obtaining such information were not available until recently.

So as more babies were given cow's milk and there were fewer completely breastfed infants in a doctor's practice, it was gradually forgotten that babies on their mother's milk alone seldom develop diarrhea, and that death from intestinal or respiratory infections is rarer still. At the same time, the conviction persisted that illness and death among artificially fed babies would yield to improved techniques in the manufacture of formula. In any case, the doctor had the new antibiotics to fall back on when disease struck. Breastfeeding's full contribution to the baby was therefore not evident until it was no longer a part of the picture. In a sense, no one really knew what was lost until it was gone and new problems surfaced.

The New Order

The bottle had quickly become a status symbol, associated with the woman who could afford this newest luxury for her baby. The breast, by default, became primarily a sex symbol. Artificial infant feeding mushroomed into a big business, and the bottle was looked upon as the ready solution to any problem, great or small, that a breastfeeding mother and baby might encounter. Ads featuring pictures of chubby, rosy-cheeked babies promoted the "modern" way to feed the baby. It was also seen as a liberating device, rescuing mothers from the affairs of mothering.

New social patterns developed and, in fact, became social pressures. Regimentation of the infant became a prime goal. The number of times the baby was fed took on great importance, and the milk was judged by its

No one completely under-
stands why the importance
of breastfeeding was overlooked for a time. But Lisa
Parks is glad the trend has
been reversed. (Photo by
Michael Parks.)

ability to "hold" the infant for the prescribed length of time, usually four hours during the day with one feeding at night (for a few weeks only). If the baby needed to feed before the prescribed time, it was concluded that there was something wrong with the milk or with the supplier—in the case of breast milk, mother. Mother and her milk were not "measuring up." Standards for infant development were established based on artificial feeding. The number of ounces and pounds the baby was expected to gain and the time for starting solid foods became absolutes that were applied across the board to bottle-fed and breastfed babies alike.

Hands Off!

The new method of feeding also brought with it a different way of "bringing up baby." Infant care became a matter of schedules, scales, and sterilizing, an undertaking that was more mechanical than loving, more scientific than social. Attention was fixed on things, and the emphasis in mothering subtly changed. The natural inclination of a mother to hold and cuddle her baby was secondary to the schedule. In the heyday of the strict routine, the impulse to respond to the baby's cry was sternly stifled. The fear of "spoiling the baby" was instilled, and to some extent, continues to haunt us.

Groping For Answers

Meanwhile, in their laboratories, scientists were engrossed in the ongoing challenge of upgrading formulas. Often by trial and error (some of serious nature), adjustments were made as evidence of too much, too little, or a total lack of something became obvious. When corrections were made, the changes were widely acclaimed and promoted—"Vitamins Added, Iron Enriched." In the excitement, the chilling fact that the new method of feeding the baby continued to hold many unknowns and that a generation of mothers and babies was serving as experimental subjects was almost completely overlooked.

A Lost Art

Unbelievably, the exception had become the rule. In the United States and some other countries, the exceptional baby who would benefit from an alternative to breast milk was replaced by a majority of babies receiving only second best. Society no longer saw a reason for any baby to have his mother's milk. The crutch was so unquestioned and commonplace that it was routinely used. And the art of breastfeeding skipped over several generations of mothers.

When the mother of the 1940's and 1950's did opt to breastfeed, she could call on little in her background to prepare her for the experience. She probably had never seen another mother breastfeeding her baby. Even the dolls she played with as a child came packaged with miniature bottles. Breastfeeding—like mothering itself—can be a natural, almost instinctive response, but it is also an art that is enhanced by observing others involved in it. In times past, this understanding of breastfeeding was picked up in the course of day-to-day living. When all babies were breastfed, there were ample opportunities for a young girl to see the loving give-and-take of a mother and child and to absorb the many nuances of the nursing relationship.

A new mother who wanted to breastfeed in the U.S. in the 1950's often found herself in an alien world. Society in general greeted her desire to nurse her baby with predictions of failure. Most likely she would give birth to her baby in a hospital, and for the hospital, breastfeeding was a real inconvenience. The nursing staff had been trained in the management of a central nursery, an arrangement that was geared to bottle feeding and is, in fact, a by-product of this technical approach. Dubbed a "displaced person's concentration camp," by an astute physician and father, the central nursery was originally conceived as a cost-effective way of using hospital space and personnel. Part and parcel with hospital procedures was an emphasis on germ control. The ordered and sterile way of caring for the baby was a necessary extension of other hospital practices geared to protecting the sick from one another's germs. When this approach is transferred to the breastfeeding situation and the nursing couple, the outcome is frustrating and, at times, almost comical.

One mother who had her babies in the mid 1950's still remembers clearly the various programs in different hospitals for "getting ready" before the babies were brought in for a nursing. It was a no-nonsense procedure, and with her first baby, a pad smelling of a strong alcohol solution was handed to her with strict orders to scrub her nipples. With the next baby, there was a larger pad, also saturated with what was surely a super germ killer, but this time it was for cleaning her hands.

A small pitcher of clear liquid that was to be poured over the nipples was distributed with another baby. But there was to be *no* scrubbing. What stands out in her mind was the next hospital stay with a new baby, when she was confronted with both a pitcher and a pad and had no idea of which was to be used where. She was sure she had missed the instructions for their use, and the busy nurse was already on her way to deliver another armful of babies, some for their once-a-day visit to their non-nursing mothers.

Undaunted, this mother poured the liquid into a plant and buried the pad under the mattress. Better, she decided, to get on with feeding her hungry baby.

Reversing the Trend

In recent years, a ground swell of mothers and fathers who are quietly insisting on the natural way of nurturing their young have reversed what was considered an irreversible trend toward artificial infant feeding. For the first time in decades, surveys by several manufacturers of infant formula in the U.S., Canada, and Australia reveal the dramatic increase in mothers who are breastfeeding their newborn babies—good news indeed!

WORLDWIDE IMPLICATIONS

At the same time that the widespread practice of artificial infant feeding has begun to recede in some areas, there is heartbreaking evidence that it is continuing to displace breastfeeding in other parts of the world. The infant bottle and formula are profit-making commodities in an ever-enlarging export package to what are commonly labeled "underdeveloped countries." The term fails to acknowledge that in some instances, such as infant feeding, the new developments have the potential to leave the people poorer still.

Monetary Concerns

While bottle feeding a baby may be a strain on the budget of a young couple in an industrialized country, it can be devastating for their counterparts living in a less economically developed part of the world. The cost of processed cow's milk formula takes as much as one-third or one-half of a laborer's wages in some areas. To parents trying to better their children's lot, the bottle symbolizes the fabulous world of technical progress and the promise of a better life. Yet the dramatic increase in infant mortality in the bottle-fed baby, plus births in rapid succession to the non-nursing mother, all drain a family's—and a nation's—resources. In the 1973 Science issue of *Saturday Review,* Alan Berg, a nutrition planner, wrote on "The Economics of Breastfeeding." He states, "The all-but-silent disappearance of such a major resource [breast milk] must be counted a catastrophe on a global scale."

When you look at your six-month-old breastfed baby, who will most likely have doubled his birth weight and then some on your milk alone, you can reflect with all due pride on your contribution to the world economy. You have produced approximately 400 quarts (about 377 liters) of milk. If you had used a cow's milk formula instead of breastfeeding, approximately 463 quarts of cow's milk would have been required in order to produce a comparable amount of formula. Processing the cow's milk into formula would have required the use of machinery and energy. Packaging, including bottles and artificial nipples, would use up additional resources. These items would then become waste products that need to be disposed of. And getting the product from cow to baby would undoubtedly have involved transporting it a number of miles, using more valuable sources of energy.

The cost of artificial infant feeding can be steep. When figures were obtained in 1968 in the Philippines, it was estimated that the loss in breast milk for that one year cost the Philippine people thirty-three million dollars. Dr. Derrick Jelliffe, who has traveled extensively in the Third-

Surveys by formula companies show that breastfeeding is on the increase among mothers in Australia. Dulcie Ames is one of the lucky babies contributing to that happy statistic and her t-shirt proclaims the fact that "breast fed is best fed." (Many League mothers find that the type of infant seat in this photo—with a fabric back on a slightly springy metal frame—is more comfortable for babies than hard plastic types.)

World studying infant nutrition, calculated that in order to replace breast milk with cow's milk in India in 1968, it would have required 114 million additional dairy cows. The cows would have to be fed, of course, and growing the necessary grain would remove arable land from the production of other foods. In areas of the world where food supplies are often scarce, using grain to feed milking herds would mean less food for some portion of the population.

When weighing the costs of different methods of feeding the baby, it must be said that breastfeeding is not as costly as some formerly believed. "The financial cost of human milk for feeding babies," Dr. Jelliffe says, "has been consistently overestimated because of an unrealistic and unnecessary emphasis on the need for large amounts of expensive animal protein in the diet of the lactating woman—a need that can be met largely by mixtures of locally available inexpensive plant foods."

If a mother is undernourished, it has been shown that supplementing her diet will quickly increase the amount of milk she has for her baby. When there is a critical food shortage, it just makes good sense to feed the mothers and so enable them to feed their babies. Doctor Jelliffe further explains, "The high efficiency rate of conversion of food energy into breast milk in the mother, and the very low requirement of protein, added to the biological ability to store energy during pregnancy, enables mothers who are subsisting on marginal nutrition to breastfeed their infants for prolonged periods."

Population Problems

Nor is the economic drain the only consideration. With the decline of breastfeeding in a population, there inevitably follows an overall increase in births—a population explosion. The mother who is not breastfeeding can become pregnant sooner. "In terms of national development," Alan Berg points out, "lactation has another major economic asset—its link to family planning." Breastfeeding is now recognized as an important controlling factor in the growth of a population. In his article, "Breast-Feeding and Population Growth," John Knodel of the Population Studies Center at the University of Michigan, wrote in 1977 in *Science,* "Recent estimates suggest that the total woman-years of protection against pregnancy provided by breastfeeding in the Third World is quite substantial and may well be larger than the total amount of contraceptive protection achieved through family planning programs. . . ."

In Taiwan, scientists estimated that breastfeeding limited the increase in births by twenty percent. If the nursing mothers of India all decided to bottle feed their babies, there would be approximately five million more births each year.

A Natural Resource

A number of governments, recognizing the importance of breastfeeding, are taking steps to protect their newborn infants and to preserve the natural resource that is mother's milk. The Jamaican Ministry of Health, for one, publishes a variety of helpful pamphlets on infant nutrition, all promoting breastfeeding exclusively in the early months of the baby's life. Billboards located throughout the island proclaim "The Breast is Best," and spot radio messages carrying the same message are heard regularly.

Emily Will, who taught a nutrition program to high school students in Jamaica for several years, writes that now, as a nursing mother at home, "I still have the opportunity to promote good nutrition in a highly personalized way." The fact that Emily is breastfeeding three-month-old Peter "fascinates" the students who visit her and her husband, Mark. "Some even ask me to feed Peter while they are visiting," Emily relates. "While this makes me feel as though we're staging a show, I've decided that the educational benefits outweigh such personal considerations." She adds that visitors "inevitably ask what else I'm feeding Peter. 'Does he get tinned feed (formula), too?' Most seem unwilling to believe that an infant can really be fat and happy on nothing but breast milk." Emily notes, "Somewhere, somehow, Jamaicans have picked up the notion that although the breast is good for baby, it's not enough." She suspects that "although infant formula is no longer advertised, the insidious fears about the breast being insufficient for baby were sowed in the recent past when formula was pushed."

In Papua New Guinea, the national breastfeeding organization, the Susu Mamas ("susu" means breast milk in New Guinea pidgin) have kept alive an appreciation of breastfeeding's value. Due to their efforts, the national parliament passed a bill restricting the import and distribution of nursing bottles, nipples, and formula. Bottles and nipples may be sold to mothers only on the written authorization of a registered health professional after it has been determined that such items are necessary and the mother knows how to use them correctly. There is a stiff penalty for violations. It is hoped that this legislation will halt the recent shift to artificial infant feeding with its attending problems among the urban mothers of Papua New Guinea.

Babies' Health

As important as economic loss and population explosions are in an appraisal of infant food, the bottom line is the health of the baby. In this regard, the evidence is irrefutable. There are few things that are more important to a newborn than to assure him, as much as possible, the benefits of his mother's milk.

In the tropics particularly, where the climate makes the control of infectious diseases an uphill battle, the infant who does not have the protection of his mother's milk is in jeopardy. Most unfortunate are the instances when the baby's nursing bottle holds a very dilute mixture of a little powdered formula and the only water available, which may be contaminated. If the mixture looks like milk, the mothers believe it nourishes as does milk. They scrimp to buy it for their babies in the well-meant but mistaken belief that it is the best thing they can do for their children. The return to breastfeeding cannot come too soon. The implications for the next generation are incalculable.

Chapter XIII

Fact, Fiction, and Fancy

The birth of a baby is no ordinary event, and in keeping with its specialness, societies throughout the world have developed ways to ensure the well-being of the new infant and mother. The rather elaborate set of customs that usually surrounds their care is meant to be helpful, and in many ways, it is just that. But the prescribed practices are also a reflection of the society itself. Differences abound. The words of advice that are directed to a new mother are often a colorful mixture of fact, fiction, and fancy. Through our contacts with League people in a number of different parts of the world, we have learned about some of the commonly held beliefs in many lands. The descriptions of mother-baby care are often enlightening and sometimes amusing, but they're always interesting.

Ideas about food almost always figure prominently in the period immediately after the mother gives birth and while she is nursing her baby. In some areas, a traditional dish is made for the new mother. In Italy, an old recipe for bread soup made with whole-grain bread, milk and eggs is often served to new mothers.

Often, mothers are also warned against eating certain foods. A quick glance at the selection reveals that there is little rhyme or reason to the choices. Breastfeeding mothers in the United States may hear that eating chocolate will give their babies diarrhea. While there is little reason to recommend chocolate to a new mother, it can safely be said that chocolate eaten in moderation is no more likely to cause problems than any other foods. (Moderation is a good rule to follow in regard to all foods.)

Nursing mothers in New Zealand are told to avoid cabbage and tomato soup. A mother in Italy, however, can enjoy dishes made with tomatoes with never a second thought, but she can expect to hear that she should be eating generous portions of white foods, such as pasta and white wine. The assumption is that milk, being white, is best produced by eating foods of the same color.

Shanda Bertelli and Jenny della Torre report from Italy that the laws governing maternity leaves there are "among the best in the world." An Italian mother who quits her job to have her baby will receive compensation for some time after her baby is born, and she can stay home for about three years while still being assured of getting her job back. But Italian mothers also have their share of old wives' tales to contend with. Shanda and Jenny explain that one such story is particularly hard on the breastfeeding mother who wears glasses. She will endanger her eyesight, it is said, if she continues to nurse her baby for any length of time. This unfounded bit of hearsay claims that the retina will detach! On a more positive note, Maureen Hamilton of New Zealand tells how the Maori mothers there have traditionally treated "sticky eye" in new babies by bathing the eye with breast milk. "It really clears it up," she writes. "Obviously, those antibodies in the milk get to work."

In all societies, once bottle feeding is introduced, it is almost inevitable that mothers begin to doubt their own ability to nourish their babies. Rosalie Walker of New Zealand notes that in her country the idea has surfaced "that breastfeeding will be taking too much out of a mother, especially as the baby gets older." She is quick to add, though, that the misconceptions begin to fade as more mothers nurse beyond six or nine months. In families where the babies had been bottle-fed and breastfeeding is now the new innovation, the older generation is "being converted by their bonny grandchildren."

In some areas, the sight of an older nursing baby is frowned upon, but this isn't true everywhere—sometimes for unexpected reasons. An American mother in Poland, Nancy Sherwood, writes, "People here are not upset that I am nursing a two-year-old—they are just amazed that it can be done." Nancy describes how the Polish mothers are now hearing the negative refrain that was so prevalent until recently in the United States—"Life is too stressful for a modern mother to be able to breastfeed her baby." As could be expected, the mothers resort to bottle feeding more and more often. Further compounding the problem, the strict feeding schedule has gained a foothold. In a conversation with a Polish-American doctor whose wife was nursing, Nancy was able to explain that at two months, their son "didn't need fruit juice and tea, that breast milk is enough, and it is okay for the baby to nurse more often than every four hours as prescribed by pediatricians here." She was pleased to tell us that "when his wife started nursing more often and discontinued the fruit juice and tea, the baby and mother were both much happier."

Another difficult situation for mothers worldwide develops when material goods begin to compete with the baby. As housing becomes a status symbol in a culture, women are often expected to devote a considerable amount of time to keeping house. Holding the baby and nursing frequently are no longer regarded as important aspects of good mothering. Sad to say, the house beautiful may then become an added burden rather than a place to nurture the family.

In almost all of the industrial nations, there is pressure on mothers to work outside the home. Phillippa Seymour belongs to a League group in

Luxembourg that is made up of mothers from a number of countries, and she explains that in areas where there is a highly developed system of nurseries provided by the state for working mothers, as is the case in Iceland, "most women go back to work very soon after having a baby." She further notes, "There would be strong social pressure against any woman who wanted to stay at home and care for her children full-time."

Perhaps the greatest differences in mothering patterns can be seen in those areas in the world where a technologically advanced portion of the society lives side-by-side with a group that still mothers in a traditional manner without bottles. The former can usually be identified by the fact that the babies are kept apart from the mother, at least some of the time, while in the traditional communities mothers and babies remain together. Breastfeeding flourishes in the one and is laden with problems in the other. Gail Brown writes from South Africa: "The majority of white mothers 'lose their milk' anytime in the first couple of months, if they breastfeed at all. This is fostered by baby clinics that still advise supplementary formulas at the first setback and relatively early solids."

Gail then describes the difference when a black mother gives birth to her baby. "The mother is completely 'mothered' for the first two or three months, in that she is waited on hand and foot, with everything done for her. She feels important and secure with all the attention, and there is no

Mothering a new mother is an important part of the traditions in Africa. Cecelia Weedor reclines comfortably in a hammock while her husband Peter brings Korlu to her for a feeding.

question of failing at breastfeeding." Scheduled feedings are unheard of, Gail says. "It is just natural that when the baby is hungry, the mother feeds him." She explains that the whole attitude toward birth and baby care is supportive and relaxed, though she points out that the black mothers in the cities must often leave their babies in order to work to support their children. "But," she says, "it is still the custom for a black woman working in the city to return to her tribal homeland and family to have her baby. She stays as long as she can afford to."

In the tribal kraal, there is always a watchful—but not worried—eye kept on toddlers by an adult or older sibling. Part of the older childrens' duties is to look after the younger children who can leave their mothers. Gail believes that this is the reason why "the African blacks grow up knowing exactly how to handle and get along with children." She notes that "black fathers always take time to chat with the children and play with them if possible, and are always concerned and understanding." She explains that while the actual physical care of the baby is traditionally left to the mother, "she doesn't really have to work at making the father feel needed and involved. He is, by tradition."

Another League mother in South Africa, Nan Jolly, notes that the mothers of the Xhosa tribe "abba" their babies, that is they carry them around everywhere on their backs, securely tied on with a blanket. And, she reports, "The babies scarcely ever cry." Nan goes on to say that, "Tragically, these people are abandoning their naturally good mothering ways for imported techniques. With the use of that status symbol, the bottle, gastroenteritis and malnutrition are widespread."

In Zimbabwe, Nikki Galbraith learned of black mothering traditions from an experienced nurse in the area, Sister Mapondera, who traveled twenty miles to meet with Nikki. Sister stressed that the needs of the new mother and baby are of prime importance. "When the mother discovers that she is pregnant," Nikki writes, "she engages the services of a traditional midwife. The midwife looks after the mother during labor and delivery and afterwards does the mother's household chores." Sister Mapondera explained that payment for the midwife's services may be "a parcel of firewood, a chicken, and mealie meal (dry porridge made from crushed maize.)" The mother stays in the house until the baby's cord falls off, usually about the seventh day. Nikki writes that mothers will fully breastfeed on demand for a year and then introduce solids and continue breastfeeding for two to three years. An unfortunate custom among these mothers is to wean the baby "straight away," even when the baby is still fully breastfed, if the mother becomes pregnant. "It is believed that the milk will become poisonous," according to Nikki.

Fleur Parlidis, who lives with her Greek husband and young daughter, Dimitruly, in Athens, explains that a Greek mother will good-naturedly accept the uncomplimentary comment, "tsou tsou" or "little dirty one," that a passerby may direct to her baby. Everyone knows that the opposite

All over the world babies are happiest when they are close to their mothers. Martha Hume and Sydney, from Zimbabwe, show us a type of baby carrier used there. (Photo by Pat Crosby.)

of what is said is meant. The speaker really considers the baby to be "lovely." An admirer is intent on outwitting the "evil eye," a character from Greek folklore. If the person were to mention how sweetly the baby sleeps, for instance, why no sooner would the words be out, than sure enough, the baby wakes up—pinched awake, no doubt, by the "evil eye." If admiring relatives and neighbors do risk attracting the "evil eye" to the baby by too many unguarded compliments, all can be quickly set aright by the mention of garlic. Fleur points out that "like many other 'nasties,' the 'evil eye' is allergic to garlic!"

From her travels for La Leche League in Latin America, Betty Ann Countryman of Indiana has gained a keen appreciation of mothering in that part of the world. She writes:

We have so much to learn from the Indian mothers—indeed, from all of Mayan family life. The infants I saw were snuggled close to their mothers' bodies, nestled in rebozos (a type of shawl used by the Indian mothers to carry their babies). Sleeping peacefully on mother's back or nursing contentedly at her breast, every baby was clearly satisfied and secure. I grew accustomed to the sight of a bright-eyed little one peering over his mother's shoulder at the world in front of him or viewing from his perch on her back the places and people passing by. Even the child of two or three is carried by an older sibling whenever he grows tired or needs some comforting.

Touch—always the magical security of touch! If not in arms or snug on mother's or sister's back, then holding hands with one of them or with father or big brother.

To the list of breastfeeding's unique characteristics, we add yet one more—its universality. The baby at the breast represents the common language of mothering. Babies have basic needs that do not change, regardless of when or where they are born. And the beautifully natural act of nursing your little one has this same timeless quality. It is a link to other mothers and a sign, even, of womanly power. The ability of a mother's body to nurture her child is a source of strength to her. And through breastfeeding's gentling effect, an island of peace is secured. It is a small miracle, belonging rightfully to mothers, babies, and families the world over.

The baby at the breast represents a common bond with mothers everywhere. Veronica Castillo finds an island of peace as she nurses seven-month-old Sebastian. (Photo by Richard Ebbitt.)

About La Leche League

La Leche League began with a wish—a dream, really—that all mothers who want to breastfeed their babies will be able to do so. The seven of us who founded La Leche League had overcome varied difficulties before we were able to breastfeed with ease and confidence, and we knew of too many mothers who were unable to breastfeed at all simply because they had no one to turn to for information and advice.

It was at a church picnic that Mary White and Marian Tompson decided that there had to be a way to help their friends who wanted to breastfeed their babies but found only frustration and failure when they tried. With their own nursing babies cradled in their arms on that summer afternoon in 1956, Mary and Marian wanted to find a way to help those women so that they, too, could know the deep fulfillment of the nursing bond.

In the weeks that followed, Mary talked to Mary Ann Kerwin, her sister-in-law, and Mary Ann Cahill, who casually mentioned the idea to Betty Wagner. Marian contacted Edwina Froehlich, who got on the phone to call her good friend Viola Lennon. Each of us had nursed one or more babies. We had no grand plans on how to go about helping our friends, but we were willing to try. Two local physicians, Drs. Herbert Ratner and Gregory White, were an important source of information on aspects of breastfeeding and mothering that were commonly associated with the medical community.

Confident of our information, and enthusiastic about the natural way of mothering, we gathered our pregnant friends for a meeting at Mary White's house one October evening in 1956. What we offered to interested neighborhood mothers then—and what the 18,000 La Leche League Leaders who have followed us continue to provide—was information, reassurance, and the personal mother-to-mother warmth and caring that assures success for any woman who wants to breastfeed her baby. Although La Leche League now has grown into a worldwide organization with over 4,000 La Leche League groups in forty-three countries (located in communities throughout the United States and Canada, parts of Europe, New Zealand, Africa, and other parts of the world), our focus still remains on the personal one-to-one sharing of information and encouragement that provides the new mother with the confidence she needs to nurse her baby.

Today La Leche League stands as the internationally recognized authority on breastfeeding. La Leche League has been contacted by mothers, fathers, doctors, nurses, and various professionals throughout the world for our expertise on breastfeeding. Over the years it has been La Leche League's privilege to help hundreds of thousands of mothers nurse their babies.

To us, La Leche League is nothing more and nothing less than a mother with a baby in her arms and a smile on her face, proud of herself and eager to share all that she has learned and experienced. The heart and soul of La Leche League are mothers, like you, who find fulfillment and delight in nurturing an infant.

La Leche League Leaders everywhere rejoice in the knowledge that through helping mothers to nurse their babies, they are playing a part in strengthening and deepening the love ties formed in infancy that will last a lifetime.

Our Organization

Statue of Our Lady of La Leche in St. Augustine, Florida.

Our name, La Leche, is Spanish and is pronounced la lay-chay. Simply translated, it means "the milk." The name for our organization was inspired by a shrine in St. Augustine, Florida, dedicated to the Mother of Christ under the title "Nuestra Senora de la Leche y Buen Parto," which translates freely, "Our Lady of Happy Delivery and Plentiful Milk."

Our international office, located in Franklin Park, Illinois, USA, is staffed by over 50 employees. Every year they open thousands of pieces of mail and answer countless phone calls from the many people throughout the world seeking breastfeeding help or information. In addition to more than 14,000 active La Leche League Leaders throughout the world, we have a Professional Advisory Board composed of more than 40 professionals with expertise in all areas of breastfeeding and maternal-infant health. Members of the Professional Advisory Board review all medically related information used in our publications and are available to provide help with unusual breastfeeding situations.

An LLLI branch office, with its own staff, is located in Ontario, Canada, and handles all Canadian orders. The address is: La Leche League International Canadian Supply Depot, Box 39, Williamsburg, Ontario, Canada KOC 2HO.

This book, THE WOMANLY ART OF BREASTFEEDING, is in its third edition. As of this printing, over one million copies have been sold. We also publish more than 140 pamphlets and information sheets dealing with a wide variety of topics related to breastfeeding, childbirth, parenting and nutrition. For a complete list of our publications, write to us at our Franklin Park address and request the General Price List.

We also distribute a number of books designed to meet the needs and interests of breastfeeding mothers. (See the Book List.)

La Leche League Meetings

La Leche League meetings offer a wonderful source of information and encouragement, and they provide a ready source of new friendships among mothers with whom you have so many things in common.

LLL meetings are held in the relaxed atmosphere of a member's home. A series consists of four meetings, one a month, each with its own topic: (1) Advantages of breastfeeding to mother and baby; (2) The art of breastfeeding and overcoming difficulties; (3) The baby arrives; (4) Nutrition and weaning.

The group Leader shares her knowledge on each of these subjects and encourages mothers to ask questions and share their experiences. For every question or difficulty that might be brought up, there are usually several mothers at the meeting to offer various solutions or suggestions. It is both exciting and reassuring to watch the other babies in the group thrive and grow. It is fun to see how different each baby is from the others, and the wonderful, warm way in which each mother and baby relate to each other. Babies are always welcome at LLL meetings.

As well as breastfeeding information, LLL meetings are a wonderful place to learn more about the world of mothering an infant from other women who have "been there" and are delighted to pass along their insights.

Our Leaders are primarily mothers who have breastfed their own babies and are willing to share their knowledge and enthusiasm about breastfeeding with mothers who look to them for help. The personal experience and special training of each Leader prepare her for this role. Every LLL Leader has completed a specific application process before she is considered qualified to act as an official representative of La Leche League.

How To Find a La Leche League Group

With over 4,000 La Leche League groups meeting every month all around the world, the chances are excellent that there are one or more groups in your community. Group Leaders make every effort to publicize their meetings so that mothers will be able to find the local LLL group quickly and easily.

Nearly all groups place meeting notices in the local newspapers. Watch your paper, or simply call the newspaper office and ask if they know how to get in touch with the La Leche League groups in the area.

In some of the larger cities, you will find La Leche League listed in the white pages of the telephone directory. If there is no listing, try calling the maternity wards of the larger hospitals or some of the obstetricians and pediatricians in your area. Childbirth instructors often have information about La Leche League groups in the community.

Don't forget to ask around among your friends and neighbors who are pregnant or have young children. You will likely find one or more such women who have been to League meetings and would be delighted to put you in touch with the local Leader.

If you should have difficulty finding the La Leche League Leader closest to you, or if you need immediate help, call or write to us at our Franklin Park, Illinois, office, and we will give you the name and telephone number of the La Leche League Leader in your area.

Our address is: La Leche League International, 9616 Minneapolis Avenue, Franklin Park, Illinois, 60131, USA. Our telephone number is (312) 455-7730. Our regular business hours are from 9:00 A.M. to 3:00 P.M., central time. At other times, a prerecorded message will refer you to another number for immediate breastfeeding help.

ABOUT THIS BOOK AND ITS AUTHORS

When the seven of us wrote the first edition of THE WOMANLY ART OF BREASTFEEDING in the 1950's, we were all mothers at home full-time. Writing was done in between other chores, while the baby napped or played nearby, perhaps with a preschool brother or sister. More often than not, the desk was the family dining table, and manuscript pages had to be hastily gathered up at mealtime.

We had mutually agreed that our families were our first priority. It was an understanding that freed us to set aside League work when our families needed us. As our children grew up and circumstances changed, some of us then took on salaried jobs with the growing organization of LLLI.

Betty, Edwina, Viola, and Mary Ann Cahill are currently employed by La Leche League, and Marian is engaged in related work. But the interest that we shared twenty-five years ago has not abated. All of us continue to serve on La Leche League's Board of Directors, which at the present time numbers seventeen members.

An office staff and numerous others supported us in writing this revision of the manual. Drs. Good, Ratner, and White all read at least one version of the manuscript and often patiently went over rewrites as well. Other professional consultants, including Dr. Lawrence Gartner, Dr. James Baggott, and nutritionist Mary Goodwin have reviewed sections of the book. While you won't find footnotes and references in the text—it isn't that kind of a book—you can be assured that we have sound authority behind the statements we make.

League members Judy Sanders and Judy Kahrl also read the manuscript and we benefited from their insight. Gwen Gotsch and Mary Lofton, in the League office, made an all-out effort to research needed material. Mary Ann Cahill's son, Tim, a medical student, also helped to research some of the technical material. In the preparation of copy, Joyce Kasheimer and Carol Hutto from the LLLI office staff worked long hours and came in on Saturdays to complete the typing. Kaye Lowman was a constant source of encouragement, as well as being a contributing writer. Mary Carson, who edited the second edition of our book, was a much-appreciated critic. Indexing and final copy editing were done for us by Jane Meinike. And without the unstinting efforts of Judy Torgus, who edited the manuscript, planned the layout, and handled last minute details, the book would not have been ready in time to meet the publication date. Judy was assisted in her efforts by Marybeth Doucette, Carol Carson, and Shirley Biancalana of the LLLI Publications Department. We also want to thank the parents whose stories are used in these pages and those who posed for photographs, as well as the photographers who allowed us to use their photos. A special thanks to Joan McCartney for sharing the delightful cartoons about parenthood from her forthcoming book, *The Other Side Makes Chocolate.* We are deeply grateful to each of the above and to the many others—too numerous to mention—who helped make this new edition possible.

While the 1981 book looks quite different from the familiar manual with its plain blue cover, the philosophy underlying it is the same. It is based in good part on what we have found through experience to be most valuable. For this reason, we include some information about us as individuals.

When we started the League, each of us knew one or more of the others, but some of us were getting acquainted for the first time. We were far from being carbon copies of each other. Some had bottle fed the older children, others had been fortunate enough to have been able to breastfeed their first babies. There is a span of sixteen years in our ages. What solidly unites us is our belief that "Good Mothering through Breastfeeding" is an important concept and a most worthwhile goal.

MARY ANN CAHILL, Libertyville, Illinois: Mary Ann was well along in her first pregnancy when she found a copy of Grantly Dick-Read's book, *Childbirth Without Fear*, on a sale table in Marshall Field's basement in Chicago. "I read passages aloud to Chuck over that summer before Elizabeth was born," she recalls. "I was convinced that our baby would be born naturally and, of course, I would breastfeed." Unfortunately, the dream of a natural delivery vanished with the routine administration of a spinal, and breastfeeding amounted to "a noble try." When the Cahills

(Photo by Richard Ebbitt.)

moved to Franklin Park in 1951, they learned of the "radical Dr. White."

Under his care, the rest of the Cahill babies arrived without medication and thrived on mother's milk. The family moved to Libertyville in 1960, and eventually nine children filled the red brick tri-level: Elizabeth, Robert, Timothy, Teresa, Mary, Joseph, Margaret, Charlene (Charlie), and Frances, the youngest, now fifteen. Following Chuck's death in 1978, Mary Ann has worked in various capacities for the League. Most recently, she has been devoting her time to writing, researching, and compiling the information in this book.

EDWINA FROEHLICH, Franklin Park, Illinois: Edwina was one of the few women in the 1950's who devoted considerable time to a career and married late. She was thirty-six years old when she and John began their family. There were dire warnings from all sides about the perils of having a baby at such an "advanced" age. And certainly, it was said, no woman over thirty could produce enough milk to satisfy a baby. Paul was born naturally at home, and those aged mammary glands produced an abundance of milk for him and the two brothers, David and Peter,

(Photo by Richard Ebbitt.)

who make up the Froehlich family. Early in her mothering, Edwina found it quite a struggle to give up the organized approach to life that had served her so well in the business world. It was only after she relaxed and accepted the unscheduled needs of her baby that she was able to truly enjoy motherhood. The Froehlich boys are now grown and on their own. Edwina works full-time for the League in the position of Executive Secretary.

MARY ANN KERWIN, Denver, Colorado: When Mary Ann and Tom Kerwin became parents for the first time in 1955, Mary Ann didn't even know how to hold a baby comfortably. The combination of her inexperience and a sleepy baby made it difficult to get started with breastfeeding. Helpful advice and support were forthcoming from Greg and Mary White (Mary is Tom Kerwin's sister), and Mary Ann and baby Tommy were soon a contented nursing couple. Mary Ann's major regret regarding her breastfeeding experience is that Tommy was weaned at nine months. It

(Photo by Richard Ebbitt.)

was a painful and upsetting time for both mother and baby, and Mary Ann learned from the experience. All of the other babies were allowed to wean at their own pace. The Kerwins have eight children: Tom, Ed, Greg,

Mary, Anne, Katie, John, and Mike. A ninth child, Joseph, who was born in 1959, died at six weeks, a victim of Sudden Infant Death Syndrome. Mary Ann is presently the Chairman of La Leche League's Board of Directors and is a guiding influence on the League's work all over the world.

(Photo by Richard Ebbitt.)

VIOLA LENNON, Chicago, Illinois: Vi's ten little Lennons came in all sizes, and just to prove that no challenge was too much for her, she even produced a set of twins in 1961. It was considered quite an accomplishment to nurse even one baby in those days, so Vi caused quite a stir in the neighborhood when she calmly proceeded to totally breastfeed both Catherine and Charlotte. Cathy was wakeful as an infant, nursing at least every two hours, while sleepy Charlotte nursed much less often, but gained more rapidly than her sister. She also weaned five months later than Cathy. The twins were sixth and seventh in the lineup, with Elizabeth, Mark, Mimi, Rebecca, and Matthew preceding them, and Martin, Maureen, and Gina following. Mimi was colicky as a baby, and Vi assumed that indicated a high-strung personality, but Mimi has grown into an easygoing, serene young lady. Vi is now the Resource Development Director for the League, helping to secure outside funds to finance La Leche League's ever expanding work.

(Photo by Richard Ebbitt.)

MARIAN TOMPSON, Melrose Park, Illinois: Even though she changed to a new doctor with each of her first three babies, Marian was unable to breastfeed for as long as she would have liked. Each doctor gave her the standard advice of the time—nurse no more often than every four hours, offer supplementary bottles, and start solids at six weeks. It was with their fourth baby, in 1955, that Marian and her husband, Tom, found Dr. Gregory White and more supportive help. Baby Laurel was nursed until she weaned herself, as was true for the succeeding babies. The seven Tompson children, Melanie, Deborah, Allison, Laurel, Sheila, Brian, and Philip, are all grown now. Marian was La Leche League's first and only president. During the twenty-four years of her presidency, she spoke out clearly and with love in many parts of the world for breastfeeding mothers and babies. Currently, Marian writes a popular column for *The People's Doctor Newsletter*. She is also the Executive Director of Alternative

Birth Crisis Coalition, and she serves on a number of advisory boards for organizations concerned with nutrition, childbirth, and family life.

(Photo by Richard Ebbitt.)

BETTY WAGNER, Franklin Park, Illinois: Betty breastfed all of her children, beginning back in 1943, thanks in large part to her mother, who was able to give her the practical help she needed. It was baby number six who presented Betty with new challenges. Dorothea cried a good deal and wasn't happy anywhere but in her mother's arms. Betty found it necessary to curtail all outside activities and rearrange her life around this little one who needed her so intensely. Dorothea was past her third birthday before she would venture very far from her mother, but about the time she was three and a half, she blossomed into a very self-confident, outgoing little girl. The Wagners had seven children—Gail, Robert, Wayne, Mary, Peggy, Dorothea, and Helen, who recently turned twenty. Betty's daughter Mary was the first of the founding mothers' daughters to become a La Leche League Leader. As the Chief Executive Officer of LLLI, Betty is responsible for the day-to-day operation of the League.

(Photo by Richard Ebbitt.)

MARY WHITE, River Forest, Illinois: Mary's first attempt at breastfeeding was just like that of most mothers in the 1940's—disastrous! In a short time, baby Joseph was a bottle-fed baby. When her second baby was born, her doctor husband, Greg, was home from the Army, and she had the support that a nursing mother needs. Bill and the eight sisters who followed, Peg, Katie, Anne, Jeannie, Mary, Clare, Molly, and Liz, along with brother Mike, were all breastfed with never a bottle in the house. Only the three oldest were hospital births; the others were born at home. Mary was forty-seven years old when the youngest, Elizabeth, arrived. Mary's devotion to the special kind of mothering that is so much a part of breastfeeding has always been a guiding influence in La Leche League. If you were to ask Mary, she would tell you that she believes her most important job as a mother is to instill in her children a love and trust in God for all of their lives. Over the years, the volunteer hours that Mary has devoted to the League would truly be an impressive number—if only someone had kept count.

Book List

Most new or expectant parents are eager to learn as much as they can about their new role. Fortunately, there are many books currently available on the subjects of childbirth, child care, breastfeeding, and nutrition. The following list includes only a small selection of the books which we have found especially helpful to new parents.

You will probably be able to find many of these books in the Group Library of your local La Leche League. This is just one of the services LLL groups offer to mothers.

Many of the books we recommend can also be purchased from La Leche League International or from your local LLL group. Profits from the sale of these books help LLL to continue serving mothers. (Books which are available from LLLI are so noted on this list.) Other excellent sources of books on childbirth and parenting are Birth & Life Bookstore and ICEA Bookcenter. (Addresses are included at the end of this chapter.) Your local bookstore or public library will probably also have some of these books.

Although we encourage you to read and learn as much as you can about your role as parents, remember that no book can offer a blueprint

Most expectant parents are eager to learn as much as they can about their new role. Cassandra and Joe Mariano prepare for the birth of their baby in the best possible way—by reading THE WOMANLY ART OF BREAST-FEEDING!

of how to raise *your* children. Each family is unique, and what works for someone else may not work for you. So don't try to do things "by the book." Relax and enjoy your baby.

PRENATAL CARE AND CHILDBIRTH

The Rights of the Pregnant Parent by Valmai Elkins.
   Two Continents Publishing Group: 1980. Softcover.
   Available from LLLI

Encourages careful selection of doctor and hospital for the wonderful event of childbirth. Every aspect of the hospital birth experience is explored, and fathers are encouraged to participate fully. Tips included on how to talk to the doctor, and what to ask when "shopping" for a doctor.

A Child Is Born by Lennart Nilsson.
   Delacorte Press: 1966. Softcover.
   Available from LLLI

Photographs of fetal life, originally published in *Life* magazine.

Nourishing Your Unborn Child by Phyllis Williams.
   Avon Books: 1974. Softcover.
   Available from LLLI

A basic introduction to good nutrition for the pregnant mother and the whole family— enjoyable reading and valuable information.

The First Nine Months of Life by Geraldine Flanagan.
   Simon and Schuster: 1962. Softcover and Hardcover.
   Available from Birth & Life and ICEA

An interesting book for prospective parents that covers the period from conception to birth. It has excellent illustrations and photographs showing prenatal growth.

Why Natural Childbirth? by Deborah Tanzer and Jean Block.
   Doubleday & Co.: 1972. Softcover.
   Available from Birth & Life and ICEA

A psychologist's report on the benefits to mothers, fathers, and babies. Philosophy rather than technique. Very readable.

Methods of Childbirth by Constance Bean.
   Dolphin Books: 1982. Softcover.
   Available from LLLI

Revised edition includes a comprehensive and up-to-date discussion of prepared childbirth, hospital procedures, and parents' responsibility in choosing their doctor or midwife and the place of their child's birth.

Husband-Coached Childbirth by Robert Bradley.
   Harper & Row: 1974. Hardcover.
   Available from Birth & Life and ICEA

Dr. Bradley sees the doctor's role as prenatal instructor, encourages the husband to help his wife with physical conditioning, and to be present in the delivery room. His often humorous, masculine approach to childbirth and breastfeeding are appealing, although his attitude of male superiority may be objectionable to some readers. LLL takes exception to his views on routine episiotomies, home delivery, and advocacy of a regular night out for parents without the baby.

Childbirth without Fear by Grantly Dick-Read.
 Harper & Row: 4th ed. 1979. Softcover.
 Available from Birth & Life and ICEA

Dr. Dick-Read was the pioneer in the field of natural childbirth. His trailblazing book has been revised by Helen Wessel and Harlan F. Ellis, MD, and has been reorganized and "Americanized," including some excellent new material.

Childbirth without Pain by Pierre Vellay.
 E. P. Dutton & Co.: 1959. Hardcover.
 Available from ICEA

Dr. Vellay, associate of Dr. Lamaze, together with others, presents a series of basic lectures on the psychoprophylactic methods of childbirth. First half is technical—second half consists of warm reports from new mothers sharing their experiences using this method. The photographs should convince even the most skeptical that it is possible to give birth joyously.

The Experience of Childbirth by Sheila Kitzinger.
 Penguin Books: 4th ed. 1978. Softcover.
 Available from Birth & Life and ICEA

This book is an excellent blend of feelings and facts, giving a warm account of childbirth plus detailed accounts of the physiology of pregnancy, development of the fetus, and normal labor. Reflects the teachings of Dick-Read, Lamaze, and Vellay, and stresses the emotional preparation of the mother, with the father as coach, and points out how beautifully breastfeeding satisfies the emotional needs of the baby.

Home Birth by Alice Gilgoff.
 Coward, McCann, & Geoghegan, Inc.: 1978. Hardcover.
 Available from ICEA

This book explores the many reasons, both medical and emotional, that are leading more and more couples to consider home birth, which is described as not only a physical location, but also a state of mind and philosophy of life.

The Home Birth Book by Charlotte and Fred Ward.
 Inscape: 1978. Softcover.
 Available from Birth & Life and ICEA

A comprehensive book on a subject which is of increasing interest to many couples and the professionals who serve them. Includes first-person stories of home birth written by parents and health professionals.

Having a Cesarean Baby by Richard Hausknecht and Joan Heilman.
 E. P. Dutton & Co.: 1978. Softcover.
 Available from LLLI

Good overall discussion of cesarean birth. The book's approach is caring, sensitive, and conveys real understanding of how cesarean parents feel, both physically and emotionally. The father's presence, repeat cesareans, choosing doctor and hospital, and risks and rights are all thoroughly discussed.

Emergency Childbirth by Gregory White.
 Police Training Foundation: 1969. Softcover.
 Available from LLLI

Although this book is a manual for policemen and others who may need to assist in an emergency delivery, it is also excellent reading for prospective parents. Dr. White, a member of LLLI's Professional Advisory Board, describes the birth process clearly and concisely.

Circumcision: An American Health Fallacy by Edward Wallerstein.
Springer Publishing: 1980. Softcover.
Available from Birth & Life

A very definitive book, covering twelve years of research. The author feels that circumcision is a solution in search of a problem. Extensive arguments against routine circumcision are presented in a most readable manner.

BREASTFEEDING

Nursing Your Baby by Karen Pryor.
Pocket Books: 1973. Softcover.
Available from LLLI

The author's lively, readable style makes this book a favorite among LLL members. Extensively researched, this book presents scientific information along with practical tips. Highlights the joys of the close inter-personal relationship of the mother and her nursing baby. Worthy of endorsement in all aspects except its approach to tandem nursing and toddler weaning, both of which are approached with greater concern for the needs of the mother than of the dependent little one.

You Can Breastfeed Your Baby . . . Even in Special Situations
by Dorothy Patricia Brewster
Rodale Press: 1979. Softcover.
Available from LLLI

Gives reassurance and specific advice about nursing in a variety of situations. Includes experiences of over 500 mothers, plus advice from medical experts on nursing twins, premature babies, sick babies, allergic babies, adopted babies, and much more. Throughout the book the emphasis is on how to continue breastfeeding despite obstacles which might at times seem insurmountable.

Breast Is Best by Andrew and Penny Stanway.
American Baby Books: 1982. Softcover.
Available from LLLI

An excellent book from Great Britain with a distinctly British flavor. The Drs. Stanway offer thorough, practical, down-to-earth information on breastfeeding. LLLI takes exception to several points including separation of mother and infant for a night out, the use of syntocinon, rubber nipple shields, contraceptive pills, concern over "fat babies," and the inability to breastfeed for genetic reasons.

Breastfeeding and Natural Child Spacing: The Ecology of Natural Mothering by Sheila Kippley.
Penguin Books, Inc.: 1975. Softcover.
Available from LLLI

This book encourages good mothering through breastfeeding. Subtitle appropriately describes the contents. Rather than a point-by-point "how to," it presents a philosophy of mothering—one of fostering infants' rights to love, care, and the best nutrition.

Human Milk in the Modern World by Derrick and Patrice Jelliffe.
Oxford University Press: 1978. Softcover.
Available from Birth & Life and ICEA

The Jelliffes are eminently qualified to summarize recent research and new knowledge available on human milk and breastfeeding. From a scientific sub-structure, they proceed to argue the case for a reappraisal, on a global basis, of the role of human milk in overcoming world health problems, and suggest ways and means to increase breastfeeding.

Mothering Your Nursing Toddler by Norma Jane Bumgarner.
La Leche League International: 1982. Softcover.
Available from LLLI

Practical, reassuring, informative, and supportive book for the mother of a nursing toddler. Emphasis on meeting child's needs. Discusses importance of breastfeeding relationship, natural weaning, temporary changes in lifestyle, society's expectations vs. child's and family's needs. Reinforces LLL approach to weaning.

Breastfeeding and Drugs in Human Milk by Gregory and Mary White.
Veterinary and Human Toxicology: 1980. Softcover.
Available from LLLI

Comprehensive summary of research/information currently available on the topic of medications in human milk. Prepared primarily for the use of the prescribing physician so that an informed judgment can be made on the risk/benefit factors relating to the use of a certain drug for an individual lactating mother. Includes listing of drugs by brand name, as well as drug class or generic name, with appropriate comments and references.

The Joy of Breastfeeding by Linda McDonald.
Oaklawn Press: 1978. Softcover.
Available from Birth & Life

The question and answer format of this easy-to-read book makes it good first reading about breastfeeding. Contains beautiful illustrations.

CHILD CARE AND PARENTING

The Child under Six by James Hymes.
Prentice-Hall, Inc.: 1974. Hardcover.
Out of Print

Excellent, warm, inspiring book containing beautiful concepts about the young child's need for love. Philosophic disagreements with LLL are found in the author's acceptance of the practice of leaving the infant under six months at home without mother, and in the recommendation for nursery school attendance for all from age three.

How To Really Love Your Child by Ross Campbell.
Victor Books: 1977. Softcover.
Available from LLLI

All about the importance of showing our children that we really love them. Good discussion of discipline and many positive reinforcements of LLL principles throughout the book. The author's personal religious convictions may be offensive to some.

Raising Your Child, Not by Force But by Love by Sidney Craig.
The Westminster Press: 1973. Softcover.
Available from LLLI

With a very positive, love-oriented, philosophical approach, the author presents new insights on family interaction with special emphasis on motivating children to become responsible human beings without incurring inappropriate feelings of anger, frustration, and possible self-hatred.

Your Child's Self-Esteem by Dorothy Briggs.
Doubleday & Co.: 1975. Softcover.
Available from LLLI

Emphasizing the importance of self-esteem, a crucial ingredient of mental health. The author points out that every child must know "I am lovable" and "I am worthwhile." Written to show specifically how to build a child's self-esteem through positive forms of discipline and plenty of love.

Good Things for Babies by Sandy Jones.
  Houghton Mifflin Co.: 1976. Softcover.
  Available from Birth & Life

A catalog of baby-oriented items which evaluates their safety and suitability. The mothering attitudes stressed throughout the book parallel LLL's approach.

Oneness and Separateness: From Infant to Individual by Louise Kaplan.
  Simon & Schuster: 1978. Softcover.
  Available from LLLI

Underlines the importance of mother-infant togetherness by sensitively portraying why and how a mother's presence and understanding along with her unconditional, unscheduled love are necessary for maximum development of the child. While clinical in its information, the book is very readable and person-oriented.

The Family Book of Child Care by Niles Newton.
  Wm. Morrow & Co.: 1957. Hardcover.
  Out of Print

Relaxed approach to child rearing by a mother of four. Dr. Newton's book is dedicated to maximizing mothering and minimizing housework. Pregnancy, childbirth, and breastfeeding are carefully explored—although certain sections seem more geared to the bottle-fed baby, and the section on weaning is not in accord with LLL recommendations.

The Family Bed: An Age Old Concept in Child Rearing by Tine Thevenin.
  Privately printed: 1976. Softcover.
  Available from LLLI

Discusses pros and cons of children sleeping with their parents and/or siblings. Historical perspectives as well as personal experiences provide very helpful reading for parents who worry about sleep problems. Reflects and reinforces LLL ideas throughout.

Look at the Child by Aline Wolf.
  Parent Child Press: 1978. Softcover.
  Available from Parent Child Press

Maria Montessori's beautiful philosophy is expressed concisely in brief statements and photographs of children.

Gerald the Third by Faye Young.
  La Leche League International: rev. 1980. Hardcover.
  Available from LLLI

La Leche League's own book for children. Written as a first-person story giving a six-year-old's view of family life and the birth of his new baby sister.

The Rights of Infants by Margaret Ribble.
  Columbia: rev. 1965. Softcover.
  Available from Birth & Life and ICEA

One of the classic books on the basic needs of babies which helped to swing child care away from the old can't-pick-them-up-or-you'll-spoil-them theories. A true milestone in child care literature, first published in 1943.

Touching: The Human Significance of the Skin by Ashley Montagu.
  Columbia University Press: 1971. Softcover.
  Available from Birth & Life

A comprehensive survey of research and opinion documenting the importance of skin stimulation in the development of the human being. Encourages mothers to give in to their natural impulse to cuddle their babies and emphasizes the importance of breastfeeding.

Parent-Infant Bonding by Marshall Klaus and John Kennell.
  C. V. Mosby Co.: 1982. Softcover.
  Available from Birth & Life and ICEA

The authors report on their research into the importance of early contact and interaction between a mother and her infant. Considerable attention is also paid to paternal bonding and the inter-relationships of the whole family.

Woman at Home by Arlene Cardozo.
  Doubleday & Co.: 1976. Hardcover.
  Available from LLLI

A book which proclaims itself to be "for the woman who chooses to stay at home, and for whom forming close human relationships is the first priority." Emphasizes the needs of children and recognizes the personal fulfillment available to the woman who chooses to stay at home while addressing the potential for development and outreach of the mother as her children grow.

Motherlove: Natural Mothering, Birth to Three Years by Alice Bricklin.
  Running Press: 1979. Softcover.
  Available from LLLI

Presents a philosophy of mothering which stresses early mother-baby closeness including breastfeeding, bonding, and birth at home. Explores the emotional interaction between mother and child in the early years. Most LLL mothers would disagree with the author's conclusions about breastfeeding and a woman's sexual responses.

FOOD AND NUTRITION

Whole Foods for the Whole Family by Roberta Johnson.
  La Leche League International: 1981. Spiral-Bound.
  Available from LLLI

La Leche League's new cookbook. Includes mother-tested recipes full of good, nutritious ingredients. A complete cookbook, recipes use no processed foods or brand names; use of sweeteners is minimized even in desserts. Protein and calorie counts are listed for all recipes.

Mother's in the Kitchen by Roberta Johnson.
  La Leche League International: 1971. Softcover.
  Available from LLLI

La Leche League's first cookbook of recipes submitted and tested by League mothers. Emphasis is placed on good nutrition, economy, and ease of preparation.

Supermarket Handbook: Access to Whole Foods by David and Nikki Goldbeck.
  Signet Books: 1976. Softcover.
  Available from LLLI

A supermarket shopper's guide to nutritious foods. The authors specify brand names which they believe to be most nutritious, and brands which avoid additives, food coloring, and over-processing.

The Book of Whole Grains by Marlene Bumgarner.
  St. Martin's Press: 1976. Softcover.
  Available from St. Martin's Press

About cereals as the people of ancient times knew them. There are 250 recipes for breads, main dishes, vegetable treats, salads, soups, beverages, and snacks—all made with grains, nuts, seeds, peas, and beans. Recipes are economical and easy enough for school-age children to prepare.

Around the World Cuisine: LLL-ATW Cookbook by Catherine Storlie.
Around the World Division of LLLI: 1980. Spiral-Bound.
Available from LLLI

Delightfully unique collection of around-the-world recipes submitted by LLL mothers from many countries.

Nutrition in Pregnancy and Lactation by Worthington-Roberts et al.
C. V. Mosby 2nd edition: 1981. Softcover.
Available from Birth & Life

Concise, practical information for health professionals on nutrition and reproduction. Includes summaries of research and clinical information on lactation, nutrition during pregnancy, and the nutritional needs of the pregnant adolescent, as well as discussion of nutrition education issues.

Laurel's Kitchen by Robertson et al.
Nilgirl Press: 1976. Hardcover. Bantam Edition: 1978.
Available from Birth & Life

A natural foods cookbook and nutrition reference which is delightfully written and filled with mouth-watering recipes. Presents helpful information about vegetarian diets.

ABOUT LA LECHE LEAGUE

The LLLove Story by Kaye Lowman.
La Leche League International: 1977. Softcover.
Available from LLLI

The history of La Leche League from the early days to the present. Includes many photos and anecdotes. Tells the story of the founders and their families.

WHERE TO OBTAIN BOOKS

La Leche League International, 9616 Minneapolis, Franklin Park, IL 60131
Telephone: (312)455-7730

LLLI Canadian Supply Depot, Box 70, Williamsburg, Ontario KOC2HO

Birth & Life Bookstore, Inc., P.O. Box 70625, Seattle, WA 98107
Telephone: (206) 789-4444

ICEA Bookcenter, P.O. Box 20048, Minneapolis, MN 55420
Telephone: (612) 854-8660

Parent Child Press, P.O. Box 767, Altoona, PA 16605

St. Martin's Press, 175 Fifth Avenue, New York, NY 10010

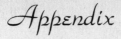

Many of the organizations listed below have local groups affiliated with them. Look in your local telephone book to see if a group is located nearby.

CHILDBIRTH AND/OR FAMILY-ORIENTED GROUPS

AAHCC — The American Academy of Husband-Coached Childbirth
Box 5224 — Department CB
Sherman Oaks, CA 91413

Founded by Robert Bradley, MD and Jay and Marjie Hathaway for the purpose of making childbirth information available through films, classes, lectures, and workshops.

ACHO — American College of Home Obstetrics
664 North Michigan Avenue, Suite 600
Chicago, IL 60611

Formed to gather together those physicians who wish to cooperate with families who choose to give birth in the home.

ASPO — American Society for Psychoprophylaxis in Obstetrics, Inc.
1411 K Street NW, Suite 200
Washington, DC 20005

A group of physicians, parents, and professionals offering training and certification of prenatal class instructors in the psychoprophylactic method of childbrith preparation (Lamaze method).

CIH — Children In Hospitals, Inc.
31 Wilshire Park
Needham, MA 02192

A group of parents and health-care professionals concerned about the need for ample contact between children and parents when either is hospitalized. It encourages hospitals to adopt flexible visiting and living-in policies.

C/SEC — Cesareans/Support, Education, and Concern, Inc.
22 Forest Road
Framingham, MA 01701

An organization seeking to provide information on many aspects of cesarean childbirth, in order to make couples more aware of what the procedure involves and what options may be available to them.

CCL — The Couple to Couple League
P.O. Box 11084
Cincinnati, OH 45211

An interfaith organization offering couples help with the practice of natural family planning. CCL teaches ecological breastfeeding and the full sympto-thermal method.

HOME — Home Oriented Maternity Experience
511 New York Avenue
Takoma Park, MD 20912

An organization devoted to helping couples achieve the optimum experience of a safe home birth. Trained leaders conduct meetings on preparation for home birth throughout the U.S.A.

ICEA — International Childbirth Education Association
P.O. Box 20048
Minneapolis, MN 55420

A volunteer organization which brings together persons interested in family-centered maternity and infant care.

LLL — La Leche League Groups

Send a stamped, self-addressed envelope to LLLI and request a copy of No. 504, LLLI Directory. This publication lists two key representatives of every area in the U.S.A. and forty-three other countries. Contact the particular representative for names and addresses of groups nearest you.

Midwest Parentcraft Center
627 Beaver Road
Glenview, IL 60025

Founded to teach Grantly Dick-Read techniques. Groups in greater Chicago area hold childbirth classes for parents-to-be and referral service to wider area.

NAPSAC—InterNational Association of Parents and Professionals for Safe Alternatives in Childbirth
P.O. Box 267
Marble Hill, MO 63764

Parents, medical professionals, and childbirth educators who promote education enabling parents to assume more responsibility for pregnancy and childbirth.

POP—Parents of Prematures
13613 NE 26th Place
Bellevue, WA 98005

An excellent support group for parents of prematures.

VBAC — Vaginal Birth After Cesarean
10 Great Plain Terrace
Needham, MA 02192

Provides classes, lectures, and seminars for couples interested in learning about vaginal delivery after a previous cesarean.

SPECIALIZED HELPS IN BREASTFEEDING AND MOTHERING

Breast Pumps

There are a number of electric and hand-operated breast pumps available, both for sale and rental. The most commonly known companies are:

Egnell
765 Industrial Drive
Cary, IL 60013

Marshall Electronics, Inc.
5425 W. Fargo
Skokie, IL 60077

Happy Family Products
12300 Venice Blvd.
Los Angeles, CA 90066

Medela
457 Dartmoor Drive
Crystal Lake, IL 60014

Loyd-B Breast Pump (LOPUCO)
1615 Old Annapolis Road
Woodbine, MD 21797

Ora Lac
9256 8th NW
Seattle, WA 98117

Breast Shields

Plastic, two-piece shields (from LLLI) are for use by mothers with flat or inverted nipples. Wear during pregnancy/between feedings after baby is born.

Baby Carriers

Information needed to make your baby carriers, baby slings, etc., is contained in the LLLI *Baby Carrier Packet.* The packet also contains a number of advertisements from commercially available baby carriers and backpacks.

Blind and Visually Handicapped

A large number of LLL publications are available, free of charge, in Braille, on cassette tape, and reel-to-reel. Ask for LLLI's *Special Publications List.* To obtain this list actually printed **in** Braille, ask for *Special Publications List–BRL.*

Lact-Aid Nursing Supplementer

Resources in Human Nurturing, International
Box 6861
Denver, CO 80206

Further information available on the use of Lact-Aid to help mothers who are interested in relactation or nursing adopted babies.

LLLI Information Sheets and Reprints

Over 200 information sheets, reprints, and booklets are available from local LLL groups and from LLLI. These cover many aspects of breastfeeding and child care. Some are written by doctors and other health professionals; others are written by experienced mothers. A *Catalogue* (No. 501) will be sent on request. Please enclose a stamped, self-addressed business size envelope. For information in languages other than English, ask for the *Translation List* (No. 508).

Here is just a sampling of the items available.

3 **La Leche League International Fact Folder**
Facts about LLL publications, Professional Advisory Board, membership, meetings, growth, etc.

13 **Breastfeeding Your Premature Baby**
Complete information to help mothers nurse their premature babies, includes references and personal experiences.

27 **Manual Expression of Breast Milk—Marmet Technique**
Detailed information and illustrations on a special method of hand-expressing milk.

28 **Sore Nipples**
Suggestions for relieving nipple pain and preventing its recurrence.

29 **Sore Breasts**
Treatment and prevention of plugged ducts and breast infections.

51 **Breastfeeding the Down's Syndrome Baby**
Basic information about Down's Syndrome and advice on how to help these special babies develop their full potential. Photos, stories from parents, and list of helpful resources.

52 **Mothering Multiples**
Booklet on breastfeeding and mothering twins or triplets. Helpful advice on all aspects of mothering multiples.

80 **Breastfeeding After a Cesarean Birth**
Compiled from experiences of mothers.

SPECIAL GIFT ITEMS

ESPECIALLY FOR YOU
The first baby record book designed for the breastfed baby. Includes full color illustrations and poems written by parents. With a washable, padded cover.

LLLI CALENDARS
Each year, LLLI publishes an appointment calendar with full color photos of parents and children along with poems about parenthood.

LLL DIAPER BAG
This multi-purpose tote bag will take mother and baby anywhere in comfort and style. High-quality vinyl (12" x 12" x 5") with zipper closure and adjustable shoulder strap, also large outside zipper pocket for wallet and keys.

Index